Soteriology and the End of Animal Sacrifice

Soteriology and the End of Animal Sacrifice

GIOSUÈ GHISALBERTI

WIPF & STOCK · Eugene, Oregon

SOTERIOLOGY AND THE END OF ANIMAL SACRIFICE

Copyright © 2018 Giosuè Ghisalberti. All rights reserved. Except for brief quotations in critical publications or reviews, no part of this book may be reproduced in any manner without prior written permission from the publisher. Write: Permissions, Wipf and Stock Publishers, 199 W. 8th Ave., Suite 3, Eugene, OR 97401.

Wipf & Stock
An Imprint of Wipf and Stock Publishers
199 W. 8th Ave., Suite 3
Eugene, OR 97401

www.wipfandstock.com

PAPERBACK ISBN: 978-1-5326-5206-6
HARDCOVER ISBN: 978-1-5326-5207-3
EBOOK ISBN: 978-1-5326-5208-0

Manufactured in the U.S.A.   08/08/18

To the memory of
Kent Underhay Enns, 1964–2016

Contents

Abbreviations | ix

Introduction: Jewish Prophets, Greek Philosophers, and the Denunciation of Animal Sacrifice | 1

CHAPTER 1
Socrates's "Impiety" | 20
   1. The Indictment | 20
   2. Athens's Tragic Theology | 24
   3. Socrates's Private Conversation | 39
   4. Socrates's Declaration in Court | 52

CHAPTER 2
The Case of Alcibiades | 63
   1. The "Nagging" Speech of Apollodorus | 63
   2. The Illness of the Cave Dwellers | 74
   3. The Alcibiades Dialogues | 78
   4. Socrates's Therapeutic Philosophy | 87

CHAPTER 3
Physiologia and the Psychodynamics of Epicurean Theology | 96
   1. Did Epicurus Condone Animal Sacrifice? | 96
   2. The Origin of Epicurus's Thought | 101
   3. Epicurean Theology | 108
   4. Lucretius Contra Philodemus | 117

CHAPTER 4
Epicurus's *Logotherapeia* and the Health of the Psyche | 138
   1. True Philosophy, True Health | 138
   2. Feelings and Perceptions | 149
   3. Chance, Necessity, and Justice | 156
   4. Cicero without Consolation | 164

CHAPTER 5
Jesus' *Soteria* | 171
  1. *Healing Words* | 171
  2. *A Teacher* | 180
  3. *Afflictions of the Self, Afflictions of Society* | 186
  4. *Levitical Illness* | 190

CHAPTER 6
Jesus' Anti-sacrificial Acts in the Temple of Jerusalem | 209
  1. *The Essenes of Qumran* | 209
  2. *Opposition to the Temple Leadership* | 218
  3. *Jesus' Rejection of Animal Sacrifice* | 221
  4. *The Eucharist* | 243
  Postscript: A Dialogue with Paula Fredriksen on the Cleansing of the Temple | 246

Conclusion: Christians, Jews, Polytheists, and the End of Animal Sacrifice | 255

Bibliography | 267

Abbreviations

Ancient Sources

Aristides
Or.	*Orations*

Aristophanes
B.	*Birds*
Cl.	*Clouds*
Fr.	*Frogs*

Athenaeus
Deip.	*Deipnosophists*

Augustine
Sol.	*Soliloquy*

Cicero
Leg.	*Laws*
Nat. D.	*On the Nature of the Gods*
Pis.	*Against Piso*
Rep.	*The Republic*
Tusc.	*Tusculum Disputations*

Diogenes Laertius
Lives.	*Lives of the Eminent Philosophers*

x   Abbreviations

Donatus
Vita.   *Vita Virgilii*

Empedocles
Pur.   *Purifications*

Epicteus
Dis.   *Discourses*

Epicurus
Ep. Men.   *Letter to Menoeceus*
Ep. Hdt.   *Letter to Herodotus*
Ep. Pyth.   *Letter to Pythocles*
PD.   *Principal Doctrines*
VS.   *Vatican Sayings*

(The last two are not standard. I used the English instead of the, sometimes, customary Latin)

Euripides
Hipp.   *Hippolytus*

Heraclitus
Fr.   5

Hesiod
Th.   *Theogony*

Iamblichus
Vita   *On the Pythagorean Life*

Isocrates
Ar.   *Areopagiticus*

Josephus
Ant.   *Antiquities*
War.   *Jewish War*

Abbreviations xi

Lucretius
DRN. *On the Nature of Things*

Ovid
Fast. *Fasti*
Met. *Metamorphoses*

Philo
Alleg. *Allegorical Interpretation*
Prob. *Every Good Man is Free*
Hy. *Hypothetica.*
Vit. Cont. *On the Contemplative Life*

Philodemus
P. *On Frank Criticism*
Piety. *On Piety*

Plato
Al. *I Alcibiades I*
Al. *II Alcibiades II*
Ap. *Apology*
Chrm. *Charmides*
Cr. *Crito*
Euthphr. *Euthyphro*
Grg. *Gorgias*
Ion *Ion*
L. *Laws*
Lach. *Laches*
Lysis *Lysis*
Phaedo *Phaedo*
Phaedrus *Phaedrus*
Prot. *Protagoras*
Rep. *Republic*
Soph. *Sophist*
Sym. *Symposium*

Theag.	*Theages*
Theat.	*Theaetetus*

Pliny

Ep.	*Letters*
Nat. His.	*Natural History*

Plutarch

Adv. Col.	*Against Colotes*
Non Posse	*That Epicurus Actually Makes a Pleasant Life Impossible*

Porphyry

Abst.	*On the Abstinence of Eating Animal Flesh*
Vita	*Life of Pythagoras*

Pythagoras

GV.	*Golden Verses*

Usener

Ep.	*Epicurea*

Seneca

Ep.	*Letters*

Sextus Empiricus

Pyr.	*Outlines of Pyrrhonism*

Tacitus

Hist.	*Histories*

Thucydides

War.	*The Peloponnesian War*

Virgil

Catal.	*Catalepton*

Xenophon

Ec.	Economic
Cyr.	The Education of Cyrus
Mem.	Memorabilia
Sym.	Symposium

Contemporary Sources

AJP	The American Journal of Philology
AP	Ancient Philosophy
APQ	American Philosophical Quarterly
A	Apeiron
BMCR	Bryn Mawr Classical Review
CA	Classical Antiquity
CBQ	Catholic Biblical Quarterly
CJ	The Classical Journal
CP	Classical Philology
CTR	Criswell Theological Review
CQ	Classical Quarterly
CR	The Classical Review
CBR	Currents in Biblical Scholarship
BTB	Biblical Theology Bulletin
ET	Expository Times
GR	Greece and Rome
GRBS	Greek, Roman, and Byzantine Studies
H	Hermes
HTSTS HTS	Teologiese Studies
I	Interpretation
HJ	The Heythrop Journal
JHP	Journal of the History of Philosophy
JBL	Journal of Biblical Literature
HTR	The Harvard Theological Review
JHS	The Journal of Hellenistic Studies
JP	The Journal of Philology
JTS	The Journal of Theological Studies

Abbreviations

LCL	Loeb Classic Library
M	Mnemosyne
NTS	New Testament Studies
PF	The Philosophical Forum
PAPS	Proceedings of the American Philosophical Society
RBS	Roman and Byzantine Studies
SBL	The SBL Handbook of Style
SH	Studia Historica. Historia Antigua
RIPS	Royal Institute of Philosophy Supplement
TP	Transactions and Proceedings of the Journal of the American Philological Association
VS	Vatican Sayings
ZNW	Zeitscrift für die Neutestamentliche Wissenschaft und die Älteren Kirche
ZPE	Zeitschrift für Papyrologie und Epigraphik

Biblical Sources

KJV	King James Version
Acts	Acts
1 Cor	1 Corinthians
Gal	Galatians
John	John
Luke	Luke
Mark	Mark
Matt	Matthew
Phil	Philippians
Rom	Romans

Introduction
Jewish Prophets, Greeks Philosophers, and the Denunciation of Animal Sacrifice[1]

DURING THE CONTINUOUS DIALOGUE between Yahweh and Moses and the prophet's repeated plea to the pharaoh for the Jewish people to be released from Egypt so they may serve their God according to tradition and there-

---

1. An initial note is here necessary if only to, first, state my argument and, second, admit that it will be in dialogue with some current positions regarding the ancient practice of sacrifice that attempt to disavow the violence and killing inherent in the ritual. In a lengthy article, "Sacrifice in the Ancient Mediterranean," Daniel Ullucci begins with questioning the definitions of sacrifice and the theories associated with the religious ritual. Such definitions, he argues, are "dangerous when they are presented not as scholarly creations but as fundamental, universal or natural categories, as many earlier discussions of sacrifice presumed (for example, the assumption that blood sacrifice was categorically different from other types of offerings)" (393). That I completely ignore such "sacrifice" as the burning of incense or the offering of grain or honey makes my position, to begin with, unequivocal; slaughtering an animal and offering farm produce cannot be equated; their difference is not an "assumption." As will become evident, I am not here concerned so much with the origin of the practice as for the long tradition (Jewish, Greek, Roman, Christian) of its criticism and, ultimately, its historical end. In the notes to "The Religion of Plant and Animal Offerings Versus the Religion of Meanings, Essences, and Textual Mysteries," Stowers makes the attempt to challenge "conceptions of sacrifice that define it as a kind of killing, destruction, and violence" (51). The slaughter of an animal (slitting its throat with a knife, severing the neck with an axe, and butchering it) during a religious ritual is not a "kind of killing" and is certainly not a "conception" but a historical fact. Better yet, in his "Discussion" in *Violent Origins*, Walter Burkert calls these the "hard facts. Animal sacrifice, at least the form most practiced in ancient Greece, Israel, and many other contexts, is a scandal, because it makes killing animals and eating them a sacred affair, a religious act, or even *the religious act*," 177. In *Violence and the Sacred*, René Girard states that "sacrifice is an act of violence inflicted on a surrogate victim," 7. Finally, in "Théorie générale du sacrifice et mise a mort dans la ΘΥΣΙΑ grecque," Jean-Pierre Vernant writes that "le meurtre de la victime constituent le centre autour duquel gravite toute la cérémonie," 4.

fore sacrifice by providing "burnt offerings" (Exod 10:25),[2] the final plague to be inflicted on the land, its people, and animals will involve nothing less than the interrelated deaths of every single first-born Egyptian child and animal, as well as the accompanying slaughter (and a shared meal, what the "Paris school" calls commensality[3]) of a sheep whose blood will be used to mark the two side posts and upper post of the door of a Jewish household and initiate the "pass over" and its commemoration. The death of sacrificial animals and the display of their blood will finally make possible a renewed future in freedom and the restoration of their worship and most fundamental ritual—the sacrifice of animals that, in Egypt, was prohibited due to the nature of the hybrid/animal deities revered by the population. According to Jon Levenson, the freedom experienced in Exodus "is not freedom in the sense of self-determination, but *service*."[4] Or stated otherwise, liberation and the resumption of a religious tradition long abandoned due to their captivity are absolutely related. The liberation of the Jews means the ability to once again provide a service to God through the sacrifice of animals. The creation of Passover will require the perpetual recollection of the event, as well as a festival to repeat a foundational ritual. "And this day shall be unto you for a memorial; and ye shall keep it a feast to the LORD throughout your generations; ye shall keep it a feast by an ordinance for ever" (Exod 12:14). Yahweh's instructions on the nature of the feast will be meticulous and precise, beginning with the requirement to provide "this service," (Exod 12:25) a word often repeated and referring to the animal sacrifices to commemorate the event and, in particular, when the blood of the lamb on the signposts of the door to a Jewish house serves as protection against impending death. The liberation of the Jewish people from Egypt led to other significant traditions being instituted, once again after a significant lapse, at Yahweh's request or demand. The foremost among the divine instructions, to fulfill plans and intentions, are given to Moses and with the imperative that, in the future, "ye shall be unto me a kingdom of priests, and a holy na-

---

2. The decision to use a particular translation of the Bible is not an easy one. After much deliberation, the King James Version will be used throughout. There is much to be said for the hermeneutic struggle of reading enigmatic passages rather than the more accessible translations.

3. See, for example, the opening essay by one of the two most well-known scholars of the "Paris school." In "Culinary Practices and the Spirit of Sacrifice," Marcel Detienne mentions the "relations with divine powers through the highly ritualized killing of animal victims, whose flesh was consumed collectively according to precise strictures," 1.

4. Levenson, *Hebrew Bible, the Old Testament*, 128. Despite italicizing the word "service," Levenson does not pursue the consequences of its meaning as it relates specifically to the worship of Yahweh by sacrificing animals. Service will become a description of singular importance.

tion" (Exod 19:6). Moses will fulfill his responsibility, but without knowing at this time how a kingdom of priests and a holy nation may not always be compatible, a problem if not an irreconcilable contradiction eventually emphasized by several prophets and, ultimately, by Jesus himself when he repeatedly confronts certain *individuals* of the temple leadership of Jerusalem. The human and the holy may be in proximity in intention and effort, but the human priest and the people he addresses with divinely sanctioned authority will not always be able to represent the holy, not when violence, the shedding of blood, and death (and what Burkert calls "the strange prominence of animal slaughter"[5]) are demanded as representative of piety and worship. Its biblical origins in the offerings of Cain, the farmer of the land like his father, and Abel, the shepherd who sacrifices and butchers the animals from his flock, provide no explanations whatsoever and are shrouded in an enigma no theological imagination has adequately clarified; reasons are neither intimated nor given.

Once freed and moving in the Sinai with uncertainty if also with a promise, of geography and otherwise, Moses creates the ordinances that will govern his people, including the precise and meticulous instructions for building the sacrificial altar and the step-by-step ritual killing of animals. The institution of sacrifice will continue to be more precisely developed. The Book of Leviticus, what was originally known in the Hebrew as *wayyikra*, the "call" and summons of God, begins with an extended description of the sacrificial ritual and its essential role in the offerings for sin and peace, trespass and atonement. The death of an animal provides a change in the moral condition of the sacrificer. The law of the burnt or "ascent offering" (*qorban olah*) will take up the beginning of Leviticus 1–7, with the next three chapters devoted to the appropriate animals to eat (and the distinction between the clean and the unclean), as well as the issues of menstruation and childbirth, the problems of skin blemishes—the "plague of leprosy" to become central in Jesus' *teaching*—followed by a detailed list of further laws and ordinances, statutes, and judgments. The threat of disorder from within the vulnerable human body and from the social instability of a community cannot be allowed to undermine their newfound freedom and the resumption of a fundamental theological dedication. And so the offering of the *qorban* is equated with *qarab*, the assumption of "drawing near" to Yahweh and ensuring a binding relationship, as if ascending smoke mediated a relationship.

However, at a certain juncture in history, beginning with the insistent *voices* of the prophets, their speech demanding to be heard and understood,

---

5. Burkert, *Homo Necans*, xv.

there will be a necessary reevaluation of the previously noted "holy nation" and instead a harsh judgment will be passed on what the prophet deems to be a "sinful nation," (Isa 1:4) a "sin" to be understood as a particular kind of affliction and not simply reducible to a moral transgression in violation of a precept or commandment. The malaise cannot be reduced to an act or a thought; it has become a condition of being, estranged from an original image and likeness. Human thought has alienated itself from Yahweh and creation. Isaiah recognizes how the people he most wants to address are ill in head and heart, psychologically stricken. How did this come about? Isaiah's answer (as well as the response of other prophets from Jeremiah to Micah) will be consistent and unwavering. The laws, statutes, and judgments first proclaimed in Leviticus have not been maintained as originally intended; perhaps, as Jeremiah tells us, directives may have been misconstrued. Relying on an observance to provide the people with peace and atonement, they have depended exclusively on the performance of an act by priestly representatives rather than on the more important personal responsibility of being just and living up to the standards, not simply the ordinances, outlined in Leviticus.

Leviticus continues with the foundation of the kingdom of priests and the holy nation first announced in Exodus, now with a precise and well-defined articulation of the responsibilities of the priests in terms of the exercise of rituals. Sons will inherit a position and a responsibility. However, and in a problem to be directly addressed by Jesus in his deliberations with the Torah, both the central observances of the Mosaic law (animal sacrifice and considerations of purity) are called into question. Indeed, as the Jewish prophets will make clear again and again, when the performance of rituals can for some become mere habitual duties and lead to the disregard of one's ethical responsibilities, then the priesthood—at least certain individuals if not the entire institution—can no longer remain without scrutiny; they too will have to be reexamined with regard to their legitimacy and purpose in the life of a people. Tradition cannot guarantee their authority. The prophets will not hesitate to call the priests to a thorough self-examination of their lives, of their duties. Furthermore, the central act of piety, first of all, can no longer remain unquestioned due to its foundational nature and as a guarantee of tradition and its continuity. It has become objectionable, and for reasons not entirely made explicit.

Ephraim Radner[6] rightly identifies a reader's "ambivalence" with regards to Leviticus, at once expressing an outline of the minutiae of animal sacrifice, the priestly duties of attending to the unclean, and that most

---

6. Radner, *Leviticus*, 18.

important of commandments, "thou shalt love your neighbour as thyself," (Lev. 19:18) an ambivalence defying easy resolution. And ambivalence may not be entirely apt. "How does one 'explain' and 'apply' a book that devotes seven chapters to the bewildering, if not seemingly bizarre, requirements of ancient Israel's sacrificial system and five chapters to details of ritual purity."[7] Perhaps incomprehension more accurately defines a reader's reaction to the seeming contradictions of Leviticus. How does one reconcile the slaughter of an animal as a religious act devoted to God, and the love of one's neighbor as an ethical responsibility the prophets believe to be more indicative of authentic piety? Religion may itself be polarized by this distinction: the violent killing of an animal on one hand, and the love of others as intrinsic to the theological imperative of antiquity on the other. Some commentators may provide explanations and rationale, but they are hardly satisfactory. Jacob Milgrom writes that "behind the specific laws of sacrifice is a profound design for creating a sense of spiritual connectedness."[8] The spiritual connectedness, once it requires death and *blood*, seems all the more peculiar and (surely for modern sensibilities even more jarring than for the Jewish prophets) alienating. "Blood joins the human and the divine in a sacred moment,"[9] surely a thought that is hardly self-evident. Blood appears as a euphemism. The creation of the sacred by killing an animal and sprinkling its blood on an altar leaves one with the gravest of doubts. "The blood of the sacrificial victim makes atonement for the worshiper."[10] Such *beliefs*, so often repeated, nevertheless make their reevaluation possible, as becomes evident with the Jewish prophets, one reason they in turn will suffer the ultimate punishment, as if their deaths were necessary so that sacrifice would continue uninterrupted and as a guarantee of the people's piety. And when a desire and a need are attributed to Yahweh—who demands an act of killing at the very moment of worship, blood at the very moment of devotion—then a certain belief becomes most vulnerable and difficult to sustain. When an objection is made and a substitution proposed, the purpose of sacrifice no longer seems to be that of a ritual which ensures stability. Jewish wisdom will emphaszie that, "to do justice and judgment is more acceptable to the Lord than sacrifice" (Prov 21:3).

The prophets enter history to disturb, unsettle, provoke, and call into question the past of tradition in order to rethink both theology and humanity in the present. Reciprocity has been severed, at least as previously

7. Balentine, *Leviticus*, 1.
8. Milgrom, *Leviticus*, 17.
9. Owens, *Leviticus*, 13.
10. Rooker, *Leviticus*, 53.

conceived and as it has been practiced and handed down from one generation to another, without choice or deliberation. The prophets believe another future has become possible and is in fact necessary if Yahweh is to be served as originally intended. The prophets may denounce and castigate, but they will also (as in Isaiah) speak with an unparalleled urgency and poignancy, exhorting, compelling, and above all healing listeners from an intolerable condition. The words of the prophets are intended to rouse those who are suffering from a condition of lassitude and indifference, a people who have become numb and hard-hearted, as Jesus will recognize in a prevailing *anaesthesia* of thought, of emotion. The prophets do not speak on their own behalf, as individuals, alone; they repeat the utterances they have apparently heard from Yahweh, as a conversation and an appeal, and with one purpose. It has become urgent, the times are critical. The prophets do not so much anticipate the future as reassess the present from the perspective of a past ordained by Yahweh, one now compromised and at least partly unfulfilled. The obligations for leading a proper life as found in Leviticus (moral, certainly, but also psychologically healthy) have been forsaken and conveniently, and exclusively, replaced with the performance of mere rituals, easily repeatable as an observance by a priestly class with the exclusive mandate for all religious acts. The prophets enter history in order to reexamine it, insisting that the fundamental and irrevocable tenets introduced into the world by Yahweh have been neglected and almost completely forgotten. Responsibility has been disavowed, obligations relinquished. Animal sacrifice has become a convenient ritual that for many (the population and the priests among them) has replaced the need for that self-reckoning that is essential for any relationship. The prophets repeatedly call for the abolition of animal sacrifice and its replacement with a new form of piety. Their proclamation amounts to the introduction of a decisive before and after into history, one with no eschatological expectations whatsoever and made possible with nothing less (and nothing more) than a certain kind of speaking. The spoken word, originating at the moment of creation and with the unparalleled utterance of God saying "let there be light," will replace the act of killing. The language of compassion for others will replace an act of violence, bringing forth a renewed conception of life. The creative word of the divine will now be spoken not to create matter, the physical presence of the cosmos or nature in the world; it will be speech and breath and once again (as in the creation of human beings) inaugurate a world where the Spirit will be revived. Language and the speech from one human being to another will inaugurate a new world.

Isaiah begins his appeal to the people of Israel with "Hear, O heavens, and give ear, O earth: for the Lord hath spoken," (Isa 1:2) stressing from the beginning the need to hear, to listen, to understand the spoken word. And when Hermann Gunkel tells us that "the prophets were not originally writers but speakers,"[11] he draws attention to their speech and their voices, their ability to move the hearer with a particular effect, one far more important than conveying a message, a mere form of knowledge. From the beginning, speech was intended to heal. As the prophet Isiah views humanity, he sees catastrophe and destitution, and one *diagnosis* in particular stands out: "the whole head is sick, and the whole heart faint" (Isa 1:5). The prophets are motivated by the wisdom of healing. Isaiah does not simply point out moral wrongdoing, concentrating exclusively on sin as an act, original or one most evident in the present. The theology of moral culpability cannot fully explain the psychological frailties, so often self-inflicted, of human beings. People have become psychologically ill, in head and heart, suffering from an illness far worse than being "unclean," merely on the body and superficial, as if a lesion could adequately define the whole of a stricken life. When Isaiah implores everyone to "hear the word of the Lord," (Isa 1:10) the *very first words* spoken by Yahweh are specifically in relation to their most important ritual and observance. The people have become psychologically unstable and they will not be cured by their handed-down traditions, as if offering animal sacrifices could somehow cure them, restoring their health, providing them with the *peace* so necessary for their well-being. *Shalom* can no longer come from the death of a sacrificed animal; on the contrary, violence exacerbates the feeling of being divided from oneself, others, and God. A prophet now recognizes the need to attend to an internal disposition of the spirit (which is now ill, in need of a cure), while simultaneously calling for the abolition of sacrifices. Sacrifices and healing will be in opposition, as they will for Greek philosophers. The sacrificial death of an animal can in no way restore a human failing of the spirit. "To what purpose is the multitude of your sacrifices unto me? saith the Lord: I am full of burnt offerings of rams, and the fat of fed beasts; and I delight not in the blood of bullocks, or of lambs, or of he goats" (Isa 1:11). Isaiah has been given the responsibility of communicating with his people and telling them the words of Yahweh verbatim. He reveals to them how all previous acts of devotion now have to be abandoned; these are many and varied, including feasts, assemblies, and meetings, all the moments of all the days recalled for the purpose of commemoration. The periodic events intended as celebrations of the divine/human relationship are now, so it seems, to be discontinued and replaced with a more constant devotion. Festivals of worship have become irrelevant. The most important religious ritual, the animal sacrifices offered

---

11. Gunkel, "Prophets as Writers and Poets," 24.

daily and on special occasions, is now considered unacceptable. "When ye make many prayers, I will not hear: your hands are full of blood" (Isa 1:15). Even prayers are no longer desired or accepted. Animal sacrifice is not only to be abolished. Their blood has become, when actually seen and perceived, evidence of violence. More importantly, sacrifice must be replaced, as if the prior substitution (a dead animal in place for one's fault) now had to come to an end. "Learn to do well; seek judgment, relieve the oppressed, judge the fatherless, plead for the widow" (Isa 1:17) Yahweh instructs, specifically asking humanity to dedicate itself to a new form of piety—no longer the ritual of animal slaughter but the devotion to the well-being of others and most especially those vulnerable and in need.

In Isaiah, one conclusion above all must be emphasized: the relationship between the abolition of sacrifice and words of healing. Previously, people could not see, nor perceive, but now, in and through Isaiah's prophetic message, they will be able to "hear with their ears, and understand with their heart, and convert (*teshuvah*), and be healed" (Isa 6:10)—with the double-meaning of *teshuvah* explicit, at once a turning back to God and a change in oneself, a conversion, the consistent term to echo in Acts, the letters of Paul, and the gospels of Jesus with the Greek *metanoia*. Finally, when Yahweh implores them to "remember ye not the former things, neither consider the things of old," (Isa 43:18) one striking difference can be heard—and with the all-important idea of *serving*: "Thou hast not brought me the small cattle of thy burnt offerings; neither hast thou honoured me with thine sacrifices. I have not caused you to serve with an offering" (Isa 43:23). Yahweh has not requested to be *served* with sacrifices. On the contrary, Yahweh has reinterpreted the meaning and purpose of service as a fundamental obligation: "But thou hast made me to serve with thy sins" (Isa 43:24). The previous service, provided by animal sacrifice, has now been assumed by the divine so that the idea of service leading to *healing* becomes explicit in Yahweh's relationship with the human world. As René Girard tells us:

> Throughout the prophetic period . . . the prophets address the chosen people and, invariably, what they advocate is the substitution of love and harmony for the sterile and symmetrical conflict of doubles—the violence that sacrifice is no longer capable of *curing*.[12]

Again and again, the Jewish prophets attempt to convey the messages Yahweh has given them, first by saying "Hear, O earth" (noticeably, without

---

12. Girard, *Things Hidden Since the Foundation*, 199, my emphasis.

national distinctions) and then, similar to Isaiah, with the declaration that "your burnt offerings are not acceptable, nor your sacrifices sweet to me" (Jer 6:20). Rather than the performance of a ritual thought to be central to piety and devotion and worship, Jeremiah advises that Yahweh most wants people to devote themselves to each other, taking care of people who are experiencing difficulties, like strangers, orphans, widows, "and shed not innocent blood in this place," (Jer 7:6) an important declaration insofar as, for the first time, the victimized animals are described as "innocent." Jesus will describe them, in Matthew 12:6–7, as "guiltless," specifically using judicial language (the language of justice) to provoke those who sacrifice to reconsider their ritual:

> But I say unto you, That in this place is one greater than the temple. But if ye had known what this meaneth, I will have mercy, and not sacrifice, ye would have not condemned the guiltless.

The animal can no longer be victimized; it must be shown mercy, as Hosea will also demand. Reflecting both the Jewish prophets and Greek philosophers, Jesus will be the singular individual who will both denounce animal sacrifice and act against the temple as the supposedly sacred place where a perpetual slaughter occurred; drawing from Isaiah and the difference between sacrifice and human healing, Jesus says: "They that be whole need not a physician, but they that are sick. But go ye and learn what that meaneth, I will have mercy, and not sacrifice: for I am not come to call the righteous, but sinners to repentance (*metanoian*)" (Matt 9:12–13). Here Jesus juxtaposes a new piety—being a physician and curing others—with the teaching of *metanoia*, with the old practice of sacrificing guiltless animals. Jeremiah makes an even more startling pronouncement, reporting that Yahweh

> Spake not unto your fathers, nor commanded them in the day that I brought them out of the land of Egypt, concerning burnt offerings and sacrifices: But thus commanded them, saying, "Obey my voice, and I will be your God, and ye shall be my people: and walk ye in all the ways that I have commanded you, that it may be well unto you." But they hearkened not, nor inclined their ear, but walked in the counsels and the imagination of their evil heart, and went backward, and not forward." (Jer 7:22–24)

Reporting on the words of Yahweh, Jeremiah reveals what could only be understood as remarkable and astounding: when the Jewish people were released from Egypt, Yahweh *did not* ask them to perform sacrifices, as they had assumed. On the contrary, he specifically commanded them to adopt a new devotion based on obedience to what Yahweh most wanted to fulfill in the world. Jeremiah appears to refute the claim made by Moses. The prophets announce a fissure in Judaism, not thereby to wrench it apart in a final divisiveness much less destruction. They urgently call the people back to their fundamental obligation of developing themselves rather than remaining limited by the performance of a ritual now increasingly without meaning or relevance, its intention now no longer capable of being fulfilled.

Hosea likewise begins with "Hear ye," asking for Yahweh's words to be heard, but this time with an important audience, "O priests,"[13] (Hos 5:1) specifically conversing with the group of people directly in charge of performing sacrifices. "And the revolters are profound to make slaughter, though I have a rebuke of them all" (Hos 5:2). Yahweh expresses a prevailing idea, juxtaposing the sacrifice of animals with another request altogether—one, parenthetically, in principle open to everyone rather than a class with both duties and privileges. Piety and worship cannot in principle be restricted to a class of priests who inherit their positions via the father. Piety has no exclusive particularities and cannot be enjoyed by someone simply through genealogical privilege. Priests cannot be representatives of a nation, a people; individuals are called to represent themselves. The prophets are despised and killed precisely because they dare offer the people an alternative communication and relationship to Yahweh, one without the need for the priests as intermediaries. "They will go with their flocks and with their herds to seek the Lord; but they shall not find him; he hath withdrawn himself from them" (Hos 5:6). Yahweh and human beings have become separated, estranged from each other in part because of the presumption that sacrifice could somehow suffice. Yahweh therefore makes a demand, or rather hopes that by finally acknowledging their "affliction," they will be able to change themselves. A proper devotion to Yahweh will lead to being healed. "He will heal us," (Hos 6:1) and such a healing will take place *only when* sacrifice will be replaced by a much more important example of human devotion. Following Isaiah and with far-reaching implications, Hosea announces that as long as animal sacrifices are performed—as long as killing and the spilling of blood is required—all peace, all health, all individual and social well-being will be impossible. Violence and killing must be disavowed. "For I desired

---

13. Although some of the prophets address their sayings in a critical manner to priests (as does Malachi 2:1 when he emphasizes that "this commandment is for you"), H. H. Rowley's comment in *From Moses to Qumran* should be kept in mind: "to think of the prophets only in terms of the best and priests only in terms of the worst is unwise," 137. Such an observation will be made, remarkably, in the gospel of John when he clearly comments on the divide of the Jewish temple leadership with regard to Jesus.

mercy and not sacrifice," Yahweh says in a juxtaposition to be repeated by Jesus as he himself prepares, for the first time in history, to actively interfere with the temple sacrifices of a politico-religious society, "and the knowledge of God more than burnt offerings" (Hos 6:6). The demand for "mercy" cannot be restricted to human relationships: an entire tradition (obvious, as we shall see, with the Greeks, starting with their aversion to killing and the vegetarianism of Orphics, Pythagoreans, and Empedocles) makes the demand that all sentient beings should be shown mercy and compassion as well; to recognize the existence of the animal independent of any human instrumentality is to develop a previously denied ethical consciousness.

Amos too writes as if directly quoting Yahweh's words of anger and reproach, unequivocally expressing feelings and saying, "I hate, I despise your feast days, and I will not smell in your solemn assemblies" (Amos 5:21). Specifically referring to the "sweet savor" of roasted meat that he seemingly enjoyed in the past, Yahweh now both hates the occasions of the feasts and turns away, with more than indifference, from the smell of sacrificial meat. Yahweh continues: "Though you offer me burnt offerings, I will not accept them: neither will I regard the peace offerings of your fat beasts" (Amos 5:22). Yahweh's refusal, at this point in Jewish history, cannot be compared to the first rejection of a sacrifice, that is Cain's offering of produce from the earth. Rather, Yahweh makes it clear how sacrifices can no longer be considered adequate; the blood of a slaughtered animal can in no way compensate for the way his people are now leading their lives.

Micah again begins with "Hear ye now what the Lord saith," (Mic 6:1) and then, calling into question the nature of piety and worship, proceeds to present his argument rhetorically: "Shall I come before him with burnt offerings, with calves a year old? Will the Lord be pleased with thousands of rams" (Mic 6:6–7)? Yahweh does not require the slaughter of animals. Among the character traits most in need of being developed, Micah too (like Hosea) asks his readers to "love mercy," that is, to rethink one's relationship to others and, by acting justly, ethically, and psychologically, contribute to their well-being. Isaiah, Jeremiah, Hosea, Amos, and Micah, these are only five prominent prophets who repudiate the practice of animal sacrifice and emphasize, directly through Yahweh, a different kind of life altogether, one that stresses the ethical and psychological attributes of human beings most in need of being recalled and developed. By substituting animal sacrifice with healing, they do nothing less than transform the symbol of the served animal to "the prophetic expectation of the servant."[14] The abolition

---

14. Lucas, "Sacrifice in the Prophets," 72.

of animal sacrifice makes possible the transformation of a human being as a religious individual within a new community of believers.

The Jewish prophets, however, are not alone in their reassessment of animal sacrifice as a specifically religious ritual, nor in their emphasis on healing a stricken humanity. In the Greek world, beginning with the pre-Socratic philosophers,[15] there was an equally repeated and consistent argument against the killing of animals as a religious observance—one that served to define the relationship between the gods and human beings insofar as they were citizens of a *polis* such as Athens. The philosophical reexamination (and outright rejection) of animal sacrifice in the Greek world was part of a multifaceted tradition involving several individuals who also founded schools of thought, or sects, with religious characteristics. Philosophy, if not generated out of its dialogue and critique with traditional religious piety and its rituals, nevertheless understood itself as, in part, assuming this obligation—just as Epicurus, for example, will study *physiologia* (all *physis* or natural phenomena) so as to undermine superstition and its role in civic life. Jan Bremmer argues that "except for Orphics and Pythagoreans, few philosophers seem to have been critical of animal sacrifice before Theophrastus' *On Piety*,"[16] associating such a critique only with the successor to Aristotle after his death in 322/21, thereby ignoring a multifaceted tradition of Greek thought, including first and foremost, as we shall see, Socrates. Even a cursory glance at early Greek philosophy makes the concern with the inappropriateness of animal sacrifice—indeed, killing animals and eating meat as such—not simply a peripheral concern. It is important to note that a philosophy of vegetarianism as an ethic was inseparable from the rejection of animal sacrifice. Obviously, individuals or groups who did not eat meat would not participate in any of civic festivals involving ritual slaughter, the fundamental expression of piety and worship of the polis. In the two references to Orphism from the classical period, one striking similarity in terms of lexicon requires commentary. The Orphics, Plato tells us, viewed animal

---

15. In *Therapy of the Word*, Lain-Entralgo believes that "logotherapy is as ancient as Western culture itself" (32), and attempts to trace a psychotherapeutic intent back to Homer; such a genealogy cannot be sustained due to the omnipresence of the gods and the need to perform sacrifices. There may well have been what he calls a "cheering" speech in Homer, but when he also adds "charms" and "conjuration" (practices associated with superstitious religion and much criticized, eventually, by Lucretius and others), a therapeutic philosophy developed by Socrates and Epicurus in the Greek world is simply not possible in Homeric times.

16. Bremmer, *Greek Religion*, 90. A central argument of the study to follow will be to examine the textual evidence (most especially in Plato, Epicurus and his followers, and the gospels of Jesus) concerning the long-held view that animal sacrifice could not be an appropriate expression of piety.

sacrifice as an "unholy" act. More importantly, they make a distinction between an "unsouled" (*apsychen*) and "ensouled" (*empsychen*) being:

> The custom of men sacrificing one another is, in fact, one that survives even now among many peoples; whereas amongst others we hear of how the opposite custom existed, when they were forbidden so much as to eat an ox, and their offerings to the gods consisted, not of animals, but of cakes of meal and grain steeped in honey, and other such bloodless sacrifices, and from flesh they abstained as though it were unholy to eat it or to stain with blood the altars of the gods; instead of that, those of us men who then existed lived what is called an "Orphic life," keeping wholly to inanimate (*apsychen*) food and, contrariwise, abstaining wholly from things animate (*empsychon*).[17]

And in the conversation between Hippolytus and his father in Euripides's play, he tells his son that

> the gods are not such fools as not to be able to see what you're truly like. Go on, then, by all means, spout out all you want about your vegetarian diet (*apsychen boras*) like a quack. By all means, let Orpheus be your master! Enjoy, no, revere, if you wish, all his idle musings, all of his many books.[18]

In making such a distinction, Euripides calls attention to a vegetarian who defines his diet as *apsychen*, without a psyche/soul, as opposed to a diet that includes eating animals *with a soul*.[19] Walter Burkert adds that the recognition of "a *psyche* within" leads to a new conception of a human being furthermore, and that due to this fact "the essential mark of the human person is indeed a revolution."[20] Once the psyche was a characteristic of all sentient beings, the revolution in question therefore became much more comprehensive and included a reconsideration of animals and, of course, the gods themselves and what they had historically required as worship. The

17. Plato, *L.*, 782cd.
18. Euripides, *Hipp.*, 952–55.
19. There is a similar distinction in Genesis. Three references must here suffice: when God first creates "every living creature" (Gen 1:21) the "creature" is, more precisely, a *nephesh hayah*, a living soul. When God then creates Adam and breathes life into his nostrils, he too becomes "a living soul," a *nephesh hayah* (Gen 2:7). And now, even more striking when compared to Noah post-deluge, though not without its ambiguity given the preceding passage: "but flesh with the life (*nephesh*) thereof, which is the blood thereof, shall ye not eat" (Gen 9:4). Is God commanding Noah not to eat animals, who have a living soul? Or, as many translators have it, one cannot eat an animal without first draining its blood?
20. Burkert, *Greek Religion*, 300.

distinction, first of all, calls into question the naturally assumed hierarchy between animals and human beings (with the gods, of course, preeminent) and instead asserts a fundamental commonality characterized by a body and a soul.

Orphics were vegetarians. What remains to be explained (and becomes equally evident with Pythagoras) is the motive for adopting such a renunciation. It is important to note that the Orphics were not simply vegetarians, as if their decision was merely dietary. Although they were concerned for the welfare of animals, so that Orphic ethical consciousness extended to all sentient beings, their refusal to eat meat was inseparable from their rejection of animal sacrifice as a religious ritual within a political context; or to be more precise, the rejection of animal sacrifice was simultaneously a religious and political act. As Marcel Detienne has forcefully argued, the refusal to eat meat is inseparable from the rejection of a system of thought making the sacrifice of animals a state-sanctioned ritual that establishes a proper relationship, and an irreducible division, between human beings and the gods.[21]

> Orphism is a movement of religious protest that defines itself by an attitude of refusal, refusal of the whole politicoreligious system organized around the Olympian gods and the distance that separates them from men... to change one's diet is to throw into doubt the relationship between gods, men, and beasts upon which the whole politicoreligious system of the city rests.[22]

Let us repeat: sacrifice is essential in the maintenance of a "politicoreligious system." Werner Jaeger calls the Orphic abstinence from meat a "commandment."[23] Such a commandment was adopted in explicit contradistinction to the traditionally accepted beliefs and practices of the time and was inseparable from an opposition to the city as then constituted. In this case, an *individual* commandment rejected polis religion. A foundational political act, initiated by philosophical thought, was therefore the critique and rejection of animal sacrifice; in effect, philosophy substituted itself for the religion of the polis.

The philosophical life—and more particularly, the "Pythagorean way of life"[24]—was comprehensive and so well-known that Plato feels no need to explain its particular features. Noticeably, the expression reoccurs in Josephus's *Antiquities* and in the context of establishing a relationship

21. Detienne, *Gardens of Adonis*.
22. Detienne, *Dionysos Slain*, 70.
23. Jaeger, *Theology of the Early Greek*, 216.
24. Plato, *Rep.*, 600b.

between Pythagoreans and the Essenes of Qumran, the community that composed the Dead Sea Scrolls. The Essenes, Josephus writes, "practice a way of life introduced to the Greeks by Pythagoras."[25] As the purported inventor of the word *philosophia*, he was also the founder of a religious society whose characteristics were opposed to state cult. Both Iamblichus of Chalcis in *On the Pythagorean Life* and Porphyry of Tyre[26] (the author of *On Abstinence from Killing Animals*[27]) provided much more detailed descriptions of Pythagoras's teaching and life. The Pythagorean aversion to the killing of animals (interpreted, by some, as a consequence of his theory of metempsychosis or the transmigration of souls) was much more than an ethic of eating or simple vegetarianism. As a founder of a community, Pythagoras was expressly separating himself from his immediate society, from its beliefs and practices. "As long as man continues to be the ruthless destroyer of lower living beings," he argues in a quote attributed to him, "he will never know health or peace."[28] In other words, fundamental to his ethical philosophy was the relationship between killing animals (and more so, in the context of a religious ritual) and a psychologically unhealthy human being, and, by extension, a social world increasingly unaware of itself, its beliefs, and its practices. "Pythagorean vegetarianism was also based on concern for both health of body and health of *psyche*."[29] Vegetarianism and their metaphysical belief in the transmigration of souls were but two ideas developed in contradistinction to the accepted norms. "The refusal to kill animals was particularly radical, as it cut Orphics and some Pythagoreans off from animal sacrifices, the essential religious ritual of the Greek states."[30] In addition to a vegetarianism that had effectively made the group independent, and different from, the majority, Pythagoras introduced one more essential aspect of his teaching: like the prophets of Israel, he established both the importance of specific utterances (his "golden words") and how they

25. Josephus, *Ant.*, 15.371.

26. In the *Life of Pythagoras*, Porphyry testifies that Pythagoras "not only abstained from animal food but would also not come near butchers and hunters," 7.

27. In the Introduction to her translation of *Porphyry*, Clark draws attention to the title and the original—*peri apokhes empsukhon*—and the meaning of *animals with souls*.(Clark, *Porphyry*, 2).

28. As cited in Manning and Serpell, *Animals and Human Society*, 136.

29. Dombrowski, "Philosophical Vegetarianism and Animal Entitlements," 538. This important affirmation requires some expansion. This will be the main argument to follow: the concern most especially with the health of the psyche only began when the previous dedication to the gods turned to human beings taking care of each other; not accidentally does it begin, also, in philosophical schools and communities. In *Golden Verse* 66, Pythagoras makes healing the soul all important in avoiding afflictions.

30. Price, *Religions of the Ancient Greeks*, 123.

would contribute to changing the life and thought of others. The Pythagoreans were divided into two groups, and while the *mathematici* emphasized numbers and music theory, the *acusmatici* or "hearers" were students who memorized his precepts and put them into practice. Constantine Vamvacas defines them as "allegorical aphorisms."[31] W. K. C. Guthrie calls them "sayings" and "precepts."[32] If not the sole originator in the Greek world of the importance of a particular kind of speech, a tradition of healing speech (more precisely, therapeutic philosophy) nevertheless developed out of sayings. These became evident in the teachings of Socrates, Epicurus's *doxai* as principles of his philosophy, and Jesus' *rema* or, literally, "that which is said," the sayings memorized first by his mother Mary (Luke 2:51).

Among the most important of the objections by pre-Socratic philosophers was one by Heraclitus who, in his fifth fragment, also defines religious rites of sacrifice as "unholy" and exposes those who "when defiled they purify themselves with blood, as though one who had stepped into filth were to wash himself with filth."[33] By equating the spilling of sacrificial blood with filth, Heraclitus defines the ritual itself as a form of pollution, *miasma*. Empedocles must certainly be counted as sharing in these sentiments; moreover, he identified himself as a philosopher as well as healer, as attested in his practice of his "healing utterances."[34] His *Purifications*, intended first and foremost as a philosophy of healing in the present, is specifically contrasted with a past age (a Golden Age) when Aphrodite, the goddess of love, was worshipped without sacrificing animals: "[her] altar was not wetted with the unmixed blood of bulls, but this was the greatest abomination among men, to tear out their life-breath and eat their goodly limbs."[35] Empedocles makes the difference between the inappropriateness of animal sacrifice and the therapeutic speech of the philosopher essential to his teaching and life.

As a philosopher and a poet, Empedocles would have considerable influence (along with Epicurus) on Roman poets, Lucretius,[36] Vergil, and Ovid who, in Book 15 of his *Metamorphoses*, has a detailed critique of meat-eating, specifically in relation to Pythagorean teaching:

31. Vamvacas, *Founders of Western Thought*, 57.
32. Guthrie, *History of Greek Philosophy*, 183.
33. Heraclitus, *Fr.*, 5.
34. Empedocles, *Pur.*, 1.
35. From Porphyry's *De Abstinentia* (the incomplete Latin title), as cited in Inwood's *Poem of Empedocles*, 146.
36. As an Epicurean, Lucretius's numerous critiques of animal sacrifice in *On the Nature of Things* will be examined in detail and in relationship, first, to Epicurus's own attitude toward state cultic ritual and, second, compared to Philodemus's arguments in *On Piety*.

> Human beings, stop desecrating your bodies with impious foodstuffs. There are crops; there are apples weighing down the branches; and ripening grapes on the vines; there are flavoursome herbs; and those that can be rendered mild and gentle over the flames; and you do not lack flowing milk; or honey fragrant from the flowering thyme. The earth, prodigal of its wealth, supplies with gentle sustenance, and offers you food without killing or shedding blood.[37]

Beginning with Lucretius, the Roman poets will no longer sustain the belief that sacrifice (the Latin *sacer facere*) has any relation at all to that which is *made sacred*. The belief that sacrificial slaughter "points to humanity's desire for renewal: to 'make sacred' and participate in the very source of life,"[38] will be exposed most especially by Lucretius the Epicurean poet in his critique of Roman *superstitio*, and in one scene of remarkable pathos in *On the Nature of Things*.

Describing both individuals and families as they sacrificed, Martin Perrson Nilsson writes that "he might bring a votive before a god and offer it together with his family, various reliefs represent family sacrifices of this kind, significantly, *most of them are to the physician-god Asklepios*."[39] Nilsson makes the important observation that sacrifices were most often made as appeals to restored health, though once again perpetual illness or eventual death made all adherents to the cult aware of divine inconsistency in their responses. If Greek philosophers emerged when they understood the concerns of the epic poets, wondering not so much whether the gods existed or not, but about their perceived ability to effect the human world, they began to reconceive the gods, and therefore themselves and the possibility of a new self-understanding. And if philosophers began to think at least in part when they understood the ambiguity present in the epics of the poets, a tradition of thought would soon be developed with its first detailed exposition in the thought of Socrates and Epicurus in the Greek world and, identifying with the call of the prophets, Jesus as another historical individual whose life and teaching would become a consistent reevaluation of forms of piety and worship as practiced in the temple of Jerusalem. In the teachings of Socrates, Epicurus, and Jesus, there are two consistent and

---

37. Ovid, *Met.*, 15.60.

38. Sedley, "Sacrifice, Transcendence, and 'Making Sacred,'" 268.

39. Nilsson, *Greek Piety*, 13, my emphasis. If, as Nilsson points out, many sacrifices were done specifically to ask for healing, the transformation of consciousness by philosophers was exemplified in this one deviance from tradition: healing could not be accomplished through an appeal to the gods. Healing became a human responsibility and duty.

interrelated ideas: the reevaluation of religious piety as currently practiced, and the emphasis on taking care of the health of others.

The transformation of a traditional religious sensibility resulted in a far-reaching consequence: when the custom of providing a service to the gods began to be questioned, resisted, and for some abolished as a civic requirement, all the previous care for the gods (and always expecting the reciprocal relationship to be continued in sacrifice and prayer) turned into providing a service *to others*. The transformation in antiquity did not result, as Michel Foucault argues, in "the care of the self,"[40] in those individually motivated practices of asceticism, the care of the self as a narcissistic pursuit of discipline and self-control. Rather, once the gods were reconceived and their meaning fundamentally altered, the emphasis was now on how human beings would provide service to *each other*. In his response to and critique of Foucault, the Epicureans in particular are singled out by Pierre Hadot[41] as exemplary in their practice of "mutual affection," and not simply to other Epicureans in their school or elsewhere. What occurs in antiquity, especially in the three figures of Socrates, Epicurus, and Jesus, is a rethinking of human relationships and how best to achieve what Epicurus called *ataraxia*, the freedom from the disturbances of the psyche now made possible by one's philosophical/therapeutic vocation.

While some have analyzed the origin of a new piety (or, in Guy Stroumsa's words, "a new religiosity or piety"[42]) during the third and fourth centuries CE, the principles of its emergence had already been established in the prophetic writings of the Hebrew Bible and in the philosophy beginning in fifth-century Greece, which Stroumsa acknowledges but does not individually interpret. It will now be necessary to counter Bremmer's assertion that opposition to animal sacrifice was rare before Theophrastus (371–287 BCE) and instead provide a detailed reading of some exemplary Platonic texts where the philosophy of Socrates specifically raises the question of the meaning of traditional piety and, central to his arguments, the relevance of prayer and the associated practices that sustained the polis: animal sacrifice. While Stroumsa is at least partly correct in associating the radical ideas of Christianity to Judaism (he writes that "such a transformation was only conceivable among philosophers and among the Jews—in very different ways,

---

40. Foucault, *Care of the Self*.

41. Hadot, *Philosophy as a Way of Life*. See, in particular, "Reflections on the Idea of the 'Cultivation of the Self,'" 206–13. Hadot's main argument is that "Foucault is propounding a culture of the self which is *too* aesthetic," 211. One could add "too aesthetic" and neglecting an ethic of the self not concerned with oneself (in culture, care, or cultivation) but with the care of others.

42. Stroumsa, *End of Sacrifice*, 4.

in each case, of course"⁴³), he does not, as a historian, provide a *hermeneutic* reading of the philosophical texts most representative of what he calls the "religious revolution" in question. If the critique of animal sacrifice in the Jewish prophets and the pre-Socratic philosophers led to a fundamental rethinking of the meaning of piety in antiquity, it is now necessary to turn to specific texts reflecting both traditions and see how the lives and teachings of Socrates, Epicurus, and Jesus (as well as their followers) ultimately led to the end of animal sacrifice and its replacement with a new service to the divine. Only when the purpose of animal sacrifice as a religious ritual was exposed to a sustained philosophical critique did it become possible to envision a wholly different and new piety that involved a dedication to people's healing or *soteriology*.⁴⁴

---

43. Stroumsa, *End of Sacrifice*, 18. In at least one way (and I argue it may very well be the most fundamental) there was a profound similarity in both, that is, in the critique of animal sacrifice and its substitution by a certain kind of speaking related to healing.

44. In *Drudgery Divine*, and especially in his concluding chapter "On Comparing Settings" (116–43), Jonathan Smith presents the concept of soteriology as essentially divided between a "this worldly" and "other worldly" *salvation*—a word that, in the New Testament, has been metaphysically interpreted in relation to the divine—though not without ambiguity, as is evident in Paul's letters. In the study to follow, however, and in one of the most consistent arguments of the entire work, soteriology can also be translated (as in Epicurus's *Vatican Sayings*) as a specifically psychotherapeutic healing in contradistinction to all metaphysical associations; in other words, my attempt throughout will be to specifically stress the confrontation of individuals to their ancient religions, and to provide what they perceive to be the only response possible: a "healing" that can be accomplished in the here and now and rejects any appeal to a metaphysical origin.

Chapter 1

Socrates's "Impiety"

1. *The Indictment*

DESPITE THE WELL-KNOWN ACCUSATIONS made against Socrates and the subsequent judicial charges leading to his trial and ultimately to his execution (they include three perceived crimes, all of them related to impiety: refusing to acknowledge the gods of the city, inventing new gods, and corrupting the young) one of the more specific of his impious beliefs has not been sufficiently considered: Socrates's unsettling philosophy for the citizens of the polis cannot be understood without acknowledging his implicit critique of Athenian religious *practice* (first and foremost, the ritual of animal sacrifice[1]) as well as *his* conception of a fundamentally new expression of piety in and through a *logoi* dedicated to the psychical well-being of others as individuals and as citizens of Athens. His supposed impiety, most in evidence in his private conversation with his friend and self-styled expert in religious matters, Euthyphro, and even more succinctly if indirectly in the all-important myth of Aristophanes in the *Symposium*, cannot be disassociated from how the Athenians conceive and relate themselves to the gods in their beliefs and observances. The most central of these is the necessary

---

1. In "The Impiety of Socrates," M. F. Burnyeat rhetorically asks: "What would be left of traditional (fifth century) religion, hence what would be left of traditional (fifth century) Athenian life, if the city accepted Socrates' view that divinity demands from human beings is not propitions and sacrifices, festivals and processions, but the practice of moral philosophy?," 6. This position was articulated by Gregory Vlastos in *Socrates: Ironist and Moral Philosopher*. It is this idea of "moral philosophy" that needs to be more precisely defined to reflect Socrates's ideas on a new piety.

ritual of animal sacrifice, that is, *thusia*, and all its convenient euphemisms ("making smoke," or "burnt offerings") instead of the much more graphic and visceral *sphagia*, the violent slaughter of an animal by means of slitting its throat with a knife, or in the case of an ox, severing its vertebrae with an axe, blood-letting and sprinkling on the altar, skinning and gutting, dismemberment, roasting of the *splanchna* and butchered parts, and eventual consumption as a *religious ritual* especially important to the identity of the city-state.[2] In the introduction to their co-edited *Greek and Roman Animal Sacrifice*, Christopher Faraone and F. S. Naiden argue that the Greek language does not have a *vox propria* for "animal sacrifice," that is, a precise term to define the cultic slaughter of an animal. They write: "the common term *thuein*, for example, meant to 'make smoke,' not to slaughter and consume an animal victim."[3] The rhetoric itself betrays the denial of the animal's death as the culmination of the ritual. The ascending smoke is produced from fire and the sizzling parts of the animal are now of course referred to with another euphemism: meat. That they ignore the *olakautein* (the total burning of the animal, or holocaust) allows them to more completely deny a historical reality.[4] By reading *thuein* as simply, innocently, to "make smoke" (leaving aside the other common translation, "burnt offering"), modern readers are in jeopardy of accepting the euphemism and thereby ignoring the animal as a sacrificial victim. Jean-Pierre Vernant could not be more eloquent when he writes, "The distance between the candid nakedness of the practice and the fallacious masquerade of discourse is a measure of that part of the ideology governing social consciousness."[5] For Vernant, as with other notable critics of animal sacrifice (namely Walter Burkert and René Girard), the violent death of the sacrificial victim is precisely at the center of the entire ceremony; killing and death at an altar are its culmination. Despite emphasizing the feasting and celebration of the human participants during a particular festival (for example, the two most important in Athens are the

---

2. Although Socrates's affiliation to any Orphic-Pythagorean group remains a matter of debate, his independence from the polis religion of Athens is attested in many dialogues—as we shall see in what follows. The theory of Socrates's religion being unofficial—and inspired by Orphic-Pythagorean ideas—was first presented by Alfred Edward Taylor in his *Varia Socratica*. Although Socrates does not necessarily have to be dedicated to either Orphic or Pythagorean ideas, he was certainly familiar with them. There are no indications of Socrates being a vegetarian, nor does he have a particular ethical regard for the life of an animal, as did both these sects; in any case, these are ancillary issues. Socrates calls into question (in fact, shows to be entirely inappropriate) *animal sacrifice as a religious practice indicative of piety*.

3. Faraone and Naiden, *Greek and Roman Animal Sacrifice*, 3.

4. For the iconographic evidence, see van Straten's *Hierà Kalá*.

5. Vernant, *Mortals and Immortals*, 294.

Panathenaea and the Dionysia) Sarah Peirce admits that "no definition of thysia is possible that excludes the slaughter."[6] When Detienne adds that "political power cannot be exercised without sacrificial practice,"[7] Socrates's charge of impiety includes a simultaneous religious and political subversion of an ancient custom, and now its substitution with an innovative form of piety and worship. Moreover, if "sacrifice was a mechanism for honoring one's superiors,"[8] as defined by the values of the polis, Socrates undermined the hierarchy inherent in the ritual, the first and foremost of which were the wealthy landowners who were considered benefactors when donating animals for sacrifice. That "the primary function of sacrifice is to define hierarchies"[9] was true in Athens as it would be in Rome—and more so in the context of empire and the succession of Caesars. With few exceptions, Socrates has been neglected as a philosopher who specifically examines the meaning and purpose of animal sacrifice as a form of religious worship to the Olympian gods and, evident by the judicial charges against him, was perceived to be a threat to the religiopolitical establishment of the polis. Socrates's philosophy threatened to undermine the foundations of civic life insofar as it was supported by a human relationship to the gods that had been perpetuated by a long-standing tradition. W. R. Connor is one of the few to add:

> in the political atmosphere of 399 his [Socrates's] insistence on the categorical commands of justice rather than the traditional piety of prayer and sacrifice would have seemed a strong political statement and provided thereby the basis for his indictment at the hands of worried politicians.[10]

During consistent declarations and statements (though, in the *Euthyphro*, these are most often expressed as ironic questions intended to provoke reflection), Socrates will present a thorough if subtle critique of the practice of animal sacrifice as an intended service or *therapeia* to the gods, repeatedly calling into question the purpose for such a ritual, that is, the exchange of reciprocal gifts and its mutual benefit known as *charis*[11] and what the

---

6. Peirce, "Death, Revelry, and Thysia," 221.
7. Detienne, "Culinary Practices and the Spirit," 3.
8. DeMaris, "Sacrifice, an Ancient Mediterranean Ritual," 70.
9. Rüpke, *Religion of the Romans*, 145.
10. Connor, "Other 399," 55. Again, as in the previous affirmation of Vlastos's moral philosophy, Connor's "categorical commands of justice" are made explicit by Socrates most especially, as we shall see, during his trial in the *Apology*.
11. In "A Religious Revolution?," Lännström argues that *do ut des* and the reciprocity of *charis* should be understood differently. Her important point is: "regardless of

Romans would later define as the *do ut des* relationship ("to give so you may give"). Socrates was charged with being impious according to the beliefs of the Athenians (as other philosophers and playwrights, including Euripides, were in the closing decades of the fifth century and beyond[12]) due to his attempt to reevaluate the rituals to the gods and put into doubt the very desire of their anticipated response, whatever blessings they could bestow. Only when such a service to the gods is abandoned, Socrates will argue, will human beings be able to properly take care of each other and thereby fulfill an obligation that no less than Apollo, the god of healing among his other abilities and responsibilities, has imposed on the conversational philosopher as his most important duty. The healing of others will become the quintessential philosophical responsibility requiring a rethinking of *ethos*. Indeed, if Apollo has been understood to be a law-giver and, above all, providing "the greatest, the finest, and the first (*prota*) enactments," (and the emphasis should not go unnoticed) the ones now specifically mentioned are "the founding of temples, sacrifices (*thusiai*), and other services (*therapeiai*) to the gods,"[13] principles Socrates will subvert, above all during his trial, by reconceiving the meaning of Apollo and reinterpreting his role in the pantheon of the gods. Whether Socrates disregards all the others gods for a Greek proto-monotheism remains, at least, a suggestive possibility in the *Apology*.

Socrates has been charged with the capital crime of impiety for undermining the supposed foundations of the city's edicts, calling into question the purpose of sacrifice, and for transforming the idea of religious *therapeia*. When Socrates begins to inquire about "What would be the general lines about the gods (*peri theologias*)?,[14]" he asks the question so as to philosophically evaluate the human conception of the gods (the *logoi* than can be said

---

what Socrates himself intended, these views could easily be extended into a call for a virtual abolishment of sacrifice," 273. Socrates may not have *directly* called for the abolition sacrifice; his discussions, however, and the beliefs of his students and friends, make his position unequivocal.

12. A list of the intellectuals who were suspected of impiety or actually charged with the crime would be extensive. To name but one prior to Socrates, and who could not be counted as an influence on Socrates's consideration of the gods and religion, is Protagoras of Abdera. According to several testimonies—for one, in Cicero's *On the Nature of the Gods* (1.23.63)—Protagoras began his treatise on the gods with the statement: "About the gods I am unable to affirm either how they exist or how they do not exist." His agnosticism led to his banishment from Athens and the public burning of his books. Persecutions of radical thinkers continued well into the fourth century. See, for example, O'Sullivan's "Athenian Impiety Trials."

13. Plato, *Rep.*, 427b.

14. Ibid, 379a.

about them) and, equally as important, how such an idea will influence and determine the life of an individual no less than the city of Athens, which is the very reason it is necessary to examine the speech of Aristophanes in the *Symposium* prior to Socrates' pre-trial conversation with his friend Euthyphro. Ironically, the speech by the famous comic playwright and his representation of a momentous event in the relationship between human beings and the pantheon of the gods (rebellion first, followed by a peculiar punishment) will expose Athens's theology as tragic from beginning to end. In the speech of Aristophanes, Plato will turn the comic playwright into a tragic theologian and thereby expose the polis and its traditions.

2. Athens's Tragic Theology

Among the most noticeable difference between Socrates's private conversation with a friend in the *Euthyphro* and his much more public speech during his trial in the *Apology* are the specific words he uses when describing human service, either to the gods or to others. The distinction will be repeated and often emphasized with an unmistakeable lexicon, in the first consistent, in the second specifically defining one's civic duties and responsibilities as a *servant*, parenthetically the same word, *uperetes*, used in the gospels to describe the ministry of Jesus. In his conversation with Euthyphro, Socrates repeatedly uses one specific term (*therapeia*, and its relationship to animal sacrifice, *thusia*) that *not once* does he use when addressing the jurors of his trial, that is, the citizens of Athens. In the Areopagus, Socrates's speech is measured and precise, demanding to be heard differently (and in comparison to) his philosophical conversation. Plato's composition of the two interrelated dialogues demands such attention. The shift in vocabulary—surely not accidental, and evidence of Plato's sensitivity to readers' *perception* of Socrates—cannot be overlooked. In order to attempt to define Socrates's transformation of the idea and practice of piety, quite different from what has been inherited from the *archaic* past and perpetuated with customs, traditions, and observances in the present, Socrates's vocabulary will be noticeably altered during his trial. His service will be related to the social responsibilities of a citizen. In the *Apology*, Socrates never uses a term central to his discussion prior to his public trial. What, then, are the main differences between the two Platonic works and what specific terminology does Socrates use in each?

Before providing the examples, and their implications for understanding Socrates's critique of Athenian ritual, turning to another composition, the *Symposium*, will allow us to notice an event (the banquet in celebration of Agathon's victory at a dramatic festival in 416 BCE) that describes some crucial points of Athenian religion and, specifically, the relationship between human beings and the gods in a conflictual, *agonistic* beginning. The dialogue most associated with different speeches dedicated to praising Eros—be it the god or love—also presents a reevaluation of Athenian religion as well as a conception of Socrates's theology and its relation to his philosophy. By the time of Socrates's trial, Apollo will do nothing less than supersede Eros as the god of love and inaugurate a new form of piety along with a kind of speech described in significant dialogues, noticeably in Aristophanes's *Birds*, as *psychagogy*,[15] a "leading of the soul" that will be accomplished between a speaker and a self-reflective listener. This notion will also later be defined, in the philosophy of Epicurus, Paul's letters, and the gospels of Jesus, as both *paressia* and *paraklesis*. By portraying the tragic theology of the Greeks in a speech by a comic playwright who, in the past, turned Socrates into a philosopher to be ridiculed as a buffoon, Plato will literally have the last laugh. By so doing, Plato will follow the critique of Athenian religion with the examination of piety in the *Euthyphro* and with a culminating speech in the *Apology* that will substitute Socrates himself as a gift instead of the previous offering to the gods in the form of sacrificed animals and prayer. The entire logic of sacrificial reciprocity will be abandoned in favor of a gift given for the sake of others (for their *soteria*, their healing) and with no expectation of an equal return. The soteriological speech of the philosopher will replace animal sacrifice as an expression of piety.

In Plato's *Symposium*, the dramatic presentation of a gathering of Athenians all intent on praising the god of love, and Socrates's philosophical teaching and therapeutic relationship to others—best described, as we shall see, in the apparently "drunken" speech by Alcibiades[16]—is expressed in contradistinction to all the other speeches. The best example of this is the one attributed to Socrates himself in his representation of the *mantis* Diotima, the woman who postponed a plague by instructing the Athenians about what sacrifices to make and who believed that spirits shuttle between human beings and gods "conveying prayer and sacrifice from men to gods, while for men they bring commands from the gods and gifts in return for sacrifices."[17] But the speech that is most exemplary of the tragic conception of the gods will be revealed, if unwittingly, by the comic playwright Aristophanes—who attended Socrates's trial and was mentioned as one of

---

15. Aristophanes, *B.*, 1553.
16. This will be the subject of chapter two.
17. Plato, *Sym.*, 202e.

Socrates's detractors if not an outright accuser.[18] However, if the speech of Aristophanes is to be understood and related to Socrates the philosopher as a critic of traditional religion, it is first necessary to provide a framework for his speech in a much neglected comment by Agathon in the "Introductory Dialogue," the first that will indirectly establish the human relationship of *therapeia* to the gods as analogous to slaves towards their masters, a service based on inequality, coercion, and exploitation—a problem already evident in Hesiod's *Theogony* and in the events surrounding Prometheus's disobedience and punishment.

As Agathon and his guests are already reclined on their couches and waiting to be served, Socrates has yet to arrive. While walking toward Agathon's house and the symposium with his friend Aristodemus,[19] he has been suddenly compelled to stop "to think about something" and, at the same time has "lost himself in thought,"[20] not so much distracted as enticed. In the following descriptions of Socrates's eccentric behavior—which emphasizes him as preoccupied, drawn toward a thought or perhaps the voice of his *daimonion* he can neither ignore nor disobey—the uniqueness of his character is portrayed, one much admired by his friends and students, much maligned by conservative individuals he has offended by exposing their pretenses of wisdom or goodness or ability to practice a particular

---

18. In Aristophanes'ss *Clouds*, Socrates is portrayed as someone interested in explaining natural phenomena and, more significantly for my argument, is directly associated with the critique of animal sacrifice. During one memorable conversation, Socrates tells Strepsiades: "will you not, pray, now believe in no god, except what we believe in—this Chaos, and the Clouds, and the Tongue—these three?" Strepsiades adds: "absolutely I would not even converse with the others, not even if I met them; nor would I sacrifice to them" (423–26). This will not be the last time one of Socrates'ss friends or students specifically rejects the practice of sacrifice; that "Tongue" is substituted for sacrifice will become much more telling during the trial. Subsequent philosophers will become the almost stock characters of comedies: see, for example, chapter 1 of Pamela Gordon's *Invention and Gendering of Epicurus*.

19. Aristodemus is a crucial presence here, not only as a student of Socrates, but also someone who appears in Xenophon's *Memorabilia* as an example of an individual who refuses to observe the religious ritual of animal sacrifice. Xenophon writes that Aristodemus "did not sacrifice to the gods (*thuonta tois theois*) or make us of divination (*mantike*) but even laughed at those who did" (1.4.2). A student of Socrates is clearly represented as the opposite of what is considered pious. The charge of "corrupting the young," then, is no longer ambiguous: it is specifically related to Socrates'ss teaching to avoid the ritual animal sacrifice and the associated belief in manticism or divination. It is inconceivable that one of Socrates'ss students would have rejected animal sacrifice if he had been taught otherwise; and as we shall see in *Alcibiades II*, prayer will also be open to Socrates'ss critique—and for the interesting reason that the desired-for outcome of a prayer may, in fact, lead to unwanted consequences.

20. Plato, *Sym.*, 174d.

skill necessary for the well-ordered city. His character and individual *spirit* will soon be on trial, judged by others to be neglecting the gods of the polis and instead listening to his personal *daimonion* and, as he will reveal in the *Apology*, for ignoring traditional observances and only obeying a god who gives him one all-important command. Obedience to his god Apollo will define his piety, with dedication to the *psyche* of others his most important duty as a philosopher. When Aristodemus tells Agathon that at one point he "turned around" (*metastrephomenos*) to look for him but Socrates was "nowhere to be seen," (174e) there are two additional meanings beyond the merely literal description of the scene. First, when Aristodemus "turns around," the *metastrepho*[21] has the added meaning of a necessity that he has yet to fulfill. He must still turn his soul or convert, *change himself*. And second, Socrates is nowhere to be seen. He is metaphorically invisible; he demands to be perceived, but the majority of Athenians are not up to the demand. His teaching, and his character, remains inaccessible to most. He has not been understood because custom, what Hippias called "the tyrant of mankind,"[22] makes him unrecognizable to everyone except those most devoted to his teaching and who are willing to expose themselves—and what they have inherited from their city—to a thorough self-examination. Socrates is different than his times; as an individual (that is, by being an example) he introduces an idea that is essential to the conception of human beings, to the idea of human nature to be so decisive in *Alcibiades I*: human beings can change and therefore become different than merely being reflections (mere copies, and for instrumental reasons) of their time and place.

When Agathon describes Socrates as "strange," (*atopos*, 215a) Alcibiades, at the end of the *Symposium*, will also describe him in a similar way. Being *atopos* is a reflection of his character in terms of being strange, weird, and bizarre because he is "out of place," in opposition to the regulations of the city. Phaedrus, for example, tells Socrates that he is "remarkable . . . you're like a complete stranger (*atopotatos*)—literally, as you say, as if you

---

21. In *Philosophy as a Way of life*, Pierre Hadot defines the ultimate aim of Socratic thought as "a conversion (*metastrophe*) brought about with the totality of the soul," 96. In a footnote, Hadot quotes from the *Republic* and adds that "education is the art of turning this eye of the soul." He adds one more, again quoting from the *Republic*, "always accustom the soul to come as quickly as possible to cure the ailing part. . . making lamentations disappear by means of its therapy" (604b-d). Finally, the idea of "turning a soul" (*peristrophe alla psyches*) should be also related (521c). The turning of the soul as the culmination of Socrates'ss teaching once he reenters the cave will be discussed at a later point.

22. Plato, *Cr.*, 337d.

were a visitor being shown around, not a local resident."²³ Alcibiades succinctly describes Socrates as

> unique; he is like no one else in the past and no one in the present... this man here is so bizarre (*atopian anthropon*), his ways and his ideas are so unusual, that, search as you might, you'll never find anyone else, alive or dead, who's even remotely like him" (221d).

Finally, in *Alcibiades 1*, Socrates is described by the dialogue's main protagonist as "extraordinary" (*atopoperos*, 106a).

Socrates is perceived to be unique, certainly without contemporary equals and, therefore, an individual whose life and teaching are in direct opposition to the customs and traditions of the city of Athens. By virtue of his character and philosophy, Socrates does not belong in the city of Athens despite being a citizen; he has, at best, a very precarious social position. In the *Apology*, he will be described similarly as *perissos*, someone who is extraordinary, who has separated himself from others, a quality admired by some and resented by others. His way of life and teaching make him a threat to the well-run city since all his conversations, direct or ironic, probing and relentless, are consistently motivated by one comprehensive intent: not simply to expose the ignorance of Athenian citizens—as if he was a mere epistemologist interested in knowledge, allowing others to know—but to radically, completely transform both *psyche* and *polis*. Aristodemus, who only partly understands his words, tells Agathon that it is one of Socrates's "habits" (*ethos*) to stand motionless, in thought, and be "absent." Despite Socrates, for the moment, not being literally present and reminding everyone that they too need to find themselves, that they can change and discover a part of themselves not determined by what they have inherited from parents and teachers and those in positions of authority, Agathon's next seemingly simple order has consequences that will continue throughout the symposium (in the speech of Aristophanes), and, equally importantly, will also be prominent in two dialogues: one before Socrates's trial, the other one during the trial. Why is Agathon's order to his slaves so significant especially in relation to Socrates's perceived impiety?

The seemingly unimportant comment to his slaves (literally, children and *minors*), establishes several pairs of unequal relations: slaves and the free, children and adults, and, most significant of all, human beings and the gods, a relation that in both the speech of Aristophanes and in the pre-trial dialogue the *Euthyphro* will begin to reveal Socrates's subtle and indirect

23. Plato, *Phaedrus*, 230c.

but nonetheless noticeable reevaluation of Athenian piety, which is no less than the foundational ideals of the city. Equally important is the observation made by Socrates when in the *Crito* he speaks for "the Laws" and they remind him and his friend that as an Athenian citizen "you were our child and slave."[24] Socrates makes an important juxtaposition when he rhetorically asks Callicles "Am I to withstand the Athenians with the idea of improving them, like a doctor, or to behave like a servant whose object is simply to do his master's pleasure?"[25] Slavery and healing are here juxtaposed; as they will be from now on, often and repeatedly.

Before the beginning of the symposium, Agathon orders the slaves to "go ahead and serve the rest of us. What you serve is completely up to you; pretend nobody's supervising you—as if I ever did! Imagine that we are all your own guests, myself included. Give us good reason to praise (*epainomen*) your service (*therapeute*)" (175b–c). The *symposiasts* will soon turn to praising the god of love for his apparent service to human beings, as if he could be a benefactor, giving gifts as a sign of divine/human reciprocity. But by following the speech of Aristophanes and relating it to what occurs later, we can appreciate Socrates's philosophy insofar as it comments, and critiques, the specific *practices* of Athenian religion—one in particular that involves humans being butchers, cooks, and servants feeding the gods. That is to say, precisely in the same position as the household slaves attending to their masters at a banquet. A certain conception of the gods has thereby *domesticated* human beings, imposing on them a limited identity and ability: that of mere servants and slaves of masters, subordinate and exploited and ordered about with impunity, the reason for gods and mortals "negotiating" at Mekone[26] and due to a dispute that will be noticeable once again in the speech of Aristophanes.

If the relations of master/slave, child/parent, human beings/gods must be maintained in the city of Athens, one of the first and most significant comments made by Socrates involves exposing the foundations of social relations, and in particular his evaluation of the acts performed by human beings in service of the gods. Does Socrates argue that the slaves who serve guests at a symposium are analogous to human beings who slavishly serve the gods? Just as slaves feed humans, so do they in turn feed the gods in a civic ritual, for in giving a gift to the gods in the form of animal sacrifice they know (in Homer's *Iliad* no less than in Genesis 4) that the expected and hoped for exchange may in fact be denied and withheld. Sacrifice may

---

24. Plato, *Cr.* 50e.
25. Plato, *Grg.* 521a.
26. Hesiod, *Th.* 535–6.

be rejected. The offering of a sacrifice is fundamentally ambiguous since the expected acknowledgment may be categorically refused. As a consequence, human apprehension is constant and unavoidable unless philosophy intervenes to undermine the presuppositions of such a belief, restoring humanity to itself by transforming (if not, yet, entirely eliminating) a certain conception of the gods.

Prior to beginning his speech, and in part a response to the physician Eryximachus—the socially conservative speaker who preceded him, a physician of the body and restricted to empirical observations and prescriptions—Aristophanes must have reflected on the speech and wondered how best to respond. Argue? Persuade? Attempt to dazzle with rhetorical eloquence? Eryximachus had concluded his speech in a peculiar way, mentioning "the rites of sacrifice (*thusiai*) and the whole area with which the art of divination is concerned, that is, the interaction (*koinonia*) between men and gods" (188b–c). There are, then, two complementary parts to a pious observance: animal sacrifice and being prophetic and oracular insofar as it is necessary to anticipate the desire of the gods. To be a seer (as Euthyphro will claim to be) is essential. This is the remarkable claim Socrates will also make for himself during his trial when he reveals how he is in direct communication with the god Apollo. There is also a proper love in relation to the gods in terms of *koinonia*, a concept that can be rendered as fellowship. "What is the origin of all impiety (*asebeia*)?" (188c) the physician asks, a question that will need to be related both to the *Euthyphro* as well as Socrates's defense as represented in the *Apology*. For Eryximachus the physician, who seems to have some knowledge of health and healing (at least, of the body), he believes that piety involves proper "interactions between men and gods," (188c) and, in particular, devotion to a healthy love. Piety for him is the dedication to serve the love that heals, one that has a double purpose: "the bonds of human society, concord with the gods," (188d) a definition that Socrates explicitly questions and rejects in the *Euthyphro*. Not once during his speech does Eryximachus evaluate either the beliefs or the practices of Athenian religion; they are simply accepted due to tradition and viewed as self-evident because they are supported by a foundational if inaccessible past. His rational discourse cannot recognize its mythic influence. The sacrifice of animals, as a show of reverence and love to the gods, providing them with a specific kind of offering, cannot be called into question. Nor can the practice of divination, the specific kind of knowledge that anticipates the desire of the gods, the knowledge proper to someone, like Euthyphro, who is a *mantis*. That such manticism can be achieved through reading the entrails of sacrificed animals (hieroscopy was the interpretation of *hieara* as signs[27]) may be too ironic for Socrates to even mention: the human future can only be told once the life of an animal has been terminated and its entrails examined for signs. Eryximachus therefore concludes with an admission, one that does not cause him sufficient concern: "perhaps I, too, have omitted a great deal in the discourse on Love," (188e) he tells his listeners, and Aristophanes in particular, who now has been cured of his hiccups and can therefore begin his own speech and possibly "complete the argument" (188e) provided by the physician. However, Aristophanes will neither complete the argument nor analyze, as necessary, the meaning of being impious and the associated rites of sacrifice. The comic playwright will unwittingly present the speech in the *Symposium* as the most representative of the tragic theology of the city of Athens. He is not worried about being funny (after all, he admits, that would be consistent with his Muse), but he is most worried about saying something "ridiculous," (189b) something absurd, as if he senses—but cannot quite understand, certainly consciously—the implications of his prepared speech.

Before beginning his speech proper, however, Aristophanes makes some introductory comments, beginning with his belief that "people have entirely missed the power of love" (*erotos dynamin*) (189c). According to Aristophanes, human beings have been unable to see his dynamic ability; he seems to be enigmatic, elusive, not through any dissimulation on his part, but from a human flaw and inadequacy. If they had understood this power and what it could accomplish (a power, furthermore, dedicated to them) "they'd have built the greatest temples and altars and made the greatest sacrifices" (189c). Aristophanes speaks as if human beings *had not* fulfilled these obligations and responsibilities. The sacrifices, made upon altars, seem to be the most direct expression of reverence and piety—a ritual repeatedly questioned by Socrates (as we shall see) in his conversation with Euthyphro. Furthermore, Socrates's impiety may also be related to his evaluation of commemorative festivals, the significant days of the year that perpetuate the traditions of the past and therefore make any change or innovation impossible. Festivals are observances of a mythic past. If only they were aware of the power of love, human beings would build the largest altars and make the biggest sacrifices to the gods. "For he loves the human race," (literally, he is the god with the most *philanthropia*) because he "stands by us in our troubles, and cures those ills we humans are most happy to have mended" (189d). Aristophanes describes this god in several different ways as essentially a healer, someone who helps in terms of *iatreuō*, healing. The god of love then heals human affliction, an initial position that is soon to

---

27. See Bonnechere, "Divination."

become impossible to sustain and eventually will put into question Aristophanes's myth from beginning to end. Gods cannot heal; only a human being dedicated to being an *epikourous* (189d) can treat the afflictions of others and provide them with *soteria*.

Aristophanes then begins his speech proper by emphasizing how human nature now is not as it used to be "in the beginning," (189d) a time when human beings were whole, complete, but not, as some have argued, "perfect."[28] Others have described the protohumans as "self-satisfied and self-sufficient.[29] On the contrary, they can neither be perfect nor self-sufficient because, as Matthew Meyer adds, they are in "conflict with the reigning deities."[30] Despite the *physical* attributes of wholeness and being complete ("completely round") they have a life that makes difficult demands on them, at least in part because they are not independent. Not only do they lack freedom, they are in fact in a position of submission and *servitude* to the gods and are therefore in a perpetual state of restlessness and dissatisfaction. They are ultimately compelled to defy the gods so as to define themselves. The protohumans neither revere the gods nor are in awe of them. They simply desire to undo the terms of their relationship, this time doing more than attempting to settle a dispute between them as described in Hesiod's *Theogony*. Humans may be justifiably angry, now perceiving the demands made upon them by the gods to be a form of extortion and with a cynical disregard for their well-being. Leo Strauss makes an important comment: "it seems that originally men had honored the Olympian gods and *brought sacrifices to them prior to their rebellion*."[31] Aristophanes continues with his description of human characteristics and adds, first of all, that "they were like their parents in the sky" (190b)—presumably, parents are the gods—and that *therefore* they were strong, powerful, terrible. If they were children however, certainly younger than their parents and still in a position of inferiority and dependence, they could not be as strong, powerful, or terrible as Aristophanes portrays them, except perhaps in emotion, intelligence, and will. When they "made an attempt (*epexeiresan*) on the gods," and "tried to make an ascent to heaven so as to attack the gods (*epithesomenon*, 190b–c)," an incident represented by Homer in both the *Iliad* and the *Odyssey*, the sense of a *physical attack* is by no means certain. *Epitheō* simply has too many meanings to unequivocally understand the nature of the ascent. Per-

---

28. See, for example, Saxonhouse, "Net of Hephaestus."
29. Meyer, "Peisestairos of Aristophanes's Birds," 288.
30. Ibid., 288.
31. Strauss, *On Plato's Symposium*, 125, my emphasis. I would add: they rebelled precisely because they no longer wanted to offer sacrifices to the gods.

haps the best approximation is to "run after," that is, pursue, catch up with, and stand beside them and be their equal. If they indeed made an attempt to ascend to Mount Olympus—though not to "attack the gods," physically, but rather to be their equal—no one has sufficiently considered their reasons for doing so. Human beings had "great ambitions" (190b), but the aim of that ambition has not been recognized—certainly not by the speaker—not for someone who accepts as naturally ordained the social relationship of slave to master, child to parent, and human being to the gods, all of which are relations of hierarchy and inferiority best represented in the vertical supremacy of the gods on Mount Olympus.

The ascent by Aristophanes's protohumans (who were whole and indivisible) can be compared to an episode in Genesis and the people who at one time were also unified and spoke one language. "And the whole earth was of one language, and of one speech," (Gen 11:1) the narrator tells us, and when they finally found a place to dwell, they gathered up the elements of the earth and began to build places to live first of all, and then something that had meaning beyond mere physical need. "And they said, Go to, let us build us a city and a tower, whose top may reach unto heaven," (Gen 11:4) now repeating, if not precisely emulating, Cain when he too "builded a city" (Gen 4:17). By building a tower that could reach heaven, they were expressing themselves beyond their mere material needs, the sand, clay, and stone imposed on them by the facts of existence. By attempting to reach heaven, they were not necessarily attempting to defy God—in any case, they do not mention either Yahweh or Elohim—but in building such a structure they were making a declaration to themselves as being architects and builders and therefore more than simple dwellers. They were also attempting to understand their abilities, what they were capable of imagining, hoping for, and achieving with nothing more (and nothing less) than themselves. In both cases, in the Hebrew Bible and Aristophanes's myth, the human beings were punished by the divine who evidently misunderstood human intentions, the first by the loss of one language and their subsequent dispersion, the second by the loss of a whole self. In both cases, the divine seems insecure, anxious about its supposed supremacy, and constantly unsure about the extent of human abilities and how they will determine their existence and, consequently, their sense of self for the present and the open-ended future. The divine punishes by dividing, making incomplete, imposing an irretrievable loss that by necessity forces human beings to adapt to their new circumstances and *initiate a new kind of life*. The Stoic philosopher Seneca would develop the philosophy of ascension insofar as the individual guided by wisdom "is the equal of the gods; he strives toward heaven, mindful of his origins." His addition seems to respond directly to the dilemma of the protohumans in the myth of Aristophanes and, at least thematically, to Genesis 11. "No one is wrong in attempting to ascend to the place from which he has descended."[32] In Seneca's view, the ascension is therefore a return—a Stoic theology inconsistent with Socrates's understanding of the myth.

Nowhere does Aristophanes define either the nature of the ambition or its origin, much less speculate on a justifiable reason; the motivations of the human ascension are unexamined. The myth, remarkably, is represented solely from the perspective of the gods, and then by name only in relation to Zeus and Apollo, the first as the head of the pantheon and the second by his double-role as a law-maker and god of medicine who, in un-Hippocratic fashion, will perform the operation to divide people as their punishment. The event presented by Aristophanes involves human beings making "an attempt" (190b) on the gods not out of some misguided ambition, nor can they be accused of what Anthony Hopper calls "warmongering,"[33] in effect defending and supporting the gods and necessarily misinterpreting a human act, accusing them of violence. Rather, human beings confront the gods in order to put an end to their servitude, one wholly determined by prayer and sacrifice, by a relationship of anticipated but not always fulfilled reciprocity. For Socrates, Athenian piety and all the rituals associated with religion and reverence to the gods are also and necessarily a perpetuation of a state of dependency, indeed, slavery, the very reason Agathon's simple instruction to his slaves actually established several relations of inequality. Therefore, when Hopper presents deficiency as an aspect of human nature, a distinction should be made between a constitutive deficiency (that is, an ontological one), and one resulting from a metaphysical belief and relationship to a *specific idea* of the gods. Socratic impiety results from the recognition that the practices necessary to serve the gods are, in fact, undermining human beings and perpetuating a state of dependence. The deficiency is historical since human beings determine themselves in relation to a metaphysical belief, one accompanied by a certain place or *topos*, the world below and the perpetually imposing Mount Olympus above. Without understanding their motivations, which are clearly established once Zeus and the rest of the gods consider their punishment, then the reason for the myth, what it calls into question (hence, Socratic impiety) cannot be understood, as it will also be misunderstood and wilfully distorted when Epicurus relegates the gods to a *topos* completely unrelated to the world, either in its natural state or as a reflection of human endeavor.

---

32. Seneca, *Ep.* 92.29.30.

33. Hopper, "Greatest Hope of All," 577. He later adds the accusation of human "pointless warmongering."

What is the reason that the gods did not *kill* human beings? The answer, given by the gods themselves, is most revealing: if human beings were killed, their death would "wipe out the worship they [the gods] receive, along with the sacrifices we humans give them" (190c). The gods themselves provide the reason that human beings ascended to Mount Olympus: it was not so much the beginning of a war but an act of defiance and a proclamation of independence against the gods as sources of authority who demanded to be *served* domesticated animals, the reason why in the beginning of the *Symposium* the precise word used when slaves are serving the guests at the symposium is *therapeia* and whose meaning Socrates will completely transform. Instead of killing the now-vulnerable human beings, Zeus comes up with the plan of cutting them in half, in part so human beings will "become more profitable," (190d) more useful, and exploited in terms of providing twice as many sacrifices. Splitting human beings in half results in an equally bizarre equation: twice as many animals will now be sacrificed, as if they too will be punished as a consequence of a human act. In effect, they have doubled the economy of the god/human relationship, now extracting twice as many gifts without, however, stating what they will reciprocally provide. A customary and often repeated punishment of inflicting blindness has been rejected by Zeus and the other gods.[34] Cutting human beings in half doubles their servitude, at once renewing the economy of what is received by the gods (a relationship of exchange, though what human beings actually receive from the gods here is unknown), while also reestablishing the religious identity of human beings as butchers, cooks, and waiters, thereby perpetuating their identities as domesticated servants. That the gods organize human domestication reflects how animals have been domesticated so as to be ritually slaughtered. René Girard's unique insights deserve reflection:

> The domestication of animals requires that men keep them in their company and treat them, not as wild animals, but as if they were capable of living near human beings and leading a quasi-human existence. What could be the motive for such behavior toward animals? . . . An immediate motive was necessary, one powerful and permanent enough to encourage treating animals in such a way as to ensure their eventual domestication. The only motive could have been sacrifice.[35]

---

34. Tatti-Gartziou, "Blindness as Punishment." She outlines several categories of punishments; among them were punishments for those that had crossed the limits of human behavior in relation to the gods.

35. Girard, *Things Hidden Since the Foundation*, 69.

When Zeus comes up with a plan to allow human beings to keep living but to "stop their misbehaving," (190c) their "licentiousness" and "intemperance" are directly related to their desire for freedom, that is, to be free from their slavish condition of both praying to the gods and, more importantly, providing sacrificial animals for them. The gods, however, merely look at human desire as simple debauchery, refusal to be disciplined, onerous will. Humans are *unrestrained*. The Socratic presence in Aristophanes's speech involves his direct and unequivocal denunciation of Athenian religion because it once again establishes a condition of dependency. Without being free of the gods (free of a certain *belief* in their existence and characteristics), human beings will themselves remain bound to a certain tradition, to the customs that make a new conception of existence or social life in the city of Athens impossible. Arlene Saxonhouse's argument[36] that the original human beings were "perfect" cannot be sustained because they desire to either be equal to the gods or (though the text here is ambiguous) perhaps even to "kill" them and therefore become truly independent—a murder, of course, more profoundly symbolic than actual. Doing away with the gods would of course liberate them from the obligations of piety, prayer, and above all, the practice of offering animal sacrifice. The gods, however, simply dismiss the human desire for freedom by regarding them as immoderate, impetuous, and youthful; they are treated as children and punished accordingly, the gods now insisting on imposing an inescapable vulnerability on them.

The speech juxtaposes healing and sacrifice, even if the speaker fails to recognize the implications of his words, which is odd for a playwright, to be sure. And if the sacrifice of animals is considered the most significant service of all, Socrates makes the single most important affirmation of his impiety by first rejecting the practice, and second, and as a direct consequence of his impiety, the therapeutic service in the future will be entirely a human interrelationship, humans therapeutically serving each other so that the attributes of the gods will be, finally, reinternalized. By withdrawing the service to the gods in the form of slaughtering animals (killing, butchering, roasting, serving), human beings will henceforth be able to provide specifically therapeutic care to their own well-being such that any previous idea of healing as a dispensation of the gods (as several speakers in the *Symposium* believe), will no longer be tenable as a belief or a practice. Human healing, for Socrates, cannot occur as a process of religious exchange, as if the death of a sacrificed animal and the healing of a human being were reciprocal acts, one following the other. Only when animal sacrifice is abandoned will human beings be able to better serve themselves, the single most important

---

36. Saxonhouse, "Net of Hephaestus."

argument made by Socrates and initiating nothing less than the possibility of a religious revolution announced, as we will see, during his judicial defense. Socrates's therapeutic language will represent an alternative to the bureaucratic manipulation of speech in its social context, whether judicial, political, or religious.

Without a fundamental opposition to the idea of the gods and their meaning in human life, the still-unfulfilled possibilities of human nature cannot be realized. They remain bound and limited by the inheritance of poetic myths, by an entire world inherited from the *phantasma* of the poets. In the myth of Aristophanes, after realizing that the original separation led to inconsolable suffering and, often, death itself, Zeus decided to "move their genitals around to the front" (191b) so that they would be able to both enjoy the pleasure of sexual intercourse as well as engendering children—that is, the creation of a human world. Socrates no doubt viewed this punishment as ironic. The gods punished human beings and they, consequently, began to feel desire, passionate love, and eros—both the physical and emotional sort. "This, then, is the source of our desire to love each other. Love is born into every human being; it calls back the halves of our original nature together; it tries to make one out of two and heal the wound of human nature" (191d). The importance and prominence of healing is indeed achieved through love, but in a way that Aristophanes cannot comprehend. He cannot understand how Socrates's philosophy, being *therapeutic*, has displaced the prominence of the gods for humanity. Only Socrates—the iconoclastic therapist, so-called corrupter of the young, and introducer of new deities in the city of Athens—will be able to reveal the double meaning of philosophy as both the love of wisdom and, eventually (in the ecstatic speech by Alcibiades) the wisdom of a certain kind of love, one that is more comprehensive than merely erotic. Aristophanes's myth is presented, but without any interpretation capable of recognizing, especially at the end, how his conception of love (its aim and goal) cannot and *should not* be achieved.

The irony of the punishment, of course (no different than the punishment of Adam and Eve in Genesis 3), is in the creation of love, sex, desire, passion, the birth of children. In the myth of Aristophanes, the attraction to others has the aim of becoming whole again, complete, and therefore restoring the unified and complete self. However, when Hephaestus is introduced as the god capable of putting the two divided selves back together, Aristophanes describes him as talking. He appears when two lovers "are lying together" (lying or, in fact, having sex), preceded by the complicated statement that "it's obvious that the soul (*psyche*) of every lover longs for something else; his soul cannot say what it is, but like an oracle it has a sense of what it wants, and like an oracle it hides behind a riddle" (192d). According to Aristophanes, lovers are not ultimately motivated by physical desire or sexual pleasure. There is another kind of desire, sensed by the psyche, but not understood. If the psyche is like an oracle and hiding behind a riddle, then it must be possible to interpret the words of the oracle and understand it. Far from mere physical desire and sexual pleasure, the psyche of human beings senses, vaguely, that it has another desire altogether. What is it? The appearance of the god Hephaestus, the craftsman (a maker of *things*) is fundamentally misplaced here in part because, as a materialist, he represents a literal and not allegorical understanding of the myth. He begins to speak to the two lovers and asks: "What is it you human beings really want from each other" (192d)? The human beings, who are "perplexed," do not answer. They have no idea, or perhaps they restrain themselves from answering, knowing that telling the god what they think may have unforeseeable consequences. He then asks them another question. He has the ability to weld them together, so that they will be forever joined, in life and in death, in the world and in Hades, a promise of the infinite which Socrates ultimately rejects in the *Apology*. Aristophanes, insofar as he tells the story, represents it, seems to believe that if human beings were given such a choice—from Hephaestus or anyone else—they would "surely" take it. He has no doubts. The god presumes, underestimating what the new humans have already perhaps understood.

> No one would find anything else that he wanted. Instead, everyone would think he'd found out at last what he had always wanted: to come together and melt together with the one he loves, so that one person emerged from two. Why should this be so? It's because, as I said, we used to be complete wholes in our original nature, and now "Love" is the name for our pursuit of wholeness, for our desires to be complete (192e).

He makes the claim with absolute certainty. No one, during the speech, interjects. But if Hephaestus *the god* is necessarily related to the other gods and the original punishment devised by Zeus, carried out by Apollo, human beings would have to immediately reject his proposal. If a human being accepted his proposal, to be put back together by a god, he or she would necessarily reconfirm their dependency as well as reestablish an archaic relationship. The absolutely necessary act of rebellion would be nullified. The ascendancy to heaven was intended as an act of defiance and an affirmation of the human desire for independence. Prior to being divided by the gods (literally, as punishment), they were always and already incomplete due to their relationship to the gods and their worship, prayer, and sacrifice to them.

The first significant act by human beings was indeed one of impiety, an act inseparable from the desire for freedom. Before turning to the conclusion of Aristophanes's speech, one that repeats the devious temptation by Hephaestus (he seems to believe that human beings desire to return to an original state, which confirms that the gods *have never understood* them at all) it is now necessary to turn to two related dialogues concerning Socrates's impiety. By following the dialogue on piety in the *Euthyphro* and Socrates's sustained critique of Athenian religion insofar as human *therapeia* is always defined by a "burnt offering," a *thusia*, his views in the *Symposium* while listening to the speech will become more clear and lead (first in the *Apology* and then in several dialogues in chapter two) to a decisive realization of the beginning of therapeutic philosophy and of Socrates's first patient, Alcibiades, a relationship that will be one "dedicated to love"[37] and involve one fundamental analytic necessity: to "give an account of his present life-style, and of the way he has spent his life in the past."[38]

3. *Socrates's Private Conversation*

The single most important difference between the private conversation between friends in the *Euthyphro* and the public declaration in a court of law in the *Apology* can be recognized in Socrates's specific discussion of piety and the relationship of human *therapeia* to the gods and the ritual of a "burnt offering," the *thusia* as animal sacrifice, a fact *not once* mentioned during Socrates's trial. In the *Euthyphro*, a dialogue with his friend, Socrates establishes one fundamental relationship in his discussion of the meaning of Athenian piety, at least as observed by the many: the practice of *thusia* insofar as animal sacrifice is the most consistent expression of *therapeia* to the gods, a word soon to be complemented by *upereteō*, a "service," that implies a certain kind of dedication.

Unlike Mark McPherran, who argues that "Socrates would hold that acts of traditional sacrifice performed with the correct intentions are pious, but do not constitute the whole of proper religious practice as he conceives it, since piety above all requires that we engage in the practice of philosophy,"[39] the relationship of the two dialogues to be examined reveal that sacrifice and philosophy are incommensurable, though McPherran may be relying on Xenophon's testimony and, as such, be the first and not the last (as we shall see in the case of Epicurus) indication of a prevailing dilemma in an-

---

37. Plato, *Phaedrus*, 248d.
38. Plato, *Lach.*, 118a.
39. McPherran, *Religion of Socrates*, 71.

tiquity.⁴⁰ The *Euthyphro* shows a consistent and repeated reevaluation of the beliefs and practices of Athenian religion. The one specific observance of animal sacrifice is repeatedly questioned by Socrates for no more obvious reason than to reevaluate the purported relationship between human beings and the gods. The repeated use of the word *thusia* (a "burnt offering," or, as a more literal translation, to "make smoke") can be understood as a euphemism; he does not use the more graphic *sphagia*, the act of slitting the animal's throat that, in the case of an ox, was preceded by severing the cervical vertebrae with an axe. If Socrates's personal views on being impious are to be sufficiently understood and appreciated, they will be found in personal conversation with a friend rather than during a formal procedure where Athenian laws (essentially related to the city's metaphysical/theological foundations), are also explicitly reevaluated.

The location of their conversation could not be more significant; they are standing outside the office of the so-called King Archon, the civic official and distinguished citizen who, amongst other responsibilities, observed the dates of festivals and regulated all public sacrifices. Athens did not have a priestly class, but they did, however, appoint individuals who presided over civic rituals. For Socrates to literally show up on his front doorstep to philosophically discuss the meaning of piety and holiness demonstrates how he does not have the slightest concern with the possibility of being found guilty and executed. His possible death is irrelevant; all that is important is the philosophical life and how, in this particular place, he will direct his analysis to the King Archon *in his role as a civic priest*. The philosopher and the priest are separated, their identities opposed, their responsibilities divided, the first adhering to his individual conscience, the second obeying the *nomos* of the city. By necessity, the philosopher has a precarious relationship to the laws of the city.

On the eve of his trial, Socrates has no fear or apprehension, which would be understandable given his situation, being prosecuted under a

---

40. In the opening of the *Memorabilia*, Xenophon's very first defense of Socrates against the charges brought against him is clear: "everyone could see that he sacrificed (*thuon*) regularly at home and also at the public altars of the State; and he made no secret of using divination (*mantike*)" (1.1.2). Can this testimony be trusted, especially in light of the previous description of one of Socrates'ss students as well as the portrayal in Aristophanes'ss *Clouds*? There is no indication in any of Plato's writings that Socrates ever attended a public or private sacrifice of an animal. As we will see, Xenophon will not be the last to write an apologia for a philosopher specifically concerning his participation in public sacrifices; for the first time, and to be often repeated (as we shall see, for example, in the different testimonies by Lucretius and Philodemus of Gadara about Epicurus), adherence or refusal to sacrifice becomes a fundamental aspect of a philosophical ambivalence.

graphe, a public indictment with potentially grave consequences. He is, above all, analytical in this dialogue concerned only with raising questions about the meaning of piety and holiness as the Athenians (so different from him) understand, and putting these social ideas into practice. In the discussion of the charges brought against him, Socrates first mentions being a corrupter of the young—corrupting them to be different from what Athenian socialization demands—and then, to be judicially specific, he tells his friend that a certain Meletus is accusing him being "a manufacturer (*poieten*) of gods... that I create new gods and don't recognize old ones" (3b)[41]. He has been charged with presenting ideas inimical to the polis religion of Athens. Therefore, Socrates's new conception of the gods—made much more well-defined in the *Apology*—has implications for the observance of ancient rituals. Instead of adopting the gods as if they have been handed down by custom and tradition and the laws of the city of Athens—the *archaic* gods, from time immemorial—Socrates has been accused of creating (inventing on his own) ideas of new gods, at least in part because of a personal relationship with his *daimonion*, which *speaks* to him. Socrates has a personal oracle within him. The specific charge of impiety (*asebeia*), however, has not yet been specifically mentioned. For now, it is important to stress how Socrates's personal *daimonion* should be contrasted with the tradition of oracles such as the Pythia at the temple of Apollo in Delphi. Nock's assertion that "*mantike* was an integral part of his [Socrates's] theism"[42] will become most evident during his trial. His manticism, however, should not be traditionally understood as a kind of divination; rather, it is Socrates's ability to philosophically imagine an entirely different future.

We also learn that his friend Euthyphro, who believes himself to be a "diviner" or *mantis*, has brought the serious charge of murder against his own father—this after his father was responsible for the death of one of his servants. As someone who can anticipate the desires of the gods, the murder charge against his progenitor is less about justice than averting the possibility that pollution or *miasma* will infect the family for subsequent generations. However, the present legal case[43] may, in Plato's dialogue, represent a more important fact: if a son can bring legal charges against his father, then one can begin to think about bringing an indictment against the gods, or at least putting into doubt the beliefs human beings have about the gods and

---

41. In his *Laws*, Cicero will repeat this one important aspect of the social and political aspect of religion: "no one shall have gods to himself, either new gods or alien gods, unless recognized by the State" (2.7.19).

42. Nock, "Religious Attitudes," 476.

43. For a specifically legal reading of the dialogue, see Panagiotou, "Plato's Euthyphro and the Attic Code on Homicide."

their characteristics. According to Euthyphro, his father's murder of a servant has created a severe danger: that of "pollution," *miasma*. As someone who believes himself to be knowledgeable about religious matters, he fancies himself an expert, and boasts of the fact despite being labelled "crazy," (3c) like other friends of Socrates.[44] Euthyphro believes prosecuting his father is a holy act approved of by the gods, a belief soon to be questioned by Socrates precisely because Meletus, he tells his friend, has "indicted me for impiety" (5c). The meaning of *asebeia* should not be narrowly understood in its religious and political context. Equally important is Socrates's impiety toward parents—to be more specific, his lack of reverence or respect for the fathers of his students whose knowledge and authority have been seriously undermined by his philosophy. Fathers ensure tradition; the critique of what has been handed down, then, leads directly to the fathers being responsible. Their wrath, soon to be made even more obvious by the majority vote in court, has led to his indictment. Socrates may be perceived, and judicially accused, of being impious in relation to the gods. His impiety toward fathers, their social position, and their place in a genealogical succession ensuring continuity, seems to induce much more resentment against him.[45] They appear to defend the gods, but in fact they are protecting their privilege and their authority in the family and the city with much more vehemence. Socrates displaces authority, both divine and human, and undermines their *related* legitimacy.

Socrates begins the dialogue proper when he asks his friend, who claims to be an authority on the matter, "What do you say piety (*eusebes*) and impiety (*asebes*) are?" (5c). For Eryximachus, as we have seen, to be pious and reverential, one had to above all practice the arts of divination and offer sacrifices. What does Euthyphro answer? Now using a related though different term, Socrates asks him: "What do you say holiness (*osion*) is, and what is unholiness (*anosion*)" (5d)? As a state of being, holiness is

---

44. The other notable example is, again, from the *Symposium*. In the "Introductory Dialogue," Socrates'ss friend Apollodorus is called a "maniac" (173d). Another reason Euthyphro may be considered "crazy" is his status as a diviner. According to Sarah Iles Johnston's *Ancient Greek Divination*, Euthyphro may be a self-styled and independent diviner and therefore not enjoying the status offered by institutional oracles. Being defined as "crazy," in both cases of friends of Socrates, has overt social/political significance.

45. Nancy Jay's *Throughout Your Generations Forever* uniquely emphasizes the importance of sacrifice as an institution ensuring the male succession of generations. Socrates'ss corruption of the young (evident by Aristodemus not sacrificing) involves repudiating the real meaning of inheritance—which transcends its economic function. That Socrates is charged with corrupting the young means fathers are outraged that he is undermining their rightful authority and making their sons independent.

made possible by being free of guilt after making an offering to the gods. As Socrates shows, an act initiating a relationship of exchange is supposed to be pious and holy. In both cases, to be pious and holy involves a direct relationship of service to the gods, specifically the sacrificial act of animal slaughter, an act that some people, including Orphics in the *Laws*, describe as "unholy":

> The custom of men sacrificing one another is, in fact, one that survives even now among many peoples; whereas amongst others we hear of how the opposite custom existed, when they were forbidden so much as to eat an ox, and their offerings to the gods consisted, not of animals, but of cakes of meal and grain steeped in honey, and other such bloodless sacrifices, and from flesh they abstained as though it were unholy to eat it or to stain with blood the altars of the gods; instead of that, those of us men who then existed lived what is called an "Orphic life," keeping wholly to inanimate food and, contrariwise, abstaining wholly from things animate.[46]

In this case, Socrates should at least be considered as someone with sympathies toward, if not outright adherence to, both Orphic and Pythagorean objection to animal sacrifice, thereby contributing to a countercultural phenomenon extending down to Epicurus, the Essenes of Qumran, and eventually, Jesus and early Christianity.

Socrates makes the observation that one of the reasons people of Athens resent him is when he points out their taken-for-granted lives, their emotions, actions, and their specifically religious beliefs. "Whenever somebody talks like this about the gods, I find it very difficult to accept," (6a) he tells his friend without, however, detailing what precisely he finds difficult to accept—Socrates has serious misgivings about how gods are represented by creative poets like Hesiod and Homer. Socrates wonders if the poets are able to know about both vice and virtue. Moreover, can they really know anything about the gods?

> We must therefore investigate whether they have been deceived on meeting these imitators, and when they see their works they do not realize that these are at a third remove from reality and are easy to compose without knowledge of the truth; they are but images (*phantasmata*), not reality.[47]

---

46. Plato, *L.*, 782cd.

47. Plato, *Rep.*, 598e–599a. Phantasmatic images will become especially important when analyzing, in chapter two, the allegory of the cave.

The poets, however, cannot by themselves be held responsible for how human beings view the gods. There are others (perhaps even more damaging than poets) that use the gods to exploit others, obviously for financial gain. Again, in the *Republic*, Socrates reminds us that

> what men say about the gods and virtue is the most amazing of all, namely that the gods too inflict misfortune and a miserable life upon many good men, and the opposite fate upon their opposites. Begging priests and prophets frequent the doors of the rich and persuade them that they possess a god-given power to remedy by sacrifices and incantations at pleasant festivals any crime that the rich man or one of his ancestors may have committed. (364b–c)

There were, then, a class of "begging priests"[48] who exploited the superstitious and persuaded them to make sacrifices (in this case, it would have been a *patrioi thusai*, or "ancestral sacrifice") in order to exonerate themselves from any real or perceived wrongdoing. E. R. Dodds examines religious experience in antiquity and writes: "this does not mean that he [Socrates] proposed to abolish ritual purification altogether,"[49] but instead to merely regulate the practice of sacrifice and make it unlawful for these wandering priests to prey on the superstitious. The threat of divine punishment, in life and after, remained a persistent dread, the reason these itinerant priests could so easily convince the superstitious of their powers and why, eventually, Epicurus would deny any metaphysical influence in his theology.

In the *Euthyphro*, Socrates goes on to make a remarkable statement, one anticipating an equally important declaration during his trial. "What more could we say, when we admit for ourselves that we know nothing about them," (6b) Socrates says, quoting verbatim from the beginning of a well-known book by Protagoras,[50] a philosopher also accused of impiety and forced to leave Athens. For Socrates, the conduct of the gods as they are currently conceived cannot possibly teach human beings how to act appropriately, which is the reason he turns to his friend again and asks him for a definition of the holy, its "special feature" (*eidos*) and "single standard" (*idea*) (6d) and *paradeigma* (6e) or example—three consecutive and differ-

---

48. These begging priests, described by Bracht Branham in *Unruly Eloquence* as "religious entrepreneurs," will be the subject of the satire *Alexander the False Prophet* by Lucian of Samosata. In Lucian's work, the Alexander presenting himself as a religious prophet will be contrasted with the rationality and teaching of Epicurus.

49. Dodds, *Greeks and the Irrational*, 22. Again we notice how Socrates, in this case, is only a religious reformer.

50. As reported by Cicero in *On the Nature of the Gods*. "Protagoras declared himself uncertain." 1.2.

ent concepts—so as to point out its complications. The holy does have a "paradigm" but no one seems to know it except Socrates himself. Equally significant is his desire to know which "actions" are deemed holy. Impiety is not simply a belief; impiety involves an observance (especially during festival days of commemoration) deemed necessary for the health of the city, establishing its origin, defining its purpose, and insuring its continuity. Therefore, when Robert Parker tells us that "in practice, no doubt, the Athenians rarely moved against verbal impiety,"[51] one must then consider what act (or, more likely, the omission of an act) has led to Socrates being impious and how he has substituted a ritual for a new form of piety. In the testimony before his peers, insofar as they are citizens of Athens, Socrates will present an innovative (and therefore impious, according to his listeners) definition of the will of a god which is no less than the foundation for a new "religion" or *religio*, here understood as related to the Christian *ekklesia* and Jewish synagogue as the bonds of a community, one founded on a particular precept and speech.

In the *Euthyphro*, the dialogue between the protagonist and Socrates concerning impiety continues when Euthyphro believes that the concept of the holy must be defined and approved of by the gods. "What is agreeable to the gods is holy, and what is not agreeable is unholy," (7a) he claims, anticipating the question posed by Socrates, one that presents a dilemma: "Is the holy approved by the gods because it's holy, or is it holy because it's approved" (10a)? His definition, then, depends on the determination of the gods, which is difficult to accept for Socrates since it presents a first problem for the self-declared philosopher who knows nothing: How do human beings *know anything* about the gods? How can what is agreeable to them be actually known? Indeed, Socratic impiety—and along with it the philosophical life—is nothing if not directed at the reevaluation of all belief, most especially the belief that determines how human beings make choices based upon their apparent knowledge of the gods. Much has been written about the gods (including their disagreements and disputes or, even more seriously, the jealousy of the father and the rebellion by the son, including murder), and therefore puts into doubt whether the gods themselves could in principle reach a consensus on the nature of the holy. Socrates may profess ignorance on the matter, at least in his conversation. During his trial, however, he will present a well-defined and, for him, incontrovertible knowledge of a specific god as well as the one preeminent commandment.

Socrates's question, which at the formal level puts into doubt the validity of Euthyphro's claims, more importantly begins his defense of the

---

51. Parker, "Trial of Socrates," 152.

charge of impiety, as if he has already begun an apology, (in fact, exposing the vulnerabilities of Athenian theology) in this case to a friend and outside the formal procedures expected in a court of law. What the dialogue makes clear here no less than in the *Symposium* is Socrates's argument that our conceptions of the gods are mistaken and, consequently, the actions deemed holy and pious are also, necessarily, unfounded and wrong, thereby perpetuating a *phantasma* of the gods whose *images* prevent one from seeing the human condition and its possibilities. The traditional conception of the gods distorts, and limits, human self-understanding and actually prevents the self-examination necessary for the philosophical life. More injuriously, as Epicurus will systematically argue in his own ethics, such a conception of the gods has entirely egregious consequences for human life and for the health of the psyche. If the holy is that which is "divinely approved," (*theophiles*) (7a)—literally, what is loved by the gods—there is no way to know with certainty, for example, that it is right and just to prosecute a man who has killed someone, as is the case for Euthyphro's father. For Socrates, the ultimate point of his argument is not so much to determine for now any characteristics of the gods (concerning anything about them at all), but to make the point that the conceptions of the gods are created by human beings and, therefore, require a rethinking of the meaning of being human much more than the meaning of the divine. *Theology* exposes how the human imagination has effectively determined both an individual and social nature. In the *Alcibiades II*, it will above all be the nature of human beings, and the imperative to know oneself, that will be the foundations of his philosophy. Socrates's *theologia* becomes an analysis of the human imagination, of the poets, and of the people. Any thoughts about the gods necessarily reveal human characteristics, such as the quarrels and disputes and jealousies of the gods. They never seem to agree, therefore making it difficult for Euthyphro to sustain his initial definition. Unlike Socrates, "Euthyphro's theology is, so to speak, vulgarly Olympian,"[52] and therefore still traditional. Socrates's impiety involves nothing less than recognizing that if all the attributes of the gods are created by human beings, then our conceptions of the divine are, in fact, expressions of a human desire, a need. Socrates must then also argue (and this is the importance both of the beginning and ending of Aristophanes's speech), that if our conceptions of the gods are mistaken, the civic rituals associated with providing service to the gods are also, necessarily, misguided. They serve no actual purpose in terms of providing a service to the gods: the sprinkled blood on the sacrificial altar

---

52. Allen, "Comment" to his translation of the *Euthyphro*, 32.

Socrates's "Impiety"   47

they cannot see, the aroma of the smoke they cannot inhale, or the meat and viscera they cannot taste or eat.

When the dialogue turns to the relationship between the holy and the just, Socrates argues that the two not only do not go hand in hand; quite the opposite. Something considered holy can be unjust. At the moment that Euthyphro relates holiness as the justice that serves the gods, Socrates begins to wonder about the reason service is given to the gods in the first place, what possible reason such service was begun, and the reasons for tradition continuing the practice. What is the purpose of animal sacrifice? Euthyphro says: "I believe that this is the part of the just which is pious and holy, the one concerned with looking after the gods (*theon therapeian*), whereas that concerned with looking after men is the remaining part of the just"[53] (12e). What does he mean by the "remaining part?" Is he implying that providing service to the gods is primary, and whatever is left is then used to serve others? Socrates wants to know precisely what it means to look after a god. He leads his interlocutor to one unavoidable affirmation, that "it's for the improvement and benefit of the thing looked after, " (13b) a statement with far-reaching implications. For one, Socrates of course questions how "looking after" a god (for example, by killing an animal) could possibly improve or benefit a god. The gods seem to require some support, some assistance, as if the sacrificial death of an animal provided them with a lack, a need, the fulfillment of some desire. The ultimate consequences of Socrates's deceptively presented *argument* will be that once human beings stop providing a service to the gods (that they cannot need), then the part of human beings that wants to look after each other will become the sole meaning of service. Therapy will not replace theology, but it will become a more relevant expression of piety. "It was for this very reason that I asked you what you mean by 'looking after' (*therapeian*) the gods" (13cd). Socrates's radical theology involves nothing less than overturning a previous service to the gods (in sacrifice, first of all, but also in that ubiquitous form of speech, prayer) and instead now providing *therapeia* to others in a form Plato will describe, in many dialogues, specifically in terms of a particular kind of *new speech*. Socrates invents the therapeutic speech of *psychagogia* as the replacement of animal sacrifice and its associated prayers.

---

53. In a noteworthy footnote (#58) to "Elenchos and Exetasis," Tarrant writes: "Justice toward animals is seldom recognized by the Greeks; exceptions would usually involve some special doctrine, like the Pythagorean doctrine of transmigration, by which a soul, after leaving the human body, might enter an animal one. In this case the animal which one maltreats could turn out to be one's own ancestor." Granted, Socrates does not seem to express any concern for the life of the animal; his singular concern—consistently implied in the dialogue—is what religious purpose does animal sacrifice serve?

Noticeably, in the discussion of "looking after," Socrates's examples are animals, as in people who look after horses, dogs, and cows. Indeed, there must also be people, of a priestly type, who look after animals for the sole purpose of later using them for sacrifice. The domesticated animals are looked after, of course, to their detriment, to be slaughtered for some human idea related to the need of a god, which for Socrates is clearly a conception that needs to be reevaluated and abandoned because of the relationship established to gods, others, and domestic animals. When Euthyphro must agree that looking after the gods cannot mean improving them in any way, making them better, nor providing any benefit to them, Socrates begins his conclusion, and when Euthyphro answers that "it's like slaves looking after (*therapeouousin*) their masters," (13d) he has essentially admitted without wanting to that the human relationship to the gods is analogous to slaves serving masters, as was also evident in the *Symposium*. Socrates has thereby connected slaves and masters to human beings and gods, with the killing of an animal in ritual sacrifice being the one act perpetuating such a relationship. "I get it—it would be a kind of service (*uperetike*) to the gods," (13d) Socrates says, this time not using the consistent term *therapeia* but a related term that implies being a public servant, the same one used in the gospels to define being "ministers (*uperetai*) of the word" (for example, in Luke 1:2) and one of the interconnected terms Socrates will use during his trial to portray himself as someone dedicated to serving others. His interlocutor agrees.

Socrates's next example is decisive. "Could you then tell me, what goal does 'service to doctors' help to achieve? Don't you think it's health" (13e)? Socrates's example is hardly incidental; it has become central to his argument, each comment interconnected, from the *therapeia* of the gods to taking care of animals and finally to the necessity of human health. Socrates has begun a *diagnosis* of the city of Athens and a possible *remedy*. His therapeutic philosophy does not limit itself to treating the ills of one individual or a group of philosophical adherents, like his students, for example, but rather, it has a much more comprehensive aim and intent. As we will see, the philosophical argument now leads from the idea of *therapy* (as in taking care of others, that is, in a particular kind of *love*, an *eros* related to *erotan*, to ask questions) and its distinction from the idea and practice of *thusia*. The two are intimately related for the time being; by the end of Socrates's argument, human therapy can only properly begin (human beings serving the needs of each other for the purpose of health) when the practice of sacrificing animals for the gods is stopped, the ritual abolished. Laszlo Versenyi agrees when he writes that "the sole function of Socratic thought is therapy," and yet he misidentifies the nature of the therapy, reducing it to a merely intellectual capacity. He

Socrates's "Impiety"   49

adds: "A therapy that is to begin with a therapy of thinking: a clearing up of confusion and eliminating of contradictions within our various, so often internally incoherent, beliefs and opinions."[54] Socratic therapy cannot be reduced to a simple change of ideas, as if human affliction was merely epistemological; it must involve, as he intimates, an individual's *psychological* well-being. Therefore, if *thusia* and *therapeia* are the most important and juxtaposed concepts of the *Euthyphro*, Socrates's argument will soon lead to his most important if indirect affirmation; and by shifting from *therapeia* to civic service, Socrates stresses how the service provided by human beings perpetuates their subordination, which is precisely why the protohumans in the speech of Aristophanes in the *Symposium* made an ascent to heaven, an ascent which soon transformed (unfortunately) into a metaphysical ideal by the priestess Diotima in her conception of the so-called "ladder of love." Socrates too wants to make an ascent to heaven, but not, however, to initiate a conflict with the gods, much less reach the Platonic forms, but rather to proclaim human independence from the Athenians' conception of the divine and thereby end all the consequential religious acts and observances.

Socrates continues, pressing the issue further. "To what goal's achievements would service to the gods (*theois uperetike*) be contributing? It's obvious that you know, seeing that you claim that no one knows more than you about religion" (13e) he adds, again emphasizing a decisive shift in lexicon, one which will become all-important in the *Apology* as the irreducible difference between taking care of the gods and taking care of others *in the city*. And in this instance, he surely knows the answer and only wants his interlocutor to recognize it as well: What possible end could there be in our subordination to the gods? What does the relationship serve? Socrates makes two simultaneous and related arguments: in providing service to the gods, human beings cannot provide anything to them whatsoever and, more consequentially, they remove something from their own lives. Human life is thereby diminished not because of religion per se, but in the specific observances recommended, in and through observances of the law, by Athenian society, an observation which is also repeatedly made by the Jewish prophets.

Euthyphro nevertheless continues with his explanation and reaches another singular juncture. The dialogue has had successive stages of argumentation; it has been precise, detailed, and with one singular emphasis: "if one knows how to say and do things gratifying to the gods in prayer and in sacrifice, this is what's holy, and such conduct is the salvation (*sozei*) not only of private households but also of the public well-being" (14b). Salvation,

---

54. Versényi, *Holiness and Justice*, 17.

health, and being rescued from a perilous condition can only be achieved, according to Euthyphro, when the people of the city pray and sacrifice to the gods—a claim Socrates completely rejects when he ironically points out, not for the last time, how the relationship is founded on a dubious exchange: "surely sacrifice is making a donation to the gods, while prayer is requesting something from them" (14c). Socrates now begins to expose the interconnectedness of sacrifice and prayer as a specifically economic exchange, one he will soon compare to a marketplace of buying and selling. Provoking Euthyphro to reach the conclusions he has been moving toward, Socrates tells him, with a question, that the idea of the holy is "a kind of science of sacrifice (*thuein*) and prayer, isn't it?" (14e) again stressing the relationship of prayer and sacrifice, a request and an offer, the appeal involving the hope of reciprocity. The intimate relationship between the slaughter of an animal and the logos of a prayer will be definitively abandoned when the beautiful words of the therapeutic philosopher will be turned toward the health of the individual. The healing speech of the philosopher will be the sole substitute for a traditional form of piety no longer recognized as relevant or efficacious.

Once again Socrates stresses how religion, its belief, and practice, has the intended aim of taking care of the health of individuals and the community as a whole. Religion should be salvific and concerned with healing; however, Socrates's friend has yet to define precisely the benefit either prayer or animal sacrifice contributes to the gods. How are the gods therapeutic? Socrates's statement may well be worth repeating: "surely sacrifice (*thuein*) is making a donation to the gods, while prayer is requesting something from them," (14c) Socrates continues, asking and arguing—calling into question—the relationship based on an exchange of gifts. His interlocutor agrees, yet Socrates remains dissatisfied with his answers, pushing his viewpoint to the extreme (to attempt to make Euthyphro see the consequence of his belief) by finally equating religion with a kind of "trade" (*emporike*) where human beings offer killed animals—as if the gods actually needed them—and then respond to prayers by giving human beings what they request. The Gospel of John uses the same terms, and is the only one that specifically mentions an emporium or marketplace in the context of Jesus' acts in the temple of Jerusalem. "Make not my Father's house an house of merchandise (*emporiou*)" (John 2:16). If Socrates is the first philosopher to equate the supposed purpose of animal sacrifice with a transaction at a marketplace, it will be Jesus (as we shall see in all four gospels) who becomes the first individual to not simply criticize the practice, but to *act* against it, and for reasons which extend beyond the economic, the simple objection to the buying and selling of animals.

Socrates's "Impiety"   51

The gods then, above all need human beings to kill animals for them—a proposition Euthyphro, of course, cannot recognize. And he also cannot sense Socrates's irony when he tells him that "nothing is good for us except what comes from them" (15a). Socrates seems to echo the views of the symposiasts, but in actuality states that the human good can only be achieved by self-sufficient rather than dependent and slavish human beings. The irony: nothing comes from the gods, a decisive idea soon to be of utmost importance in Epicurus's theology as foundational to his ethical philosophy. The indifference of the gods and their nonparticipation in the world will also expose him to accusations of being impious during his life and, much later both in early Christianity and rabbinical Judaism, to being an atheist.

At one point (asking a question, perhaps wondering for the first time and therefore partly understanding Socrates's argument) Euthyphro asks: "Do you really suppose, Socrates, that the gods are benefited as a result from what they get from us?" (15a) Does he express doubt? As the dialogue comes to a close, without an apparent conclusion, the reader has to return to the beginning. The central argument of the dialogue has been evident since the start, and at different points in their exchange Socrates has made his views obvious without ever stating then directly. It is not necessary, as Socrates says, that "we must enquire again from the beginning about what the holy is," (15c) though this is what he tells Euthyphro. Instead, the reader of the Platonic dialogue has the responsibility of returning to what has been written and read in order to find out precisely what Socrates said about religion without *directly* stating his views. R. E. Allen believes that "the search for definition in the Euthyphro ends in failure. The dialogue does not say what holiness is, or what religion ought to be."[55] To reach *his* conclusion, Allen has to necessarily ignore all the statements made by Socrates in and through his questions here and in other *associated dialogues*, most especially the speech in the *Apology*. As Euthyphro runs off to an important engagement, Socrates ironically expresses disappointment that his friend has not been able to teach him about the holy, or about religion, and he will therefore be unable to defend himself against Meletus's charges that he denies the gods of the city, invents new ones, and corrupts the young. In other words, Socrates does not represent the traditional and old understanding of religious principles. However, in the *Apology* Socrates will argue that the

---

55. Allen, *Plato's Euthyphro*, 6. Several commentators agree with his position; among them, Roslyn Weiss in "Euthyphro's Failure." The dialogue ends aporetically only if one ignores how a subsequent dialogue (which cannot be read independently of the *Euthyphro*) should be regarded as the second and accompanying part; reading the dialogues back to back is essential if one is to understand Socrates's philosophical position and the reason he is brought to trial.

religion that most needs to be created (he is, then, a religious innovator and obviously unorthodox) will involve a god who commands human beings to serve each other—more precisely, *love* each other—in a way the Athenians cannot yet conceive of or understand.

4. Socrates's Declaration in Court

Unlike the private conversation with Euthyphro and the specific mention of sacrifice and other services to the gods (his "impiety" is explicit and specific), in the *Apology* Socrates is represented as not so much criticizing Athenian religion as presenting his specific belief, justifying his philosophical life of examining himself and others as not only consistent with piety, but in fact done in obedience to the command of a particular god—Apollo, the god of healing. Although the parallels[56] between the dialogue in the *Euthyphro* and Socrates's defense in the *Apology* have often been emphasized, there is at least one significant difference between the private conversation between two friends and the more formal, and obviously precarious, speech in front of a jury that includes enemies who are intent on delivering a guilty verdict in order to rid the city of him once and for all, either by exiling or executing him. In the *Apology*, Socrates does *not once* mention the two most important (and interrelated) ideas of his philosophy insofar as it re-evaluates Athenian religion and its practices. By excluding from his speech both *therapeia* and *thusia*, he has presented his philosophy by substituting an interrelated lexicon for words specifically related to the service of *social obligations* and duties—being a hired laborer, a rower on a ship, a troop inspector, and finally, a "benefactor," each of them a substitute for *therapeia*, which allows Socrates to define himself as a servant to others in the city and to fulfill a religious obligation. Not once does he mention the specific services prescribed by Athenian custom and law (in particular, burnt offerings) and instead details his own individual relationship to his *idea* of a god and how he serves it—that is, by taking care of others and the city of Athens. Noticeably different from the *Republic*, where Apollo is defined in his role of safeguarding the laws of the city, as well as "the greatest, the finest, and first enactments," those specifically related to religion, "the establishing of temples, sacrifices, and other forms of services to the gods," (427b) in the *Apology* Socrates presents the god with a different emphasis and, equally important, declares himself to have privileged access to the god who obliges him to speak to others not simply for the sake of knowledge, to rid them of ignorance, but to cure and heal. Socrates's way of speaking (not simply

---

56. On some of these parallels, see Diamon, "Parallel Trials."

his rhetoric) will become fundamental. To understand Socrates's profound animosity toward the Sophists one must take into consideration the difference between the teaching and learning of rhetoric (for its juridical or political use) and what he will soon call psychagogy and "leading the soul."

Socrates's speech in front of the Athenian jury, far from an *apologia* (it is not a defense, an argument for his innocence, and certainly not an appeal for his life) precisely and systematically outlines the fundamental ideas of his philosophy as it relates to the judicial charge of impiety. In the speech, he will thoroughly undermine the most time-honored beliefs of the city of Athens concerning sacrifices, manticism, prayers, and the institution of civic priests. More significantly, he will redefine the nature of the divine pantheon and reach, finally, an extraordinary conclusion, one that will decisively overturn the prevailing gods/human relationship and establish the foundations of a new religious sensibility based exclusively on himself being a servant who speaks to others with particular *logoi*—to be described, in many different but interrelated ways, by one of his students, as therapeutic words that "touch my soul."[57]

How does he begin to represent himself—or at least his claims—as "just" (*dikaios*), when in fact he will argue indirectly that to observe the customs and traditions of the city is in many ways unjust and inimical to an authentic religious life? Socrates's speech during his trial includes a remarkable series of culminating declarations (not questions, as in the *Euthyphro*) intended as affirmations of his knowledge of the god Apollo which are not unrelated to his claim in the *Symposium* and the *Theages* that all he knows is the "art of love." His speech culminates with the extraordinary claim that he knows precisely what the gods of healing have commanded him to do. It is a responsibility that is inseparable from his knowledge of the art of love or, otherwise stated, philosophy as the wisdom of a love that can only be conveyed through a certain kind of speaking, and certainly not with the oratory as practiced in law-courts, political assemblies, or the incantations of a cultic ritual.

He begins his speech not by addressing the charges of the moment—a particular form of impiety of not acknowledging the gods of the city, inventing his own, as well as corrupting the young—but earlier accusations and rumors and gossip, what he calls "the earliest charges that have been falsely brought against me," (18a) the ones dealing with him being a scientific philosopher and someone who had "theories about the heavens" (18b). These were true in his youth, as is admitted in the *Phaedo*, but now, as a therapeutic philosopher, these have long ago been abandoned. Socrates knows

---

57. Plato, *Ion*, 535a.

that anyone associated with an interest in natural philosophy—in a material rather than a metaphysical explanation of phenomena—is often also suspected of not believing in the gods, that is, the customary, lawful gods, the gods representing the *nomos*. Socrates distances himself from a tradition of long-standing and, in particular, from individual thinkers such as Anaxagoras and Protagoras whose ideas about the heavens or about the gods made them vulnerable to prosecution. Socrates also makes a significant point when he tells his now-mature jurors that they were corrupted when they were young and adolescents by others who resented his teaching; others, the older generation, are guilty of corrupting the young much more than he in the present. He has long been considered an atheist by his enemies, obviously with no justification except for resenting his nonconformism to traditional beliefs and practices, including someone here only described as a "playwright" though clearly identifiable and later named as Aristophanes. "The history of Plato's feelings toward the real Aristophanes continues to elude us,"[58] K. J. Dover writes; but as we noted earlier, in the *Symposium* these feelings are more than evident, and as we shall see in the conclusion to Aristophanes's speech, they may be more obvious than previously assumed.

In Socrates's first defense, he tells the jurors that he has no interest in either the phenomena in the sky or below the earth. The science of *physiologia*, as Epicurus called it and made it essential to his overall philosophy precisely to undermine religious belief, does not interest him at all. He has only one true concern: to find out "who is the expert in perfecting the virtues (*aretes*) of people in a society" (20b). More precisely, by bringing everyone to their own excellence through a "skilful leading of the soul (*psychagogia*) by means of words, not only in public gatherings such as the law courts."[59] When he begins his defense proper—and very few in attendance can understand the extent of his words—he first of all attempts "to rid your minds of a false impression which is the work of many years," (19a) a statement which must also be heard as an attempt to rid them of their *superstitions*.

When he then turns to another of the reasons Socrates has been considered a suspicious citizen, he tells the jurors that he has long been judged to be "abnormal," (*perissos*) as in the examples in the *Symposium* when he becomes much too attentive to his *daimonion* and stands riveted in one spot for unusually (for others) long periods of time, even in the interim of a military campaign. As someone who is described as *perissos* (along with the description of him as *atopos* in the *Symposium*), Socrates is considered unorthodox, a nonconformist, an iconoclast. For many, he is simply

---

58. Dover, "Aristophanes's Speech in Plato's Symposium," 50.
59. Plato, *Phaedrus*, 261a.

stigmatized with the term "crazy," as was Apollodorus (a namesake of the god Apollo) who was considered a maniac. Socrates himself is *atopos*, "out of place" in the city of Athens, and considered a threat to its identity and beliefs because of his individuality. Socrates's character is also on trial; as *perissos*, he is also perceived as an individual (an *idiotes*), as opposed to a citizen (a *polites*), someone who does not represent the gods of the city and ignores them to the detriment of civic life. He believes that his false notoriety and *reputation* come from the fact that he has been inspired by a specific kind of wisdom. "What kind of wisdom do I mean? Human wisdom (*anthropien sophia*)," (20d) he answers plainly, though hoping to be understood as making a claim that human wisdom, serving others, should be the proper way to conceive of his life and teaching. "I really am wise in this limited sense," (20e) he says, an ironic statement that ultimately means that human wisdom (unlike the one attributed to the gods) is the only wisdom that makes any difference and has impact in the human world, in the lives of human beings. Unlike in the *Theaetetus*, when he says that "I have no wisdom in me,"[60] here he does admit to being wise—as he will claim to know the "art of love" in the *Symposium*. But like the *Theaetetus*, a noticeable similarity, he also knows what the god commands him to do, especially for others. "The god compels me to act as a midwife," (150c) he says, a belief he now repeats and develops during his trial when he calls as his witness no less of an authority than "the god at Delphi," (20e) that is, Apollo, the god who will compel him to redefine piety and the religious life.

The rest of the trial will be a repetition of this one fundamental belief. A belief in the gods (and therefore the expression of piety, indeed its highest expression) is recognized first and foremost in one's love for others, the only authentic way one can heed the "divine command" and "assist the god" (23b). When he makes the claim about his particular religious belief and action, it is nothing other than "searching in obedience to the divine command," (23b) that is, following the gods' real desire in exposing human ill-health (as necessary before searching for authentic wisdom) and thereby providing what Socrates calls "my service (*latreian*) to God" (23c), a word used by Paul to juxtapose it with sacrifice, to "present your bodies a living sacrifice (*thusian zosan*), holy, acceptable unto God, which is your reasonable service (*latreian*)" (Rom 12:1). The early Christian rejection of sacrifice and its substitution with the love of others is here introduced as essential to Socratic teaching. Here Socrates does not use the word *therapeia* (as in the *Euthyphro*, when it was fundamentally related to the act of sacrifice as service), and instead relies on a much more humble reference to himself

60. Plato, *Theat.* 150c.

as a hired laborer, one meaning of *latreia*, the first of several interrelated concepts for being a *servant*. Socrates now begins to make far-reaching philosophical arguments, placing himself, as an individual, in the service of one particular God and soon to define himself in a remarkable way.

In his defense against his present accuser Meletus, he first of all restates the charges, the ones initially discussed with his friend in the *Euthyphro*: "Socrates is guilty of corrupting the minds of the young, and of believing in supernatural things of his own invention (*daimonia kaina*) instead of the gods recognized by the State" (24bc). The charge is now more succinctly defined as the invention of a new deity, though it must have been clear to his listeners that the god at Delphi was Apollo. Why Apollo of all the gods? The reasons are many. First of all, if he partly derived his name from the yearly assembly called the *apellai*[61] (the day when youths became full-fledged adults), Socrates's obedience to this god means his relationship to the young does not, in fact, corrupt them; on the contrary, he *initiates* them more comprehensively than the more formal rituals of the city. Second, Apollo, as the god of healing, conforms to the Socratic concern with examining others for the benefit of their health. The philosopher diagnoses and offers a *remedy*, both a change from a previous condition and, more precisely, a cure.

When the cross-examination turns to Meletus and the charge of impiety, Socrates reiterates the charge, that of teaching the young to believe "in new deities (*daimonia kaina*) instead of the gods recognized by the state" (26b). The first argument he makes is important: if Socrates is teaching the young about gods (any gods) then clearly he is not an atheist. He begins to lead to his conclusion (in fact, he has had but one fundamental belief) that he must live his life as a philosopher precisely because he believes he is fulfilling an obligation imposed on him as a command by a god: none other than Apollo. Emphasized as the god of medicine and healing rather than as a legislator and overseer of religious rituals, the identity of the god has been transformed, his many responsibilities given up for the sake of one command. The philosophical life is dedicated to nothing other than the well-being (to the cure) of others. He says to the jurors that "God appointed me . . . to the duty of leading the philosophic life, examining (*exetazonta*) myself and others" (28e). In making the claim of the responsibility of leading the philosophical life—a leading related to a military position prior to a battle—Socrates once again affirms his specifically social responsibility to the citizens of Athens. Although Harvey Goldman argues that *exetasis* "is implicitly, connotatively, and inextricably linked to the military meaning,

---

61. Bremmer, *Greek Religion*.

to station, service and review of the troops,"⁶² the particular term must be related to the entire lexicon of serving in the *Apology*, literally in terms of one's social responsibility to others and, metaphorically, preparation for the "battle" or *agon* to come, one which is wholly internal. Socrates, he stresses, is not an *idiotes*, that is, either an individual indifferent to the citizens or city of Athens, nor is he a private soldier, a related meaning of the term *exetasis*. Parenthetically, when Paul uses similar military rhetoric such as "to put on the armour (*endusometha*) of light," (Rom 13:12) the *enduō* can refer to the preparation for battle insofar as it involves putting on armor and the beginning of a struggle with one's previous self, one that will directly involve a *self*-confrontation. Harold Tarrant further argues that Socratic "*exetasis* is especially associated with the examination of the extent of somebody's knowledge,"⁶³ a belief that does not sufficiently consider the more comprehensive idea of *exetasis* as an examination not merely of what an individual *knows*, but of his or her whole life. So when Socrates tells everyone that "the unexamined life is not worth living,"⁶⁴ the examination must be comprehensive.

Socrates continues and makes the statement that he is indifferent to death, indifferent that he may be killed due to his one all-important obligation. He also tells everyone present that their belief in life after death, in a post-mortem existence of either rewards or punishments, is by no means certain. To know about life after death is one of the most obvious ways that one is ignorant. Any belief in life after death cannot be considered a part of religious belief or knowledge, an idea to become essential in the teaching of Epicurus and in the *tetrapharmakon*, the "four-part" cure, for in thinking that "death is nothing to us,"⁶⁵ as Epicureans affirm, one shows complete indifference to the belief in post-mortem divine reward or punishment. What is most important, and what he continues to stress, is obeying not the dictates of the city, but what he believes is the command of God: to contribute to the perfection of the *psyche*. "This, I do assure you, is what my god commands; and it is my belief that no greater good has ever befallen you in this city than my service (*uperesian*) to my god" (30a). Again, Socrates avoids the specific word *therapeia* he used in his conversation with *Euthyphro*, and here instead uses a word commonly associated with being a rower on a ship, serving as part of the crew, a socially important responsibility, as with the earlier military reference. What, for Socrates, is the service

62. Goldman, "Re-examining the 'Examined Life,'" 33.
63. Tarrant, "Elenchos and Exetasis," 72.
64. Plato, *Ap.*, 38a.
65. Epicurus, *PD.*, 2.

to his god? It is dedicating himself "for the highest welfare of your souls (*psyches*)" (30b). He has already reached the most significant aspect of his speech. In the remainder, he will only reiterate this one fundamental defense of his life, thought, and teaching, repeatedly stated during his trial and in other Socratic dialogues. For example, when discussing taking care of people's character in the *Laches*, his is defined as a *technikos peri psyches therapeian*" (185e). Similarly, in the *Charmides*, and now making a crucial addition, Socrates affirms that when one begins to "treat the soul" (*therepeuesthai de ten psychen*), such a treatment must involve "beautiful words," (157a) a language wholly attentive not simply to wisdom as such (nor of course to the rhetorical eloquence of the sophists), but to the particular psychological affliction of each individual. In the *Phaedrus*, he specifically uses his ability to perfect a *techne psychagogia*, "guiding" or "leading" the soul. Finally, in the *Gorgias*, when Socrates asks his interlocutor if oratory is the kind of speech "which tells the sick how they must live in order to get well" (449e)—Gorgias answers "no"—he has defined his speech, against the sophist, as therapeutic rather than merely eloquent, much less argumentative or persuasive. When James Beckman defines Socrates's philosophy as "fundamentally religious,"[66] the definition of what is religious (or pious or holy *in Athens*) has been completely rethought. C. D. C. Reeve describes Socrates's teaching as a "mission."[67] As Socrates will soon reveal (with one remarkable word to expand on being commanded) he will be the individual overturning all previous conceptions of the divine; and by doing so, he will represent a *philia* much more significant that Miletus's "patriotism" or *philiapatria*.

Socrates recognizes that the claims he is about to make will bring him closer to a guilty verdict than anything he has previously said; it was inevitable and far from avoided. He cannot restrain himself; he cannot speak apologetically, and certainly not in fear. He is absolutely certain of his convictions and therefore is indifferent to the judgment of others, even when they have the power to end his life. By telling the jurors, more than once, that "God has assigned to me to this city," (30e) Socrates is doing nothing less than claiming he represents the will of the gods and, in part, carries out their intentions. "God has attached me to this city," (30e) he repeats, in order to fulfill his responsibility as a philosopher; but in so doing, he has also made a claim considered extraordinary—and itself impious—by the majority of his jurors who would be outraged by his claims. By claiming to be in direct communication with the god, Socrates has declared himself to be not only equal but actually superior to that important institution of interpreters

---

66. Beckman, *Religious Dimension of Socrates's Thought*, 43.
67. Reeve, *Socrates in the Apology*, 72.

or *exegetai*, individuals in the service of Delphi who were either named by the oracle or elected by the Athenian people.[68] He has, in addition, displaced the god Hermes as the one who interpreted the enigmatic words of the gods and made them understandable for human beings.

The normally restrained philosopher's next declaration must have seemed unbelievable to many of his listeners, because by stating that he has been "sent to this city as a gift (*dedosthai*) from God," (31a) he has made himself into a *didomi* and thereby completely reversed the gods/human relationship insofar as sacrifices and prayers were offerings to the gods. By calling himself a gift from God, Socrates comes close (or can the belief be actually attributed to him?) to calling *himself* a sacrifice. Or at the very least, his *life* now will be a sacrifice for the sake of others. *Didomi* will again resound in the gospels of Jesus when his life will also be described as a gift, in particular when he will "give his life (*dounai ten psyche*) a ransom for many," (Matt 20:28, Mark 10:45) implying, in this case and prior to any christological interpretations of his crucifixion, a giving of himself in terms of mind, heart, and soul. In both cases, being a *didomi* from God is the absolute reversal of all sacrificial systems and the beginning of their abolition, for when Socrates and Jesus call themselves gifts from God, all previous gift giving and reciprocity has been nullified by the one supreme declaration by a man. One more important point: by the time Paul and his most trusted co-author Timothy began writing their letters, their teaching involves the "good news" being "delivered," (*paradoka*) (1 Cor 11:23) such that the *paradidomi* has the sense of initiating a new teaching and, therefore, a new tradition. The inheritance of past traditions has been nullified and made it possible to inaugurate anything less than a new history. The singular importance of Socrates being the first gift implies the *beginning* of a religious revolution that will extend itself (if in different ways determined by the individuality of each movement) into the Hellenistic philosophy of Epicurus, the Gospel of Jesus, and the teaching of early Christianity.

As he continues with his speech, being a gift from God also distinguishes him from everyone listening to him, the reason he now contrasts himself and the responsibility of a citizen, both as a common man and someone, usually wealthy, known as a benefactor. He also admits that he has never participated in public affairs, in "matters of state," (31c) a responsibility of citizens he has consciously avoided due to his *daimonion*. Socrates tells everyone that he has avoided "public life" and refused to "engage in politics" (31d) without providing a reason. The single most important part of his speech involves believing that Socrates has been specifically chosen

---

68. Guthrie, *Greeks and their Gods*, 186.

to represent the will of God, that everything he does as a philosopher and citizen is in "obedience to God's commands" (33c). By making such a declaration, Socrates knows he runs the risk of being considered impious and of introducing himself as an intermediary of the gods, in fact a unique representative, specifically called and therefore with more authority and legitimacy than any civic-appointed priest.

After being found guilty, Socrates has the task of proposing a penalty other than execution. And yet, he makes no alternative possible. After reaffirming that he has never pursued the goods considered important to Athenians, he again makes the statement that he has only followed one fundamental duty: "to be the greatest possible service (*euergetein*)" (36c), and he repeats again a word (service, in this case being a benefactor) so often repeated in the *Apology* and other dialogues related to Socrates's impiety. Socrates's final and perhaps most important self-definition of embodying *eurgetism* means he was both a benefactor to the city as well as someone who was a *soter*, certainly a healer, and perhaps a savior who could save and rescue them.[69] Nothing could be more important. Rather than the service that is provided by human beings to the gods (in return for favors and gifts) he believes that, as a servant of the gods, his service is in fact divinely inspired. More importantly, by specifically using the word "benefactor" in reference to himself, he views himself as much more important than the wealthy citizen who contributed sacrificial animals at his own expense, as Xenophon tells us in relation to a wealthy farmer who is obligated "to please the gods by offering sacrifices and having stock for their own disposal."[70] Vincent Rosivach makes the addition that "in inscriptions the generosity of the benefactor is sometimes attributed to piety."[71] Socrates has argued, repeatedly and consistently, that the most important good to pursue is "well-being," a therapeutic well-being related to the examination necessary for the proper understanding and conduct of life. In the *Apology* (unlike in the *Euthyphro*), Socrates has used various ways to describe his service to others while simultaneously providing a reevaluation of the city's conception of the gods. Socrates is finally justified, however, not after the conclusion of his

---

69. In *Essays on Religion and the Ancient World*, Arthur Nock provides several examples of the simultaneous use of *soter* and *eurgetes* for individuals, dignitaries, and Roman emperors. The language was later appropriated. Nock writes that "*soter* was a title which belonged specially to Christ; in liturgical texts, he is occasionally *soter* and *eurgetes*," 731. Although Socrates does not call himself a *soter* in his defense, several other dialogues (as we have shown) clearly indicate his philosophy and speaking were fundamentally intended to heal.

70. Xenophon, *Ec.* 5.3.

71. Rosivach, *System of Public Sacrifice*, 129.

trial, but in the speech of Aristophanes and the conception of the gods that must be rejected in order for human beings to recognize (and claim), their proper humanity. It is now necessary to return to the end of Aristophanes's speech so that Socratic therapeutic philosophy, exemplified—as we will see in the following chapter—by the speech of Alcibiades, is opposed to the tragic metaphysics of Athenian religion and polity.

Aristophanes therefore begins his conclusion without understanding the original problem, which is fundamentally theological. "There's a danger that if we don't keep order before the gods, we'll be split in two again" (193a). The dependence on the gods has been reestablished, thereby instituting an element of fear, uncertainty, and perpetual insecurity in their relationship to the gods—always vulnerable to the whimsical and inconsistent vagaries of their unpredictable personalities despite (as in the case of Agamemnon before battle in the *Iliad*) following protocol as established by an earlier pact between the gods and humans. Transgression or disobedience leads to punishment in the world, in the afterlife. The bind is absolute. Morality therefore depends on the polis religion and rejects Socratic individual conscience; and the order of the world, the relationship between humans and the divine, remains a perpetual threat. "We should encourage all men, therefore, to treat the gods with due reverence, so that we may escape this fate and find wholeness instead" (193a–b). For the first time, and consistent with Hephaestus's questions, Aristophanes argues that if human beings revere the gods and continue to perform sacrifices to them (that is, continue to be pious and reverential), then it might be possible to be restored. "If we are to give due praise to the god who can give us this blessing, then, we must praise Love" (193d). In order to be given the blessing of being restored, it is necessary above all to worship the god of love, Eros, at least for the time being. Love is merely temporary; indeed, love itself is incomplete, so Aristophanes seems to argue. "Love does the best that can be done for the time being; he draws us toward what belongs to us" (193d). By this account, love is therefore both temporary and itself incomplete; it cannot accomplish the goal of being made whole and complete again.

> But for the future, Love promises the greatest hope of all if we treat the gods with due reverence, he will restore to us original nature, and by healing (*iasamenos*) us, he will make us blessed (*makarious*) and happy (*eudaimonas*)." (193d)

But as Socrates must have argued repeatedly and consistently in the past, it is impossible to achieve either happiness or self-flourishing by relying on the intervention of the gods—waiting, apprehensively and without certainty—that they may bless us. Indeed, to desire our original nature would merely repeat a prior event and condition: the need to confront the gods and claim independence from them. Such expectation could only be maintained by ignoring the example of their unpredictability and often irrational behavior. Rather, if human beings are ever going to achieve freedom, they must reject the customary view of the gods, as well as the prayers and sacrifices offered to them. Only through the specific care of others in *therapeia*—as Socrates soon makes evident in his relationship with Alcibiades, in and out of the allegory of the cave, the two dialogues named after the notorious statesman, and at the end of the *Symposium*—will it be possible to fundamentally alter the human conception of the gods and, more significantly, human lives both individually and in the polis.

CHAPTER 2

The Case of Alcibiades

1. The "Nagging" Speech of Apollodorus

AT THE APPARENT CULMINATION of the *Symposium*, when Diotima proceeds to define the so-called "rising stairs" and its ascending steps, "the end at this lesson,"[1] seems unequivocal: the first purpose of the ascension in love should lead to a certain kind of "learning," though as Socrates knows it cannot simply be equated with knowledge as such, some epistemological proficiency, the mere overcoming of ignorance. Education, Socrates will tell us in his own words and in conversation with someone continuing to be enticed by the images of the cave, involves a certain commitment to the psyche of another and requires a specific "turn around," the *epistrepho*, implying a shift in self-consciousness. Diotima does recognize the process of learning and being "lead by another," so that the accomplishment of education should lead someone "to know just what it is to be beautiful (*esti kalon*)," (211d) implying a possible change in *being*, inside and out, in thoughts and acts, one more significant than either an ethical or aesthetic beauty. The dynamism of philosophy depends on its ability to transform human beings; it demands nothing less of itself than this one effect: to first resist passively inheriting the handed down ideas of tradition or to reflect the ideals of the city. The second purpose of the ascension in love indicates that in order to "see the Beautiful itself" it is first necessary to overcome the body, all the senses, a perception "not polluted by human flesh," (211e) and if one had the ability (the *dunamis*), it would be possible to "see the divine beauty

---

1. Plato, *Sym.*, 211c.

(*theion kalon*) itself in its one form (*monoeides*)" (211e). For Diotima, here so unlike Socrates[2] and his court speech, the human world and the divine are separated; they are irreconcilable—the first prototypical conflict again to involve a confrontation between Athenian gods (and the polis as such) and Socrates's impiety, that is, his individual attempt to transform how the gods and the city they support are conceived, perceived, and venerated. In order to see divine beauty or the ultimate good—which cannot be accomplished by the mere human sense of sight, a beauty or goodness not contained and bound in a thing, earth or heaven, an animal, a human being—Diotima believes it is necessary to ascend, "always upwards" and transcend everything in the world and achieve *areten alethe*, "true virtue," (212a) what must be distinguished from *eidola aretes*, "images of virtue" (212a). The fascination with *eidolon*, images and idols, has been noted if not entirely renounced. They will certainly be put in their place once the prisoner leaves the constraints of the cave, and Alcibiades, in his drunken speech, defines Socrates as an *eikon*,[3] though the ambitious Athenian will be unable to understand the reason for his desire, above all, to be idolized as a renowned citizen of the city. Despite being forced out of the cave (Socrates will literally have to drag him out) Alcibiades makes a choice with unintended consequences: not to return and talk to others about the difference between inside and outside, deception and truth, but to accept the reality of the cave, accept and embrace it as the way to fulfill his greatest desire. For Alcibiades, everything depends on achieving honor and immortal renown.

When the Diotima speech concludes, followed by loud applause which makes it impossible for Aristophanes to respond (this in relation to one of his prior arguments), the reader encounters what at first seems to be a rude interruption by the "plastered" Alcibiades who barges in on the symposium and will soon provide the single most important declaration on the meaning of love by Socrates. He defines himself to Alcibiades as "one who loves your soul (*psyches eron*),"[4] a love exceedingly far from any *monoeides*, so much lower than the highest step in Diotima's stairs and in utmost proximity to the human world of thought and feelings and, perhaps, best expressed

2. Although it is not the scope of this chapter to argue for the difference between Plato and Socrates (more specifically, the difference between the metaphysics of the *monoeides* and what I will call here Socrates's wisdom of love), I do not agree with Paul Friedländer's *Plato, Vol. 1* that "there is no struggle between Plato, the metaphysician, and Socrates, the ironic inquirer" (170), or Charles Kahn in *Plato and the Socratic Dialogue* that "from Plato's point of view, there is no fundamental discrepancy between the philosophy of Socrates and that of Plato" (100).

3. I am indebted to the work of Jean-Luc Marion for the distinction between the icon and the idol. See, especially, *God without Being*.

4. Plato, *Al. I*, 131d.

by descending back into the cave to establish a relationship (and a dialogue) with those most chained to themselves and their distorted perceptions.[5] Socrates will reveal the ultimate nature of his love by first forcing one of the prisoners of the cave to leave (to leave not so much an incomplete and deceptive reality but the illusory nature of the city and how it can distort human self-conception), and second, returning and attempting to persuade others to consider their irrational and ailing condition. Socrates cannot enjoy his singular freedom; he has feelings for the other prisoners, has empathy for them and loves them enough to subject himself to a return to the cave despite knowing full well the risk and danger. The resentment of the cave dwellers will be immediate and reactionary. Nothing provokes murderous rage more than exposing the delusions of others (their self-righteous ideas, apparently, with moral infallibility) and holding their lives accountable.

Although the interlocutors in the cave are anonymous, at least unnamed, Plato leaves sufficient possibilities for us to speculate on their identities and to recognize their characteristics—one a philosopher, the other an ambitious citizen of a polis who will be taught to examine the nature of his desire for both public and private acknowledgement and provide a testimony for Socrates's teaching and, in particular, the effect of the philosopher's beautiful words on his psyche.

Prior to Alcibiades's speech and the culmination of the *Symposium*, however, several interrelated preludes are necessary, each of them combining to comprehensively understand how Socrates *treats* Alcibiades. Despite the uncertainty about the authorship of the two dialogues named after the notorious Athenian statesman (especially *Alcibiades II*), the philosophical relationship of the Platonic dialogues to follow can be read as thematically organized, beginning with the remarkable "Introductory Dialogue" of the *Symposium* and the presence of two perhaps underappreciated students who together recount the events and speeches of the evening: Aristodemus (who, according to Xenophon,[6] refused to attend public sacrifices) and Apollodorus as both the narrator of the story and someone who nags both others and himself. And if Apollodorus represents one of Socrates's students who now can reflect on himself and his place in the city, it will then be important to follow Socrates into the cave and his dialogue with a prisoner for the sole purpose of the "curing" (*iasin*) of their "ignorance," (*aphrosunes*)[7] literally healing them of their irrationality, an illness, and tribulations of

---

5. In *The Fragility of Goodness*, Nussbaum writes that "Socrates and Alcibiades compete for our souls," 198.

6. Xenophon, *Mem.*, 1.4.2.

7. Plato, *Rep.*, 515c.

their psyche. The conversation in the cave will be intermixed with the *Alcibiades I* and the occasion when for the first time Socrates's *daimonion* finally allows him to talk to the ambitious Athenian about the most important of philosophical concerns: to analyze the nature of a human being and fulfill the Delphic dictum at the temple of Apollo to "know thyself." The *Alcibiades II* will then complement, and actually complete with declarations instead of questions, the fundamental problem of piety, prayer, and sacrifice first made evident in the *Euthyphro*, and lead finally to the end of the *Symposium* and the plastered speech by Alcibiades as he reveals Socrates's most important philosophical lesson to him.

In the "Introductory Dialogue," when Glaucon encounters Apollodorus and asks him to tell him the story of the famous symposium, one of the first and significant revelations concerns Apollodorus and how, knowing Socrates—that is, knowing especially "what he says and does" (173a)—has resulted in a significant change in his life. Socrates's words and acts have been enough to begin a process of self-examination leading, for him, to a reappraisal of everything he was in the past. Apollodorus now represents the *mathetes*, the student and "disciple" (as translated in the gospels of Jesus) who first changes himself and then devotes his life to the same transformation of others, thereby fulfilling a responsibility, as we will see, consistent with the one who has left the shadows of the cave and, after experiencing the perception of reality rather than the images created in the world, can return and speak to others for their own freedom, even with the danger that he will be ridiculed, persecuted, and perhaps even killed. Before Apollodorus knew Socrates, he "simply drifted aimlessly," (173a) that is, he simultaneously walked metaphorically, in no specific direction but also, equally importantly, discussed, talked with others without knowing precisely the reason for the dialogue. Ideas went round and round without purpose, in a kind of senseless, gossipy chatter with no real intent or *telos*, so different from the turn around evident in the particular learning of a *psyche*. Apollodorus admits he was completely lost; he neither knew himself nor his proper place in the city, in part due to the insignificant topics most important to those self-conscious about their status and reputations, the very people he is now talking to and beginning to provoke. While not yet nagging, Apollodorus begins a testimony of the philosophical life. Philosophy attends to others by initiating a process of self-accounting, one more significant, more long-lasting, than the ephemeral admiration of others due to one's perceived abilities or the status pursued with such commitment by the citizens who identify with the city's values and desire to be recognized for their unique place within it. Philosophy does not make you simply a good man, morally, providing examples of virtue. Philosophy makes it difficult to be self-delusional, hence

The Case of Alcibiades 67

Carlo Pancera's definition of Socratic teaching as a "psycho-pedagogy,"[8] a "teaching of the soul" that will become most significant in post-Socratic philosophy and eventually be of critical importance in Epicureanism and early Christianity. When Socrates defines his own kind of speaking or rhetoric as "a skilful leading of the soul (*techne psychagogia*) by means of words"[9]—and let us remember that they had to be "beautiful words"[10]—he has essentially defined the intimate relationship between philosophy as a certain kind of speaking, a unique dialogue to be understood in part as distinct from the history of prayer and its appeal to the divine for beneficial intervention. Unlike Gregory Vlastos, who believes that "for Plato, as for Socrates before him, the supreme goal of all human endeavor is the improvement of the soul—and that means its *moral* improvement,"[11] Alcibiades's description of Socrates will ultimately emphasize his ability to analyze the ailing *psyches* of individuals and lead them toward therapeutic health, an end exceeding moral goodness. Indeed, moral goodness cannot be achieved if people in the city continue to be compromised by their ailing *psyches*. Virtue cannot suffice; moral goodness is not comprehensive enough. "Excellence then seems to be a kind of health (*ugieia*) and beauty and well-being of the soul."[12] If one is psychologically unhealthy, if one experiences perpetual conflict, chronic doubt, debilitating anxiety, so that the self is experienced as prone to influence (from within and without), one is far more likely to disrupt the lives of others, a problem Epicurus understood so well when first commenting on an unfounded conception of divine wrath. Socrates concerns himself first and foremost with the *psychical* good. Without the psychological health of individuals, the city will continue to suffer from all of its most evident afflictions and thus make it impossible to transform both its self-conception and its most important institutions—including, for example, the institution supposedly most concerned with justice, the "shadow of justice,"[13] as he calls it in the *Republic*, that led to his execution. The city will merely be able to reflect its past, but in doing so, it has closed off all possibilities for a future yet to be imagined, conceived, and actualized. The *moral* good can only be one and by no means the only consideration of the good, not when *arete* is understood as a virtue, certainly, but more comprehensively as a human

8. Pancera, *La formazione dell'uomo in Socrate*.
9. Plato, *Phaedrus*, 261a.
10. Plato, *Chrm.*, 157a.
11. Vlastos, *Platonic Studies*, 14.
12. Plato, *Rep.*, 444d.
13. Ibid., 517d.

excellence that has a specific end of health, that is, to be cured from the psychopathologies of the city.

When Apollodorus says "my greatest pleasure comes from philosophical conversation, even if I'm only a listener," (173c) he also knows the most important philosophical act cannot simply be the dialogue, listening, and talking *with others*, but must also include the ability to turn inwards, into oneself, so that the conversation can also become a silent soliloquy, a reflective self-examination conducted through words, precisely how Augustine (in 386–387, shortly after his conversion) defined the nature of the *soli loquia*.[14] Apollodorus can be here compared with someone described in the *Phaedrus* and his "passion for hearing speeches (*peri logon akone*),"[15] a listening someone else defined in terms of its effects: "somehow your words touch my soul."[16] As a consequence of the way he has been affected by Socrates's speech, he now has the ability to have a conversation with himself, the "silent inner conversation of the soul with itself."[17] In the *Theaetetus*, the self-reflective dialogue is described as "the talk (*logon*) the soul (*psychen*) has with itself."[18] Apollodorus has learned one of Socrates's fundamental philosophical lessons: listening should first lead to self-reflection, on being, living a certain life ("to live well"[19]), and then turning to others with an equal dedication for conversation and dialogue, one with an essential motivation and purpose.

The self-dialogue is crucial since Socrates's voice has been internalized as a permanent characteristic of Apollodorus's analytic psyche: there are, then, two aspects of the psychotherapeutic conversation, one in relation to others, one in relation to oneself. Apollodorus has been much neglected as a student of Socrates. He represents someone who, first of all, has been changed by his conversations with Socrates and, equally if not more importantly, is someone who now can carry out his own simultaneous self-analysis and conversation with others. Commentators have not been generous and instead have been noticeably drawn to one overriding perception: some refer to his "complete, almost comic devotion to Socrates."[20] He has been labeled a "gushing youth, reveling in uncritical enthusiasm" as well

---

14. Augustine, *Sol.*
15. Plato, *Phaedrus*, 228b.
16. Plato, *Ion*, 535a.
17. Plato, *Soph.*, 263e.
18. Plato, *Theat.* 189e.
19. Plato, *Cr.*, 48b.
20. Corrigan and Glazov-Corrigan, *Plato's Dialectic at Play*, 17.

as an "overzealous little student."²¹ He has also been derided for "his shallow devotion of a parroting acolyte."²² True, he does express himself in the tone of a rebellious youth in opposition to the *status quo*, especially when he dismisses the wealthy who are interested in business and the pursuit of riches. His particular kind of speaking, however (described as "nagging" and therefore resembling *parresia*), shows an ability to understand the full extent of Socrates's philosophy, both admonishing and exhorting, criticizing and encouraging.

Apollodorus's acquaintance with Glaucon, however, betrays his lack of understanding when Glaucon tells him: "you'll never change (*omoios*), Apollodorus! Always nagging (*kakegoreis*), even at yourself" (173d). There are two points to note here. First, Glaucon tells him that he will never *change* (he will always be, stay, the same), which is precisely what the Socratic conversation and subsequent self-dialogue is intended to accomplish—to become different. And second, the philosophical lesson achieves its intended purpose when the self can "nag" not "even at yourself," but especially at oneself. The meaning of *kakegoreō* (to speak ill of one) is precisely the opposite of the subject of the symposium—an *epaineō* or *eulogeō* on Eros, as deity, as human disposition, a distinction also to be made in Epicurean philosophy. But what Apollodorus understands by this nagging is nothing less than the self's ability to evaluate, analyze, and change oneself in what Alcibiades, at the end of his speech, will call *parresia* (222c), that "bold speaking" and "frank criticism" not so much related to that most important of social privileges in Athens—free speech—but to the speaking that is essential to Epicurean philosophy that can be conducted in a specifically therapeutic dialogue and during one's self-examination.²³

One of Socrates's students (this prior to the speeches praising Eros), shows how one of the essential teachings of the therapeutic philosopher involves not the desire for praise from others—as if flattery led to feeling honorable—but a relentless and critical analysis of one's self. Speaking ill of oneself is intended as the beginning of a self-transformation. Character cannot be bestowed on one by others—what Alcibiades, for one, craves to the detriment of his self. It can only be created internally, as an aspect

---

21. Pieper, *For the Love of Wisdom*, 37.

22. Scott and Welton, *Erotic Wisdom*, 183.

23. In one aspect of "frank criticism" evident in the Epicurean Philodemus of Gadara, he points out how the "sage" is someone intimately related with the process of constantly evaluating one's thoughts so as to ensure the perpetual state of that highest ideal—*ataraxia*, or to be free from the disturbances of the soul. In Fragment 1 of *On Frank Criticism*, Philodemus point out that "A wise man and philosopher speaks frankly" about his or her "errors" (*hamartias*).

of character. Apollodurus is therefore the most *psychologically significant* character in the *Symposium*—with one exception, and precisely because he introduces him and anticipates him as the culmination of the speeches on love. Apollodurus is a "maniac," (173d) suffering from a *mania*, because he is most excellent at "raving," (173e) speaking to others (and also himself) with the particular audacity of *parresia*. He acts and speaks like a madman, an ultimate irony since what can be deduced from his dialogue is much less his raving than the psychopathologies of the city. The ultimate meaning of this nagging will only be revealed at the very end of the *Symposium*, precisely at the moment Alcibiades's speech is defined as "frankness," *parresia*, a kind of philosophical language intended to provoke and antagonize the listener into realizing how his character and life are shameful and, through the shame, initiate the transformation leading to a more self-sufficient life. The relationship of shame to *sophrosune* (emphasized twice in the speech) will soon be decisive.

When Socrates arrives at the symposium halfway through dinner, he takes his seat beside Agathon (accepting his request), and eats with the rest of the guests. Immediately, following tradition and the "whole ritual" preceding the evening, "they poured a libation (*spondas*) to the god" (176a). The apparently customary ritual, as an act devoted to the recognition of the gods, is performed without fanfare.[24] That Socrates was present during the libation does not in any way suggest he believed that spilling wine on the floor had any meaning for him or the gods. However, there are two aspects of the ritual worth noting as they are interrelated. A *sponde* is a peace treaty or a truce, usually reserved for a military campaign or political agreement, as in the events of 404–403, when the democratic faction regained power after the oligarchic takeover. The truce (an associated meaning is "reconciliation") involves in principle both a political and theological relationship. For Socrates, however, a psychical reconciliation precedes (and is more crucial than) either a historical or transcendental one. Reconciliation can only be possible by a self-sufficient act, one which is independent of either the city or the gods. Several speakers at the symposium, however, all agree on the fundamental dependence on the gods. As Aristophanes tragically concluded: "if we treat the gods with due reverence, he will restore to us our original nature (*archaian phusin*), and by healing us (*iasamenos*), he will

---

24. In his "Comment" to his translation of the *Symposium*, Allen argues that the drinking itself is considered a religious act; furthermore, the symposium is, if not a religious ceremony, a gathering that involves mutual fellowship. Being with others, then, constitutes possible piety for Socrates, especially in the context of conversations. Or stated more forcefully, conversing with others (moreover, on the subject of love) constitutes one of the highest expressions of piety for Socrates.

make us blessed and happy (*makarious kai eudaimonas*)" (193d). Both Phaedrus and Eryximachus anticipate his conclusion. Nothing could be more inimical to Socratic teaching. Philosophy categorically rejects any idea of restoring a supposedly intact, better human nature in part because all previous conceptions of being human were predicated irreducibly on a certain relationship to the gods. Blessedness, happiness, and especially healing, cannot be accomplished by reverence for the gods (either in prayer or sacrifice), but only through the self-inquiry leading to one of the most significant concerns of the evening, that is, a *sophia* reflecting a particular expression of love. And just as the psyche will be turned, so too will philosophy be able to assert itself and its double meaning as both the love of wisdom and wisdom of Socratic love.

The second aspect of the libation must also be mentioned: since every *symposia* traditionally opened with three libations[25] (to the Olympic gods, the Heroes, and Zeus *Soter*), the last becomes particularly meaningful for the *Symposium*. The significance of Zeus the "Healer," which is obviously far greater than that of the mere physician Eryximachus, is directly related to the speech of Alcibiades and the ultimately philosophical/therapeutic act of Socrates. Two of the most significant ideas of the symposium—reconciliation and healing—have now been articulated. But far from attributing them to the gods, it is the plastered Alcibiades who will present a description of Socrates allowing everyone at the symposium to recognize that the philosopher's most important achievement has nothing to do with knowledge, but rather the wisdom leading to one's independence from both the gods and the city and the inner perception allowing for a transformation of the self. Socrates rejects both political and theological reconciliation. Not accidentally does the good doctor begin his advice on the "nature of intoxication" immediately after the pouring of the libations. In his mind, "inebriation is harmful to everyone," (176d) for *methe* (a drink not precisely the same as wine, with properties inducing potentially ek-static states) will soon have unexpected consequences.[26] Before the speeches then, everyone agrees not to drink according to the custom of the symposia (with someone imposing an amount) and then make a decision to "honor the god" of love in a particular way, by giving "a speech in praise (*epainon*) of Love" (177d). Socrates is the first to agree and, speaking for everyone else present, is certain no one could possibly object. He then makes one of the most remarkable statements he has, perhaps, ever uttered. The philosopher most famous for publicly stating he has no knowledge at all now suddenly claims: "the only

---

25. Quasten, *Music and Worship*, .
26. On the unique properties of wine in the ancient world, see Rinella's *Pharmakon*.

thing I say I understand is the art of love (*ta erotika*)." (177d) His admission is echoed in the *Theages*: "I always say, surely, that I happen to know so to speak nothing, except a certain small subject of knowledge: what pertains to erotic love."[27] No translation seems to be adequate to this particular *logos*; his meaning can only be recognized at a later, appropriate time, and it is not with his speech (or rather, his reported speech of Diotima) but when Alcibiades arrives and prepares the culmination of the *Symposium*. His affirmation on knowing *ta erotika*, however, is no mere play on words, *eros* and its relation to *erotan* or "to ask questions," as Reeve argues.[28] *Philosophia*, therapeutically understood, will be the wisdom of love and its expression in language and in the care of others.

When Socrates turns to Agathon and tells him about the emotional relationship between himself and Alcibiades, he reveals, with extremely disguised language, the nature of his teaching. In addition to the "jealous rage" expressed by Alcibiades, as well as his fierce passion, Socrates makes a curious request, stating from the beginning the psycho-dynamic lesson: "could you perhaps make him forgive me" (213d)? Although Strauss and others translate *diallassō* as "reconciliation"[29] instead of forgiveness, the difficult meaning of this particular philosophical expression remains. It refers, as well, to an *exchange* (as a consequence of their conversations) and implies a subsequent alteration, a change in oneself, so that Socrates, ironically, is asking Alcibiades to transform him. The opposite of course is true, but Alcibiades cannot be reconciled because of his dependence on the adoration (the idolatry) of the city; he cannot reconcile his self-division since he is drawn simultaneously to the philosophical life and to the ambitions of a political and military career.[30] He desires to be an idol, revered as an exemplary citizen—an ambition absolutely inconsistent with the philosophical life Socrates has been attempting to show him, and the disaster of the Sicilian expedition led by him in 415 will be evidence of his desire for honor and glory rather than the attainment of wisdom of the philosophical life, which would make him more self-possessed and less dependent on the opinions of others.

---

27. Plato, *Theag.*, 128b.

28. Reeve, "Introduction," xix.

29. Strauss, *On Plato's Symposium*. This translation is used throught the book.

30. Alcibiades also became famous as a victor at the Olympic Games—but not as an athlete; he was the owner of the horses used in chariot races. In a speech to the Athenians before launching the Sicilian Expedition of 415, he reminds them that he entered seven chariots and that he took first, second, and fourth place. See Thucydides, *War.*, 6.16.

Immediately Alcibiades responds and tells Socrates, everyone present, and himself: "I shall never forgive (*diallage*) you" (213d). Socrates does not seek forgiveness from Alcibiades—that is, a moral decision leading to an amicable relationship, a resolution to a prior disagreement or division—nor does he seek to be reconciled with him. Rather, and this is the psychodynamic lesson ultimately leading Socrates on, he has instructed Alcibiades about how to reach reconciliation *within himself* and thereby choose the philosophical life rather than the political and military ambitions that motivate his future actions for the sole purpose (entirely self-interested) of being recognized as a man of renown. Alcibiades is self-estranged, torn between his desire for adulation from the many and becoming self-sufficient, that is, free. Parenthetically, and with an often-repeated concept used by Paul in his letters, "reconciliation" is to be understood as specifically psychodynamic. For example, when he writes of "the word of reconciliation," *logon tes katallages* (2 Cor 5:19), the teaching is intended to provide human beings with "peace," internal conflict overcome and resolved and expressed as the ability "to make of himself twain (*duo*) one new man" (Eph 2:15). Reconciliation, both expressed by Socrates and Paul, is first and foremost a psychological concept—and a therapeutic health to be achieved—related to the always-threatening human predicament to be self-divided, torn between internal passions and external acknowledgments.

The emotions of jealous rage and reconciliation are related, and are to be understood as a psychodynamic process. When Socrates analyzes Alcibiades's jealousy, he has emphasized how he needs to possess another, to take away their individuality and freedom, to render one a slave. But the jealousy (the desire for possessiveness) only reveals Alcibiades's enslaved condition to his own lack and need—divided between his desire for acknowledgment from the city and becoming self-sufficient. The complicated multi-meanings of *diallassō* define the Socratic teaching most necessary for Alcibiades: in order to achieve any reconciliation in himself, Alcibiades must become someone other than he is, hence the other important meaning of *diallassō*, that there will indeed be an "exchange" between Socrates and Alcibiades, and it will involve nothing less than a surprising lesson intended to transform Alcibiades's *psyche*. Alcibiades therefore will begin his description of Socrates and the lesson which taught him the relationship between shame and reconciliation; before doing so, however, it is first necessary to turn to the relationship between the allegory of the cave in Book VII of the *Republic* and the dialogue, *Alcibiades I*, detailing the first conversation between Socrates and Alcibiades.

2. The Illness of the Cave Dwellers

When Plato opens Book VII of the *Republic* with the allegory of the cave, the first consideration of the images to come are intended to show how *paideia* has an effect on human nature. More precisely, how education can both free the prisoners from the cave (from the impositions and restraints of the polis) and "turn around" the *psyche*. Although the two main protagonists of the allegory are anonymous—or at least unnamed, as the god of Delphi in the *Apology*—Plato's suggestions are, in certain places, unmistakable and indicate none other than Socrates the philosopher, the first to leave the cave, and Alcibiades the ambitious Athenian who is forced and compelled to follow, if only briefly, so as to experience human freedom and *health*.

"The men have been there since childhood," (514a) Plato begins. They are in chains and the fetters also prevent them from even turning their heads. They can only see flickering shadows on the wall in front of them, a semblance of reality, but more importantly, they cannot "see anything of themselves and each other" (515a). The prisoners have only known this one, severely restrained reality, so much so that their visibility (that is, their perception of what is seen and, also, what can be imagined) has been effectively limited; they can only think as a reflection of their distorted perception, limited by the reality in front of them and the inability to perceive any of their human characteristics. They know themselves only through images. The consequences of the discussion will soon be extraordinary, beginning with the realization that human nature (or what can be known, at all, about the human beings) cannot be essentially defined but only assumed; it is, for now, incomplete in part because of the nature of the cave. The concern with knowing oneself (and understanding the possibilities of human nature as discussed in *Alcibiades I*) are here specifically contrasted with the restriction of the cave and, for Alcibiades, the inherent problem of a public, political life as opposed to the responsibility of the philosopher and his care for others. The obligation of the philosopher, and the calling of what he calls "true philosophy," (*Vatican Saying* 54) is nothing other than the care of others and, if they are unhealthy, their healing, as Epicurus will stress by equating true philosophy with true health in his *Vatican Sayings*.

Further describing the condition of the cave, the prisoners see shadows on the wall in front of them, shadows created by artifacts, such as statues and other reproductions of people and animals and things. "Do you think, in the first place, that such men could see anything of themselves and each other except the shadows which the fire casts upon the wall of the cave in front of them?" (514c) Socrates rhetorically asks, thereby making the first argument. It is not simply that human beings cannot *see* themselves or others. In fact, they can see at least parts of their own bodies. However, they cannot begin to reflect on themselves, on who they are, due to being enticed by the light of images in front of them. Their visibility has determined everything they can know—the reason Socrates the philosopher will make the extraordinary attempt to leave the cave in order to see another reality altogether (including himself and all human possibilities of being) and then return out of care and compassion to teach others. "Consider then what deliverance (*lusin*) from their bonds and the curing (*iasin*) of their ignorance (*aphrosunes*) would be if something like this naturally happened to them," (515c) Socrates tells his interlocutor as he prepares him for the release of one of the prisoners. Their condition is not simply one of being prisoners; or ignorant of some knowledge. They are ill due to being irrational, if not suffering from another more serious affliction, and that is the reason they need to be cured from an ailment they may be able to feel and sense but cannot explain; they can feel, but without understanding. They will not simply be cured of their ignorance, as if they could simply be cured by *knowing*, as if their illness could be reduced to some mere ignorance overcome with knowledge; rather, they are ill because of their inability to think about themselves, others, and the world, to reflect in a way that is different from their constant attention to the images in front of them and their customary perception. Socratic philosophy begins when human beings are first diagnosed as ill and in need of being psychotherapeutically treated to become healthy.

Socrates then seems to speculate about the possibility of someone in the cave becoming free and how they would initially feel pain, discomfort, insecurity. In fact, what he begins to describe is a conversation he has *already had* with one of the prisoners. "What do you think he would say if he was told that what he saw then was foolishness" (515d)? Socrates describes the first time he had a conversation with one of the prisoners *after his return* to the cave to tell him about all the nonsense he is seeing, and the attempt to make him leave by force. "And if one were to drag him thence by force up the rough and steep path, and did not let him go before he was dragged into the sunlight, would he not be in physical pain and angry as he was dragged along" (515d)? The questions sound as if they were only speculative, in the spirit of "What would happen if?" The possible future has to be replaced with a past event, just as the allegory of the cave will soon turn to the *psyche*. The philosopher makes the attempt to tell him that, despite being unable to see the images he had formerly seen (despite his vision appearing worse) he should trust him. Everything the prisoner has formerly known seems uncertain; and it causes him anxiety. Worst of all, the philosopher now physically drags the prisoner up toward the exit of the cave and the sunlight outside. Once outside, his condition appears to him much worse than before; the sunlight is so bright he cannot see at all. He squints, covers his eyes, turns away from the light. "I think he would need time to get adjusted before he could see things in the world above," (516a) Socrates says before pointing out how, in time, he would begin to see the sun and understand its relation to the seasons and the years. Although the comment can be easily passed over, Socrates in fact makes a crucial observation (indeed, a philosophical position) on the natural as opposed to the metaphysical origins of the earth and its place in the cosmos. Socrates also understands the sun, which Anaxagoras had called a "red-hot stone"[31]—a comment that would lead to him being charged with impiety and exiled—to be a natural element without any relation to the gods. His youthful interest in the natural sciences may have been renounced as a philosophical pursuit, but its findings have not been forgotten.

The freed prisoner, Alcibiades, now begins to understand not simply the natural world—earth and sky, moon and sun and stars—he begins to reflect on the difference between being in the world now and his former condition. "As he reminds himself of his first dwelling place, of the wisdom there and of his fellow prisoners, would he not reckon himself happy for the change, and pity them" (516c)? He does not, in fact, call himself happy (filled with *eudaimonia*), despite his own personal transformation. For the change in himself has led him to reach, for the first time, a certain *feeling*, one accompanied by an understanding of his relationship to others. He now knows that all the *wisdom* apparently possessed by those inside the cave, including the "praise and honor from each other," (516c) that is, the specific recognition and social acknowledgement apparently so important for Alcibiades as an Athenian citizen, all has to be put into doubt. Those who are recognized for their skills and rewarded because of them—such as those who can "most ably prophesy the future," (516d) those with divinatory abilities so important for the religious rituals of the city, or the ones who by virtue of power or other skills are honored—they are now to be regarded quite differently than before. All the individuals in the cave who are praised, honored, and rewarded are in fact destitute; the prisoner who has now reached freedom, understanding, and most importantly empathy, would rather "go through any suffering, rather than share their opinions and live as they do" (516d). The philosopher does not simply make the distinction between the opinions of the many and real knowledge (as Epicurus also will) but continues to stress how holding opinions of the many leads to a much more damaging life than mere ignorance. It leads to ill health.

31. Copleston, *History of Philosophy*, 66.

The former prisoner, out of compassion and love for those who remain chained and only aware of a limited and distorted reality, has to necessarily return. Once back in the cave, however, his sight is once again compromised, so much so that the prisoners ridicule and mock him for the journey out of the cave which, from their perspective, has made his sight far worse than before. "As for the man who tried to free them and lead them upward, if they could somehow lay their hands on him, and kill him, they would do so" (517a). The ones most celebrated in the polis, the ones who have earned praise and all the rewards given to the most prominent citizens can only sustain their reality—or what is called "the realm of the visible" (517b)—by persecuting the one who is *atopos*, who no longer has a place among them and is therefore the ultimate outsider. The philosopher who has been transformed and seen a different reality (in the world, in human beings) can no longer live as before and cannot occupy himself with "human affairs" (517c). Once the philosopher has attained the insights and the vision now compelling him to teach others, he can no longer live as before—acting as a juryman in a court of law, for example, where "the shadows of justice" (517d) are everywhere but unseen.

The remarkable transition from the allegory of the cave, "from darkness to light" (518a), to the related analysis of the *psyche* occurs, not incidentally, at the very point Plato invokes the trial of Socrates and, once more, stresses how the philosopher is most concerned "whenever he sees a soul disturbed" (518a) and is compelled to take care of them.

"Education (*paideian*) is not what some declare it to be," (518b) Socrates says, using *paideia*, as he had when beginning his parable, as both education and more comprehensively in the raising of a child, every child regardless of perceived capacity or ability. "The capacity (*dunamin*) to learn and the organ with which to do so are present in every person's soul (*psyche*)," (518c) Socrates says. The philosopher therefore commits his life and teaching to this one necessity. "Education then is the art of doing this very thing, this turning around (*metastraphesetai*), the knowledge of how the soul can most easily and most effectively be turned around" (518d). Socratic *metastrepho* involves nothing less than a turn-around from a previous way of being (especially within the limits of the polis), such that the transformed individual can now begin to properly serve others—authentically, that is—and not in the self-serving manner to be so evident in the tragic life of Alcibiades. And the most significant word for this service is "to take care for," (520a) the act which is essential to the life of the philosopher as he serves others, and the polis, by taking care of them. Socratic philosophy—as exemplified in the *Symposium* and in the allegory of the cave in the *Republic*—can be defined as the wisdom of love insofar as the philosopher is someone whose compassion leads him not to simply care for himself, but for their well-being, even when (as in Socrates's case) it can lead to persecution and, ultimately, death.

Socrates now begins to approach his conclusion when he mentions—again relevant for Alcibiades—how "the uneducated who have no experience of truth would never govern a city satisfactorily" (519c). Moreover, those who are educated (those who are wise philosophers) would never think about governing a city because they have a more urgent responsibility: "to take care for and to guard others" (520a) in a way not reducible to political life. Socrates's final point is even more strenuous. He makes "true philosophy" incompatible with political office, and therefore gives Alcibiades a choice, one he will struggle with (as we will see during the end of his speech in the *Symposium*) until, ultimately, he will sail for a military expedition he hopes will make him famous and wealthy. If what Socrates calls *philosophia alethe* aims at the turning of the soul, the *metastrephō* of the *psyche*, the philosopher will have this one and overriding devotion, one incompatible with Alcibiades's ambitions of becoming revered as a politician.

3. *The Alcibiades Dialogues*

In *Alcibiades I*,[32] Socrates approaches the youthful student and speaks to him for the first time because, previously, he had been prevented from doing so by his *daimonion*. The philosopher's inner voice and counsel has dissuaded him from speaking directly to the young and prominent Athenian. Now, however, Socrates has assumed the responsibility—given to him, let us remind ourselves, by a particular god as he stated in the *Apology*—of taking care of the young man, or more precisely, to *love* him in a particular way. For if "philosophy is concerned with tendance of human beings,"[33] that is, their care and ministration, all the dialogues between Socrates and Alcibiades will be determined by this one overriding preoccupation.

---

32. Plato, *Al. I*. The sub-title of the dialogue—"On the Nature of Human Being," *peri anthrophon phuseos* according to Diogenes Laertius 3.59—first of all indicates the emphasis of Socrates's therapeutic philosophy: "if the soul too is to know itself, should it look at the soul, and above all at that place in it in which the virtue of the soul—wisdom—comes to exist, and at any other thing to which this happens to be similar" (133b)? I do not take up the question of the authenticity of either of the two dialogues named after Alcibiades; they are too representative of Socratic thought to be spurious; and as I argue later, in relation to *Alcibiades II*, the dialogue is complementary to the *Euthyphro* and, ultimately, to Socrates's trial.

33. Bluck, "Origin of the Greater Alcibiades," 50.

Unlike the speeches in the *Symposium* and the praise of love, Socrates understands *eros* in a unique way: the Athenian concept of the erotic has been minimized. It has begun to dawn on the philosopher that the erotic (understood in the context of Athens) does not adequately reflect its intended meaning or allow someone to fulfill their responsibility. In part, Socrates's love will have been perfectly portrayed in the speech by Alcibiades; but in *Alcibiades I*, Socrates will continuously represent his love solely through speech, in what he calls his *ortho logos*, a proper, healing speech, beginning with his evaluation or prognosis of Alcibiades's desire (his greatest ambition) to achieve honor in the city of Athens and consequently to have extensive power—military and political—and therefore to become mired in the vicissitudes of the world. At this point, Socrates does not yet tell Alcibiades that his ambitions are the very causes of his inability to ever achieve wisdom; he only tells him that, "with the help of the god," (105e) which here has involved the complement of Apollo with his *daimonion* in a new idea of piety, Socrates will prove to be essential to his future—one he leaves, for now, ambiguous and undefined.

Alcibiades believes himself to be the individual best suited to represent the city and to be its most important adviser. However, Socrates immediately begins to question Alcibiades's abilities and intentions when he asks him: "But whether the man counseling the Athenians is poor or wealthy will make no difference to them when they deliberate about the health of those in the city, but they will seek an adviser who is a doctor (*iatron*)" (107b–c). Although Socrates again withholds the conclusion to come, he has already told Alcibiades—without, at this juncture, the young man being able to understand—that there is only one adviser of utmost significance, the *iatros* (not to be confused with the *techne* of the physician) who is able to heal the *psyche*.[34] The city, then, is unhealthy, as are its citizens, and it cannot be an individual like Alcibiades who will be able to do them any good. The conclusion to come has already been announced, and the rest of the dialogue will be conducted so as to allow Alcibiades to reach, first of all, an understanding of Socratic therapeutic philosophy and, by so doing, reject his ambitions and instead devote himself to the pursuit of the excellence of the soul rather than the honor, fame, and power available to the honored citizen. Alcibiades has one overriding need: to confront the world, agonistically, so as to overcome external obstacles and therefore sense himself as victorious and superior. Socrates, however, leads him from the affairs

---

34. In *Plato's Symposium*, Stanley Rosen defines this in two ways, as "medicinal rhetoric or psychiatry," xlvii.

of the world toward knowing himself; more comprehensively, to recognize a previously unknown self, one not simply a reflection of the world.

Socrates has long practiced a particular kind of speaking; he may be known as an irritant and insulting, a "gadfly" to some, but he knows that there is another kind of speaking (described often and in numerous dialogues) motivated by an end which is much more important than mere knowledge. In this case, defining it as being able "to converse in a fine way," (*kalos dialegesthai*) (108c) the conversation is not only intended to be rhetorically pleasant, fine, good, and beautiful, but to create in the hearer a certain disposition Socrates will soon equate with the excellence of the *psyche*, that is, its health. He goes on to make additional statements that specifically criticize the knowledge, methods, and ends of "the many," not thereby to dismiss the ideas of the *hoi polloi*—as he had earlier in their ideas of the pious and the holy—but to specifically analyze the most important aspect of human nature. "If we had wanted to know not only what human beings are but which are healthy and sick, would the many be adequate teachers for us" (111e)? In other words, one of the most important aspects of the philosophical life is not simply to define human nature, what human beings *are*. Such a study will always be incomplete unless it also investigates the nature of illness and health, its causes and remedies, and that means pursuing the Delphic adage and the Apollonian demand to "know thyself" (124b). There are several interrelated aspects of his new thinking. Socrates initiates nothing less than a new conception of the self (of human nature) now that it has freed itself from its theological obligations—at least those related to the past. Knowing oneself was previously limited by the knowledge human beings believed they had about the gods. Socrates's conception of human nature, and its possible developments beyond tradition (this is his concept of *transcendence*), could only result as a consequence of the *peri theologia* of the city he had analyzed in the *Symposium*, first of all, and in the *Euthyphro*.[35]

Socrates begins to turn Alcibiades around from a previous conception of himself in relation to the city when he asks him, while keeping in mind the self as either ill or healthy: "In what way might the self itself be discovered? For in this way we might perhaps discover what we are ourselves" (129b). Socrates has, of course, already discovered what is most essential to human beings: "Presumably we could not assert there is anything more dominant in ourselves than the soul (*psyche*)" (130d). Socrates has now

---

35. In "Did Plato Write Alcibiades I?," Nicholas Smith argues that passages from the dialogue "directly conflict with what we find in Plato's canonical dialogues," 108. I do not find his arguments convincing; on the contrary, the dialogue is consistent with the themes most important in the relationship between Socrates and Alcibiades.

begun to define the most important aspect of his philosophy insofar as it involves being in conversation with others. In so doing, the therapeutic philosopher defines, once more, the importance of a particular kind of human language because of its ability to establish a psychical relationship. "And is it not fine to believe thus—that you and I are associating with one another using speeches (*logois chromenous*), one soul toward the other" (130d)? By specifically defining his speech in relation to *chraomai*, Socrates allows Alcibiades to recognize, perhaps for the first time—at least clearly—that he is being treated, one psyche taking care of another psyche in a therapeutic relationship. Their conversation is far from theoretical, and it is not ultimately about Alcibiades's future in terms of acts, that is, participation in Athens' political and military life. Rather, Socrates asks him the most fundamental question of all: What kind of human being do you intend to become? Alcibiades may not consciously recognize his affliction. Socrates, however, has known the symptoms for some time. How does this cure and healing take place? Alcibiades must first relinquish the ambitions of being an adviser to the city—along with the ambitions and supposed honors that come with such a position—and instead turn his attention to the health of his psyche. "It is with the soul, therefore, that we bid to become acquainted by the one who enjoins us to know ourselves" (130e). Socrates's devotion is done out of love, he emphasizes, a love that will be constant—with one possible exception. Socrates has not yet led Alcibiades toward being healed. He has led him to a decision: One cannot pursue the wisdom and excellence of the soul and, at the same time, serve the city in a customary and traditional way. The city and the psyche are incommensurable:

> If you are not corrupted by the populace of Athens and become baser, I will not give you up. For I fear most of all lest, having become a lover of the populace, you be corrupted; for many and good men among the Athenians have already had this experience. (132a)

The city can corrupt a psyche already compromised by its impulses and compulsions. As Socrates leads Alcibiades toward the conclusion of the dialogue, he does not expressly tell him to avoid any dealings with the citizens of Athens, though like Epicurus, being involved in the affairs of state makes it likely one will be forced to be accommodating and compromise philosophical values for political needs and expediency. Socrates simply warns him, prepares him for such an eventuality. "Train (*gumnasai*[36]) first,

---

36. By "training," Socrates stresses how the philosophy to be learned involves a kind of exercise. In *Philosophy as a Way of Life*, Pierre Hadot specifically defines the training of therapeutic philosophy as a "spiritual exercise."

blessed fellow, and learn what needs to be learned in order to approach the things of the city, and do not do it before, so that you have an antidote and suffer nothing terrible" (132b). In this case, Socrates has not yet advised Alcibiades to avoid the enticements of the city. Nearing the end of the dialogue, however, Socrates inevitably leads him to further considerations and, finally, the decisive insight that (so it would seem, though history[37] shows otherwise) led him to devote himself, at least for a time, to the philosophical life. "Therefore, dear Alcibiades, if the soul too is to know itself, should it look at the soul, and above all that place in it in which the virtue (*arete*) of the soul—wisdom—come to exist" (133b)? Alcibiades must answer both the question and find out where there are other places where the excellence of the psyche is more difficult if not impossible to find. By stating that "the soul is more divine than that which is concerned with knowing and thinking," (133c) Socrates has both disassociated the therapeutic philosophy of the psyche from all merely intellectual pursuits and abilities. He has also stated, once more and finally, how the religious observances of the city should no longer be considered pious, holy, and sacred. Only with the proper pursuit of philosophy—taking care of the psyche of others—can the religions based on convention and tradition be relinquished and replaced with a new desire from god as Socrates stated during his trial:

> In looking to the god, therefore, we shall treat him as the finest mirror, and in human things we shall look to the virtue of the soul (*psuches areten*). In this way, above all, we may see and know ourselves. (133c)

By the end of the dialogue, and with Socrates leading him toward a conclusion, he does not dissuade him from an involvement in the city. Before he can make such a decision however, he will first have to pursue (and attain) an excellence of the psyche such that it will allow him to best serve the city and do it not to individually pursue honor and fame, but to fulfill a divine obligation. Whatever benefit Socrates's relationship may have had with the young Alcibiades, his intense ambitions could not be relinquished, and, therefore the philosophical life would ultimately be rejected. François Renaud and Harold Tarrant end their commentary of *Alcibiades I* with a provocative idea: "if we do not see in the Alcibiades what should yet be called a 'philosophy of self' it may be the very point from which some such

---

37. Alcibiades's many exploits are recounted in Thucydides's *The Peloponnesian War*. In Book Six, for example, the historian gives us two aspects of his life which are important for what Socrates has been attempting to teach him: his love of wealth (and his desires made him spend well beyond his means) and his need to have a reputation.

philosophy really did begin to grow and flourish."[38] In *Alcibiades II*, the recognition of a "philosophy of self," and certainly the therapeutic philosophy so far presented in the teaching of Socrates, became conscious only when the relationship to the gods was reexamined and the practice of animal sacrifice was rejected, if not yet abolished.

Although *Alcibiades II* (sometimes called *Alcibiades Minor*[39]) is considered spurious by the majority of commentators, it nevertheless has unique characteristics that make it especially suited to be a complement to the discussion of piety in the *Euthyphro*. In the dialogue that takes place in front of the office of the King Archon, the civic official with many responsibilities, including the festivals and processions in relation to public sacrifice, Socrates discusses the nature of piety, and in particular the *therapeia* provided to the gods. In *Alcibiades II*, Socrates will once again reexamine the nature of religious belief and observances, concentrating on the specific relationship between human beings and god(s) in the form of prayer. And if *Alcibiades I* establishes the first principle of philosophy, the foundations of knowing oneself (and to inquire into the possibilities of human nature) can only be made possible by the double critique of religion established in the *Euthyphro*—a rejection of sacrifice as a form of piety, and its necessary corollary, the substitution of prayer to the gods for the therapeutic speech between two individuals that will be made explicit in *Alcibiades II*.

Encountering Alcibiades and stopping him before he could reach a temple to pray, Socrates begins the dialogue by analyzing the nature of prayer and the expectations associated with it. He first asks Alcibiades if we are right in assuming that "whenever we pray in private or in public, the gods sometimes give us some things, but not others, and that they give to some of us, but not to others" (138b)?[40] The question at first seems straightforward; but Socrates, as usual, has already begun with his conclusion, one that will fundamentally rethink the nature of prayer and its purpose of receiving what has been requested from the gods. He does not, as in Genesis or Homer, simply present the gods as arbitrary, giving and withholding, choosing some to favor, others to ignore; the nature of the gods is significant only as an indication of human belief—which has always been, for him, the nature of what he called in the *Republic*, *peri theologia*. Socrates begins

38. Renaud and Tarrant, *Platonic Alcibiades I*, 272. See especially, 269–72, "Coda: Towards a Philosophy of Self."

39. The ancient title of the dialogue was known as *On Prayer*.

40. That Socrates is here specifically discussing the nature of prayer cannot be disassociated from its relation to sacrifice. In *Greek Religion, Walter* Burkert writes: "there is rarely a ritual without prayer, and no important prayer without ritual: *litai—thysai*, prayer-sacrifice is an ancient and fixed conjunction," 73.

a dialogue with more complicated and, according to the polis religion of Athens, more impious reasons. In subjecting human prayer and its purpose to a reevaluation, he also believes caution is an imperative, for in asking the gods, one also reveals one's desires, and these, Socrates says (anticipating Epicurus) may, "*without being aware of it,*" (138b, my emphasis) actually be detrimental if fulfilled. He will ultimately reach the conclusion that it is best not to pray at all, and for two specific reasons. First, human desire remains enigmatic, often unknown, and its origin is often too remote to fathom, and second, if a prayer has been answered, it may in fact lead to unwanted (indeed, tragic) consequences. For the time being, however, and in response to Oedipus's prayer that led to the death of both his sons, the dialogue turns to a psychological description of the difference between someone who is a "madman" (*mainomai*) or "sensible" (*phronein*). The added difference, is that someone who is either healthy or unhealthy (*astheneō*) once again establishes how many people of the city are psychologically unhealthy. The latter concept, *aestheneō*, will be understood by both Epicurus and Jesus as specifically related to human emotions that have become hardened and therefore have made it so people are unable to feel empathy and compassion. The appearance of Oedipus here testifies to the author's (whoever he or she may be) considerable ability to anticipate the reader's hermeneutics: prayer and tragedy may be much more related than previously assumed.

In a recurring diagnosis—one which is evident, for example, in the inhabitants of the cave—Socrates does more than divide the foolish from the sensible. He tells Alcibiades that many are psychologically unhealthy. "Don't you think that few in the city are sensible, but many indeed are foolish, the ones you call mad" (138c)? If many of the citizens of Athens are unhealthy, then living among them should make one feel uncomfortable, ill at ease, in part because they are praying for favors they cannot recognize to be misguided desires, such as Alcibiades's ambition to be a ruler of Athens. For the time being, he reaches one conclusion: "So you see that it is unsafe either to simply accept whatever is given or to pray oneself that it happen" (141d). In both cases—that the gods grant on their own initiative, or in response to a prayer—it is "unsafe," dangerous, a peril that Socrates tells Alcibiades has been suffered by many generals, for example, or men and women who prayed to have children; children sometimes turn out badly, through no fault of the parents. "I can find no way to deny that it is truly vain for men to blame the gods by claiming that bad things come to them from the gods" (142a). Socrates is not, here, defending the gods from the blame imposed on them; he begins to make the argument, from a philosophical position, that to pray to the gods for anything—whatever the outcome—runs counter to being self-sufficient. Prayers, then, should not be made at all precisely because one is neither completely conscious of the nature of desire nor if the prayer should in fact be answered. Furthermore, rather than understanding the human predicament between freedom and *tuche* or "chance" (as Epicurus will stress) the superstitious attribute the events of the world, both natural and human, to divine intervention. The belief in prayer serves only to perpetuate a world where the gods are the ultimate arbiters of both nature and human life and, therefore, make independence and self-sufficiency, as philosophical ideas, impossible.

So far, Socrates's examples on the foolish and the sensible, the healthy and the unhealthy, have not yet turned to the beginning of the dialogue, when Alcibiades was on his way to pray to god, and a complete reflection on prayer and, by extension, all other acts done in relationship to the gods. Since he points out that "the many are mistaken about what is best," (146c) the conclusion to come must analyze how the many, the majority of the citizens who are influential, are in fact wrong in what they do. The analogy is, again, clear: "So if either a city or a soul is going to live correctly it must get hold of this knowledge, just as one who is sick must get hold of a doctor" (146e–147a). Since, however, the citizens of the polis are unhealthy, Socrates must now define precisely why they are in this condition and offer a cure. Before providing a *remedy*, he begins to talk about the Lacedaemonians. He will use them as an example of a people who apparently have been blessed by the gods with good fortune. He adds: "If, after all, they too have not been fortunate in all things, this is not because of their prayer, but it is up to the gods, I think, either to give whatever someone prays for or the opposite of that" (148c–d). Here, moving toward his conclusion, he again reiterates a first point on the nature of prayer. The events that are consequential to a prayer are (he seems, but only *seems* to say) entirely decided by the gods.

Socrates proceeds to tell Alcibiades a story he heard from "some old men" (148d). The Athenians and the Lacedaemonians have often fought battles and, for a reason they believe can be explained, the Athenians frequently lose, whether the battle is on the sea or on land. The Athenians therefore decide to ask Ammon (the Egyptian deity identified with Zeus in the Greek pantheon) why the gods gave victory to the other side. The Athenians are perplexed since they "give more numerous and more admirable sacrifices than the rest of the Greeks," (148e) and therefore expect to be duly rewarded and compensated for their obviously generous devotion. The Lacedaemonians, on the other hand, "have never been concerned with any of this," (149a) either proper sacrifices, the adornment of temples and sanctuaries, or the most elaborate processions. The Athenians, at a loss to explain the reason that the gods do not return their show of piety, receive a surprising answer. "Ammon says this. He declares that he would prefer the reverent Laconic speech (*euphemian*) to all the sacrifices of the Greeks put together" (149b). An astounding declaration and one consistent with Socrates's testimony in the law court when deliberating his innocence or guilt. The reference to *euphemia* or "holy silence"[41] should now be related to Oedipus who made his prayer in a sacred grove where such an observance was required. God prefers a reverent speech instead of sacrifices. What is the nature of this reverent speech? Is it simply reverential *prayer* and the opposite of *blasphemia*, therefore returning us to the beginning of the dialogue and its most important subject? Socrates has no doubts about the role of sacrifice in the human/gods relationship. "So it did them no good to sacrifice and give gifts in vain, hated as they were by the gods. For the gods, I think, are not of the sort to be turned by gifts, like some bad moneylender" (149d–e). This is once again an astounding declaration and one that must be compared to the questions Socrates initially posed in the *Euthyphro*. In the dialogue with his friend, Socrates had only asked (though, of course, with a precise answer in the question) what possible benefit the gods could receive from human beings as they sacrificed. Moreover, how could they possibly need anything at all? Socrates now begins his conclusion, one that specifically puts in opposition the act of sacrifice rather than the examination of the psyche through a specific conversation and dialogue. Sacrifice and prayer are now to be rejected as the acts and words most appropriate to piety, and are ultimately to be abandoned for another form of piety—the very one he had talked about during his trial. "For it would be an awful thing if the gods looked to our gifts and sacrifices and not to our souls, to see whether we are pious and just" (150a). Rather than the so-called *aporia* presumed to end the *Euthyphro*, here Socrates complements his earlier discussion of piety and contrasts the piety of the soul rather than the act of sacrifice or the *logoi* or prayer:

> They look to this, I think, far more than to these expensive processions and sacrifices; nothing stops either an individual or a city that has done many wrongs to the gods, and many to men, from performing these every year. But the gods, as they do not take bribes, despise all these things. (150a)

Once more Socrates uses a specifically economic, financial, and monetary description to underscore precisely how, in the past and up until now, sacrifices have been viewed: as a form of exchange. So, sacrifices have been completely rejected and are now to be replaced by a particular kind of speech, a speech, moreover, that cannot be the same as prayer, at least

---

41. Travis, *Allegory and the Tragic Chorus*, 202.

the kind of prayer that asks for the gods to intervene and ensure that some specific desire will be fulfilled. Socrates therefore dissuades Alcibiades from praying at all, seeing as he now does not know (nor did he ever know) what he wants. Socrates ends the dialogue by telling Alcibiades that now is the right time to "learn" the *new* relationship "toward gods and toward men" (150d). Socrates now believes it is essential to rethink the nature of human beings no less than our conception of the gods. "So when will this time be at hand," Alcibiades asks Socrates, "and who is going to educate me" (150d)? Socrates answers and tells him that the individual who will educate him is the one most concerned about him, the one who most cares for the state of his *psyche*. Alcibiades, at the end of the dialogue, commits himself fully to being treated by Socrates. What he will learn, however, will not lead him to come to know the best way to pray to the gods, nor will he simply "put off the sacrifice" (151a) until the proper time. Both sacrifices and prayers will be rejected. Alcibiades will learn that the most pious life possible will involve one's dedication to others and to their healing—the very definition and purpose of philosophy. At the end of *Alcibiades II*, many more such conversations between them will be anticipated, all of them leading to the one decisive evening when, finally, Alcibiades will both reveal the extent and meaning of Socratic love and be able to articulate (but not overcome) the difference between the life dedicated to philosophy and one dedicated to attaining honor from the city.

4. *Socrates's Therapeutic Philosophy*

Turning once again to Socrates at the symposium, the drunken Alcibiades tells him: "It is no easy task for one in my condition to give a smooth and orderly account of your bizarreness (*atopian*)," (215a) that is, his uniqueness and ability to lead others to themselves. If the idea of *atopos* is understood as Socrates intends it, and as Alcibiades will explain, it should in principle lead the reader to realize that Socrates's fundamental philosophical intention is to heal self-division and an individual's dependence. For one to become "extraordinary"[42] (to have a unique nature, an additional meaning of *atopos*) it is necessary to reject the love of the city and the gods. Socrates's most fundamental teaching—the one which leads to his arrest, trial, and execution—is nothing but the absolute rejection of the love of the city of Athens and the gods precisely to become an individual. The category of "citizen" has become suspect and much too limited.

---

42. Plato, *Phaedrus*, 230c.

Alcibiades begins his description and "praise" (*epainen*) of Socrates by using an image, an *eikon*, or rather two related images: a statue of a Silenus (like the ones sold in many shops in Athens which contain tiny statues of gods) and of a satyr named Marsyas, skinned alive for challenging Apollo to a musical competition. Now that Alcibiades has described Socrates as an individual *eikon*, the previous description of the *eidolon* is be explicitly contrasted. Unlike the *eidolon*, (a mere image, to be seen) Socrates as an *eikon* presents himself to be a reflection, that is, an example leading to a specific kind of *arete*. The image of a Silenus, so similar (it seems) to Socrates's face, can mislead and deceive. Alcibiades begins to speak in a way Plato would not dare; he cannot bring himself to do it, not overtly, directly, so he finds a substitute. Alcibiades becomes Plato's proxy—giving himself the opportunity to represent Socrates differently than someone who reported on a speech by Diotima. He uses Alcibiades to reveal one of Socrates's most essential teachings on the "art of love," that is, *philosophia* as the wisdom of love descending back to earthly love and its significance. He descends the ladder of love. Once the Silenus/Marsyas duo is revealed, that is, that they have a concealed inner meaning hidden by their appearance, it becomes possible to begin defining precisely how Socrates should be seen, an *eikon*. "But the resemblance goes beyond appearance," (215b) Alcibiades makes sure to add, therefore telling everyone present that they too must recognize their own condition, that they too have characteristics inside themselves which they do not see and cannot recognize precisely because appearances are so enticing. Socrates's words have "the power to possess," (215c) to demand so much attention, that one is simultaneously held and brought elsewhere, to a completely different state of mind. Alcibiades continues and tells Socrates that, unlike Marsyas and the music of his flute, the music Socrates plays is linguistic; his words give everyone the sensation of being "transported, completely possessed" (215d). Alcibiades's repetitions are intended to emphasize Socrates's ability to make everyone so self-aware that they are no longer able to maintain either their self-deception or their dependence on the illusions perpetuated by the city. Alcibiades accuses everyone at the symposium of being idolatrous, praising the image of Eros and the emotion of love only as a reflection of their own narcissism. As an *eikon*, Socrates leads others to a particular kind of awareness, perception, and consciousness, not one remotely interested in the *monoeides* but in overcoming the limits imposed on oneself, the city, and the gods. Unfortunately, for the listeners, they cannot properly understand the implications of his words; they hear them superficially. Alcibiades attempts to inform others of Socrates's language and his ability to make others self-possessed, independent and self-sufficient. Socrates condemns idolatrous pedagogy. There is an education more important than *paideia*.

Finally, returning once more to the *Symposium*, Alcibiades[43] speaks of the "extraordinary effect his words have always had on me," (215d) when mentioning Socrates. What is the nature of this effect in addition to being possessed? There are several. First, as soon as Socrates begins to speak, Alcibiades admits that "I am beside myself," (215e) in such a state of emotional instability, similar to anxiety—he even mentions crying and a rapid heartbeat—that his previous sense of self becomes threatened. Socrates's words unsettle him. As Alcibiades continues with his own speech, he attempts to convey how Socrates's words force one into a self-examination which can only reveal how his self (indeed, what he calls his whole *life*) is founded on self-deception. Such are the effects of Socrates's words that, Alcibiades says, "my very own soul (*psyche*) started protesting that my life—my life—was not better than the most miserable slave's" (215e). Alcibiades is enslaved—to himself and the ambitions he believes, deceptively, to be capable of freeing him; his attempt to make himself achieve notoriety is a result of being profoundly unsure about his own self, what he is made of, what his character is like. "He makes me admit that my political career is a waste of time, while all that matters is just what I most neglect: my personal shortcomings, which cry out for the closest attention" (216a). Socrates teaches him that seeking self-gratification from the citizens of the city (those who most base themselves on their social position) are fated to be forever vulnerable to the opinions and whims of the many. One's character is thereby determined by the accolades from the external world, while Socrates insists that the most important pursuit of a human being is self-recognition—the analysis conducted by the self, first in dialogue and then in introspection. "He makes me feel ashamed," (216b) Alcibiades tells everyone. The crucial experience for Alcibiades, and the one causing him the most intense psychical pain, is shame, and it is crucial to realize that this shame is not related to the opinions of others, or the social judgments made by those in the city. It is a wholly internal shame, an overwhelming feeling that one's self is essentially compromised by its own delusions and by its need for the acknowledgment of others. As soon as Alcibiades forgets Socrates's crucial lesson (to feel shame as the beginning of changing his life, and to create a character independent of the city of Athens) it is then that "I cave in to my desire to please the crowd" (216b). Here Alcibiades tells his listeners how the values

---

43. Alcibiades's testimony here should be compared to the beginning of another dialogue when Socrates tells a friend that Alcibiades is well disposed toward him, "particularly today, since he came to my assistance and spoke up for me at some length." Plato, *Prot.*, 309b.

of the city of Athens (to be respected and adored by the many) are in fact the opposite of authentic self-recognition; rather than crave adulation, Socrates teaches introspection, the need to reevaluate oneself. For the second time, Alcibiades mentions the effect Socrates has on him. Unlike the young Phaedrus, who argued for a social relevance of shame (and who merely understood it in contrast to honor), Alcibiades begins to explain the psychical significance of shame, the motive for someone transforming themselves. "When I see him, I feel deeply ashamed, because I'm doing nothing about my way of life" (216b). Socrates always reminds Alcibiades that his desire to please the crowd shows him to be empty, shallow, seeking approval from the citizens of Athens in order to fulfill himself in and through reputation. Alcibiades continues with his revelation of Socrates by telling his listeners that "none of you really understands him. But, now I've started, I'm going to show you what he really is" (216d). Speaking about Socrates and telling others what he really is can only be the beginning of his own self-disclosure. Alcibiades begins to provide an analysis of his own character at the same time as he describes Socrates. Like Apollodorus, he has understood himself only by listening and paying attention to Socrates. Previously, he has prepared his listeners with an *eikon* of Socrates, of a Silenus and Marsyas, two beings intended as examples to be emulated, one showing his multifaceted and complicated interiority, the other willing to confront the ability of a god in order to assert his own independence. Now Alcibiades deepens his analysis of the Socratic teaching (his acts, his words) and makes one of his most important declarations: the relationship between shame and *sophrosune*.

Once again Alcibiades returns to his description, that is, Socrates and his similarity to Silenus—at least "on the surface." (216d) He has a psychological depth no one has fully recognized; and when he tells his listeners that Socrates is "crazy about beautiful boys," (216d) which is only the first statement in need of being revised (to see through the appearance) Alcibiades begins to reveal the intent of the philosopher. Socrates has no interest in the beauty of young boys; he does, however, want to corrupt young boys, teach them other values than the ones defended and extolled with such enthusiasm at the symposium and in the city of Athens. Such a teaching could only be understood as both defying the parental authority of the father and, more seriously, the very laws of the city. In his conversation with Crito, for example, and representing the Laws in his speech, Socrates shows the relationship between the laws and corrupting the young. "For any destroyer of laws might very well be supposed to have a destructive influence upon young and fooling human beings."[44]

44. Plato, *Cr.*, 53bc.

Alcibiades tells everyone how Socrates, showing himself in public to be infatuated with beautiful boys, is actually uninterested in their beauty, just as he is uninterested in wealth, fame, status—all of which are part of the ethos so essential to Athenian society. There are characteristics of Socrates that have never before been recognized precisely because he has been superficially interpreted by his contemporaries When Alcibiades calls him a "temperate" (*sophrosunes*) man, the description has to be understood in a particular way; the characteristic has nothing to do with his apparent self-discipline. Rather, if *sophrusune* is understood as related to *so* (to "heal") and coupled with *phren*, heart,[45] then Socrates's ultimate meaning as a philosopher is to heal the heart, that is, attend to the psychological states of others and to heal them from the afflictions they suffer from due to their character and the ones imposed on them by the city. His healing, however, has nothing to do with the *techne* of the physician; his advice for moderation—unlike Eryximachus—leads others (with both his allegorical acts and philosophical words) to heal themselves from being enslaved to their own desires, their distorted desires and passions, and to the ideals of the city.

If Socrates had merely been infatuated with the beauty of young boys, pursuing them for aesthetic reasons—or, for that matter, for sexual gratification—he never would have been charged with corrupting the young. If pederasty was the norm and socially encouraged, at least within a particular segment of society, it was by no means universally approved. Wives, we assume, had doubts about their husbands' infatuations. The corruption, in Socrates's case, refers to his attempt to sway the youth of Athens that the ideals of the city are vacuous and maintained by a small group of wealthy and influential citizens—precisely those who will accuse him. Alcibiades, in this case, is telling everyone about Socrates's true intent, and his method: "His whole life is one big game—a game of irony" (216e). Far from being interested in the beauty of young boys, he is attracted precisely to their flaws, the ones they have inherited from their educators. This is the reason Alcibiades mentions the psychology of shame so often. Unlike Phaedrus, the young lover whose speech on social shame was intended to impress his older teacher/lover Eryximachus (his speech is, in fact, a praise of the physician and self-interested flattery), Alcibiades knows the teaching of Socrates must necessarily lead him back to himself—a self which withdraws from the adulation of the many to reflect on the nature of the self. Alcibiades's drunken speech becomes an indictment of everyone present. One can only transform the city of Athens by disinheriting young boys from their so-called educators, the ones who tell them achieving maturity can only

---

45. This is Jamey Hecht's translation in *Plato's Symposium*.

be accomplished by perpetuating custom and tradition. Ultimately, when Socrates is charged with this capital offense, he represents the philosopher as the individual whose ultimate purpose in life is the transformation of the social/political world (that is, history) while simultaneously putting into doubt the relevance of the specific teachings and rituals concerning the gods.

Alcibiades begins the culmination of speech by talking about his former self, the one which assumed there was a correlation between intimacy and pedagogy: "All I had to do was to let him have his way with me, and he would teach me everything he knew" (217a). Alcibiades returns to his past in introspection and in and through the memory of his experience attempts to inform others of his own transformation; he soon leads everyone away from an idolatry of Eros precisely through the experience of Socrates rejecting him. He recollects his attempt to seduce Socrates—alone, at the gymnasium, at his house for dinner—all leading to his perceived failure. When he then continues with his praise of Socrates and "one of his proudest accomplishments," (217e) we soon learn of the most effective of Socrates's psychotherapeutic methods, the one he uses simply by being himself.

Alcibiades finally has Socrates lying next to him; he expects a scene of seduction, sexual pleasure, the gratification which is, in essence, an acknowledgment of his self—body, heart, soul. But unexpectedly, for Alcibiades, Socrates acts with indifference, an attitude much worse than a simple rejection. The culmination of the speeches has been announced. Only by spurning Alcibiades does Socrates teach him about his lack and need, a psychological insight developed from *Lysis*. When Socrates says "that thing which desires desires what it is in need of,"[46] he does not mean the origin of the desire can be fulfilled objectively outside the self, by a human being or a thing. On the contrary, to understand the nature of desire requires Alcibiades—in recognizing his shame as a consequence of being spurned—to return to himself, to analyze how his dependence on both the many and the one (Socrates) has made him destitute.

When Socrates spurned him, rejected him as a lover (with a psychological motive only he truly understands), Alcibiades again emphasizes his feeling of shame. By acting indifferently to Alcibiades's sexual advances, Socrates believes his shame, for being rejected, will force him to recognize the reason for his desire, that is, his incompleteness. "I was deeply humiliated," (219d) he says, a shame that should, in principle, begin his own process of self-transformation. When Alcibiades adds, once again emphasizing Socratic *sophrosune*," but I couldn't help admiring his natural character, his

---

46. Plato, *Lysis*, 221d.

moderation (*sophrosunen*)," (219d) Alcibiades realizes his rejection of him should lead him to an understanding of himself. By being acknowledged as a lover (to be requited and wanted) Alcibiades could continue to feel important. Being rejected by Socrates initiates the self-reflection which will lead him to realize how the values of Athens are themselves to be rejected. Socrates spurns Alcibiades, leading him to realize the philosopher is also, more importantly, putting into doubt all the ideals most held by Athenian society. It is important to stress the relation between shame and *sophrosune*. Since shame is usually experienced as painful, something to be avoided, Alcibiades makes his most important statement: shame becomes the condition for his own transformation, that is, his healing. Socratic *ta erotika* can now be defined. It cannot be fulfilled in the erotic relationship of the older pedagogue with a young boy, nor, equally importantly, does it serve the gods. Rather, Socrates the philosopher teaches him to become independent of others, the city and the gods, and by so doing, transform philosophy into a healing of the *psyche*.

In a reading provided by Michel Foucault in the introduction to his *The Use of Pleasure*, he attempts to define a characteristic of Socrates and, in so doing, fails to see the psychotherapeutic/philosophical reasons for his act. When he writes that Socrates was "the one whose wisdom everybody sought to appropriate—a wisdom that manifested and proved itself precisely in the fact that he was himself able to keep from laying hands on the provocative beauty of Alcibiades,"[47] he has misinterpreted the meaning of Socrates's intentions and his philosophical wisdom. The wisdom of Socrates is not, as Foucault seems to assume, that he restrained his sexual interest in the younger, beautiful man—this, parenthetically, in a sub-heading called "a model of abstention"—but that the sole purpose for being unresponsive to the other man's advances is to teach him, precisely, the origin of his desire. Alcibiades feels ashamed and humiliated precisely because he realizes he is a slave to himself. "No one else has ever known the real meaning of slavery," (219e) an enslavement both to his individual incompleteness and, consequently, his needs and his reliance on others and the city of Athens to feel self-worth. He feels humiliated precisely because he realizes, effectively, his need for others in order to feel significant. Seth Benardete believes Alcibiades hears a moral call in Socrates's words: "Socrates for him is fundamentally a preacher, whose exhortations to repentance cannot but give Alcibiades pleasure as he wallows in self-contempt."[48] In this case (as was evident with the Greeks—as it will be with early Christianity), the very

---

47. Foucault, *Use of Pleasure*, 20.
48. Benardete, *Plato's Symposium*, 93.

idea of repentance was not simply moral but psychotherapeutic, involving the process of *metanoia*. For example, in *The Education of Cyrus*, Xenophon writes: "but when we reflected. . . we were thus compelled to change our minds (*metanoein*)."[49] In *Allegorical Interpretation*, Philo adds: "He repents (*metanoei*) and recovers as from an illness."[50] Socrates is not a moral philosopher—much less a metaphysician; he realizes the unhealthy individuals and citizens of Athens must first be cured of their ailments as the condition necessary before transforming the city. Alcibiades, for all his intelligence and cunning, cannot ultimately realize (in more than mere cognitive apprehension) the purpose for Socrates refusing his advances; the ensuing shame, which he feels from being spurned, was intended to reach what would later be called *metanoia*, the "change of mind," allowing first for a moment of prolonged self-awareness, and second, the beginning of a transformation of the self—which of course he never achieves despite the Socratic lesson. Socrates's apparent sexual restraint has nothing to do with abstinence; by rejecting Alcibiades, he hopes to teach him how to begin analyzing the nature of his desire as a need. The lack experienced by Alcibiades cannot be filled up, as compensation, by someone external to him—whether it is erotic, aesthetic, or political. Alcibiades needs to be idolized; but Socrates teaches him (a lesson, though it goes unheeded) to first and foremost become himself, a lesson he simultaneously realizes and denies. Alcibiades decides to deny his psychical destitution by establishing himself as a commander—of others, involved in an external *agon* of opposition and vanquishing in order never to admit to being dependent.

Alcibiades concludes the speech, described in the "Final Dialogue" as *parresia*, by emphasizing Socrates's uniqueness. "He is unique; he is like no one else in the past and no one in the present—this is by far the most amazing thing about him." (221c) Socrates, then, is incomparable because he is unlike anyone else; he can only be compared to *eikons* who themselves reveal more than they seem: Silenus and Marsyas. As the individual who believes *philosophia* to be the wisdom of love and that teaching others their desire for fulfillment must first begin in oneself, Socrates becomes unique; by representing himself as someone who raises doubts about the values of the city as they are internalized by youth, he desires to overturn prevailing wisdom in order to introduce a level of transformation that was previously thought to be impossible. Although Alcibiades never once mentions Athenian religion and the need to worship (and sacrifice) for the gods, he explicitly rejects both the idea of a divine healer—Zeus Soter—and the conclusion by several

---

49. Xenophon, *Cyr.*, 1.3.
50. Philo, *Alleg.*, 2.60.

speakers, including the very first: Phaedrus. According to him, the god Eros is "the most powerful in helping men gain virtue and blessedness" (*aretes kai eudaimonias*)" (180b). Self-division and incompleteness cannot be sutured by a benevolent god or by the adulation of others; rather, Socrates rejects both the gods and the values of the city by insisting on the unique need to pursue wisdom. "This man here is so bizarre, his ways and ideas are so unusual, that, search as you might, you'll never find anyone else in the world, alive or dead, who's even remotely like him" (221d). The culmination of the speeches turns away from the singularity of the *monoeides* and instead concludes with the unique Socrates, the philosopher who teaches others to find themselves. Unlike the conclusion of *Laws*, when the Athenian and Clinias agree that it is the art of politics that best serves to treat "the natures and conditions of men's souls," (650b1) at the end of *Symposium* it is Socrates who has the last word: only the psychotherapeutic abilities of philosophical *ta erotika* can treat the *psyches* of human beings, the necessary prerequisite condition then of establishing a city as he envisions it. Neither the gods nor the politics of the city can attend to the health of human beings; such an attempt can only be made by the philosopher who has dedicated his life to the health of the *psyche* of others, as he argues in his dialogue named after perhaps his most important student. The end of the *Symposium* has been reached, but the importance (the centrality) of Alcibiades as a student of Socrates has only begun. The dialogues named after this historical character will contribute to the relationship—a crucial detail for Socrates—between the end of sacrifice as a previous form of piety and worship and the dedication of the therapeutic philosopher to the health of the *psyche* of others. Or as Epicurus opens his "Letter to Menoeceus: "Let no one delay the study of philosophy while young nor weary of it when old. For no one is either too young or too old for the health of the soul (*psyche*)."[51] By the time Epicurus began living and teaching in his school in Athens, the attitude toward the public life—political and civic—would become firm, his doctrines more and more pronounced and with one overall intent. Epicurus's dictum of *lathe biosas* (to live unknown) would be decisive in his philosophy to avoid any involvement in the city; and it would begin, as it had for Socrates on the eve of his trial, with a thorough examination of the gods of the city and the rituals associated with their pious and sacred worship.

---

51. Epicurus, *Ep. Men.*, 10.122.

Chapter 3

Physiologia and the Psychodynamics of Epicurean Theology

1. Did Epicurus Condone Animal Sacrifice?

IN THE DECADES FOLLOWING the death of Socrates and the historical period E. R. Dodds has called "an age of persecution,"[1] other philosophers came to prominence who continued the tradition of reevaluating the beliefs and practices of the city-state of Athens, thereby fulfilling their responsibility as philosophers—to be independent, critical thinkers who could face the hostility of fellow citizens and the judicial threat of prosecution, exile, or execution.[2] Among the more intriguing philosophers, and one who exerted considerable influence on Lucretius, the Epicurean poet and author of *On*

---

[1]. Dodds, *Greeks and the Irrational*, 189.

[2]. Among the philosophers who were sentenced to death for impiety in the decades leading up to the end of the fifth century, there are the cases of Diagoras of Melos and, perhaps, according to Richard Janko in "Reconstructing (Again) the Opening of the Derveni Papyrus, " the unknown author of the papyrus that was found in the remains of a funeral pyre at Derveni, Greece, in 1962. In his review of Betegh's *The Derveni Papyrus*, he believes that the treatise was written by a follower of Anaxagoras. In the "Reconstructing" article therefore, Janko establishes the connection between Anaxagoras and Socrates due to the fact that Anaxagoras's student Archelaus of Athens was Socrates's teacher. In Philodemus's *On Piety*, he mentions Socrates's execution and other philosophers, though unnamed, who were prosecuted, exiled, and killed for their beliefs and teachings.

Physiologia and the Psychodynamics of Epicurean Theology   97

the Nature of Things, was Theophrastus of Eresus,[3] author of *On Nature* and the philosopher who inherited the leadership of Aristotle's school in Athens, was widely recognized to be critical of any kind of animal slaughter, and extremely so in the context of Athenian festivals of supposed piety and holiness. According to Demetrius of Magnesia, when Epicurus arrived in Athens from the island of Samos to complete his two years of mandatory military service (an obligation of all citizens and also imposed on residents of colonies), he attended one, possibly more lectures in the Lyceum by Theophrastus, at the time in charge of the Peripatetic school due Aristotle's exile in Calchis.[4] There were, then, prominent individual philosophers like Theophrastus whose studies were encyclopedic—ranging from botany to stones in addition to the standard subjects of philosophy—and who were simultaneously concerned with the relationship between civic life and the understanding of the natural world, in part because, following a tradition extending to the pre-Socratics, providing a rational account of nature could dispel the all-powerful and enduring myths concerning the gods. Although there were subsequent philosophers after the death of Socrates who related themselves to the unique features of ancient learning as continued by the two thinkers who founded influential schools (Plato and Aristotle, as well as their most important pupils who inherited leadership roles), the philosophy of Epicurus pursued what Socrates had for some reason purposefully avoided: making the study of nature, or his *physiologia*, essential to his philosophy overall. The sect was of concern to the authorities from its very beginnings.[5] Later Epicureans would face even more civic hostility and danger.

3. Theophrastus was notable in his day for advocating a vegetarian diet as well as rejecting the religious ritual of animal sacrifice, as attested by Porphyry in his *On the Abstinence from Killing Animals*, 2.5 There is, however, a dissenting view. See Dirk Obbink's "The Origin of Greek Sacrifice." Obbink, as we shall see, has similar observations in relation to Epicurus, in part due to accepting Philodemus of Gadara's writings, especially his own *On Piety*. For an opposing view in relation to Theophrastus, see Nilsson, *History of Greek Religion*.

4. Laertius, *Lives*, 10.13.

5. In "Epicurean Contubernium," Norman DeWitt writes that a charge of impiety led to "the forced migration of the young sect to Lampsacus, presumably under pressure exerted by the Greek *censor morum*, the gymnasiarch," 55. Could the reasons for such persecution be identified? Himerius (c. 315–386) has a declamation on Epicurus being accused of a specific form of impiety. "You have done away with sacrifice as a whole," as cited in Robert Penella's *Man and World*, 173. This noticeable testimony, more than six centuries after Epicurus's death, reveals to what extent the Hellenistic philosopher continued to be a subject of interest and, in this case, specifically regarding sacrifice. Himerius will here be recalled so as to provide a first evidence for a long tradition of Epicurus and his relation to sacrifice. Epicurus was central to an argument of long standing, one apparently never sufficiently settled.

According to A. E. Taylor, "There appears to have been actual persecutions, and perhaps even martyrdoms, of Epicureans in various Greek cities."[6] If the reference to martyrdoms is overstated, there are reports that Epicurus was certainly accused, if not judicially charged, with impiety.

In the extant writings of Epicurus, we find for the first time a related concern. On the one hand, the study of natural phenomena in conjunction with a thorough (and critical) reevaluation of the current conception of the gods, and on the other, the one overriding concern of his thinking, school, and life: philosophy dedicated comprehensively to the health of the *psyche*, and therefore to exposing the reasons—internal and external—for the particularity of psychological illnesses within the polis, including the effects of religious beliefs and observances. However, in order for human beings to achieve both the self-sufficiency so necessary for human freedom from no less than the psychological equanimity defining what Epicurus deemed most essential for human life, it was first necessary to *simultaneously* study natural phenomena as well as rethinking the common view on the lives, characters, and the supposed influence of the gods. Mythopoetic thinking continued to dominate and limit human life. *Physiologia* and theology were necessarily interrelated, and his views are both unwavering and systematic, proceeding from the evident matter of the world to the need to rethink the current or popular conceptions of the gods as well as the irrelevance of death, especially given its association with a belief in the afterlife and how gods determined the human place either in Hades or on the Islands of the Blessed. For if death was final, with no possible extension or continuity, finitude becomes the very reason for one's absolute dedication to the best possible human life for oneself and for others. For all intents and purposes, life after death ceased to exist. Leo Strauss makes a noticeable if hyperbolic statement about Epicurus: "The history of criticism of religion has every reason to devote particular attention to the *only thinker* who saw in criticism of religion his highest task, the fulfillment of his intent."[7] As a critic of religion, traditionally understood and related to the polis's foundation and continuity, Epicurus's philosophy would find many opponents—none more significant than Cicero, the Roman orator and statesman who (thankfully,

---

6. Taylor, *Epicurus*, 31.

7. Strauss, *Spinoza's Critique of Religion*, 42, my emphasis. Strauss overstates the case in two ways: Epicurus was not the only thinker to criticize religion and such a critique was not "his highest task" though, to be sure, it was essential. Strauss adds: "it is the case that in Epicureanism a universal human motive for rebellion against religion finds its expression," 42. The "rebellion" (that is, the systematic critique of religion) has but one overriding purpose: to regain for individuals and the city what they had previously abnegated.

despite his general critical relationship to the philosopher) has left us with a considerable exposition and polemic.[8]

With Epicurus, the study of nature and a reevaluation of Greek religion lead to the philosophical life and its essential concern with the psychological health of others, the *soteria* or healing emphasized by his philosophy. Taking care of the psyche becomes the essential philosophical responsibility and the authentic expression of *sophia*. Although Socrates's views on sacrifice as well as psychological healing are related (as we saw, in many dialogues ranging from the *Euthyphro* to *Alcibiades II*), the case of Epicurus seems much more difficult and ambiguous to precisely define if only the extant writings are consulted, whether it be his three letters, *Principal Doctrines*, or the associated *Vatican Sayings*. The doxography (by Cicero and Plutarch, for example, his two most vocal critics) does little to clarify the situation; on the contrary, a consensus view seems next to impossible, a peculiar situation and one completely polarized by both classical commentary and modern scholarship. Unfortunately, there are no explicit references to sacrifice in any of the remaining works by Epicurus himself, though, as follows from his critique of traditional theology, it is implicit if in need of being more fully revealed by interpretation and argument.[9] Epicurus's theology is without ambivalence or confusion; it is direct and consequential. There is simply no way to consider sacrifice as an acceptable observance if the consequences of his beliefs are analyzed. And yet, Epicurus remains the most misunderstood thinker of antiquity, his character maligned, his ideas distorted and falsified. When other Epicureans are consulted (the two most prominent will be the Roman poet Lucretius and the teacher at Herculaneum, Philodemus of Gadara)

---

8. Throughout both chapters devoted to Epicurus, the works of Cicero will often be cited for two reasons: one, to compare the Hellenistic philosopher's views with those of a Roman who had considerable stakes in religion and the state (in Rome, of course, absolutely interrelated) and, two; to trace how Epicurus's ideas were received in Rome and in the transition from republican hopes to the rule of the emperors. Cicero's own critique, therefore, allows us to better define Epicurus's philosophy overall.

9. In *Herculanensi,* Drummond and Walpole write: "the atheism of the Epicureans seems not to have been questioned by any men of learning, though *their exoteric doctrines were so well disguised* as not to offend the multitude," 123, my emphasis. I am indebted to Dirk Obbink for this reference. See his "Epicurus and Greek Religion." To the best of my knowledge, this is the first time that Epicurus's works are divided between exoteric and esoteric, that is, between what is openly stated and the views that are only accessible to those familiar with Epicurus's teachings. The critique of animal sacrifice by Epicurus is, therefore, part of his esoteric doctrine—and certainly hermeneutically accessible, as I will argue, by inference. In "The Athenian Garden," Diskin Clay further contributes to the sense of Epicurean writings being esoteric and only comprehensible to initiates: "Epicurus deploys a technical vocabulary that would be incomprehensible to anyone save his closest associates," 21.

the dilemma becomes much more noticeable, a solution difficult to foresee. There appear to be contradictory positions when, first of all, Philodemus and Lucretius are compared. Modern scholars are equally divided.[10] The condemnation of animal sacrifice, both as a religiously sanctioned practice and as the violent slaughter of animals that would be ritualistically eaten, was a well-known philosophical position, one obvious in the pre-Socratic philosophies of Pythagoras, Heraclitus, and Empedocles, no less than in the beliefs of the Orphics. Socrates, as we argued from several dialogues, must be included as a significant philosopher who questioned the efficacy and relevance of sacrifice overall. Theophrastus, though head of the Lyceum and the immediate successor of Aristotle (who did not himself condemn animal sacrifice) nevertheless included an ethical disposition to animals in his philosophy as well as advocating a vegetarian diet. The ethical consideration of animals was widespread and continued throughout antiquity; and it was to become even more prominent in the pastoralism of the Augustan poets. Parenthetically, similarities of viewpoints—despite their metaphysical differences—were noticed between Epicureans and Christians. For example, while writing in the second century CE, Lucian's satire shows that the religious entrepreneur Alexander of Abnoteichus began one of his rituals by exclaiming "away with the Christians," which his followers echoed with "away with the Epicureans."[11] Epicureans and Christians shared at least one belief much opposed by the polytheistic majority. The guiding question now becomes: Did Epicurus, as a Hellenistic philosopher, also condemn animal sacrifice and (as will be argued) see its abolition as inherently related to the development of new consciousness that necessarily transformed the ideas and traditions of Greek religion and, like Socrates, reconceive the meaning of piety? Once Epicurus's theological writings are examined in more detail, principally those devoted to a critique of the conceptions of traditional polis religion, then his rejection of animal sacrifice necessarily follows; it is deliberate, unequivocal. Prior to reading the relevant writings however, it is necessary to learn of Epicurus's original inspiration for turning to philosophy. He did so from an early age, obviously compelled by a spirit of wonder and inquiry consistent with the earliest pre-Socratic philosophers. What led

---

10. In "Aspects of Epicurean Theology," Japp Mansfeld summarizes the problem when he writes: "the extant texts at our disposal are not numerous, and some of the more important later reports about his views are notoriously difficult and even hard if not impossible to reconcile with each other, and perhaps to make sense of," 172. Epicurus's philosophy concerning the gods and religion is, as I will argue, clear; it is these "later reports," both ancient and modern, that present the greatest difficulties in terms of clarity and consistency.

11. As cited in Taylor, *Epicurus*, 31.

him, first of all, to begin a life dedicated to philosophical inquiry on the nature of the cosmos, the natural world, and human beings and, associated with these three interrelated concerns, develop a unique and controversial theology that became notorious? Ultimately, and despite the interrelation of his intellectual pursuits, promoting the health of the psyche became his life's purpose. By emphasizing the philosophical life as the pursuit of the health of the psyche, the supposed benefits of prayer and sacrifice became irrelevant or unnecessary.

2. The Origin of Epicurus's Thought

In *The Life of Epicurus* by Diogenes Laertius,[12] a remarkable document both for its biographical information on the Hellenistic philosopher and for his decision to include some of his most important writings—namely, three letters to Herodotus, Pythocles, and Menoeceus, as well as his *Principal Doctrines*—Epicurus turned to the study of philosophy, alone and seemingly without someone instructing him, so independent was he, when one of his schoolteachers was unable to explain the concept of "chaos" in Hesiod's *Theogony*. At a young age, Epicurus already has the sense of himself as both enticed by learning and motivated by an individual pursuit of knowledge and wisdom; philosophy compels him to wonder about the world and his place in it. "The first power to come into being was Chaos,"[13] writes the epic poet who was, along with Homer, the individual who catalogued the origin and characteristics of the Olympian gods and made them understandable, relatable, and capable of extraordinary feats though also betrayed by very human passions. Epicurus would soon distinguish matter, nature, *phusis* from any relationship to the divine. The world and the gods would be forever separated and, by doing so, reclaim a human autonomy long ago forsaken as a possibility when the fantasy of epic poets determined reality and human consciousness. Unable to know how chaos could come into being, Epicurus was therefore motivated to inquire into the origin of the cosmos. His conclusion—no doubt startling for many, and conventionally understood to be impious—tended to regard all matter as always already existing and therefore not created by divine will, intention, and design, an idea making him much criticized by Romans such as Cicero, not to mention virtually all church fathers as well as rabbinical writers—the latter who interchanged Epicurean and atheist.[14] His physics undermined the meta-

---

12. Laertius, *Lives*, 10.
13. Hesiod, *Th.*, 116.
14. See Fischel, *Rabbinic Literature and Greco-Roman Philosophy*.

physical foundations of theology. The hostility he provoked was predictable and understandable given the consequences of his belief. For Epicurus, a world without a creator necessarily made one free and self-sufficient. For others in the polis dependent on divine favor and support and adhering to the guarantee of tradition, it made them as outraged as when Socrates dared to defy the politicoreligious order of the community. Without a creator who, furthermore, participated in human affairs, life had lost its foundation and meaning. Not so for Epicurus. Eliminating the gods from the world was nothing less than an inception. Without the gods, human life could be reconceived.

"The first point," an indication of a foundational idea on matter and the world, "is that nothing comes into being from what is not," (10.38) Epicurus writes in his *Letter to Herodotus*, a unique principle and distinct from, for example, Anaximander's *apeiron*, the "boundless" that was itself uncreated but from where all things were generated. Lucretius adds, again stressing a "first principle of our study" and how "no thing is ever by divine power produced from nothing... nothing can be created from nothing."[15] By disassociating the creation of the world from any divine initiation and power, all of existence could then be evaluated out of itself and without reference or appeal to a transcendental origin or design. Epicurus created what Giovanni Reale called a religion of the immanent, at once denying all metaphysical foundations and restoring human life to its preeminent role. Understanding nature to be self-generated—which he clearly observed in the lives of plants, animals, and human beings—had significant consequences for the rethinking of the nature of human life, what it understood about itself, and what it could aspire to become. "The totality [of things] has always been just like it is now and always will be," (10.39) Epicurus asserts, establishing a foundation without an origin, being without the divine. The gods were consigned to a separate existence. They could not interfere in human creation at all.

Countering the accusation leveled against him for impiety, Laertius comes to his defense and tells us that "his [Epicurus's] piety to the gods (*theou osiotetos*) and love for his country were too great for words," a piety and *holiness* that once again seems to testify to his respect for the polis religion of Athens but must also raise considerable doubts; this may well be an *apologia*, as it will be for Philodemus. Despite Laertius's claim, Epicurus's *philopatria* remains at least uncertain given the fundamental precept not to be involved in public life. He may have loved Greece, but less as an idea than related to its most significant representatives, the philosophers who defied its most cherished values. When Laertius further adds that Epicurus did

15. Lucretius, *DRN.*, 1.149–157.

not participate in the political life of the city, in its *politeia*, or in the fulfillment in the obligations of a citizen, the description unfortunately remains ambiguous: one can infer that he did not attend any specifically political assemblies in matters of voting, or more likely he did not fulfill his obligation as a citizen and participate in the duty of a jury man during a trial, especially given his pejorative evaluation of rhetoric and how its techniques could lead to dissembling and mendacity. His concept of justice made him categorically reject the judicial system and its rhetorical manipulation. More importantly for our main concern here: Did he philosophically refuse to attend the period festivals and processions culminating in the central ritual of Athenian religion—animal sacrifice? For now, the question can remain suspended. A thorough reading of Epicurus's *physiologia* and his theology are first necessary before a decisive argument can be made and defended against ancient and modern critics.

The Epicurean school, we know, was located outside the city walls of Athens and not far from the Academy. The Garden was established to be relatively isolated, outside the city proper, and above all independent. For all intents and purposes, the community was established to be an alternative to the social relations of the polis. It was also unique in quite a few aspects, including the admission of women as respected philosophers, among them Themista of Lampsacus and, more noticeably, the Leontium who wrote, among other works, a treatise against Theophrastus. Cicero called her a *meretricula*, a whore, or, if more circumspect, a "courtesan."[16] Were the individuals living in the Garden nevertheless members of a *deme*, one of the political and geographical divisions of the city? Would any individual participate in the Boule, the council of five hundred members (fifty from each tribe) that met virtually every day in the Bouleuterion to vote on matters of the city's administration? Laertius's double description is meaningful insofar as he makes religious piety and love for his country absolutely related; *philopatria* was both civic and religious. Due to his independence, did Epicurus also refuse to attend to the specifically religious ceremonies and observances that were essential to the political responsibilities of a citizen, most especially the rituals associated with sacrifice and in the belief (clearly thoroughly rejected by him if his thought is to be consistent) that there could be any kind of exchange of favors, or *charis*, between the divine and human beings? He certainly had no interest in the reasons—assumed if not explicit—for offering sacrifices (to name but three) so as to promote community identity, perpetuating hierarchies, and a commensality based

---

16. Cicero, *Nat. D.*, 1.93.

on the recognition of status.[17] For a philosopher who stressed the need to be independent of the polis (a central reason for establishing his Garden community in the first place), and who did not at all rely on a relationship with the divine—certainly not with the expectation of reciprocity—it is difficult, indeed impossible, to regard Epicurus as both "counter-cultural"[18] and also someone who observed and participated in the superstitious rituals of the polis. Eric Brown makes the argument that Epicurus is not apolitical; rather, "he adopts counter cultural politics."[19] Epicureans had a "counter-cultural conception of salvation,"[20] that is, a psychological healing unrelated to, and quite inimical to, the virtues of the city. Stanley Stowers writes that "even a superficial look at nonsacrificers in Greco-Roman society shows that withdrawing from sacrificial practice meant also forming alternative societies."[21] He goes on to add: "Particular nonsacrificers will likely share conditions that distinguish them from sacrificers." Richard Hibler writes that Epicurus "outlawed myths, superstitions, and religious rituals."[22] Numerous arguments should be considered when attempting to decide if Epicureans did or did not sacrifice; the creation of their own rituals, such as commemorating birthdays, for one, was an alternative to those prescribed by the festival calendar of the polis. Their community was, for them as well as their critics (indeed, they were vilified for it), an alternative to the way most other people lived. The Stoic Epictetus—and, as we shall see in detail, writings of Cicero—accuses Epicureans as a whole as being "subversive of the state"[23] as well as destructive of the family. No wonder that in antiquity Epicureans and Christians were both referred to as *atheists* because of their independence from state-sponsored religion. If Epicurus and his followers attended the periodic festivals that included sacrifices, his theology would seem wholly contradictory to his acts. Furthermore, given how several comments indicate Epicurus advised people to eat frugally, and avoid unnecessary indulgence, it is highly unlikely he would have eaten sacrificial meat even if his vegetarianism cannot be definitively proven. The feasts typical of periodic

---

17. Without here arguing for Epicurus being a vegetarian—though all references in his works to eating do not involve any animals, with the possible exception of fish—it is nevertheless relevant to cite Johanees Haussleiter's *Der Vegetarismus in der Antike* and his argument for "der individuelle vegetarismus des Epikur" (272), even though, as he adds, later Epicureans did not follow their teacher's example.

18. Pascual, "Epicuro y Atenas."

19. Brown, "Politics and Society," 180.

20. Baltzly and Eliopoulos. "Classical Ideals of Friendship," 41.

21. Stowers, "Greeks Who Sacrificed," 331.

22. Hibler, *Happiness through Tranquillity*, 35.

23. Epictetus, *Dis.*, 3.7.

Physiologia and the Psychodynamics of Epicurean Theology   105

and much-anticipated festivals were wholly contrary to the Epicurean way of life; excessive indulgence, despite his philosophy of *hedone* or pleasure (ultimately related to equanimity) did not contribute to a fulfilling life.

Jon Mikalson, on the other hand, makes the claim that "Epicurus did pray as well as sacrifice to the gods, and this led his supporters to claim his piety and his opponents to charge him with hypocrisy for concealing from the public his real belief."[24] The contradiction is often noticeable in commentators. For example, Peter Adamson can write that "Epicurus seems to be radicalizing the theological critique developed by Plato"—and the textual evidence on Epicurus's sustained critique of religion can in no way be disputed—and then add: "Epicureans generally did not avoid participating in traditional religious ritual."[25] In this case, the specific reconception of Athenian piety by Socrates and confirmed by Plato is both recognized by a modern commentator and then immediately disavowed. An ancient writer seems more reflective of the historical reality. Noting that in Homer people offered first-fruits to the gods before eating, Athenaeus (writing between the second and third centuries AD) tells us "but with Epicureans there is no libation, no preliminary offerings to the gods."[26] Needless to say, the contradictory statements by modern commentators are one indication of Epicurus's place in the history of Western philosophy. He may very well be the most misunderstood philosopher in antiquity, his ideas distorted to serve the purpose of ancient polemics.

Unlike Socrates, who turned away from his youthful interest in the study of natural phenomena, Epicurus made the inquiry into phenomena of the earth and sky essential to his overall philosophy—in part to counter the prevailing ideas on the nature of the gods and their necessary and mostly beneficial and benevolent interaction with the human world, what Cicero called "the direction and government of the world."[27] However, Epicurus's interest in a rational account of natural phenomena—for example, in the cosmos, eclipses, and, in nature, rainbows or earthquakes—had a practical aim: not simply to *know*, pragmatically, as if epistemology itself was a

---

24. Mikalson, *Greek Popular Religion*, 44–45. Such a claim could only be made by relying (as I will argue) on only a singular source, one that will be highly doubtful and more like an apologia.

25. Adamson, *Philosophy in the Hellenistic*, 42.

26. Athenaeus. *Deip.*, 179b; Usener, *Ep.*, fr. 56. Throughout the chapter I will be presenting (beginning, as I did, with the fourth-century philosopher Himerius) several testimonies that make it certain that Epicurus himself, and later Epicureans, did not in any way participate in cultic activities. By doing so, I hope to definitively disprove critics (especially modern ones, and because only one ancient critic runs counter to my positions) who assert that Epicurus was a religious conformist.

27. Cicero, *Nat. D.*, 1.2.

significant philosophical discipline, but to alleviate the anxieties of the times insofar as popular belief held that events on earth and in the heavens were ordained by the gods, thus making human beings not simply dependent on the gods, but also vulnerable to their often puzzling desires, intentions, and whims. The epics certainly portrayed them as far from predictable and, for philosophers, in no way deserving of prayer or worship much less emulation. As he writes in *Principal Doctrine XI*, "If our suspicions about heavenly phenomena... did not trouble us at all and were anything to us... then we would have no need of natural science." Predicting a solar eclipse, as Thales apparently did in 585 BCE, was not enough; it was also necessary to provide a rational explanation of its occurrence as an alternative to any and all metaphysical claims that also sustained a social and political status quo, for the heavens above were used to legitimate the world below, as if the human world reflected divine aspiration. Even Aristotle's mechanistic model of the universe nevertheless included as essential a so-called prime mover, so that the universe and its structure were divinely ordered and perpetuated in an endless and well-ordered cycle. In a remarkable series of lectures, E. R. Dodds emphasizes the uniqueness of the Epicureans when he writes that "so much was common ground to all philosophical schools save the Epicureans."[28] In terms of the structure of the universe and the belief held unanimously by his contemporaries, Epicurus was alone in regarding the world of matter as well as natural phenomena (i.e. earthquakes) as independent from the gods, though again he shares his philosophy in common with predecessors such as Protagoras and Xenophanes, thinkers who had defined superstitious assumptions and argued for a rationally understood *kosmos* and *phusis*. Epicurus both inherits and uniquely develops philosophical ideas and thereby contributes to a countercultural tradition of thought.

Epicurus was unique in his understanding of intimidating phenomena such as eclipses of the sun and the moon:

> When it comes to meteorological phenomena, one must believe that movements, turnings, eclipses, risings, settings and related phenomena occur without any [god] helping out and ordaining or being about to ordain things. (10.76)

The movement of the *kosmos* is self-sufficient. One further note: it is striking to notice how Epicurus, when referring to the divine, never uses a proper name not only to disassociate Zeus, for example, from his responsibility as a rain-giver, but to make it more difficult for his readers to imagine any god as fulfilling a prior conception. Unnamed gods are more easily

---

28. Dodds, *Pagan and Christian*, 6.

disassociated from earthly relations; without a name, they can no longer be referred to traditionally, embodying meaning, a preconceived *theologia*. Without a name, an identity, and a purpose, the gods are divested of all preconceived significance and effectively banished to their own particular *topos*, an *intermundia* no longer with the lofty privilege of Mount Olympus.

Epicurus's often provocative declarations were not simply intended as affirmations of his belief. For example, when he insisted (unlike the virtually universal held belief) that the gods did not in any way participate in the *kosmos*, nature, or the lives of human beings, that was a philosophical position consistent with his philosophy of *autarkeia*, the self-sufficiency and philosophically motivated human freedom. It is inconceivable that Epicurus could write, in *Vatican Sayings* 65, that "it is pointless to ask from the gods what one is fully able to supply for oneself," (obviously negating the theological assumption of *charis* or reciprocity) and then participate in any religious ritual, much less offer sacrifices. As Dirk Obbink rightly stresses, Epicurus chose to emphasize "the persistence and regularity of individual conceptions of the divine, and the effect (primarily social and psychological) of these conceptions upon life in the world."[29] If Epicurus, in the firsthand writings that remain, could so repeatedly criticize traditional conceptions of the gods, by the many, how could he then be portrayed by apologists such as Philodemus (writing two centuries after his death) as observing all civic rites, including sacrifice?

An initial quote will here be used to introduce Philodemus as both an unreliable source on Epicurean doctrine and *the only* philosopher in antiquity who claimed Epicurus fully participated in cultic rituals: "And in his book On Destiny there is an exposition concerning the assistance provided by them {the gods}."[30] If Epicurus was observed by the many to be practicing all the rituals associated with the polis religion of Athens, would not his public writings on the gods and Athenian religion be in contradiction to his acts—something, of course, that would not have escaped the notice of his fellow citizens, as Obbink points out, and obviously lead to being discredited for his hypocrisy? The well-known advice to refrain from any political involvement would obviously extend, it is reasonable to believe, to the participation in any cultic practice; perhaps even more so given the overly dramatic character of a sacrifice, with its festivals and processions, chanting and music, and the rituals of the civic priests that culminated

29. Obbink, "Atheism of Epicurus," 187.

30. Philodemus, *Piety.*, 1.37.1061. It would not be an exaggeration to say that all the writings we have of Epicurus makes this statement *incredible*. It is now necessary to consider whether Philodemus was an apologist in a Roman context, that is, in a society that, politically and religiously, opposed Epicurean teaching.

with the sacrifice of animals. One of the fundamental beliefs of Epicurus was the withdrawal from the many, one wholly in contradiction to the participation in the regular public festivals of the city. Could Epicureans, fiercely independent from and critical of the status quo, really participate in superstitious rituals? Epicurus's views on a specific ritual practice such as animal sacrifice remains a problem precisely because of the divergent ideas presented by Epicureans themselves—in our case, especially between Philodemus's *On Piety* and Lucretius's *On the Nature of Things*, as we will see in greater detail. One can certainly understand the suspicion and animosity aroused by his very independently minded philosophy: to become free of the gods in every way by denying that they interacted with human beings.

3. *Epicurean Theology*

In his *Letter to Menoeceus*, Epicurus writes, "the man who denies the gods of the many is not impious, but rather he who ascribes to the gods the opinions of the many. For the pronouncements (*doxas*) of the many about the gods are not basic grasps but false suppositions (*prolepseis pseudeis*)" (10.123–24). Cicero counters with the belief, stressing "prudence" as opposed to opinions or false suppositions, that "the things that are told of the immortality of the soul and of the heavens [are not] the fictions of dreaming philosophers, or such incredible tales as the Epicureans mock, but the conjectures of sensible men."[31] Epicurus and his followers may not have been as brazen as the Cynics, philosophers often spectacular in their provocations (sex in public, wearing tattered clothing, refusing to bathe, and generally insolent), but in the directness of their declarations they were no doubt regarded with aversion that could easily lead to public scrutiny and accusations, both personal and judicial. Refusal to participate in the civic ritual intended especially in relation to the gods—as supplication, appeasement, request—would have not only attracted attention, it could have been perceived as illegal, as Lucretius would emphasize at the beginning of his *On the Nature of Things*. The Epicureans were seen with suspicion and apprehension. The consequences of Epicurus's philosophy undermined the metaphysical foundations of the city. The gods were effectively banished and exiled. For once, unlike the epic poets or dramatic philosophers, the expulsion is conceived by human beings.

In his *Letter to Pythocles*, Epicurus fundamentally defines the purpose of the study of *physiologia* (indeed, he tells his friend "do not believe that there is any other goal to be achieved by the knowledge of meteorological

---

31. Cicero, *Nat. D.*, 6.3.

phenomena") as "freedom from disturbance," (10.85) that is, the anxiety felt as a consequence of the myths concerning the power of the gods in the here and now, no less than in the afterlife of eternal judgment. *Physiologia* and his critique of theology are essentially interrelated and form one central idea of his philosophy. By studying nature and the universe, Epicurus repeats in his *Letter to Herodotus*, "I bring calm to my life," (10.37) the tranquility so important to his philosophy of health and healing. Scientific knowledge, far from an end in itself, is subordinated to psychology so that, ultimately, his theology becomes psychodynamic, "for our life does not now need irrationality and groundless opinion" (10.86). Epicurus's comprehensive critique of the guiding ideas of his time and place are intended to do nothing less than provide the possibility of a reevaluation of the Hellenistic worldview concerning the particular and, for him, misguided conception of the gods and, by extension, the rituals associated with their worship. Epicurus's philosophy deserves to be recognized as a denunciation of the ideas held by Greek society and the city of Athens in particular—a denunciation leading, he believes, to much more rational and healthier human beings who, by virtue of their perception and understanding, can overcome the persistence of the custom and tradition of myths, those that continue to perpetuate a distorted understanding of the blessed gods who need nothing at all, and certainly not the offerings of ritually slaughtered animals. The religious beliefs and acts associated with the worship of the gods have substantially undermined human life, forcing it to be subservient and dependent on the apparent characteristics of the gods (which are false and only opinions) who make demands of reciprocity.

In his *Letter to Pythocles*, Epicurus repeats and emphasizes the same concerns evident in Socrates's dialogue with his friend Euthyphro as well as the speech he makes at his trial. For Epicurus, the argument has two parts: explaining "the orderliness of the cyclical periods of the heavenly bodies," he stresses that any and all explanations will not involve resorting to the gods: "let the nature of the divine not be brought to bear on this at all" (10.97). The cyclical nature of the movement of objects in the cosmos is entirely ordered on their own, as is so much else. For example, the eclipse of the sun and moon he recognizes to be caused "by being blocked by certain other bodies," (10.96) a physical theory based upon observation and deduction. Equally important, Epicurus declares himself not to be an atheist (so it seems) by adding that the divine does not contribute anything to human beings. "But let it [the divine] go on being thought of as free from burdensome service" (10.97). No more important and consequential word could be used here than "service," precisely to show how any service expected (from the gods) is both delusional and detrimental. Therefore, the service provided by human beings as part of their religious rituals in fact cannot accomplish its intended goal: to receive from the gods an expectant offering based on lack, need, or desire. Cicero's critique can serve here as a first interjection to be later expanded: "Your gods not only do no service (*beneficium*) that you can point to, but they don't do anything at all."[32] Equally important, as Socrates argued in *Alcibiades II*, asking the gods for a favor, whether through prayer or sacrifice, may in fact turn out to fulfill a desire consequently judged to be harmful. The still-prevalent idea (also discussed by Socrates) that the relationship between human beings and the gods require a service—and one that apparently involves reciprocity—is now explicitly abandoned as one of the cornerstones of Epicurean *physiologia* and theology. The gods neither require service from human beings, nor do they provide an exchange for such a service. His *Letter to Pythocles*, using the all-important service to indicate that the belief in *charis* or divine/human reciprocity has been founded on an erroneous conception of the divine, ultimately leads to a renewed understanding of the possibilities of human life. In the *Letter to Menoeceus*, Epicurus will transform the previous understanding of *charis* as provided by the divine and, instead, make it an attribute of a human being who can look back on the past with gratitude. "One should not spoil what is present by desiring what is absent, but rather reason out that these things too [i.e., what we have] were among those we might have prayed for," he affirms in *Vatican Saying* 35, thereby nullifying the reason for praying as a desire to receive something more, something different, something better. Epicurus realizes how desire has been given theological justification through prayer; by relating desire to a god, it has been rationalized. Furthermore, if, as he believes, nature generates itself, human beings (as themselves natural) have the same dynamic ability in terms of birth, social life, and history. Succinctly stated: "*physis* contre *nomos*."[33]

Like Socrates, who argued for the transformation of belief in the gods by turning away from ritual to the taking care of others therapeutically, Epicurus too devotes himself in his teaching to changing the customs and traditions of the past. At the beginning of the letter, and consistently repeated in all his writings, Epicurus wants others to learn "the lines of reasoning which contribute to a blessed life (*makarion bion*)," thoughts which are not simply concerned with epistemological certainty (knowledge, as such, is not primary), but with achieving a characteristic usually associated with the divine. What does he mean by blessedness (*makarismos*), and is it related

---

32. Ibid., 1.36.
33. Onfray, *Les sagesses antique*.

to what Socrates called *omoiosis theo*[34] or becoming in the likeness of god? Clearly, Epicurus's conception of the gods was essential in his attempt to transform the self-understanding (and the existence) of individual lives, "for a man who lives among immortal goods is in no respect like a mere mortal animal," (10.133) he writes at the very end of his *Letter to Menoeceus*, a conclusion and culmination of his teachings.

The sense of being happy, not a concern among others for philosophers, will require a more complete interpretation. For now, Epicurus wants to begin with an outline of his philosophical thinking about nature so as to insure that his students, once they have memorized these tenets, will be happy, a happiness soon to be equated with calm, tranquility, which is ultimately the aim of Epicurean thought: to achieve *ataraxia*. Epicurus made his concern for the psychological health of others his preeminent concern, therefore, when he begins to elaborate on what he calls "true physics," he knows that Pythocles and others are "entangled in preoccupations," (10.85) concerns that are far more personally troubling than theoretical. Some beliefs have psychologically harmful consequences. Epicurus teaches others to be unpreoccupied with the ceaseless anxieties of social life, with its demands and expectations, its projections and fantasies. Again, he clarifies his fundamental intent by stressing—with a "first of all" (*Proton*)—that he has one overriding concern: "Do not believe that there is any other goal to be achieved by the knowledge of meteorological phenomena. . . than freedom from disturbance (*ataraxian*) and a secure conviction (*kai pistin bebaion*)" (10.85). He explicitly mentions the nature of *pistis*—a word implying both belief and faith as a counterpoint to the ideas usually associated with religion. All scientific knowledge is subordinate to psychology. To have firm and secure knowledge results in the disappearance of the insecurity formerly experienced when natural phenomena were either explainable through archaic myths or attributed to the gods—gods who were perceived to be volatile and often prone to wrath, meddling in natural phenomena such as causing earthquakes to inflict catastrophic punishments on the lives of human beings. The very first of his *Principal Doctrines,* as well as his *tetrapharmakon* or four-part cure, stresses that a blessed being (a god) "has no trouble itself, nor does it give trouble to anyone else." And if we add the second element—"death is nothing to us"—two of the most formidable metaphysical beliefs (life after death, and a judgmental god who decides on one's eternal fate) is dispelled as inimical to a healthy life. Furthermore, in *Vatican Saying* 14, he simultaneously denies the belief in reincarnation or in any life after death at all: "We are born only once, and we cannot be born

---

34. On the concept, see Erler's "Epicurus as deus mortalis."

twice; and one must for all eternity exist no more." Nature, god, death: it was necessary for Epicurus to reconsider their meaning so that human life could then be reinterpreted and given prominence. Once god and death were interpreted from an Epicurean perspective, then human nature (the subject of Socrates's *Alcibiades I*) could consequently also be rethought and reconceived so that the idea of a good life could have an unprecedented significance. Epicurean philosophy reveals not so much the characteristics of the gods (as, for example, their blessedness) but the limits and anxieties of the human imagination, inside and out, psychologically and as an expression of civic life.

Rather than perceiving the events of the world, natural and human both, as somehow preordained, Epicurus advises that "we should not do physics by following groundless postulates and stipulations, but in the manner called by the phenomenon," (10.86) or to be more precise, how certain preconceptions (usually unacknowledged) could determine perception, an idea to be decisive for developing his therapeutic philosophy. His recommendation is, first of all, to properly observe the phenomena themselves rather than impose a prearranged theory on nature. Too many assumptions, drawn from myths, had imposed a meaning and limit to human life now in need of being radically altered for human benefit. The natural world had an order internal to itself. As always, his ultimate concern is clear: "For our life does not now need irrationality and groundless opinion, but rather for us to live without tumult" (10.87). In order to begin thinking rationally and avoid "groundless opinion," (10.87) a first requirement is to ignore what has been handed down by myths. Myths from the archaic past have been relied upon to explain natural phenomena. Now the past cannot be the foundation of explanation or truth, most especially because of their origin, one reason he believed poetry should neither be studied nor practiced. The custom and tradition inimical to the philosophical life, as it was for Socrates, is now continued by Epicurus—beginning with what a previously influential philosopher preferred to ignore: nature.

In *Vatican Sayings* 29, Epicurus goes as far as saying that he would much rather speak like an oracle (in riddles understood by no one at all) rather than "conform to popular opinion and thus gain constant praise that comes from the many." A constantly repeated piece of advice to fellow Epicureans was to avoid the socially promoted idea that one's individuality and character can be heightened by social approval, a problem that was already evident, as we saw, in Plato's *Symposium* and one of the strongest motivators for Greek citizens in the classical age as well as in Hellenistic Greece. In *Vatican Saying* 45, he writes:

The study of nature does not create men who are fond of boasting and chattering or who show off the culture that impresses the many, but rather men who are strong and self-sufficient, and who take pride in their own personal qualities not in those that depend on external circumstances.

A more revealing Epicurean ideal cannot be found, stressing character above reputation, the condition of the *psyche* rather than the transitory nature of public acclaim that, in fact, made one vulnerable since the opinions of others could always change and turn into their opposite.

In his treatise, *On Nature*, Epicurus provides a systematic description of both the *kosmos* and the nature of meteorological phenomena. He explains the appearance of movement and rotations, speculating as to the reason for their constancy, the waning of the moon, wondering why the moon's shape changes—possibly, he speculates, because the moon receives its light from the sun. Although his physical theories are often wrong (he wonders, at one point, if the movement of celestial objects depends on some kind of fuel), they are always rational and *scientific* explanations based first on observation, and second on a possible theoretical interpretation. His presentation to the student Pythocles, as well as others who would have read the letter, continually juxtaposes his theories of *physiologia* to the still prevailing theories that are for him a form of superstition, what has been handed down by tradition and now no longer has any bearing for the rational philosopher. It would not be an exaggeration to understand Epicurus's break from tradition as a first scientific revolution—and one even more significant than Aristotle's who, with his prime mover, still needed an outward force (a divine one) to insure the movement of the heavens. There had been, of course, thinkers interested in nature, beginning with the pre-Socratics and with such eminent thinkers as Anaxagoras of Clazomenae—radical thinkers who were persecuted for their provocative theories. For example, if the sun was a hot stone (as Anaxagoras taught) the celestial object could not be regarded as a god or in any way indicative of the divine. But only Epicurus made his scientific theories part of a much more comprehensive concern with the life of human beings beyond what could be known, as a fact, to include their psychological health. "It is impossible for someone to dispel his fears about the most important matters if he doesn't know the nature of the universe but still gives some credence to myths. So without the study of nature there is no enjoyment of pure pleasure," he writes in *Principal Doctrine* XII. Pure pleasure, then, cannot be associated with a *particular* pleasure, occasionally fulfilled, then desired once more, always contingent. Pure pleasure is a permanent effect on the *psyche* and involves the absence of any psychologically painful conditions such as irrational fear and anxiety. He was aware, as Socrates was before him, that as long as the cosmos, nature, and human lives depended on mythic explanations or the gods, then they would never achieve "freedom from disturbance" (10.128) but would always be vulnerable to apprehension, anxiety, and uncertainty. "Let the nature of the divine not be brought to bear on this at all," (10.97) he writes, repeating the one fundamental idea of his teaching, dismissing any metaphysical influence on natural phenomena, the reason he systematically goes through such different conditions as the formations of clouds, thunder and lightning (for so long a formidable and terrifying sign of the gods' displeasure), wind, hail, snow, dew, and again to the cosmos with explanations about comets and falling stars. Epicurus's repetitions are insistent and reaffirmed so the student will *memorize* each principle and know it by heart, easily recalled and necessary for an emotionally tranquil life.

First of all, and to defend Epicurus against any accusations of being an atheist, he writes that "god is an indestructible and blessed (*makarion*) animal (*zoon*), in accordance with the general conception of god commonly held" (10.123). Both points are significant: god has a characteristic that can be defined, including its immortality and blessedness, and both conceptions are common to the majority of people. Here he does not disagree. "Gods do exist," he writes, "since we have clear knowledge of them." (10.123) Although he believes that gods do indeed exist since we have certain knowledge of them, this knowledge varies and, therefore, can be more closely examined. Epicurus therefore makes the argument that the gods, however, "are not as the many (*hoi polloi*) believe them to be" (10.123). What does he mean by the *hoi polloi*? Does he mean people in general, including the individuals directly in charge of all the official festivals and the activities associated with them—processions, rites of initiation, and sacrifice? Defending himself without specifically implicating himself, Epicurus makes the important statement concerning the meaning of being impious: "The man who denies the gods of the many is not impious (*asebes*), but rather he who ascribes to the gods the opinions of the many (*pollon doxas theois*)" (10.124). Significantly, and here he is again sustaining Socratic ideas, Epicurus uses the term "impious" specifically in relation to someone who devotes too much of his life to the pursuit of financial gain; impiety, in this case, is related to a dedication to material interests and pursuits. Epicurus has therefore defended all the philosophers in the past who have been persecuted for their views about the gods and made his own defense explicit. Furthermore, he calls into question how piety has been defined and legitimated. As Isocrates believed, piety is defined as "not changing any of those things which their ancestors had handed down to them."³⁵ Tradition was sacrosanct and inviolable. In Athens (and, as we shall see, in Jesus' relationship to the Jerusalem temple leadership) to call into question the customs and traditions of the past was regarded with intense disapproval and could lead to judicial prosecution. For Epicurus, the important concept of piety cannot remain defined by the many, and therefore cannot be related to any of the religious acts and the participations in rituals traditionally associated with the polis religion of Athens. The philosopher becomes the individual who begins to question commonly held beliefs and (one can infer, by extension) the rituals and practices associated with a binding conception of the divine/human relationship. Can such an inference be made and justified from Epicurus's own writing? On the commonly held belief of the meaning of piety, Epicurus is consistent: "The pronouncements (*prolepsis*) of the many about the gods are not basic grasps but false suppositions (*upolepseis pseudeis*)" (10.124). The many aspects of *prolepsis* of the majority are, for Epicurus, ideas that are not real; they are judgments (*prejudgments*) that have been inherited from the past and accepted due to their tie to tradition. Part of the problem of what he calls "general education" (VS 58) involves the learning of "mere opinions" (PD XXII) as opposed to the truth. So far, his distinction between a traditional understanding of piety and his own obviously different and critical ideas has been made. In the case of Socrates, and through a reading of his own statements and the vocabulary used, his own impiety did include a reappraisal of the meaning of *thusia*. Does Epicurus offer anything comparable? Epicurus clearly argues that the ideas about the gods are false suppositions. By extension, then, he must necessarily also argue that the rituals associated with the gods are also based on false suppositions and should therefore be abolished. Epicurus may not explicitly mention the practice of animal sacrifice; but if all his theological arguments are taken into consideration (most especially his belief that the gods are not in any way related to the world of matter or the lives of human beings) then it is clear that the purpose of sacrifice—an exchange of a gift, an animal for a divine favor—no longer has any meaning or relevance. In the case of Socrates, one has to consider if the emergence of a therapeutic consciousness as the ability to take care of others was not related to the growing animosity to the continuing ritual of animal sacrifice. By withdrawing from civic rituals, and a community of worshippers bound by beliefs, traditions, and practices, one could dedicate oneself to others and to the psychagogy or the individual turning of the soul first articulated by Socrates. Epicurus's therapeutic philosophy cannot be understood without his opposition to a now archaic theology.

35. Isocrates, *Ar.*, 7.29–30.

Acts of ritualistic worship had become obsolete; the development of a new human disposition was now philosophically essential.

The conclusion of the *Letter to Menoeceus* sums up Epicurus's views on the polis religion, one that not only identifies with the idea of divine blessedness, but actually makes it possible for human beings to achieve *makarismos*, a happiness defined by a constant and unwavering tranquility. "For a man who lives among immortal goods is in no respect like a mere mortal animal," (10.133) he argues, in fact now making it possible for human beings to recognize their own capacity for being as blessed as a god. Although human beings lack one attribute of the gods (their indestructability) they can, nevertheless, share in one aspect of their *immortality*—that is, their constancy, equanimity, and *ataraxia*. Epicurus here alludes to a tradition of thought (evident, for one, in Empedocles) that aspired to become like, if not precisely equal to, the gods. Having the divine characteristics of a god, though still profoundly human, meant one was no longer accountable to the Greek pantheon and all it represented; it effectively liberated one from any and all obligations deemed religious by the polis. And if *doxa* is related to opinion insofar as what *seems*, then it is highly unlikely any Epicureans would have attended any public festival, certainly not when the drama of the ritual was so plainly obvious in terms of, for example, the sprinkling of water on the animal so it would shake and therefore assent to being killed, the wailing screams of mournful women (hired for their effect) and, finally, the ritual killing of the victim, with all its minutiae, including that strangest of all practices, the divinatory reading of their entrails. *Vatican Saying 65* is unequivocal and should be considered definitive on the question of sacrifice insofar as Epicurus stresses self-sufficiency: "It is pointless to ask from the gods what one is fully able to supply for oneself." His philosophy is unambiguous; this one principle alone, and its relation to his other comprehensive ideas, makes Epicurus in no way supportive of polis religion, in belief or in act.

Thus far, the explicit theories of Epicurus have been followed insofar as they clarify his theory of natural phenomena or *physiologos* no less than his theology; what remains to be examined are his thoughts, if any, on the role of sacrifice as a religious observance. Although the extant writings are clear on the characteristics of the gods and their influence on the city-state, there are no explicit references to sacrifice as such. The omission may be less a matter of cautious restraint than the sense of it being unnecessary since readers had no doubts about the extent of his doctrines and teaching. However, if writings by others are consulted (especially the two most prominent Epicureans, Lucretius and Philodemus) as well as scholars of antiquity, a problem arises. This, then, forms the concern of the following argument: Was Epicurus a critic of sacrifice—which certainly seems consistent with all his writings on religion, and is *repeatedly confirmed* by Lucretius's in *On the Nature of the Gods*—or is he more accurately portrayed by Philodemus, especially in his apologetic *On Piety*, as someone who was scrupulous in his civic/religious duties and therefore regularly participated in the periodic festivals and the ritual of animal sacrifice? The origin of so much uncertainty and scholarly disagreement can be located in the writings of two influential Epicureans: one a countercultural poet, the other a foreigner who needed support from a fickle Roman aristocracy who could not accept a philosophy independent of their gods.

4. *Lucretius Contra Philodemus*

An initial question needs to be raised: Are Lucretius's numerous critical comments in *On the Nature of Things* concerning animal sacrifice a reflection of his reading of Epicurus's *On Nature*? Or are they indicative of a non-Epicurean influence, namely the Empedocles poem of the same name, whose recent discovery of papyrus fragments from *On Nature* make his denunciation of all killing of animals unequivocal? Since there are no direct references to animal sacrifice in any of Epicurus's extant writings, is it possible to attribute one belief or another given our sources? Lucretius's poem and the fragments of Philodemus's *On Piety* could not be more different; the latter has Epicurus not only regularly participating in all civic rituals, but he also quotes him (apparently) from now-lost copies of Epicurus's books encouraging his followers to do so as well. John Masson succinctly describes the problem when he writes, "probably no system of thought offers stronger inconsistencies and contradictions than does Epicureanism, and nowhere are the difficulties greater than in its so-called 'theology.'"[36] Daniel Ullucci is even more heavy-handed and, moreover, cites selected sources while neglecting the most significant and trustworthy of all: Lucretius and his unequivocal presentation of Epicurean philosophy in his poem. He begins by outlining Epicurus's theology and then writes,

> One might conclude from this that Epicurus would reject the practice of sacrifice, but, in fact, *our sources* suggest the opposite. Epicurus and his school taught that sacrifice was a good and proper religious act. He practiced sacrifice himself and

---

36. Masson, "Religion of Lucretius," 149. There are, in fact, no contradictions at all in Epicurus's theology. They are as clear as they are consistent; the contradiction arises because of the later *testimonia* and, as I argue, resulting from only one source that has been much too influential and erroneous.

instructed his followers to do the same. Under the critique model, Epicurus's position is completely incoherent."[37]

The inconsistencies, however, cannot be attributed to Epicurus himself; rather, they are found in the two Epicureans who are thought to best represent his thought. Since their representation of Epicurus specifically on the question of sacrifice are irreconcilable, a possible explanation must at least be attempted, even if it may remain inconclusive especially when we take into consideration a similar problem in the doxography of Cicero and Plutarch.

If Lucretius's *On the Nature of Things* is understood to be the most faithful representation of Epicurean philosophy[38] as it has been taught continuously and through a well-defined succession of teachers and schools since his death in 270 BCE, then there may be aspects of the poem that further contribute to Epicurus's teaching as it was known at the time. In the case of doctrine, Lucretius appears consistent and unwavering in his support of Epicurus's overall philosophy, and especially in relation to religion. It will be important to confirm what has been handed down from Epicurus's own writings since, at the time of Lucretius, they were widely available. "It is perfectly obvious, although often temporarily forgotten, that Lucretius had access to much more of the written work of Epicurus than we have,"[39] Furley reminds us, and therefore forces us to consider what specific Epicurean texts he may have used, adopted, or copied from, in addition to the noted *On Nature*. There were no doubt others, perhaps numerous works giving him precise and extensive references. Carlo Giussani writes that Lucretius could not have added to, or "corrected," any of Epicurus's philosophy: "*d'un Lucrezio innovatore o correttore del Sistema bisogna bandire del tutto l'idea.*"[40] P. H. De Lacy makes the argument that Lucretius's poem was not derived solely from the work of Epicurus, which in principle is acceptable as long as the ideas are not contrary to Epicurus.[41] Recent contributions have been meticulous.[42] If a difference (or more properly, a necessary extension)

---

37. Ullucci, "Contesting the Meaning," 558–59, my emphasis. In fact, he has only one source from antiquity; and as I will argue, Philodemus's *On Piety* cannot be trusted. His citation of Cicero's *On the Nature of the Gods* 1.17.45 mentions piety but not sacrifice.

38. In *Lucretius and the Transformation of Greek Wisdom*, David Sedley argues that the poem is largely based on Epicurus's *On Nature*.

39. Furley, "Lucretius the Epicurean," 159.

40. Giussani, *Studi Lucreziani*, 10.

41. De Lacy, "Lucretius and the History." Though De Lacy traces some non-Epicurean influences on Lucretius's poem, he does not specifically mention animal sacrifice.

42. See in particular Montarese, *Lucretius and His Sources*. The study, for all its

Physiologia and the Psychodynamics of Epicurean Theology   119

of Epicurus's ideas can be noted in Lucretius's poem, it is its more explicitly social and political critique of the current status quo, that is, the Roman state, one inseparable from the evaluation of religion (obvious in Cicero) as a necessary foundation of Roman political life. As Cicero states, "We must persuade our citizens that the gods are the lords and rulers of all things, and that what is done, is done by their will and authority."[43] Unlike Cicero, Lucretius does not use religion to rationalize earthly rule. On the contrary, he often refers critically to the "utterances of priests,"[44] the very priests who, for Cicero, ensured social order, respect for the law, and continuity of the status quo. Therefore, one cannot read Lucretius's poem without considering it as "an indictment of contemporary life."[45] A more forceful evaluation can be added when Benjamin Farrington writes, "The attack of Lucretius against the gods is a political attack, one aimed comprehensively at the politico-religious institutions of Rome."[46] It now becomes necessary to read Lucretius and to specifically highlight his many and consistent references (all of them critical) to the religious practice of animal sacrifice. Nevertheless, and in relation to Lucretius, Kirk Summers calls Epicurus's support of religious observances, including animal sacrifice, a "paradoxical attitude."[47] Summers believes that the paradox can be resolved by reading a specific passage in Lucretius's *On the Nature of Things*—namely, 5.1198–1203. However, by reading *all* of the relevant passages in Lucretius on his assessment of animal sacrifice, a reader can come to a completely different conclusion, which therefore raises considerable doubt about both Philodemus's testimony in *On Piety* and subsequent scholars who rely on him for evidence of Epicurus's supposed observances of ritual. Lucretius's sustained critique of animal sacrifice as a form of evil *superstitione* (it is more of a condemnation) forms a significant and often repeated part of *On the Nature of Things* and reflects the teachings of his master, Epicurus. Independent and utterly unconcerned with his reputation—or any judicial consequences—Lucretius

---

detail, does not address our main question, that is, what writings by Epicurus, if any, directly influenced Lucretius's critique of sacrifice.

43. Cicero, *Leg.*, 2.7.
44. Lucretius, *DRN.*, 1.104.
45. Taylor, "Progress and Primitivism," 190.
46. Farrington, *Head and Hand*, 109. See in particular chapter 4, "The Gods of Epicurus and the Roman State."
47. Summers, "Lucretius and the Epicurean Tradition," 32. At issue is whether Lucretius's rejection of cult practices, and especially animal sacrifice, is in "stark contrast"(43) to Epicurus. Summers further adds: "Lucretius's stance toward cult at 5.1198–1203 diverges so starkly from Epicurus's attitude about religion that many consider it a temporary aberration," 45. Lucretius is unwavering and consistent; the "aberration" may be better applied to how Epicurus has been interpreted thus far.

dared to write a more explicit, and certainly more emotional, critique of animal sacrifice than anyone before him.

First of all, and adding a significant relation to an idea initially discussed at length by Epicurus in his *Letter to Pythocles*, Lucretius believes that the divine is "itself mighty by its own resources, needing us not at all, it is neither propitiated with services nor touched by wrath."[48] Lucretius's theology shows no difference whatsoever from Epicurus. He immediately dismisses the long-held belief that the gods require anything from human beings (they are not swayed in our favor by any acts deemed pious or holy), nor are they in any way prone to emotional changes, as if they were vulnerable to *pathe*, the feelings so intrinsic to human beings and responsible for their emotional vicissitudes. As blessed beings, the gods are not vulnerable to changes in mood; their equanimity is constant. For Epicurus, the gods are *blessed*, are characterized by a state of being that is unchanging (unmoving in themselves, unmoved by anything or anyone outside themselves), and therefore require no *eulogia*, acknowledgment, prayer, or ritual. They can have no need, no desire, because they must be necessarily complete. Lucretius's poem begins with a reevaluation of current beliefs related to superstition and attributing his belief to his teacher Epicurus whose ideas allowed others to see that "superstition (*religio*) is now in her turn cast down and trampled underfoot, while we by the victory are exalted high as heaven" (1.78–79). The ascent to heaven is now no longer a mere attempt by human beings to defy the will of the gods and to abolish the services previously given to them, as in the myth by Aristophanes in Plato's *Symposium*; nor is the ascent a turning away from the body or nature to somehow reach the *monoeides*, as in Diotima's ladder of love that announces Plato's metaphysical aspirations. Rather, in and through philosophy, human beings can now begin to rightly claim the possibility of leading a life of self-sufficiency independent of any belief in the gods, much less anxiously expecting a reciprocal exchange that, at the best of times, was volatile and certainly never guaranteed by the gods—uncertain in Homer's *Iliad* as well as Hesiod's *Theogony*, and in the Hebrew Bible as exemplified by Cain's anguished disappointment when his offering was rejected by God. Biblical Jews and pious Greeks had created a theology of service. Greek philosophers undermined such a traditional position no differently than the prophets.

The ascent to heaven described by Lucretius is repeated by one of his readers—the poet Virgil, who knew Siro the Epicurean[49] and who frequented the Villa Herculaneum where Philodemus taught as well as took

---

48. Lucretius, *DRN.*, 1.47–49.
49. Donatus, *Vita.*, 79.

care of an extensive library, volumes and fragments of which have survived the cataclysmic eruption of Vesuvius and continue to be restored. In his *Catalepton*, Virgil writes, "We are spreading sail for blissful heaven, in quest of noble Siro's learned lore, and will free our life from worries (*vitamque ab omni vindicabimus cura*),"[50] an ascent, furthermore, ending in what he calls a *cura*. The psychotherapeutic consequences of Epicurean philosophy have been inherited and acknowledged by the Roman poets, not only Lucretius, but also, significantly, Virgil and Ovid, the latter of whom, in several different works including *Metamorphoses* and in relation to Pythagoras, criticizes meat-eating and, therefore, the commensality associated with animal sacrifice. The Stoic philosopher Seneca would develop the philosophy of ascension insofar as the individual guided by wisdom "is the equal of the gods; he strives toward heaven, mindful of his origins. No one is wrong in attempting to ascend to the place from which he has descended"[51]—though Epicurus would reject any such ascension literally understood and defined by a particular *topos*. The *idea* of ascension would be nullified if it had any relation at all to a real place, a physically attainable location.

Lucretius is aware that the demands of philosophy have, since its inception and with many examples, led to individuals being persecuted and killed, hence his fear that Memmius, his first intended reader, and others subsequently reading his poem, may be in danger due to being suspected of (or even charged with) impiety when he writes, "one thing I fear in this matter, that in this your apprenticeship to philosophy you may perhaps see impiety (*sceleris*)," (1.83) a term including being accursed, evil and, most significantly in a Roman context, criminal. Impiety was a crime. The always prevalent judicial threat, historically well known and especially now from a Roman political state so intertwined with its religious beliefs, made Lucretius aware of the possible consequences of his Epicurean poem. Lucretius does not reject the important aspect of authentic *pietas*; rather, *pietas* must be separated from the tradition of Roman *religio*, as Minyard[52] points out. Authentic piety and holiness can still be possible as long as the traditional beliefs about the gods are reappraised and ultimately abandoned, at least insofar as they contribute to a certain kind of life and practice. Without the slightest hesitation, and in this case being even more brazen than either Socrates or Epicurus himself, Lucretius rather makes the argument that the actions which were deemed pious in the past have been precisely the opposite. "It is the very Superstition which has brought forth criminal and impi-

50. Virgil, *Catal.*, LCL 64:488–489.
51. Seneca, *Ep.*, 92.29.30.
52. Minyard. *Lucretius and the Late Republic*.

ous deeds," (1.83–85) he states provocatively. Lucretius begins a systematic critique of sacrifice with, first, the sacrifice of a daughter, and then includes a mother separated from her calf, sacrifices for the dead, for the desired birth of a child and, finally, to the plague of Athens.

His first example of an impious deed is none other than the sacrifice of Iphigenia, a deed performed by her father Agamemnon to ensure that the ships about to embark would reach their destination. According to David Furley, Lucretius's reference to the sacrifice of a child seems reminiscent of Empedocles (fr. B137) condemning the act of animal slaughter, and although Lucretius, as an Epicurean, rejects Empedocles's reasons (that a father unwittingly kills his son whose soul has transmigrated into an ox), he nevertheless upholds the condemnation of animal slaughter. As Monica Gale writes, "Lucretius seems to have shared Empedocles's abhorrence for animal sacrifice."[53] There is no doubt as to his abhorrence once the relevant sections are consulted and shown to be specifically organized and interrelated. "So potent was superstition in persuading evil deeds," Lucretius writes, now adding that the reader of his poem may still be vulnerable to the priests whose teachings and acts—none more intimidating than the prospects of a terrifying afterlife—can persuade others. Throughout the poem, Lucretius repeats and expands on the teaching of Epicurus, or rather provides a much-needed addition to no-longer-extant Epicurean texts. More important than a confirmation of his teachings remains the single most important question: Are there any indications in Lucretius that he rejects animal sacrifice *as an Epicurean idea*?

In one of the most moving passages in the whole of the poem, Lucretius describes the relationship of animals to each other in terms of love and empathy, in this case a mother and her calf that have been separated from each other:

> For often in front of the noble shrines of the gods a calf falls slain beside the incense-burning altars breathing up a hot stream of blood from his breast; but the mother bereaved wanders through the green glens, and seeks on the ground the prints marked by the cloven hooves, as she surveys all the regions if

---

53. Gale, *Myth and Poetry in Lucretius*, 72. Although it is not possible here to comment at length on the polemic written against Empedocles by Hermarchus, the scholarch who succeeded Epicurus, one note should be made. In the treatise entitled *Against Empedocles*, and referred to in Porphyry's *On Abstinence from Killing Animals*, Hermarchus specifically criticizes Empedocles for his defense of animals. In "Hermarchus, against Empedocles," Obbink writes: "in our more extensive passage, Empedocles comes under attack for his view that a fellowship between mankind and irrational animals exists which makes it unjust to slay or sacrifice them," 432.

she may espy somewhere her lost offspring, and coming to a
stand fills the leafy woods with her moaning, and often revisits
the stall, pierced with yearning for her calf. (2.353–367)

However much Socrates may have turned against the practice of animal sacrifice, there are no indications of any of his *feelings* involved, none of the poignancy of emotion displayed by Lucretius regarding the welfare of animals. The Roman poet, however, has no hesitation when revealing a range of intense emotions for an animal that has no corresponding example in any of Plato's writing and in the portrayal of the quintessential rational philosopher. Although Plato's dialogues are filled with references to animals (and their excellent characteristics) and are often used as examples to elaborate on a particular topic being discussed, there are no emotions for them evident, unlike Lucretius who was obviously someone with profound feelings and transformed them into poetic ideas. By the time of Lucretius, and even more intriguingly in the poetry of Ovid, the concern for the welfare of animals, especially in the context of sacrifice, had become preeminent.[54] What did this show? Two points, at least. First, in Roman society there was now an awareness by some, and surely not only poets, that by virtue of their intelligence and emotions, animals deserved to be treated with much more solicitude than was the case, both because of their wholesale slaughter in the Roman amphitheatre and in their continued victimization in sacrifice. And second, there was an accompanying validation of the importance of nature and pastoral agriculture that countered the importance of the urban center in the Roman empire.

In Lucretius, animal slaughter in a religious context is emphasized for its violence and killing, but more importantly, testifies to the emotions of the mother, who is capable of mourning the loss of her young and expressing it in visceral moaning. Animals experience emotional pain and loss. The poetic sensitivity of Lucretius therefore appeals to human emotions and the awareness of causing death and suffering to an animal that becomes a victim. As Charles Saylor writes, "the victim is totally innocent and of a wholly different order from man who sacrifices it; the animal, at least, should be beyond the realm of evil stimulated by *religio*."[55] Again stressing the animal as a victim, Lee Fratantuono writes, "the calf is a victim of the worship of the

---

54. Especially important has been Steven Green's argument, in "Save Our Cows?" that Ovid's poem takes up an already existing debate on the dubious merits of animal sacrifice and, in Ovid's case, uses the argument as a "direct political affront to the emperor" (41) Augustus. The critique of *superstitio*, then, involves a critique of the priests who were officially elected, up to and including the office of the emperor. As in Lucretius, the critique of animal sacrifice is a political and religious critique.

55. Saylor, "Man, Animal, and the Bestial," 307.

immortals and the rites devoted to them."[56] Given his earlier and repeated affirmation of the nature of the gods (that they require nothing from us, and certainly do not engage in a reciprocal exchange of gifts), Lucretius's empathic example simultaneously brings into doubt the nature of civic rituals. Far from representing mere reason as preeminent in the philosophy of Epicurus, being empathic and understanding our relationship to nature and sentient beings becomes equally important. Lucretius repeats an earlier affirmation by Epicurus, virtually quoting him verbatim, and writes that the gods are "mighty by its own resources, needing us not at all, it is neither propitiated with services nor touched by wrath" (2.650–651). The logic of sacrifice as a reciprocal service is completely undermined.

The emotional appeal only begins his several references to animal sacrifice. At the beginning of Book 3, again personally addressing his poem to Epicurus, he first of all writes that "your reasoning begins to proclaim the nature of things revealed by your divine mind," (3.14–16) so that his *ratio* leads to certain insights necessary for the enhancement of human life. Despite Epicurean teaching however, there are still many who cling to the "fear of Acheron," (3.37) who fear a particular kind of affliction and thereby lead their lives according to the expectation of calamity. How do they respond? "In spite of all, wherever the wretches go they sacrifice to their ancestors, and slay black cattle, and send down oblations to departed ghosts, and in their bitter days direct their minds more eagerly to superstition (*religionem*)" (3.51–54).

In addition to the always threatening expectation of death and other bodily afflictions, there are equally worrying calamities such as the inability to father a child, which was extremely difficult for those who wanted to be representative of a model citizen and therefore not cursed, which was so different from an important strand of early Christianity and the social and political reasons for avoiding both marriage and childbirth, that is, the refusal to contribute to the continuity of Roman society. Lucretius provides a scientific explanation for a man being unable to father a child, so that even if he is able to produce either thin or thick semen, they still cannot impregnate; and "although it penetrate, does not easily mix with the woman's seed" (4.1249–1250). What do some men do as a result? For their inability to generate life, they turn to the death of an animal offered to god as a response. With noticeable irony, Lucretius adds:

---

56. Fratantuono, *Reading of Lucretius's De Rerum Natura*, 108. Lucretius scholars (unlike many modern historians of religion) have no difficulty using specific language. Like Burkert, Girard, and the "Paris school," animals are seen as *victims*.

Physiologia and the Psychodynamics of Epicurean Theology 125

> It is not the divine powers that drive away the genital force from a man, so that he be never called father by sweet children and that he pass his days in barren wedlock, as men for the most part think, sorrowfully sprinkling their altars with much blood and making them burn with offerings, that they may make their wives pregnant with abundant seed. It is all vanity that they weary the gods' power and magic lots. (4.1233–1241)

Lucretius begins to bring his poem to a conclusion when he reiterates the one guiding principle of Epicurean philosophy, to achieve *ataraxia*. He insists that a tranquil mind cannot be achieved by a belief in the ability of the gods to intervene and bless a human being. There are no acts deemed *pious* that can beneficially influence someone's life. Outward acts are irrelevant; anticipating a fundamental idea of early Christianity and forcefully in the Pauline epistles, only the interior work of what he calls the *anima* can contribute to a healthy life:

> It is no piety to show oneself often with covered head, turning toward a stone and approaching every altar, none to fall prostrate upon the ground and to spread open the palms before shrines of the gods, none to sprinkle altars with the blood of beasts in showers and to link vow to vow; but rather to be able to survey all things with tranquil mind. (5.1198–1203)

In *On the Nature of Things*, Lucretius has been a crucial addition to Epicurean ideas that are not explicitly mentioned in any of the extant writings, however much they can be inferred from his teaching. In the several examples of animal sacrifice in his poem, Lucretius has been insistent: sacrifice can in no way be considered an act of authentic piety. Furthermore, Lucretius shows his adherence to Epicureanism by once again emphasizing the relationship of *physiologia* to theology. In one particular case and in a discussion on the natural as opposed to the superstition cause of lightning, he mentions how many consider a place struck by lightning as defiled. A place struck by lightning was called a *bidental* (related to *bidentes*, animals for sacrifice) and in order for the site to be purified an animal had to be sacrificed on the spot.[57]

Finally, in Book 6 and the account of the plague that devastated Athens, Lucretius confronts the poetic precursor who influenced the image of the gods. In Book I of the *Iliad*, with the overwhelming carnage of the plague, Achilles tells the terrified army that Apollo Phoebus, being angered, might be appeased. They believe their present calamity has been sent by him—but

---

57. I am indebted to Ellery Leonard and Barney Smith for this reference and their very erudite edition, with an introduction and commentary, of *De Rerum Natura*.

they are ignorant of the reason, human beings at a loss to understand divine motivations. Achilles needs to turn to a prophet, priest, or diviner of dreams so as to "find out from him why Phoebus Apollo is so angry with us. He may be offended at some broken vow or some failure in our rites. If so, he might accept a savoury offering of sheep or of full-grown goats and save us from the plague" (1.99–105). In his account in *On the Nature of Things*, the plague of Athens is described as a natural phenomenon and has no divine origin or intent. For all its hardship and devastation, the plague is a natural occurrence that is experienced and endured as another unavoidable aspect of life, so that human beings suffer and prevail, on their own, by virtue of the human commitment to each other, to the living and to the memories of the dead. One final indication of Epicurus's independence from the rituals and observances of Athens was the tradition (after his death, as well as other members) of celebrating the birthdays of Epicurean individuals. Stowers tells us that "only the Epicureans developed their own rituals,"[58] an important insight and one possibly replacing other, city-sanctioned festivals. In other words, Epicurean individuals were to be uniquely celebrated within the community of friends and as an alternative to the polis religion of the city. Significant individuals were more worthy of being celebrated and remembered than the gods.

Although the critique of animal sacrifice in Lucretius's *The Nature of Things* has been unequivocal and in agreement with several ancient sources, the other Epicurean that leaves us with a significant, and quite different if not completely contradictory, testimony is Philodemus of Gadara. Dirk Obbink points out that any evaluation of Epicurus's theology must take into consideration the writings of the individual whose reconstructed fragments survive from the library at Herculaneum, principally *On Piety*. Unfortunately Philodemus's allegiance to Epicurean philosophy becomes highly questionable once the relevant fragments are examined. Does Philodemus accurately represent Epicurus's theology as thought and practiced during his life? Or is he an apologist in the Roman context of necessary religious observances who, aware of the many criticisms leveled at the Hellenistic philosopher, finds it necessary to neglect some of the most important Epicurean principles and ultimately distort and misrepresent his teaching? My conclusion overall is as follows: an examination of Philodemus's *On Piety* shows him to have seriously misrepresented Epicurus's philosophy, most especially his critique of religion and, in particular, the ritual of sacrifice. Obbink's contribution is instructive because it raises one fundamental problem—the one most in need of being solved. Here then is the apparent

---

58. Stowers, "Does Pauline Christianity Resemble?," 101.

inconsistency and contradiction: How could Epicurus so reject the traditional conception of the gods and still believe that sacrifice had a specific purpose that could still be maintained? We are left with a dilemma—one that requires further consideration, most especially because the majority of modern commentators believe this to be the case. Obbink's belief that Epicurus urged his followers to participate in religious festivals (and, therefore, in sacrificial ritual) can be traced only to Philodemus. A. J. Festugière agrees and writes that Epicurus participated in "traditional acts of worship" and, more specifically, "loyally observed all the traditional feasts and sacrifices."[59] Marcello Gigante defends Philodemus's "faithful" representation of Epicurean thought, though he never mentions specifically such practices as animal sacrifice despite emphasizing the well-known advice to avoid public life and, especially, politics.[60] The conclusion presents the most difficult problem. Epicurus insisted repeatedly that the problem with theology was not the existence of the gods, but rather the conceptions the many had of them which were based on false assumptions and consequently led them to misconstrue the characteristics of the gods and, more importantly, their own lives. How could Epicurus make such an argument and then urge his followers to "demonstrate their piety by participating in public religious festivals?" How could he make his criticism of religion in terms of its belief but condone (or actually encourage) social observances?

Can the teacher at Herculaneum whose reconstructed manuscript has come down to us be decisive in our understanding of how Epicurus and his philosophy viewed animal sacrifice? The following will be an attempt to answer this one question. Whether Epicurus was indicted on a charge of impiety remains conjecture. He certainly had numerous critics. Whether Philodemus's treatise faithfully represents Epicurus's ideas also remain a matter of debate, especially considering his historical context, that is, living and teaching in Italy within the Roman state and depending on the much-needed support of a patron who could support his intellectual endeavors.[61] If Epicurus must be regarded in his writings on the gods as necessarily countercultural and certainly in opposition to the prevailing ideas held by

59. Festugière, *Epicurus and His Gods*, 59. Once again, there is only one source for this assertion.

60. Gigante, *Philodemus in Italy*, 24.

61. Gigante writes that Philodemus "did not refuse to be integrated into the social structure of the time and to conform to the conditions of the late Roman republic," 30. He also quotes from a work by Ettore Paratore who, in *Epicureanism and its Diffusion in the Latin World*, writes that Philodemus's testimony is "weakened by the suspicion of dishonest opportunism," 7. He is not the only one to bring attention to Philodemus's possible accommodation of Epicurean ideas for his Roman audience, largely made up of aristocrats and patrons.

the many, it is difficult to believe that he would have acted completely counter to his ideas in relationship to the participation in cult practices—animal sacrifice being, for us, the most important. How can Epicurus make it clear that the gods do not interact with human beings in any way whatsoever (and they are certainly not providential) while, at the same time and in obvious contradiction, advocate participation in a ritual that was wholly intended to be reciprocal? One cannot, as some have suggested, publicly write in opposition to what he calls the many while participating with them in religious observances for the sake of maintaining a stable relationship with his neighbors. In several sections of Lucretius's On the Nature of Things, the critique and rejection of animal sacrifice was clear, even when such a viewpoint would be considered impious and lead to prosecution. Philodemus was more than aware that, teaching in the Roman state and being supported by a patron as illustrious as Siro, he had to assume certain well-prescribed and expected obligations. And whereas Lucretius also knew that philosophy could be perceived as "entering a path of crime," (1.82) Philodemus avoided any such danger by revising Epicurus's teaching so that it would be acceptable to the majority of his Roman audience.

There are several sections in Philodemus's On Piety that are, in my estimation, a gross misrepresentation of Epicurus's philosophy, so when Obbink once again mentions "the Epicurean defense of such traditional religious forms as prayer, oath, sacrifice, and mystery initiation elaborated by Philodemus in the first part of On Piety,"[62] such a belief, shared by the majority of commentators (though there are exceptions) must now be reconsidered, most especially because of the highly questionable assertions made by him about Epicurus in his treatise. Since many of the points made by Philodemus are in fact notes he took when he attended the lectures in Athens by Zeno of Sidon, it seems his powers of concentration (or accuracy, or both) are dubious at best. Of course, the fault may lie with Zeno, though in his defense he does believe some extant Epicurean works may be forgeries—we will never know, as provenance cannot be verified.

In any case, two main points will be examined. First, the theological ideas attributed to Epicurus by Philodemus that I believe can in no way be sustained, and second, whether Epicurus did condone animal sacrifice and encourage his followers to attend religious ceremonies, as Philodemus suggests. For the time being, the examination of On Piety will only highlight the most pressing problems, not the least of which involves distinguishing quote from paraphrase, for one, and most especially in the context of an Epicurean work, Symposium, with fictitious characters.

62. Obbink, "How to Read Poetry," 208.

Physiologia and the Psychodynamics of Epicurean Theology 129

First of all, and expecting his readers to trust what he asserts is his primary source (that is, Epicurus himself) Philodemus quotes him when he writes that "gods are propitious,"[63] (1.33.929) a statement that clearly contradicts every single theological principle of the Hellenistic philosopher, and indeed stands in complete opposition to his many verifiable beliefs. The gods do not participate, in any way, either in the natural or human world, and they certainly do not give (much less expect to receive) any gifts. The gods cannot be propitious. Philodemus then attributes another *inconceivable* thought to Epicurus, and he does so by flagrantly misunderstanding a fundamental belief expressed in the *Letter to Menoeceus*. Philodemus writes, "and in book 13 [of *On Nature*] he speaks concerning the affinity or alienation which God has for some people" (1.37.1053) a thought so incommensurable to Epicurean thought that one wonders how, one, he could so drastically misunderstand his philosophy, and two, then attempt to disseminate this idea when others were certainly in a position to see its obvious error. For Epicurus, the gods do not feel anything for human beings; Philodemus is implying that the gods prefer some individuals and not others, thus placing them in a position of judging, an idea antithetical to the first principle of Epicurus's *tetrapharmakos*. Finally, and testifying he is referring to Epicurus's work *On Holiness*, he once again attributes an impossible thought to him: "and the person who sees also that the good and ill *sent us* by a god come without any unhealthy anger or benevolence." (1.40.1130, my emphasis) He claims as if a god could in fact send something good or bad to influence human life, but yet do so without any emotions, which the gods, for Epicurus, do not feel whatsoever. They do not have *pathe*, the feelings only felt by sentient beings in the world, of nature or society. These are but three references (there are others) in the treatise that misrepresent Epicurus's theology and, more seriously, then undermine his entire philosophy. It is now necessary to read what Philodemus writes specifically about religious observances and, in particular, the practice of animal sacrifice.

For a first consideration, and apparently paraphrasing Epicurus's *On Nature*, Philodemus makes a remarkable statement not dissimilar to Lucretius in *On the Nature of Things* in relation to the consciousness of animals. "Not even the other animals had been deprived of the analogy of disturbance, and because of this animals have the fear of death," (9.239–241) he writes. Epicurus makes the argument that animals too suffer from disturbance, that is, emotions that affect their well-being; and when he makes the related comment that such a disturbance, for human beings, includes their

---

63. Apparently the quote is taken from a letter written by Epicurus to a fellow member of the Garden, Metrodorus. The full extant quote is: "even if there should be war, it would not be terrible, if the gods are propitious."

fear of death, that must also necessarily be true for animals. In other words, animals can be disturbed by their knowledge of death; and though they might have such fear intrinsically, a certain situation of being in proximity to the smell of blood, entrails, flesh, can make them aware of death. Epicurus makes the all-important addition in relation to animals fearing death when he continues from the previous sentence (though there are several words missing) that "similar in extent to this (*one word missing*) about piety (8–10 *words missing*) because at procession and sacrifices (*thusiais*) they arrive at their view of death" (9.241–260). A quite remarkable statement. In addition to the mention of piety, Epicurus writes that animals learn about death during the procession leading to the ritual of sacrifice. He makes them sentient, intelligent, discerning, most especially aware of impending death and therefore fearful and apprehensive most especially when an animal being led to the sacrificial altar would be able to smell the slaughtered animals previously killed. Since an Epicurean was taught to avoid the experience of both psychological and physical pain, then surely to inflict pain and cause suffering was unethical and (most especially in the context of a religious ritual) should be completely renounced—as the Pythagoreans also taught. For how could the violent death of an animal be a mediation between the human and divine realms?

At issue is whether Epicurus's entire philosophy can also be extended to non-human animals, especially those to be slaughtered in apparent service to the gods. Is there an element of Epicurean philosophy, as we saw in Lucretius, that has a particular regard for the welfare of animals? Does Epicurus's teaching extend to our concern for animals? If so, Epicurus does not simply present a rational argument against animal sacrifice in the context of a religious ritual and, as a consequence, determines a certain conception of the divine. Perhaps equally important is the realization of an animal as a sentient being that should not be slaughtered at all, and most especially as part of cultic practice. By extension, then, Epicurus believes preserving the life of an animal to be more important than sacrificing its life as a supposed service to the gods. Furthermore, when Philodemus, apparently *quoting* from another Epicurean work, writes that "human fashion of the connection with the (divine) entity for which worship (*lo[goth]erapeias*) in verbal attendance in cult take place," (20.550) two points must be made. First, Epicurus has long since understood this "*logotherapeia*" to be used in human relationships, and second, the quotation is completely out of context and could, in principle, refer to an argument by Epicurus *against* such a traditional theology. The fragment is simply too ambiguous to be certain of its context, much less its meaning.

A further serious problem arises when Philodemus writes that

Physiologia and the Psychodynamics of Epicurean Theology 131

I think it is especially necessary to despise those who transgress or mock other observances as they do the traditional rites. . . . Furthermore, *it will appear* (*phanesetai*) that Epicurus loyally observed all the forms of worship and enjoined upon his friends to observe them" (25.721–22, 26.731, my emphasis).

Philodemus here makes an assertion, though it may also express doubt and uncertainty. His language is far from convincing. It is inconceivable that Epicurus would have advised his followers to communicate with the gods, (in any way whatsoever, be it through prayer, worship, or sacrifice) when taking into consideration all the unequivocal statements he makes about human beings and the gods. Philodemus, however, attempts to convince his readers otherwise by writing, "and not only did he teach these things but also by his very deeds he is found to have taken part in all the traditional festivals and sacrifices" (28.790–792). Does Philodemus provide such a testimony from Epicurus's own writings? Or, in the context of a polemical treatise also concerned with defending Epicurus while also attacking critics (and there were many) is Philodemus writing as an apologist? It is one thing to possibly attend a festival of the Anthesteria when everyone received a *chous* or wine jar, as Obbink tells us, but it is another to attend a *sphagia* or the ritual killing of animals. However, in a work by Epicurus that Philodemus seems to quote, *On Lifecourses*,[64] the philosopher writes, "'Let us sacrifice to gods', he says, 'devoutly and fittingly on proper days, and let us fittingly perform all acts of worship in accordance with the laws (*kata tous nomous*). . . moreover, let us sacrifice justly' (*dikaio*)" (31.880–891). By "justly," does he possibly mean (as in Socrates's pronouncement) that it should be bloodless, therefore returning to a time that, according to many, only involved the offering of agricultural products such as grains and fruit? This seems to be beyond doubt since a direct quote is provided. Are we left then with a problem difficult reconcile: an untraditional theology seemingly at odds with the prevailing views of the gods held by the many and, at the same time, an upholder of the *nomos* and the *dike* of the city? The direct quotation seems to be incontrovertible, unless we take into consideration one important point: as in other places, the quotations from an Epicurean work may actually be dialogic arguments between speakers (as Cicero will often use) and therefore ideas that cannot be related to Epicurus. On the contrary, he may oppose them. In a tone that dramatically changes from exposition to defense, Philodemus repeatedly stresses that Epicurus cannot be accused of impiety because he upholds the laws (*nomoi*) and com-

---

64. In the *Lives*, Diogenes tells us that the work was on ethics and, more specifically, on a fundamental Epicurean teaching—on choices and avoidances. 10.30.

mon customs of people, once again a statement completely antithetical to everything we know about Epicurus, most especially regarding customs, the very idea he philosophizes against. Are we, in this case, to believe Epicurus's critics (those who accuse him of regarding both the mysteries and festivals as foolishness and with the advice to "do away with the excuse for sacrificial feasting," 50.1428–1429)? Or are we to believe his defender Philodemus, who seems not to faithfully represent the philosophy of Epicurus but instead represents him as a *conformist*? Can we trust Philodemus when, again, he quotes from another Epicurean work—this time, *Symposium*—and attributes this quote to him: "make fine sacrifices to a god" (62.1790–1791)? Philodemus's language is not without its ambiguity. What does he mean by "just" and "fine" sacrifices? The descriptions are too ambiguous to be definitive. However, in a revealing passage (and with a direct quotation from Epicurus in one of his letters to Idomeneus) Plutarch writes, "so send us for the care of our sacred body an offering of first-fruits on behalf of yourself and your children."[65] An extraordinary statement, first because he describes his body as "sacred," and second because first-fruits are always offered to the gods, but in this case he has substituted himself as the one receiving offerings.

One fundamental difference in the presentation of Epicurean ideas remains: always writing as a representative of Epicurean philosophy, Lucretius makes it unequivocal in repeated passages (first and foremost, in his empathy for the anguish of a mother that has lost its sacrificed calf) that all rituals associated with what he calls "superstition" must be abandoned. They are criminal and evil, judgments that are without precedent in the Roman world. Philodemus, on the other hand, perpetuates one view of Epicurus that represents him as a unique thinker in relation to the gods but who nevertheless continued to follow custom and tradition and not only observed age-old practices but also advised his followers to do the same. The two positions are obviously incommensurable. However, if we again recall Epicurus's writings, most especially the relation of *physiologia* to his theology, then it seems inconceivable that he could recommend participating in *any* traditional observances—not unless he can be characterized as

---

65. Plutarch, *Adv. Col.*, 1117d. This extraordinary statement shows Epicurus to have completely substituted pious ideas about the gods as deserving of the first-fruits of sacrifice and, moreover, defined his body itself as "sacred," both ideas that no doubt would be considered extremely impious. More remarkably still, in another co-written letter by Paul and Timothy, they send thanks for "having received of Epaphroditus the things which were sent from you, and odour of a sweet smell, a sacrifice acceptable, well pleasing to God" (Phil 4:18). Both Epicures and the early founders of Christianity had rejected traditional observances and, moreover, appropriated the rhetoric of sacrifice so as to transform its meaning.

inconsistent and self-serving, indeed even cynical. To regard Epicurus as a religious conformist (*in deed*) when his philosophy articulates again and again a rethinking of all forms of religion is to regard him, finally, as no longer worthy of being read.[66] How can Epicurus be (wrongly) represented as *traditionally pious* when he writes, in *Vatican Saying* 65, that "it is pointless to ask from the gods what one is fully able to supply for oneself?" The raison d' être of animal sacrifice was to receive back from the gods—*do ut des*, the giving so that the gods would do likewise. A fundamental Epicurean philosophical position (and also a cornerstone of his theology) emphasized, first of all, the nonparticipation of the gods in the lives of human beings, and second, the *autarkeia* or self-sufficiency so necessary for a life of independence and freedom. In *Vatican Saying* 77, Epicurus writes, "the greatest fruit of self-sufficiency (*autarkeias*) is freedom." One could not, therefore, sacrifice to the gods and be self-sufficient. Furthermore, to sacrifice to the gods meant nothing less than the abnegation of one's freedom, which would be an impossibility for Epicurus and for his philosophy.

Finally, two more classical writers will be consulted—not so much to learn about Epicurus's philosophy in relation to religion in general and animal sacrifice in particular (they are too one-sided to be accepted as accurate) but to see how and for what reasons Cicero and Plutarch so vehemently criticized the Hellenistic philosopher—a criticism, moreover, that in the case of Plutarch appears contradictory. In his polemic against Colotes, one of Epicurus's more well-known followers, Plutarch concentrates on several interrelated religious ideas. Of course, Plutarch was himself a priest in the sanctuary at Delphi and therefore had both religious and personal reasons for his polemic, not, again, so different from Cicero who was also affiliated with the college of priests of Rome. In *Against Colotes*, Plutarch first of all criticizes the fundamental Epicurean idea that the gods "care nothing for our affairs,"[67] and second, accuses Epicureans "of a godless negligence and recklessness, when you tear away from the gods that appellations attached

---

66. One final note is necessary: the overwhelmingly difficult task of treating the fragmented remains of the charred papyri is an indication of how necessary a more complete reading of Philodemus's treatise on piety (and his other works) is necessary. Obbink's commentary on the text is invaluable since he recognizes how missing letters, words, and entire sections make any interpretation far from conclusive. An example is instructive. He translates one quite compromised section as "the deity that is evident and honored in ritual observance" (48.1389–90), but then adds that "ritual observance" may be "in intelligent contemplation." Here, *in nuce*, is the problem: intelligently contemplating the gods was certainly an Epicurean concern; one could share in their immortality by doing so. Honoring the gods in a ritual observance such as animal sacrifice, however, seems antithetical to all his teachings.

67. Plutarch, *Adv. Col*, 1108D.

to them and by that single act *annihilate all sacrifices*, mysteries, processions, and festivals" (1119E, my emphasis). As a consequence of his particular beliefs in the gods, Epicureans are presented as destroying the idea of sacrifices (the first in the list) and all other observances associated with religious commemoration, namely mysteries, processions, and festivals. Plutarch here presents Epicureans as refusing to acknowledge the importance of the social observances of the polis religion. Their independence from all participation in the civic life of the city was consistent with their self-imposed isolation from the status quo. Plutarch's accusation, however, is contradicted by Festugière who claims that Epicurus "loyally observed all the traditional feasts and sacrifices,"[68] a belief that can only be supported by relying solely on the writings of Philodemus (as we saw) and more importantly ignoring Epicurus's philosophy, first of all, and the writings of Lucretius in *On the Nature of Things*. Ancient and modern sources deepen the apparent dilemma. In his chapter on Plutarch, Luke Johnson writes that Epicureans "withdrew from participation in the civic cults."[69] Stanley Stowers writes that "even a superficial look at nonsacrificers in Greco-Roman society shows that withdrawing from sacrificial practice meant also forming alternative societies."[70] He goes on to add: "Particular nonsacrificers will likely share conditions that distinguish them from sacrificers."[71] This is at least one more consideration for believing that Epicureans did not sacrifice. Their community was, for them as well as their critics (indeed, they were vilified for it), an alternative to the way most other people lived.

In another polemical writing, Plutarch presents Epicurus differently, in effect accusing him of an unacceptable contradiction, indeed an unpardonable hypocrisy:

> Out of fear of public opinion, Epicurus goes through a mummery of prayers and obeisance that he has no use for and pronounces words that run counter to his philosophy; when he sacrifices, the priest at his side who immolates the victim is to him a butcher; and when it is over he goes away with Menander's words on his lips: "I sacrificed to gods who heed me not." For this is the comedy that Epicurus thinks we should play, and not spoil the pleasure of the multitude or make ourselves unpopular with them by showing dislike ourselves for what others delight in doing. . . . Here, the Epicureans are themselves no better

---

68. Festugière, *Epicurus and His Gods*, 59.
69. Johnson, *Among the Gentiles*, 110.
70. Stowers, "Greeks Who Sacrificed," 331.
71. Ibid., 331.

than they, since they do the same from fear and do not even get the measure of happy anticipation that the others have, but are merely scared and worried that this deception and fooling of the public might be found out, with an eye to whom their books *On the Gods* and *On Piety* have been composed, "in twisted spirals, slanted and askew," as in fear they cover up and conceal their real beliefs.[72]

In this case, Plutarch presents Epicurus as someone who did attend religious festivals and animal sacrifice "out of fear of public opinion." But this again runs counter to everything we know of Epicurus's philosophy and writings, most especially in the doctrine of being indifferent to the opinions of others and the beliefs of the many. Plutarch's assessment of Epicurus—what he may have read (for one, from Cicero) and heard more than three centuries after the death of the Hellenistic philosopher—cannot be sustained.

Cicero in fact anticipates Plutarch's polemic by virtually pointing out the same faults—the indifference of the gods to human life and his overturning the altars and temples of the gods:

> It is true that Epicurus wrote books about the sanctity of the gods and the need for reverence toward them. But what does he actually say? He writes in such a style that one would imagine that one was listening to some high priest such as Cronucianus or Scaevola and not to the man who destroyed the whole foundation of religious faith and *overturned the altars and the temples of the gods*—not by brute force, as Xerxes did, but by force of argument. How can you say that mankind should revere the gods, if the gods themselves not only have no care for man, but care for nothing whatsoever and have no influence on anything?[73]

"But what does he actually say?" Cicero asks, making the attempt to clarify Epicurus's belief. On the one hand, he writes on the sanctity of the gods and a pious response to them. Cicero accuses him of using a style (that is, he accuses him of sophistic rhetoric) by pointing out that he sounds like a high priest, but is in fact "the man who destroyed the whole foundation of religious faith and overturned the altars and temples of the gods." In his argument, Epicurus is portrayed as someone who rejected what had been said about the gods but, more importantly, overturned the altars where animal sacrifice has been performed. By Cicero's account, it would seem

---

72. Plutarch, *Non Posse*, 1102B.
73. Cicero, *Nat. D.*, 1.14.115, my emphasis.

that Epicurus certainly did not participate in cultic practice. But more than that, his philosophy cannot be separated from its critique of all forms of traditional religion because, in fact, it continued to determine the limits of human life and restrained its possibilities.

Finally, it is difficult to accept Kirk Summers's description of Epicurus's "paradoxical attitude,"[74] most especially when his writings are evaluated for consistency and ultimate purpose. It is ultimately impossible to accept Bernard Frischer's statement (in my estimate, correct) that Epicureanism was a "historical criticism of all existing states and of practical secession into a nearly autonomous alternative community"[75] but then to add, as writers both ancient and modern argue, that Epicurus observed the traditional observances he deemed to be mere superstition and ultimately detrimental to human life. That is not paradoxical; it is philosophically fatal. Epicurus's critique of animal sacrifice should be restored to its central place and as a ritual to be abolished and replaced with the philosophical doctrines of a thinker whose fundamental and all-important concern was his devotion to the psychological well-being of others.

Thus far, in the case of Socrates, his rejection of animal sacrifice and his philosophical rethinking of the meaning of *therapeia* were both a rejection of the civic ritual and the transformation of religious sensibility toward the psychological care of others. In the preceding discussion, Epicurus's *physiologia* and theology involved a thorough analysis of the polis religion of Athens and provided the possibility of an implicit critique of sacrifice; given the importance of Epicurus's theology in his overall philosophy, a defense (and participation) in animal sacrifice would be completely antithetical to his most fervently held beliefs. Beginning with Philodemus's *On Piety*, however, to the majority of modern commentators, there are numerous counter-claims that must be considered—a similar problem, as we shall see, in the case of Jesus. In the following chapter, Epicurus's philosophy as fundamentally therapeutic will be examined in order to include him in the tradition beginning with Socrates, one that will extend through Hellenism and become prominent in the teachings of Jesus. Once again we recall the origins of a history in both Judaism and Greece, in the words of the prophets

---

74. Summers, "Lucretius and the Epicurean Tradition," 32. At issue is whether Lucretius's rejection of cult practices, and especially animal sacrifice, is in "stark contrast" (43) to Epicurus. Summers further adds: "Lucretius's stance toward cult at 5.1198–1203 diverges so starkly from Epicurus's attitude about religion that many consider it a temporary aberration," 45. In fact, there is no discrepancy at all between Epicurus and Lucretius *unless* the testimony of Philodemus (and the contradictory statements by Plutarch) are taken to be accurate. In my estimate, they are not. Modern commentators, such as Festugière, are even less reliable.

75. Frischer, *Sculpted Word*, 35.

and the philosophers, and the rejection of animal sacrifice and substituting it with a piety based on the creation of a language dedicated to the healing, the soteriology, of others and ultimately an entire community.

CHAPTER 4

Epicurus's *Logotherapeia* and the Health of the Psyche

1. True Philosophy, True Health

IF THE SIMULTANEOUS AND related study of *physiologia* and theology was intended as a foundation of Epicurus's thought—beginning with an uncreated cosmos, a regenerative nature with its own internal and self-sufficient principles, and the blessed gods conceived differently than as currently worshipped in the *polis*—the single most important aspect of his philosophy is announced in the opening lines of his *Letter to Menoeceus*:

> Let no one delay the study of philosophy while young nor weary of it when old. For no one is either too young or too old for the health of the soul (*kata psuchen ugiainon*). (10.122)

Epicurus emphasizes two interrelated aspects of the philosophical life: the diagnosis and reasons for the maladies of the psyche (which will have two distinct origins), and the subsequent healing and, in principle, permanent health to be enjoyed as an ultimate rather than a fleeting pleasure. Once he attempted to relieve people of false suppositions and superstitious beliefs related to the gods and the services required for their worship (the animal sacrifice essential to the identity of the polis), Epicurus turned to his fundamental calling and purpose: to care for others.

Epicurus lived most of his adult life in Athens and in the Epicurean school known as the Garden (*kepos*), a name indicative of their commitment to the natural world and, perhaps, a place where they grew some of their own food, essentially creating a set of philosophical doctrines (and, more importantly, a way of life *together*) whose ultimate intent was to transform the human perception of the gods, all reality both cosmological and natural, and of the psyche so as to achieve the health of the soul, individually, and in relation to others. Philosophy as Epicurus explicitly defines it has one preeminent concern: not simply an *individual* pursuit of wisdom and all its consequences, but the taking care of the psychological health of others. "Epicurus uniquely framed *all* philosophical questions," Bernard Frischer writes, "in a psychological context."[1] More specifically, A. A. Long has emphasized "the therapeutic aspect of his [Epicurus's] psychology."[2] Many simply refer to it as a *philosophia medicans* and as a "therapy of the soul."[3] Epicurus recognized a pressing need and dedicated himself to alleviating the pain and suffering he believed to be widespread and largely avoidable, differentiating the endurable experiences of illness, disease, injury, and old age from the avoidable suffering human beings so often inflicted on themselves and others due in large part to their compulsive and therefore misunderstood desires, and an adherence to the norms and traditional beliefs of the city as it enforced a socialization almost impossible to resist. Human vulnerability was many-sided, and it one analyzes the interrelationship of Epicurus's philosophical concepts, they are all comprehensively dedicated to understanding how the psychological relationship of feelings to perception, the conditions of existence such as chance and necessity, and last but not least, a philosophical *justice* as opposed to the laws, institutions, and values of the polis, were all necessary before the achievement of *ataraxia*, being free from the disturbances of the psyche. Tim O'Keefe's belief that "Epicurus's ethics is egoistic and hedonistic"[4] can certainly be open to doubt once we realize that the ethical care for others was essential to his therapeutic philosophy. Pleasure could not be experienced if one simply accepted the pain and suffering of *others*. In order to begin the philosophical effort toward such an *ataraxia*, for an individual and in his and her relationships, Epicurus decided to establish a community of like-minded people who could collectively dedicate themselves to one ultimate aim. Once the school transferred itself from various other locations to finally settle in Ath-

1. Frischer, *Sculpted Word*, 72, my emphasis.

2. Long, *Hellenistic Philosophy*, 49. Unlike Epicurus's religious views, most especially on animal sacrifice, the therapeutic aspect of his philosophy provides no possibility of disagreement. The tradition of healing in Epicureanism extends from its origins until the end—at least in terms of the last surviving Epicurean writing, the inscription by Diogenes of Oenoanda in the second century.

3. See Voelke's *La philosophie comme thérapie*.

4. O'Keefe, *Epicurus on Freedom*, 21.

ens, Epicurus did so as nothing less, according to Giovanni Reale, than the beginning of a "spiritual revolution."[5]

First and foremost, the Garden as a community was, if not *directly* in opposition to the city, certainly independent of its values and institutions. Its location was much closer to the countryside than the *agora* or other civic places, as if their place between the city and the natural world reflected their philosophy. Partly due to his upbringing on the colony of Samos, and partly because of a naturally independent temperament, Epicurus established the community so as to reconceive the meaning of human being and social life, and it was done through relationships and in intimate conversation. Laertius describes the reputation Epicurus had in terms of his kindness to others, his solicitude, and most especially in a certain kind of speaking that, historically, had developed beginning with the pre-Socratics. For if the therapeutic logos was evident in such philosophers as Pythagoras in his "golden words" and Empedocles in his "healing utterances," and in the speech of Socrates capable of "transporting" people like Alcibiades with the beauty of his words, Epicurus's followers were "transfixed by the siren-song of his teachings."[6] It is not simply that "the Epicurean tradition lay great stress on conversation,"[7] Epicurus must have developed a language oriented to others and, specifically, to elicit from them what Philodemus would soon call the responsibility inherent in the *parresia* previously used by Socrates's students, the "bold speaking" not simply as a political expression of the free citizen, but as the ability to critically self-examine one's presuppositions, beliefs, and *convictions*. Epicurus essentially transformed the *logotherapeia* previously dedicated to the verbal worship of the gods (in prayer, for example) into a therapeutic language in the service of others, in face-to-face conversation, in the Garden, and extended in his written letters called his "communal epistolary psychagogy"[8] by Clarence Glad. Epicurus's letters were not simply intended to be pedagogical—though they certainly served to teach—but when read (and heard), his words were intended to be hortatory and salvific, a feature later shared by the co-written letters of Paul and Timothy.

For the first time—and this contributes to Epicurus being recognized as a philosopher with a much more comprehensive aim than the mere

---

5. Reale, *Il pensiero antico*, 293.

6. Diogenes Laertius, *Lives.*, 10.9. It might be appropriate to note that Epicurus's speech to those in the community was quite different than in his writings directed at other, rival philosophers. Here one can notice a polemical attitude, one emulated by other thinkers in the Garden.

7. Sedgwick, *Art of Happiness*, 141.

8. Glad, *Paul and Philodemus*, 176.

attainment of knowledge or in the catch-all word *philosophia*—he establishes his fundamental principle of healing others while, at the same time, disassociating himself from other rival philosophies. For all his reputed tranquillity, Epicurus's writings were often polemical in nature and he is not above insults and name-calling. He would have been familiar with the philosophy of his contemporary Pyrrho of Elis, and though they did share some principles in common (such as the ideal of "unberturbedness" or quietude, an ideal already evident in Democritus's *On Tranquillity*[9]) scepticism, epistemologically understood, held no attraction for him.[10] "One must not pretend to philosophize, but to philosophize in reality," Epicurus begins in *Vatican Saying* 54, in effect rejecting other competing thoughts as not even deserving of the name philosophy. As for Aristuppus and the Cyrenaics, Epicurus disagreed that the pains of the body were worse than the pains of the psyche. The psyche may be troubled by the past, present, and future, at any time oscillating between traumatic memory and apprehensive expectation. The physical pain of the past may be remembered, but rarely felt, and never with the same intensity.[11] For all of Epicurus's concern with *hedone*, with the pursuit of pleasure much misunderstood and maligned by his critics, he devoted considerable attention to pain, both physical and psychological.

"One must not pretend to philosophize, but to philosophize in reality. For we do not need the semblance of health, but true health (*aletheian ugiainein*)," (VS 54) Epicurus adds, thereby unifying true philosophy with true health. How is the ideal of true health specifically defined as the outcome of a *true philosophy*—in this case no different than Socrates in the allegory of the cave in Book VII of the *Republic*? Philosophy cannot claim to be the love of wisdom (or, as in Socrates, also as the wisdom of love, the former *eros* now transformed into *philia*, friendship, and ultimately to become the *agape* of early Christianity) unless "it does not expel the suffering of the mind,"[12] in oneself and unless it takes care of others. For Epicurus, such a *telos* could only be accomplished in a community of like-minded individuals—so different from Cicero who, often writing against Epicurus, believes that "it is impossible to live well except in a good commonwealth and nothing can

---

9. I am indebted to Jaeger for this reference. See his *Theology of the Early Greek Philosophers*.

10. In *Outlines of Pyrrhonism*, Sextus Empiricus calls Epicurus a "dogmatist." The critique of rival philosophies became traditional with subsequent generations of Epicureans. It is evident, for example, in Philodemus of Gadara's treatise on the Stoa. See Dorandi's *Filodemo*.

11. Diogenes Laertius, *Lives.*, 10.137.

12. Usener, *Epicurea*, Fr. 221.

produce greater happiness than a well-constituted state."[13] This philosophy makes human being precarious since it depends on a political order, an externality obviously susceptible to shifts and changes brought about, as in Rome, by competition and rivalry for power, with the judicial system especially vulnerable to manipulation.

The *telos* of philosophy as the attainment of wisdom and self-knowledge has been fulfilled with the aim of psychological health and in relationships founded on *philia*, friendship and affection. One cannot love wisdom without at the same time loving others; they are inseparable, each interrelated and necessary when developing relationships based on *arete*, the virtue and excellence of character. Again, the difference from Cicero is obvious: the Roman statesman is willing to forego his own tranquillity (and, as we shall see when reading his *Tusculam Disputations*, with poignant and melancholy regret) so that he can serve others within the context of the state, "for the sake of the safety of my fellow-citizens, and to secure, at the cost of my own personal danger, a quiet life for all the rest."[14] Without necessarily using the language of sacrifice—though he does advocate selflessness, an apparent altruism—Cicero nevertheless seems to forego his own tranquillity to devote himself to making possible (socially and politically) the quiet life for the Roman citizen. "All the rest," of course, may sound universal but was in fact only related to citizens of merit, the *optimates*, and therefore defined by the values of a particular political order.

Turning to Epicurus and his personal relationships in the community of the Garden, even one of his most vocal detractors could admit how he was devoted to others (personally, and not in the abstract sense of other citizens) and how he "continually cared for them."[15] In order for Epicurus to devote himself to the health of people's *psyche*—parenthetically, he may have changed his name at some point in his life to reflect his identification with being an *epikurous* or healer and helper—it must have been evident to him that, for many different reasons, people experienced significant emotional difficulties. They suffered, experienced pain, were susceptible to both internal desires and external compulsions, with only *phronesis* capable of overcoming both. Prudence and discretion, as deliberative thinking, were elements of the rational life and one response to the vicissitudes of the emotions, to their spontaneity and intensity. Epicurus therefore set himself with the task of first diagnosing the symptoms of these specifically psychological

---

13. Cicero, *Rep.*, 5.5.

14. Ibid., 1.4. One could add numerous passages on Cicero's devotion to the state, a reality much more pressing that his citizens. "The existence of virtue depends entirely on its use; and its noblest use is the government of the state." 1.2.

15. Plutarch, *Non Posse*, 1103a.

maladies, whether their origin was psychical or civic, and then offering a cure. And for physical illness, though he could not provide the healing of a physician, he nevertheless made it possible to endure even long, chronic illness with equanimity. "We must be concerned with healing (*iatreian*) ourselves," he writes in *Vatican Saying* 64 and with specific reference to the members of the sect, a healing, furthermore, which he supplements with one more significant concept, that of *soteria*, or healing. "A young man's share in salvation (*soterias*) comes from attending to his age and guarding against what will defile everything through maddening desires," (VS 80) he advises, for desires were so often compulsive and unrestrained. By adopting a varied vocabulary for an overall treatment of human beings, he could stress the interrelationship of *ugieia*, *iatreia*, and the all-important *soteria*, the latter of which would become essential in the gospels and early Christianity, even if salvation could be divided from existence by otherworldly aspirations. Epicurus's philosophy, following from the diagnosis of human ailments, was extensive. In the Garden, the writings of Epicurus himself as well as other prominent members (to name but two, Metrodorus and Leontion—the latter a woman who had been a *hetaera* or "courtesan" in the past but who became known as a philosopher and writer) would have been the subject of daily conversation, always returning to fundamental concerns: how to lead the best possible life so as to be healthy, as an individual and with others. An examination of all the philosophical principles essential to Epicurean thought would be extensive; here, only the most significant will be discussed, especially as they pertain to the obstacles to psychological health. First of all, the nature of perception and feelings (internal), the relationship of chance and necessity (external), and how its perpetual threat as intrinsic to existence has led some people to find security, for example, in the attainment of material wealth and in the recognition, in the polis, of being a citizen of honor and therefore worthy of respect. Epicurus's stress on the development of *phronesis*, on the one hand, and pleasure or *hedone*, on the other, was both an affirmation of the inherent goodness in human existence, in the here and now, and how such a pleasure could be achieved and maintained despite both internal pressures (feelings) and external obstacles, that which was deemed of value by the polis. His pleasure was not simply experienced episodically—here now, gone later. It was intended to become a permanent state of mind.

The benefit of the tight-knit community of the Garden and their independence from the *polis* allowed them to conceive of, and develop, a new set of social relations—beginning with allowing individuals traditionally excluded from participating in philosophy: women and slaves. As for teaching the young—which Epicurus mentions several times and at decisive moments in his writings, for his principles were often directed specifically at those who were young and beginning their philosophical studies—they did not follow the traditional curriculum of Greek *paideia*: there was no study of geometry, mathematics, or music, omissions that exposed him to severe criticism for ignoring tradition. And their pedagogy included a kind of teaching, in instruction and conversation, that was distinct from the traditional rhetoric so essential to the life of the polis, most especially in a political and juridical context, later to become important in the practice of declamations and the oratorical ability so necessary in the well-ordered Roman state. Forensic oratory, for example, Epicurus calls a *kakotechnia*, a "vile technique,"[16] for if the innocence or guilt of an individual depended on one's ability to speak, to persuade with arguments with no concern for the truth, then the rhetoric of the city and the language of the Garden were inimical to each other. Classical *paideia* was inseparable from its role in perpetuating civic identity and social interactions necessary for the well-ordered city.[17] In the Garden, dialogue and conversation centered on a complete self-analysis of one's character, not as a citizen but as a human being who could be more than a reflection of history. It was the prerequisite for achieving the *autarkeia* or self-sufficiency (from one's distorted desires, from the conventional desires of the *polis*) necessary for being free from the disturbances of the psyche. According to Seneca, the Garden should not be considered a school at all: "It was not the school of Epicurus that made Metrodorus, Hermarchus, and Polyaenus but their shared life."[18] The emphasis should be on this sharing, for in developing healthy relationships with others, and for a mutual benefit, one could not be undermined by social ills such as rivalry, jealousy, envy. Epicurus's philosophy was indeed a *philosophia medicans* as long as one recognizes health as an end could not be limited to an individual but extended (equally as important) to healthy relationships between people, individuals, and in the group overall.

"They must free themselves for the prison of general education and politics," Epicurus writes in *Vatican Saying* 58, contrasting the life in the Garden with the two pillars of Athenian society, *paideia* and politics. For Epicurus, the connection was essential in the well-ordered state. Education formed the citizen so he could take his place in its bureaucracy.[19] The indi-

16. Usener, *Epicurea*, Fr. 51.
17. Watts, *City and School*.
18. Seneca, *Ep.*, 1.6.6.

19. Again, Cicero's views are instructive as markers for comparison between the independent Hellenistic philosopher and the conservative Roman statesman. In *The Republic*, when discussing birth and education, he writes that the Roman state has "given us these advantages so that she may appropriate to her own use the greater and

viduals of the Garden, however, were not reclusive. They did not refuse to interact with others, at least socially, unlike, as we will see, sects motivated by concerns with purity such as the Essenes of Qumran, the Therapeutae of Egypt, or in the monastic communities of the desert in early Christianity. Although there is no sense of Epicurus himself or any of his followers engaging directly with the citizens of Athens with the intent to either convert them or to influence their society (at least directly), they did nevertheless make themselves at least partly public. Plutarch, for one, criticizes the Epicureans for writing letters to possible converts. They seemed to have actively recruited, and very successfully, it seems, since Epicurean schools were to be established in various parts of the Mediterranean world and for a remarkable period extending to six centuries. At home, perhaps also abroad, they would have made their philosophy available to everyone by selling their writings, and letters, at the "book-stalls" of the Athenian agora. Epicurus was well known for his prolific output. Plutarch himself was in possession of some of Epicurus's letters. However, the emphasis was on their independence and how they could best establish a community that reflected Epicurean ideals of friendship, of course (what Epicurus called "the greatest good" and "immortal," [VS 78]), and of a teaching and learning that included a curriculum and interpersonal relationship based on therapeutic well-being.

The community, no doubt, had its detractors. To unburden oneself of the duties of the Athenian citizen must have been regarded with suspicion and acrimony, in part because some citizens felt their way of life (to some extent) was both criticized and rejected. Nevertheless, within the Garden, each individual recognized themselves as part of a unique community, one based on a unique understanding of the meaning of friendship. In *Vatican Saying* 52, Epicurus describes this friendship in a particular way: "friendship (*philia*) dances around the world announcing to all of us that we must wake up to blessedness." *Friendship*, then, does not accurately (and certainly not completely) define the meaning of *philia*, one of the reasons the letters of Paul's gospel replace *philia* with *agape*. The vocabulary of friendship, with its ties to Greek philosophy, is replaced by *adelphoi*, brothers and sisters, in part to stress how Christianity too was initiating new social relations in the context of the Roman empire. When, for example, Richard Hibler writes that "the condition and criteria for all human conduct at the Garden was *philia*,"[20] the word should be understood and translated as *love* and its expression as the taking care of others to ensure their well-being, in part due

---

more important part of our courage, our talents, and our wisdom, leaving us for our own private uses only so much as may be left after her needs have been satisfied." 1.4.

20. Hibler, *Happiness through Tranquillity*, 43.

to the prevalence of the word *eros* and its necessary association with a deity in past Greek thought.

Later Epicureans would inherit (and, in some cases, develop) psychological health as the overriding concern of their philosophy. By development, as in the case of Diogenes of Oenoanda (who commissioned an extensive stoa in his hometown filled with an Epicurean inscription), he mentions concerns that, if not evident in the extant writings of Epicurus, were consistent with his philosophy such as the responsibility of taking care of strangers,[21] support for universality as opposed to the Stoic cosmopolitanism much less Roman citizenship[22], and an opposition to military service, the *militare* or service imposed by the Romans on colonized provinces such as his Lycia.[23] That Epicurus's philosophy survived and flourished well into the era of Roman Christianity—dissolved, eventually, after the decrees of successive Christian emperors after Constantine's con-

---

21. In the virtue of taking care of strangers, we have an apparent development of Epicurean ideals that may (or may not) have been part of the philosophy of the Garden. Furthermore, we do not know if the care for strangers was related, for example, to a possible influx of refugees during and following the last of the Jewish wars against the Romans, the Bar Kokhba revolt of AD 132–136. Let us note, moreover, that the care for strangers was prominent in the Hebrew Bible as well as in the New Testament. The message of the Hebrew Bible was clear in one's responsibility to take care of "the strangers, the fatherless, and the widow, which are in thy gates" (Deut 14:29). The documents of early Christianity are also consistent. The letter to the Hebrews urges to "be not forgetful to entertain strangers (*philoxenias*): for thereby some have entertained angels unawares" (13:2). The meaning of *philoxenia* is to show hospitality and love to strangers. Third John 1:5 repeats the same message and emphasizes to treat everyone equally: "beloved, thou doest faithfully whatsoever thou doest the brethren, and to strangers (*xenous*)." The book of 1 Peter specifically identifies the readers of his letter: "dearly beloved, I beseech you as strangers and pilgrims" (1 Pet 2:11). Finally, in extended passages of Jesus' teaching, Matthew writes of the ethical obligation to be of service to others in terms of hospitality: "when saw we thee, a stranger, and took thee in" (Matt 25:38).

22. In Diogenes's Epicurean inscription, one can notice how he has inherited the spirit of the Hellenistic philosopher (his independence from the city of Athens) and now emphasized his concern with fellow citizens that could not be equated, or reducible, to either the Stoic belief in cosmopolitanism much less the Roman assimilation of others into their empire, granting citizenship especially to aristocrats and soldiers. On the ideal of cosmopolitanism, see Neutel's *A Cosmopolitan Ideal*, as well as Lieu's *Neither Jew nor Greek?*

23. In "A Lost Epicurean Community," Diskin Clay argues that there was an "apparent lack of change and innovation in their (Epicureans) thinking" (313). However, Diogenes's inscription clearly shows several interrelated concerns that are not in any of Epicurus's writings. They do not, however, contradict the spirit of his teaching. In order to assess Diogenes's Epicurean inscription, it would have to relate Epicurean philosophy in the context of a colonized province of the Roman state and the changed conditions of the second century at the time of Hadrian.

version in 312—attests to its appeal, both historically and culturally; the number of schools in the Mediterranean world, ranging from Cyprus to Rome, could not have been possible without his philosophy being a *remedy* for the inherent difficulties in human existence and exacerbated by actual historical conditions.[24] Far from the rhetoric taught by sophists for professional advancement, economic benefits, and social acknowledgement, Epicureanism was a philosophy that fulfilled particular human needs that had little to do with knowledge as such, and with no relation to practical matters of society: economics, politics, justice. It was directly related to everyday existence, with maxims to memorize and reflect on in particular situations and for specific experiences. His ethics were so well respected that even Augustine, now writing as the Bishop of Hippo, could make one of the more unique comments in the whole of the *Confessions*.[25] The importance of psychological health, to be free from disturbances, would be repeated and stressed throughout the history of Epicureanism, especially in the three most well-known adherents and stretching from the first century BC to the second century AD. Lucretius, Philodemus, and Diogenes have left us with the most considerable body of work as all of them emphasize, if in their particular way, the therapeutics of Epicurean philosophy.

At the beginning of Book 6 of *On the Nature of Things*, Lucretius praises Epicurus as the philosopher who provides consolation by means of his teaching:

> With truth-telling words he scoured the heart, he put a limit to desire and fear, he showed what was the chief good to which we all move, and pointed the way, that strait and narrow path by which we might run thither without turning. (6.24–29)

Commenting on Lucretius, Pierre Boyancé emphasizes "the psychagogic use of the poetic form,"[26] in effect turning a conversational (and epis-

---

24. In *Epicuro*, Graziano Arrighetti translates Epicurus's *soteria* (both healing and, in the gospel letters, salvation) as *rimedio*. No different than the English, the word has the benefit of being both a specifically medical remedy as well as the ability to change a difficult situation in oneself, though it can also refer to a situation. In this case then, *soteria* can be associated with the related terms *metanoia* and *epistrepho*.

25. I draw attention (as I have before, and will again until more commentators consider its rightful place in Augustine's philosophical thought) to the last paragraph of Book VI of the *Confessions*. In a book that is extremely reticent about naming any Greek philosophers, the appearance of Epicurus by name (and what Augustine says about him) is unique in Christian literature.

26. Boyancé, *Lucrèce et l'épicurisme*, 59. To the best of my knowledge, this is the first time that the word "psychagogic" is used in relation to Epicureanism. It has, however, an antecedent (as we saw earlier) in Plato's *Phaedrus* when Socrates describes his speaking as *techne psychagogica*.

tolary) therapeutic practice into a poetic form intended to produce the same healing effect. In Fr. 1 of his *On Frank Criticism*,[27] Philodemus of Gadara writes that "a wise man and philosopher speaks frankly" (*parresia*) about their own "errors" (*hamartias*), in this case developing a concept already evident in Plato's *Symposium* and one to be instrumental in both the exhortatory and consoling speech of Jesus (to his disciples and followers) and the "bold speaking" he used when confronting adversaries and hostile critics of his acts and teaching. The Epicurean inscription by the Lycian Diogenes of Oenoanda, dated in the second century AD at the time of Hadrian,[28] makes his Epicurean philosophy reflect its centuries-long tradition and the importance of *soteria* as healing and salvation:

> I wished by making use of this colonnade to set forth in public the remedies which bring salvation, remedies of which I would say in a word that all kinds have been revealed.[29]

If, then, Epicureanism as a philosophy was essentially psychotherapeutic, what were the particular aspects of Epicurus's writings that, first of all, diagnosed the ailments of the human psyche (in the individual, in the *polis*, and in the very nature of existence) and then not only offered a cure, but equally important made an enhanced life, a good, healthy life, possible and attainable? Epicurus emphasized the totality: there was the inevitability of natural disasters and the misinterpretation of the gods. From the natural world and the gods he turned to the interrelationships of three sources for the difficulties of the human condition: one's mind (though he does not, of course, neglect the vulnerability of the body), the distorted ideals of the polis, and the nature of existence. One can begin with his single most unique insight on the nature of consciousness: the central role of feelings in perception, and how they determine not only the world (physics as such, both *kosmos* and nature) but perhaps more importantly also one's relationships with others. One can therefore begin with his ethical philosophy by first diagnosing the interrelated nature of emotions and perceptions. His *logotherapeia* develops in relation to his understanding of human beings as emotional, with feelings being primary in the act of perception and, therefore, essential in understanding one's relationship to others.

---

27. In his Introduction to *Vergil, Philodemus, and the Augustans*, David Armstrong defines *On Frankness* as a work of "Epicurean interpersonal therapy," 6.

28. Based on epigraphical evidence, James Warren dates the inscription prior to 140. See his "Diogenes Epikouros."

29. Diogenes of Oenoanda, *Fragments*, Fr. V-VI.

2. Feelings and Perceptions

Early in the *Letter to Herodotus*, when Epicurus attempts to provide his reader with a condensed but precise outline of his philosophy of the natural world so as to have a calm life, living without unacknowledged preconceptions and, more importantly, *unharmed* by false opinions, Epicurus emphasizes three interrelated aspects of his thought: the exact meaning of words and how they are used, the centrality of what he calls "sense-perceptions," (*aisthesis*) and to take into consideration "feelings" (*pathe*) when making any observation, whether about the world, oneself, or others. Prior to the actual description of nature, and with the three interrelated aspects also relevant for the understanding of human beings, Epicurus writes that, one, "we need to have grasped what is denoted by our words," two, "it is also necessary to observe all things in accordance with one's sense-perceptions," and three, "[to observe everything] in accordance with our actual feelings" (10.37–38). Epicurus's introduction in the letter sets out a systematic theory whereby the understanding (and its description in words, in meaning) takes into consideration how feelings, most especially those outside one's consciousness, can determine perception of ourselves, others, and the world.[30] Although he is concerned with establishing the *kriterion* for the observation of natural phenomena, how one judges a *thing*, he is equally (if not more) interested in analyzing the act of perception itself, what Robert Strozier calls his "consciousness orientation,"[31] and one especially relevant in human relationships. The psyche was volatile, and emotions were so often spontaneous, eluding consciousness and the will. Thoughts, daydreams, and fantasies occurred seemingly on their own (awake, during the day) as did the sudden appearance of memories and recollections, anticipations and expectations. The psyche had "distinct capacities and susceptibilities,"[32] and the human self could be overwhelmed by its own feelings and perceptions.

---

30. In "Epicurus on Self-Perception," David Glidden makes the observation that one cannot simply regard *aesthesis* as "sensation" because of its relation to *pathe*, emotional feelings. Moreover, when Glidden adds that "Epicurus suggests that primitive man first used verbal utterances to express feelings or *pathe*," (301) these utterances show that the expression of feelings, in conversation, led ultimately to the realization that human dialogue could promote not only the understanding of the source of emotions, but their possible (conscious) change. For Epicurus, language was not primarily important for its capacity to name or to categorize, but to *relate*.

31. Strozier, *Epicurus and Hellenistic Philosophy*, 4. He adds that Epicurus emphasizes "the priority of the (internal) process."

32. Von Staden, "Body, Soul, and Nerves," 86.

Prior to making his first physiological observation—"nothing comes into being from what is not"[33]—Epicurus simultaneously defines the complex nature of human being. The Epicurean *physiologia* is, then, simultaneously a protoscientific description of natural phenomena (first of all, of the *kosmos*) and a self-reflective analysis of the human psyche as it makes *judgments* about the world—of nature, of human beings, and how they interrelate. In his *physiologia*, there is always a reciprocal relationship between what is perceived and the consciousness of the one who sees, feels, perceives, and a distinction made between what is rational and irrational. His study of nature has consequences for his understanding of human beings, their relationships with each other, and for their place in the social life of the *polis*. At the same time that he discusses the nature of the atom—its shape and qualities and magnitude, for example—he also makes his reader aware of appearances, that which is seen, the reason for its specific perception:

> For if this [doctrine] is added, then it will be easier to account for what, according to our feelings and sense-perceptions, actually happens." (10.55)

What happens (what is seen to happen) cannot be separated from both senses and feelings. Indeed, and this is most important in the perception of oneself and others, feelings can influence and determine sense-perception—a recognition especially important for correctly understanding any *human* situation and experience and, therefore, for possibly recognizing a mistaken (that is, psychologically distorted) perception; the consequences of such a distortion will result in *illness*, with specific symptoms such as apprehension and anxiety, doubt and worry. Far from *physiologia* being a study restricted to the natural world, either the *kosmos* or nature, Epicurus makes far-reaching philosophical arguments concerning the relationship between the psyche and perception; the psychological conditions of character may determine perception and, therefore, its possible distortion and misjudgment. Although Epicurus seems to be primarily discussing the nature of matter (of objects as aggregates of atomic particles, for example) the more crucial observation focuses on the vulnerabilities of the psyche. Understanding the appearance of an object (for example, how a rainbow is created by light refracted in water droplets) is of course significant as a natural explanation of a phenomena, but more important than accurately perceiving the origin of a natural object is the correct perception of others, in a human situation, when conflict may arise due to difference in character, temperament, and judgment. By analyzing the irrational parts of the psyche,

---

33. Epicurus, *Ep. Hdt.*, 38.

what is *alogon*, Epicurus holds everyone accountable for their thoughts and actions and reiterates the responsibility of the philosopher as an analyst of symptoms and an eventual healer.

In what may very well be an unprecedented analysis of the human psyche—using a dream as an example—Epicurus realizes there are psychological dynamics which can alter and distort perception, but instead of remaining with his physical example of an object he instead turns to the idea of an experience:

> An error would not occur if we did not have some *other motion too in ourselves* which is linked *to the application to presentations*" (10.51, my emphasis).

Epicurus makes the claim here that the act of perception is often supplemented by an internal dynamic which can distort perception and, therefore, experience itself. Epicurus is not an epistemologist; he does not concern himself with how we *know*. He is essentially a psychologist preoccupied with how perception and experience may be distorted due to an internal dynamic which is usually (by most, certainly non-Epicureans) unnoticed. Nussbaum's stunning insight that "Epicurus discovers the unconscious"[34] can be witnessed in the thinking central to his argument in his *Letter to Herodotus*. If human consciousness is largely unconscious, and if so much of human error (as well as emotional misery, both individual and social) is directly caused by the inability to properly perceive the nature of our psychic life, then the first and most essential aspect of Epicurean teaching is to recognize, to diagnose, how the self is fundamentally constricted and limited by two opposing forces (which are themselves interrelated), that is, the internal passions and impulses of a human being and the equally forceful demands of the external world of the polis and its particular conception of reality. Human perception is thereby determined by two different forces: one internal, the other external. His significant insights into the natural world, acknowledged repeatedly by Lucretius in *On the Nature of Things*, may actually conceal the ramifications of his *physiologia* insofar as it presents an unprecedented understanding of human psychology. Diogenes of Oenoanda, in one of the most important of his Epicurean inscriptions, draws our attention to "the supremacy of these feelings which afflict the soul," (Fr. 38 I) feelings whose origin remain concealed and unacknowledged, but always dynamically influential.

Before Epicurus, no thinker had so completely exposed human consciousness to the effects of the psyche. At the beginning of the *Letter to*

---

34. Nussbaum, *Therapy of Desire*, 133.

Herodotus, Epicurus stressed how the study of nature made life calmer for the reasons—all metaphysical—already outlined. The supplement to his anti-metaphysical philosophy therefore becomes psychological. Dismissing the gods from influence does not by itself guarantee human tranquility; the source remains unexamined, that is, the source that created the gods with particular characteristics as a human need. His response was psychological. Feelings (especially when their origin is unrecognized) can influence and determine perception as such. He also separates the intellect, determined by *phronesis*, from other equally if not more forceful criteria, those that are made possible by the extrarational aspect of a human being, none of which are more important than feelings. If the two most important affirmations of the letter are at 10.39 and 10.63—"we must infer by reasoning what is non-evident" and "one must hold firmly that the soul (*psyche*) is most responsible for sense-perception"—and if he also knows and affirms that the psyche cannot be transparent to itself, then Epicurus must devote himself to an in-depth analysis of the psyche such that he will be able to understand in what particular ways it can determine feelings and perceptions. Epicurean psychology is foundational, so that when he leads the reader, in the *Letter to Herodotus* and elsewhere, to the gods, he has in fact led them to themselves and those *preconceptions* (the psychological and social *prolepsis*) which together have formed the totality of a limited world. The nature of the psyche and the nature of the *polis* have limited human life; it has been constrained. Epicurus makes sure to stress how "the natures of men" have a double-influence: the psychological, in part responsible both for feelings and sense-impressions, as well as "particular feelings and presentations, in accordance too with the various local differences among their tribes" (10.75). In other words, the ways perception may be shaped by one's immediate location, in his case, the polis of Athens and, more generally, Greece in the present and as a result of its particular history—a distinction Epicurus makes to one of his students. In *Vatican Saying* 76, he writes: "As you grow old, you are such as I would praise, and you have seen the difference between what it means to philosophize for yourself and what it means to do so for Greece."

The far-reaching consequences of his observation are to submit history to an analysis of its limits and determinations; by doing so (by recognizing local differences, that is, the relative nature of the human world) he raises the possibility of its transformation in accordance with what he soon calls nature, or more precisely, how human beings are capable of being more than a reflection of their immediate time and place. Epicurus's garden school is therefore an alternative community that analyzes how certain feelings and perceptions may be the outcome of a specific socialization in history. To recognize such a limit is the beginning of exceeding it. The *zoon anthropon* must then be understood from two equally influential perspectives—the psychological and the social. And so he must then turn to diagnosing in what ways human beings have developed, first of all, and then offer the possibility of a transformation, what he specifically calls, with different vocabulary, a cure. Society, however, has offered ways of coping with its limits in history and with the afflictions of human condition that for Epicurus are ultimately ineffective. The nature of the psyche can make human beings insecure. Creating some remedies, however (such as the attainment of wealth), cannot ultimately succeed; they are precarious since objective, *material* wealth cannot ultimately remedy a psychological affliction.

Despite the condensed version of Epicurus's thought as it represents its attention to health and healing, essentially represented in the *Letter to Menoeceus, the Principal Doctrines*, and the related *Vatican Sayings*, it is nevertheless possible to discuss the interrelationship of some of his most central tenets and to provide a systematic outline of his therapeutic philosophy. Though dedicated principally to individual healing in and out of the Garden, a consideration of some of his writings shows him to be concerned with Greek society overall and the health of the *polis* that, like Socrates, he diagnosed as in need of change. One specific problem he identified was the pursuit of wealth, what Socrates diagnosed in individual and families who have "surrendered themselves to the limitless acquisition of wealth and overstepped the boundaries of the necessary."[35] For Epicurus, the critique of wealth is by no means *economic*, at least not narrowly so; rather, he exposes a fundamental contradiction in the human condition and its flawed, failed attempt to treat the psyche's vulnerability (and its impoverishment) by means of a material fulfillment. Happiness (*eudaimonia*) could not be achieved by the acquisition of objects and the momentary pleasure or security they provided; they were external and could in no way contribute to the "self-flourishing" that resulted from the excellence of character and the philosophical attempt to exceed the limits of history without any appeals to metaphysics.

Epicurus stressed that "the disturbance of the soul (*psuches tarachen*) will not be dissolved nor will considerable joy be produced by the presence of the greatest wealth, nor by honor and admiration among the many, nor

---

35. Plato, *Rep.*, 373d. What Socrates here calls the necessary, Epicurus will call natural. While the critique of wealth and its multifaceted reasons can only be briefly mentioned here, it is obvious such a critique was essential to the philosophical life in classical Athens, Hellenistic times (as represented by Epicurus), and perhaps most strident in the teachings of Jesus. When, for example, he talks about "the deceitfulness of riches," (Mark 4:19) in this case, like Epicurus, he does not so much denounce wealth as such (though, in other places, he certainly does) but points out how it can deceive, that is, confer on a person materially while ignoring their self.

by anything which is a result of indefinite causes (*adioristous aitias*)" (VS 80). These were indefinite because they are socially created and therefore contingent and ephemeral, the attainment of wealth exceeded what was naturally necessary, and the respect from the many (being honored by others, for example) was among the most vulnerable of characteristics. The Roman Stoic Seneca read Epicurus and sometimes included his most celebrated sayings, as in a letter to Lucilius: "If you live according to nature, you will never be poor; if you live according to opinion, you will never be rich."[36] The natural and the unnatural are Epicurean distinctions that show the difference between the fulfillment of a natural and necessary desire—what nature itself indicates, such as hunger and food, along with a sense of portion— and the perhaps natural though unnecessary desire of excess, indulgence, and extravagance. As Diogenes of Oenonda puts it, "unnatural wealth is no more benefit to man than is water to a full vessel. We must realize that both run over" (Fr. 44).

In the last of the *Vatican Sayings*, Epicurus concludes with his condensed list of his most noteworthy principles by dismissing what, in his society, was long considered of the utmost importance: the wealth that apparently secured one a comfortable life and, again, being acknowledged as a significant citizen, deserving of honor, praise, and respect. The reason Epicurus puts both money and honor together is to emphasize how Athenians, at least the most prominent citizens, were primarily motivated by two pursuits—the wealth that supposedly made one secure and the honor that conferred status on an individual and his family, including the *philotimia* or love of honor created by the extravagant gesture of munificence and *eurgetism*, the practice of gift-giving later adopted and to become central for Roman emperors, first of all, and the aristocracy, both native and colonial. Diogenes of Oenoanda's dedication of a *stoa* to the people of his city was an act of eurgetism so different from what was expected of aristocratic citizens—that is, the building of baths, gymnasiums, or colonnades and, not to be neglected most especially by wealthy landowners, providing animals for sacrificial slaughter and public consumption. The second-century Epicurean, by commissioning a stoa filled with an extensive inscription of philosophical wisdom, was in effect defying convention and social expectations; rather than expecting honor, he desired only that the citizens of Lycia adopt Epicurean principles for themselves and, perhaps, ultimately influence a change in social values, certainly reassessing the influence of the Roman state and how it had imposed its own ideals on a subjected people.

---

36. Seneca, *Ep.*, 16.7.

Epicurus understood that if human beings judged their own individuality according to what he called "indefinite causes" (they were socially contingent and not based on the true needs of the human psyche), then their character would always be based either on a material cause (wealth) or on an ephemeral and by no means permanent state such as honor and admiration from the many. Above all, Epicurus realized that if we depended on an external source for our own self-understanding such as the acknowledgment and approval of the majority, then we would always be vulnerable. An outward opinion could always change, even into its opposite, with fame becoming contempt, or notoriety turning to aversion. Fame was an especially noxious characteristic since it depended on acknowledgment by others, first of all, and because of it and even worse, it could always be changed into its opposite; fame could be envied and resented. Therefore, in order to develop one's character consistent with Epicurean ideals, externals had to be ignored as much as possible, and certainly minimized in terms of their real as opposed to their perceived (that is, social) importance. *Lathe biosas*, or "living anonymously," a well-known Epicurean ideal, meant one could live ignoring the ideas most evident in society, and that gave one the opportunity to be independent and to develop one's character according to individual and not social needs, rejecting those benefits that resulted from economic prosperity or social approval. The historical critique of the pursuit of wealth, consistent from Socrates to Seneca, also makes it obvious Epicurus's own critique was somehow related to the changing world after the death of Alexander the Great, most especially with increased trade and mercantilism, pursuits that depended on fostering certain social relationships of utility. Being only nominally associated with the *polis* and always emphasizing the independence of the Garden made the community of like-minded friends much less likely to be caught up either in the affairs of state or in the pursuit of wealth deemed so important in society. Frugality was an ideal, and living with little was more than sufficient. In addition to his critique of the pursuit of wealth for the sake of ensuring one's security, "Epicurus's social philosophy necessarily transvalued those traditional virtues that were largely coordinate with the military and political roles of the citizen."[37]

He believed people, especially those with feelings of vulnerability, weakness, and insecurity, sought—outside themselves—a life where security could be achieved. As with his unique teaching on developing a proper relationship to death—it is "nothing to us"—security (what he calls the "purest security") could only be achieved by a "quiet life and withdrawal from the many" (PD XIV). First of all, he repeats a lesson from his *physiologia*: "It

---

37. Bryant, *Moral Codes and Social Structures*, 412.

was useless to obtain security from men while the things above and below the earth and, generally, the things in the unbounded remained as objects of suspicion" (PD XIII). Security provided by others could do nothing to dispel fears and the anxiety of uncertainty. Such security could only come from what he calls the "conviction" made possible by an idea, one that altered character and psyche so as to become a permanent dispostion. Although he does admit that "a certain degree of security from other men does come by means of the power to repel [attacks] and by means of prosperity," (PD XIV) the attainment of martial and economic security often has pejorative consequences and additional problems that make any such initial security vulnerable once more. Wealth could be lost; so could a war. In any case, these were contingent, accidents of history, always exposed to what he calls the two unavoidable aspects of human existence: chance and necessity. Epicurus also knows that some are drawn to the need of being respected and admired—in part to be secure, that is, protecting oneself against the anxiety of being insecure in oneself, filled with self-doubt, a psychological vulnerability some attempt to appease or overcome by gaining a reputation and being acknowledged. "Some men want to become famous and respected, believing that is the way to acquire security," (PD VII) he writes, diagnosing a prevalent attitude in Greece in general and Athens in particular. In a society at least partly founded on the virtue of the *agon*, the struggle of competition and therefore of winners and losers left many with a sense of uselessness. Epicurus realized that the attempt to ensure security had one, inescapable reason: the inevitability of death.

3. Chance, Necessity, and Justice

"The man who has made the best arrangements for confidence about external threats is he who has made the manageable things akin to himself, and has at least made the unmanageable things not alien to himself" (PD XXXIX). In this the penultimate of his *Principal Doctrines*, Epicurus draws to a conclusion another essential point: there are many aspects of life that are unexpected, contingent, and unpredictable. Nothing, then, should seem "alien," and everything which is "unmanageable," that is, cannot be influenced or changed by will and decision, must be understood from the perspective of what he calls both chance (*ananke*) and necessity (*tuche*), two unavoidable facts or conditions of existence that one cannot, ultimately, avoid except with a certain attitude of equanimity and acceptance. Epicurus systematically analyzes the conditions of being in the world, giving each their due, from the characteristics of the psyche, the values of the polis, and in this case, two unavoidable vicissitudes of life. Much of everyday life was uncertain, haphazard, making it difficult to live with a sense of assurance unless (as Epicurus taught) one developed a *psychological relationship* adequate to the uncertain circumstances of life. Intentions are often unfulfilled, expectations defied, and most significantly, the dynamic nature of desire may be such that—as Socrates argued in relation to prayer—its fulfillment would in the end be detrimental. "One should bring this question to bear on all one's desires," Epicurus stresses. "What will happen to me if what is sought by desire is achieved, and what will happen if it is not" (VS 71)?

In order to become both self-sufficient and free from the disturbances of the psyche, there are principles to understand and interpret—and one of the most important, because it is unavoidable, involves a proper relationship to the vicissitudes of life, whose randomness and unpredictability often result in painful distress. These principles (to become not simply ideas but *dispositions*) could be learned and practiced. "Do and practice what I constantly told you to do, believing these to be the elements of living well," (10.123) Epicurus writes to Menoeceus, now instructing him that a good life (a psychologically healthy one) can be achieved if his principles are thought about and put into practice. The attainment of wealth and security could not, themselves, guarantee a tranquil life, not if poverty and insecurity were *psychological* characteristics. As Konstan writes:

> That men in their ignorance seek to protect themselves against anxiety as *though* against objective danger is the cause of the compulsive acquisition of wealth and power, compulsive because no amount of riches and authority can provide security or peace of mind.[38]

Wealth, power, honor, and fame were but manifestations of how society attempted to appease the weakness of its citizens; the limits of a society and how they socialized others was effectively concealed by the pursuit of wealth as a value. However, in addition to society, there were also actual conditions of existence that required his attention. To become a free and self-sufficient human being, it was also necessary to reflect on chance (*tuche*) and necessity (*ananke*). Epicurus made the consideration of chance and necessity so as to oppose not only the poetic fantasies as conceptions of the gods who influenced and determined, but also the tragic writers who could represent an inescapable fate and destiny. DeWitt analyzes Epicurus's relationship to what would later be called the goddess Fortuna as one of

---

38. Konstan, *Some Aspects of Epicurean Psychology*, 18.

"defiance."[39] Epicurus rejected any reference to luck or the fortuitous; events were contingent, dispositions were not. Epicurus is less concerned with any theoretical principle related to cause (in nature) than to the vagaries of life—the opinion someone might have of *you*, for example—and less for any of your qualities than the other's perception, the need they had in themselves (for example, out of envy or jealousy) to perceive *their* reality.

As Epicurus emphasizes, "We must remember that what will happen is neither unconditionally within our power nor unconditionally outside our power, so that we will not unconditionally expect that it will occur nor despair of it as unconditionally not going to occur" (10.127). Such a perspective, in principle related both to the future and the past, allows one to face the contingent with equanimity, and it involves both the natural world—for example, an unavoidable event such as an earthquake—and, more commonly in one's daily life, most especially in relation to the one sure thing that is most difficult to change, others. One could not, with any certainty, expect others to relate to you in a certain way. In addition to the contingent and the unexpected, there are also the elements of life which can either be chosen as good or avoided as detrimental. None are more important in Epicurus's philosophy than developing an understanding of our desires, and again, to stress, both the ones internal and external. To achieve the *telos* of "the blessed (*makarios*) life," desires must be thought about with "unwavering contemplation." To do so "enables one to refer every choice and avoidance[40] to the health of the body and the freedom of the soul from disturbance" (10.128). Some desires are simply unnecessary; to give them up, furthermore, has repercussions for our ability to deal more easily with chance. One example (and certainly ironic, most especially today when Epicureanism is so associated with fine dining) is fitting, as Epicurus advises us that: "becoming accustomed to simple, not extravagant, ways of life makes one completely healthy, makes man unhesitant in the face of life's necessary duties... and makes us fearless in the face of chance" (10.131).

Since both chance and necessity were intrinsic to being in the world and unavoidable, Epicurus developed a philosophy of self-sufficiency or *autarkeia* such that the reality of circumstance was (as with death) considered

---

39. Dewitt, *Epicurus and His Philosophy*, 320.

40. That Epicurus wrote one of his philosophical treatises on choices and avoidance shows how much he supported the idea of human freedom—not because he believed in the freedom of the will to accomplish its intentions at all times; freedom could not be independent of chance, accidental events, the fortuitous. Therefore, Epicurus above all taught one to develop a certain relationship to the contingent such that, whatever did occur (either good or bad), one would not lose one's equanimity. Life was contingent; the psyche could be developed to be steadfast.

to have little influence on the sage who was considered so because of equanimity. "Chance (*tuche*) has a small impact on the wise man, while reasoning has arranged for, is arranging for, and will arrange for the greatest and most important matters throughout the whole of his life" (*PD*. XVI). Despite the chance events in life, which are as certain to occur as they are inevitable (and unavoidable), what distinguishes the sage is his rational relationship to being in time and how understanding the past, present, and future, he can always be aware of the greatest and most important matters. To define the one who thinks and reflects on the precepts of Epicurean philosophy as a sage depends on a certain attitude to life, the incontrovertible laws of nature which are no less than the contingent events of the everyday. "Necessity is a bad thing," Epicurus writes in *Vatican Saying* 9, "but there is no necessity to live with necessity." Seneca the Stoic again quotes him to Lucillus: "It is wrong to live under constraint, but no man is constrained to live under constraint."[41] Necessity may be a fact of life, but one can live, however, *as if* it did not exist and therefore had no bearing on one's thoughts or actions, for "chance is in fact exterior, liberty is interior."[42] Of course, there are bound to be accidents, difficult circumstances, even tragic occurrences. The events cannot be changed; nevertheless, the force of reality cannot, on its own, determine one's relationship to what has occurred. "Misfortune must be cured (*therapeuteon*) by a sense of gratitude (*chariti*) for what has been and the knowledge that what is past cannot be undone" (VS 55). The initial and understandable reaction to misfortune may be painful and traumatic. It may wound, but the experience can be alleviated, can be *cured* by being grateful to the whole of one's life and by being impervious to regret. The wise Epicurean philosopher has the personal responsibility to think in such a way that every single contingent occurrence in life be accepted. Epicurus, moreover, adds the concept of "gratitude" (*charis*) precisely to counter, once more, the commonly understood meaning of the gift given to a human being by the gods. *Charis* can no longer be understood as a divine gift or favor, and one demanding reciprocity; rather, the unwavering gratitude one feels in relation to the totality of one's existence in the here and now, and in what Jean Bollack calls "*la plenitude de l'instant*,"[43] is a grace that can be developed to become a therapeutic cure. One final point: When Lucretius argues for our *libera voluntas*, he believes that "although an external force propels many men and forces them often to move often against their will and to be hurried headlong, yet there is in our breast something strong enough to fight

---

41. Seneca, *Ep.*, 12.10.
42. Masson, "M. Guyau and the Epicurean Doctrine," 40.
43. Bollack, *La pensée du Plaisir*, 89.

against it and to resist."[44] The struggle and resistance is not, in the case of chance and necessity, an attempt to avoid and elude it. That is not possible; however, an attitude and relationship alters the psychological consequences of chance and necessity in the world. As he approaches the end of the *Letter to Menoeceus*, Epicurus writes that "chance is unstable, while what occurs by our own agency is autonomous," (10.133) an "agency" not in relation to an act, but a thought, not to contingent events but in a disposition of equanimity.

Since Epicurus's philosophy of therapeutic healing was ultimately devoted to making people free (from their internal selves, from their society) one of his most significant discussions involves his analysis of justice (*dike*), one that begins with recognizing its role in the foundations of human societies and in relationships between people—that appears, in part, as a social contract—but soon turns to a psychological characteristic. Ernst Bloch makes an important preliminary observation, when he says "Epicurean reflections were directed toward finding a law outside institutions and statutes of the status quo."[45] Such a law, then, could only be found in one place. It was neither in history nor in a society that could manipulate justice and the law to fulfill its own ends: justice, for Epicurus, had to be found in a human being. Despite never admitting any influence by Plato or any of his successors, there appear to be precursors to Epicurus's ideas, most especially in a significant passage in Book I of the *Republic*.

In the dialogue with Thrasymachus on the definition of justice, Socrates reaches some remarkable conclusions:

> It seems to follow that injustice, wherever it occurs, be it in a city, a family, an army, or anything else results in making it incapable of achieving anything as a unit because of the dissensions and differences it creates, and, further, it makes that unit hostile to itself.[46]

Injustice has a much more comprehensive meaning than related to the judicial, to actual laws; as the *Minos* argued, laws could be (and often are) unjust. A first distinction: justice and the law are not the same. They may be incommensurable. Injustice is not only or primarily social, even though the examples he uses are the city, the family, and the army. Prior to the list,

---

44. Lucretius, DRN, 2.278–82.

45. Bloch, *Natural Law and Human Dignity*, 10. While this is not the place to fully take up questions of natural law in Epicurus, it is certainly notable that two leading thinkers on the subject (Bloch and Leo Strauss) both refer to Epicurus and do so with notable respect.

46. Plato, *Rep.*, 351e–352a.

however, Socrates had pointed out that injustice has the "capacity for dissension when it occurs within one individual" (351e). The statement was made in the context of injustice leading to conflict between two people. Injustice can and does lead to enmity. The consequences of his understanding of injustice are soon to be made, first and foremost, as psychological. "Even in one individual it has the same effect, which follows from its nature. First, it makes that individual incapable of achievement (*poiesei*) because he is at odds with himself and not of one mind" (352a). The concept of injustice is here defined psychologically; Socrates does nothing less than provide a diagnosis of a specifically psychological illness. We are, once again, at the Socratic argument not so much concerning ethics, morality or virtue, at least as traditionally understood; rather, when he continues and says "we must now examine whether the just also live a better life than the unjust, and are happier (*eudaimonesteroi*)" (352d), Socrates allows us to think about the just life as being better for us, psychologically. Given his argument, the better life is defined in terms of being happy, the *eudaimonia* which is not simply a state of mind, of the psyche. It also allows one to pursue, in freedom, a specific kind of life. It allows one to *create* one's life. Psychological injustice, on the other hand, impedes, prevents one from the achievement Socrates emphasizes as essential to a healthy life.

Once again, as he had in the Alcibiades dialogues, Socrates believes that injustice has prevented an individual (and by extension, the city) from enhancing its own nature; and that is the reason he continues with a discussion of the proper function of a horse and pruning shears, always, of course, to ultimately arrive at the proper function of a human being, what he calls "one's whole manner of living" (352d). An object, an animal, a human being, they each have their function and, more importantly, their excellence, the *arete* that cannot be reduced to virtue, ethics, or morality. If, as in the Alcibiades dialogues, Socrates was concerned with reconceiving human nature—what is most possible for a human being—here he again takes up the same question and problem, that is, how such an excellence can be achieved. When he turns to the "function of the soul," (353d) as it relates to living, he then moves from its function to its *arete*. "Justice is excellence of the soul," (353e) Socrates tells his interlocutor, and the one who has an excellent soul will consequently be "blessed and happy," (354a) *makarios te kai eudaimon*.

One indication of Epicurus's independence from society and, to put it more strongly, his indifference to the *salus* of society that is so important for Cicero and the Stoics, is his unique understanding of justice. In Principal Doctrine V and its concern with living pleasantly, that is, living undisturbed, without worry or anxiety, he mentions as central the idea of justice or *dike*. He turns to one of the fundamental concepts of philosophy's concerns and analyzes the meaning of *dike* independently of either its conventionally judicial or theological meanings, the ones most prevalent in society and in relationship to both the city-state and the gods. Epicurus conceives of justice, again keeping in mind his utmost concern (the health of the *psyche*), as an individual characteristic, a psychological disposition not related to a *law*. "Justice and injustice are treated as types of psychic conditions or characteristics that either benefit or harm us."[47] For Epicurus, being just is not simply to respect and observe the law—to respect and observe the laws of the gods above and the laws of human society in the world; and though he might not, necessarily, exclude the consideration of either the gods or the city-state, his concept of justice is much more relevant to the individual. For example, a traditional understanding of justice involves the particular concern with society and the pact made between its members "neither to harm one another or be harmed" (PD XXXI). At the beginning of his most sustained discussion of justice in the *Principal Doctrines*, he seemingly introduces what appears to be a social contract theory for the benefit of society overall but eventually turns to a much more individual (that is, psychological) idea of justice. Epicurus's tenets, from this section in the *Principal Doctrines* on, are a continuous and detailed reflection of justice as it has been created for the benefit of individuals' protection and the order of society. However, a closer reading of his statements (which at first appear traditional themselves—neither new nor particularly interesting) reveals a unique understanding of justice in terms of one's consciousness and, more evidently, in relation to a *conscience* that if disturbed, may create pain and discomfort. Epicurus is first and foremost concerned with a justice in relation to the self, and though he does acknowledge that justice does not necessarily exist in either the animal world or in the relationship between different states (both can attack and kill each other), in the world of the city-state justice represents order as well as the protection of the individual.

Epicurus makes a peculiar argument when he writes that "injustice (*adikia*) is not a bad (*kakon*) thing in its own right, but [only] because of the fear produced by the suspicion that one will not escape the notice of those assigned to punish such actions" (PD XXXIV). It must have been surely controversial to argue that injustice is considered bad not because of any specific act (i.e. murder) but only because of its consequence of living in fear of being caught and punished. In this case, Epicurus seems to be indifferent to either laws as such, or in the order and safety of civil society. But if one follows the consequence of his argument and his overriding concern with the health of the psyche of every individual (rather than society), then his

---

47. Mitsis, *Epicurus's Ethical Theory*, 77.

sense of justice has nothing to do with law, judicially understood, and the sentiment of individuals who will avoid any wrongdoing not for the sake of others, those harmed, by precisely for oneself and to ensure that no action will lead to psychological tribulation. Of course, Epicurus does not concern himself with either psychopathological criminals or extreme narcissists (or, for that matter, leaders and military commanders), but only with individuals who are now being taught how to be, first and foremost, *just toward their own selves*. By being conscious of oneself and one's capacity for worry, apprehension, and disturbance, one does not refrain from breaking the law or acting justly for the sake of others; rather, the concern with one's health becomes preeminent.

Two final comments are necessary, and they contribute to as sophisticated a critique of the traditional notion of justice as can be found in antiquity, at least before Jesus:

> In general outline justice is the same for everyone; for it was something useful in mutual associations. But with respect to the peculiarities of a region or of other [relevant] causes, it does not follow that the same thing is just for everyone. (PD XXXVI)

Epicurus has now introduced a decisive problem in the existence of justice in specific regions (he does, noticeably, refer to the difference in the laws of *cities*) and thereby calls attention to its specific rather than universal characteristic. He adds:

> If what is useful in the sense of being just changes, but for a while fits our basic grasp [of justice], nevertheless it was just for that length of time, [at least] for those who do not disturb themselves with empty words but simply look to the facts. (PD XXXVII)

Epicurus recognizes how, in the social/political world of the city-state, the sense of justice and its particularities may change—whimsically, or by edict from a leader who may consider it convenient, as was evident earlier in his determination of justice being socially and historically relevant. Justice as defined in any given society may change at any time. Individual justice (or, to give it a different definition, psychological justice) can never change or be influenced by *the law*. The institution of justice (as opposed to Epicurus's psychological justice) cannot be manipulated to serve specific ends of politics or power, in time of peace or war or a calamity such as a plague. The psychological justice of Epicurean philosophy is not concerned with the justice of a society; it is only concerned with the justice of each individual and dedicating one's life to living well and pleasantly for oneself, in relation to others. Therefore, unlawful acts are not avoided out of respect for the law or society but for the health of the self. As we shall see, among the most evident arguments presented by Cicero against Epicurean philosophy is precisely his indifference to the health of the republic. Epicurus did not care about matters relating to the public or the state; he only cared about the health of individuals and how they could best lead a good life free from worry, the *ataraxia* essential to his teaching. "He who is free from disturbance within himself also causes no trouble for another," (VS 79) Epicurus writes, which can also be rewritten as "the just individual will not cause trouble for another because he or she will never do anything to compromise their freedom from disturbance." Julia Annas makes the important observation (complementing Bloch's earlier assertion) that "Epicurus's account of justice is a *philosophical* account, and as such cannot be expected to match up to any period in history."[48] Epicurus's justice cannot be a reflection of any historical period (or the laws of the polis) since the fundamental expression of his philosophy is to exceed what has been inherited from the past and perpetuated in the present. The most effective justice is therefore psychological and not at all juridical or, of course, theological. One does not act justly for the sake of the gods or society, nor to elude any real or imagined punishment, but only for the continued health of one's psyche, a philosophy of life much criticized by Cicero, a thinker whom it is now necessary to evaluate (near the end of his life) for his own relationship to philosophy and how it differed—tragically—from Epicurus.

4. Cicero without Consolation

If Cicero remains the writer and thinker who most repeatedly criticizes Epicurus, his own concern with philosophy and its contribution to human health was also preeminent if ultimately compromised by his social and political allegiance to Rome. In detailing Cicero's philosophy of consolation, one notices the difference between Epicurus's therapeutic philosophy (in the Garden and independent from the polis) and the Roman statesman's dependence on the order of the *res publica*. For if Cicero, here influenced by Stoic doctrine, "asserted more emphatically than any other schools that the individual's happiness and fulfilment depended on the service to his fatherland and to mankind as a whole,"[49] the double service to the state and to others could not ultimately be achieved, and in fact lead him to regret his

---

48. Annas, *Morality of Happiness*, 300.
49. Fuhrmann, *Cicero and the Roman Republic*, 21.

past that, most recently, had involved personal anguish, a divorce from his wife and the death of his daughter, Tullia, that had left him grief-stricken.

The *Tusculum Disputations* was written at Cicero's country villa during a period of enforced isolation—not precisely exile, but a banishment from the city of Rome for political reasons and due to events he could no longer influence by his rhetorical skills. To console himself from the separation from Rome (the separation from *himself* of being a Roman with *dignitas* and civic purpose and therefore personal honor) he makes the attempt, in five books, to argue that philosophy can be the only remedy from the distresses of life—with the conclusion that virtue is itself sufficient for leading a good and happy life. Perhaps his defense of philosophy in a Roman context recalled the incident in 155 BC when a delegation of Greek philosophers arrived in Rome, only to be expelled by Cato the censor, who worried that their novel ideas would somehow corrupt the Roman character which was now assured of itself, at least in part, because of its military conquests. The opposition between the philosopher (or, for that matter, any unique individual or groups) and the city becomes evident in Rome throughout its history, whether in time of peace or war, political stability or the turmoil during the ascension of Augustus as emperor.

During a time of intense political upheaval and uncertainty, when men of eminence and vision and, of course, military power were intent on stamping the times with their individual will, Cicero retreated to one of his country estates and argued for the relevance of philosophy. His solitude and isolation, appeased somewhat by letters to and from friends, could not have been more in contrast to Epicurus's life in the Garden, with its direct contact with others. Reading the five books of the *Tusculam Disputations,* one sees again and again the defense of philosophy above all as a discipline that promises to heal, but whether Cicero can maintain such a belief when his fundamental responsibility is civic (not so much to others as individuals but to the state) always encounters the same obstacle. For all his reliance on academic philosophy and the search for what is most probable—of certainty one simply could not expect—and for all his commitment to the psychical consequences of philosophy, Cicero the man could not effectively reconcile himself to a personal disposition, his responsibility to his idea of the Roman *res publica*. Just as his participation in the priestly office of augurs forced him to necessarily ignore rational principles of thought for the expediency of political action (one can only imagine him participating in the sacrifice of an animal and the reading of its viscera or the symbolic flight of birds for propitious or unpropitious signs) his commitment to philosophy could only be articulated in the context of the state despite writing his many treatises in the country, in a villa surrounded by farmland. Did he sense, but also deny, that in the more than a century of being exposed to Greek philosophy, the character of the city of Rome (perhaps, all cities) could not allow philosophy to have any influence on the political realities of the day, either in Cato's time or in his own? The tension of the *Tusculam Disputations* attests to Cicero's unresolved deliberations, in part because, as a Roman, he cannot assert his own individuality over tradition. At the beginning of book Two, for example, he cites a tragedy written by the Roman Ennius and one of his characters, Neoptolemus, who plays a philosopher, "but only a little way, for of doing so entirely he did not approve,"[50] perfectly expressing the general suspicion of Rome toward contemplative thought, one that could lead to a reevaluation of civic life and was therefore to be resisted.

At the time of writing, Cicero has been relieved of the two duties most essential to him as a Roman citizen: his profession as an advocate and his duties in the Senate. Philosophy, then, appears to be a pasttime pursued only with leisure, free from the day-to-day responsibilities of the citizen in the city. For all his admiration of Socrates and of Plato's writing, Cicero did not view philosophy as a practice that always and necessarily posed questions to the status of the city and its politics. Or, if he had already done so in *The Republic*, with no hope of any concrete or lasting influence except for his brother Quintus or closest friends like Atticus the Epicurean, Cicero turned to philosophy as a form of *consolatio*, the title of the first of his books on philosophy. What is the most important influence of philosophy? Despite his academic affiliation, Cicero's primary concern is not with knowledge or truth but to be free from the distresses of the psyche. The "effect of philosophy," he writes, "is a physician of souls, takes away the load of empty troubles, sets us free from desires and banishes fears" (2.4). He shows himself to be quintessentially Roman (and different from both Epicureans and, later, Christians) when he claims that "its influence cannot be the same for all: its effect is great when it has secured a hold upon a character suited to it" (2.4). The stratification of society and the hierarchies essential to the Roman identity of its aristocracy are evident even in the influence of philosophy. Furthermore, what he anticipates to be the most important aspect of philosophy, the pursuit and attainment of virtue, he etymologically traces *virtus* to certain kind of manliness, one associated with a martial capacity (2.19).

Cicero makes arguments that he cannot, ultimately, defend if one is to authentically represent philosophy. A Roman could only achieve honor and notoriety by being acknowledged by others, in particular his social, political, and economic equals. All others were merely the majority:

---

50. Cicero, *Tusc.*, 2.1

> In your case, should you become a figure in the eyes of the mob, I should nevertheless not like you to be dependent on their judgment, nor wish to accept their view of what is fairest: you must your own judgement; if you are content with yourself in approving the right, then you will not only win a victory over self, a rule I laid down a little while back, but over the world of men and things. (2.26)

Here he merely repeats the Epicurean belief in *autarkeia* or self-sufficiency, but he does so in the context of the difference between his own class of men and all others, dismissing the majority. His commitment to philosophy and the well-being of others can only be articulated within the limits of Rome's separation of citizens, with all its stratification such as the *honestiores* and *humiliores*. He thereby believes philosophy to be an intellectual attainment only possible to those who have been educated and those who have the proper character; those without access to education were simply dismissed as inconsequential. The emergence of Christian philosophy occurred in the context of Roman rule and values, hence its emphasis on a universal attitude to everyone, thus also making it distinct from the so-called Stoic cosmopolitanism which, for all its idealism, remained within a strictly Roman perspective.

Cicero seems to come to a notable conclusion regarding upbringing and education. Arguing from the standpoint of the "law of nature," some presocial constitution that guarantees an innate virtue, he makes the claim that society itself is responsible for the compromise of such an innate nature:

> The seeds of virtue are inborn in our disposition and, if they were allowed to ripen, nature's own hand would lead us on to happiness of life; as things are, however, as soon as we come into to the light of day and have been acknowledged, we at once find ourselves in a world of iniquity amid a medley of wrong beliefs. (3.1)

A remarkable statement that seems to undermine the confidence he expressed about the validity of Rome. At the beginning of Book III, Cicero seems to come to a conclusion that would necessarily force him to reevaluate everything he believes about Roman society: there is an irreducible difference between the law of nature and its influence on human beings and the process of socialization that, by necessity, leads to the adoption of erroneous beliefs, again a belief consistent with Epicureans. If Cicero developed his insight to its conclusion, he would then have to dedicate himself to a philosophy that specifically challenged all the beliefs of the status quo, teaching not only a philosophy for the purpose of everyone's psychical health, but toward the creation of a society that would contribute to the development of the law of nature rather than its dissolution in society. At the same time that he makes such an argument (that leaves him more divided and uncertain), he also recognizes the consequences for his support of Rome:

> Assuredly, there is an art of healing the soul (*animi medicina*)—I mean philosophy, whose aid must be sought not, as in bodily diseases, outside ourselves, and we must use our utmost endeavor, with all our resources and strengths, to have the power to be ourselves our own physicians. (3.3)

Cicero makes a decision here that again seems to emulate the Epicureans, namely the imperative to heal oneself and others. Rather than make the attempt to influence society as a whole, he chooses the individual who (not even needing a teacher) can heal their own afflictions. Such an endeavor, however, must become independent of society. If, as he argues, society itself is responsible for the false presuppositions that compromise a healthy human life, then one has a choice to make: either an attempt to influence society as a whole or else withdraw (as he has now at his villa) to a life where the individual pursuit of philosophy can be attempted either in isolation or, like Epicureans, with like-minded friends. Cicero has, perhaps unknowingly, inherited two aspects of Greek philosophy, two aspects that reflected his character and personal beliefs: either a Socratic philosophy committed to the amelioration of both individuals and society as a whole, or the Epicurean emphasis on a small community of like-minded friends who could remain independent of society's values and beliefs. As he writes,

> Be persuaded at any rate of this, that there will be no end to wretchedness unless the soul is cured, and without philosophy this is impossible. Therefore, let us put ourselves in the hands of philosophy for treatment, since we have made a beginning: we shall be cured if we will. (3.6)

How can he be cured if his affliction is directly related to his isolation on his farm and his inability to participate in the ongoing tribulations of the state? He knows, though cannot admit, that his cure cannot be achieved precisely because of his most time-worn beliefs, the ones that have motivated him since being socialized and educated as a Roman. He does not realize, like Augustine will leading up to his conversion, that his state of unhappiness and indecision is directly related to his attitude toward Rome—at once loyal and committed to it (and gaining some satisfaction owing to his reputation and notoriety), and also drawn away from it for his own psychical health. Again, he makes the admission:

Epicurus's *Logotherapeia* and the Health of the Psyche 169

> In dealing with scorn of office many are given of men who have not obtained office and have been happier for that very reason, and praise is bestowed expressly upon the life of men who have preferred the retirement of private life to a public career. (3.24)

Here lies then the fundamental conflict of Cicero's life: philosophy or the state and society. Both are impossible. Cicero even refers to Socrates's relationship to Alcibiades and how the older philosopher could tell the younger and very ambitious Athenian that "there was no difference, for all his high position, between him and any porter," (3.32) again affirming how character cannot be determined by social position within the city-state.

In a passage in Book V, Cicero may ultimately reveal his truest *feelings*, even if they contradict his widely-held beliefs. Here Cicero sounds profoundly regretful, as if now (isolated at his country house and with the time to reflect on the past) he has come to a sudden realization, or at least one he has no choice but to acknowledge. "The wise man will in fact despise our paltry ambitions and reject the distinctions bestowed by the people even if they come unsought," (5.36) he writes, looking back on his past and the entire course of his life and realizing that all the social and political ambitions that had motivated him, probably since childhood and during his education, now no longer had any real meaning. He had based his entire life on the certain belief that pursuing honor as a Roman citizen was the pinnacle of achievement; he was now left disappointed and forlorn. The ending of the sentence could not be clearer, nor more regretful: "but we do now know how to despise them [the ambitions and distinctions] before the time of repentance begins" (5.36). From the standpoint of the present, Cicero admits that in the past he had no ability to properly evaluate the meaning of being a Roman citizen and what was expected of him. Only now, exiled from the city, does the beginning of his repentance forcefully make him realize how wrong he had been. For all the arguments to the contrary (the philosopher must participate in the political life of the state) Cicero cannot avoid the conclusion that wisdom, to be attained, cannot be possible in a political context, and certainly not one such as the Roman state. He can only come to one conclusion:

> For what is more delightful than leisure devoted to literature? That literature I mean which gives us the knowledge of the infinite greatness of nature, and, in this actual world of ours, of sky, the lands, the seas. (5.36)

He does not extoll the greatness of the Roman state, for all the accomplishments that he must, if ambivalently, admire and respect; rather, he turns again to nature, the world made prior to all social and political institutions. Does he anticipate the literature, the poetry, of the Augustans in such works as Virgil's *Eclogues*, affirming the uncomplicated natural world and the tranquility it offers? Cicero can only come to one conclusion, however much he may resist it. He admits that "I was not only pressed to write on philosophic subjects, but provoked to do so as well" by his friend Brutus, fulfilling an obligation and responsibility. However, the conclusion to the *Tusculum Disputations* sums up his evaluation of philosophy and, by extension, being a Roman citizen:

> In doing so I cannot readily say how much I shall benefit others; at any rate in my cruel sorrows and the various troubles which beset me from all sides no other consolation could be found. (5.41)

His repentance and consolation are telling: only now, isolated on his country estate, does he realize, seemingly for the first time, that he has lived a contradictory life. Deeply troubled by the events within the Roman state that have forced him to retreat to his country estate (in part, for a safety soon to be shattered), Cicero devotes his time to benefiting others, helping others insofar as it is his source of consolation. His previous service to the state and the dependence on his social status for his own identity, he now realizes, have left him with profound regrets. He does not fully realize, however, (and this must be part of his melancholia) that there has been a fundamental and irreconcilable contradiction in both his thought and life: insofar as he was a servant of the state, he could not attend to the proper care of others; and so, perhaps even realizing the political upheaval and conflict between Mark Antony and Octavius (eventually to become Caesar) could have grave consequences for his life, he brings the *Tusculam Disputations* to a close with the kind of profound disappointment which can only experienced by someone who, approaching his end, also turns—and so unlike Epicurean teaching—to regret instead of gratitude, disappointment instead of the *charis* exemplary in the experience not of *consolatio* but of *ataraxia*.

Chapter 5

Jesus' *Soteria*

1. *Healing Words*

RATHER THAN A PUBLIC citizen of a state, and even less as someone who supported the official leadership of the Jerusalem temple (and before turning to the decisive and culminating act that will result in his arrest and crucifixion), Jesus' entire *ministry* in the countryside, villages, and towns of Galilee and its environs was, in essence, a substitution of the temple rituals for a day-to-day service to the people most in need of support. The people Jesus took care of were many: the ill, certainly, and also those most adversely affected by social conditions at the time, that is, the vast majority of people whose lives had become unbearable by the demands made on them, including the poor, the broken-hearted, the captives, and the bruised, (Luke 4:18) those who had to deal with "heavy burdens" (Matt 23:4) and "torments" (Matt 4:24), widows who lost their houses through exploitation and opportunism (Mark 12:40). His treatment was much more all-encompassing than those who needed "miracles": the "blind, lame, and paralyzed" (John 5:3). Their humanity had been compromised by an increasingly difficult life, as they had been forced to endure conditions of extreme need and were burdened with social and economic impositions such as food scarcity, taxes, and mistreatment. So instead of proclaiming an imminent and expected eschatology—a salvation from without, with its singular capacity of utterly transforming the world and redeeming it according to apocalyptic expectations—Jesus devoted himself to the succour of those most in need in the present, so as to change history from within. Jesus' acts at the temple during the Passover will soon reveal the extent of his rejection of its traditional practices and become a direct confrontation never before attempted by anyone in history, turning a centuries-old idea (prophetic, Greek, and Roman) into a decisive act of repudiation and abolition. Before carrying out his thought-out plan, and fully expecting its outcome, the approximately two-year period of teaching and *soteriology*—and, most especially, his care for the psychological well-being of all people—was all-important in terms of dedicating his life to serving others. For one, the physically damaged from birth or by accident—the blind, deaf, those unable to walk, all these individuals who would have been considered inferior and, in many cases, regarded with contempt, for their condition and their uselessness to their families and the community. Jesus' life was exemplary, demonstrating authentic piety by attending to the needs of others—the most desperate, those bereft of hope—instead of observing the ritualistic acts deemed all-important in the continuing order of society and giving it the appearance of stability. He was, above all, a servant; and he served by teaching (speaking to others in a particular way) and through his words, healing them.

Even before his birth, in the extraordinary event of an angel appearing in a dream to Joseph informing him of the birth of his son to be named Jesus, he describes him as someone who will "save (*sosei*) his people from their sins (*hamartion*)" (Matt 1:21), and though there may be many different translations of *hamartia*, one preliminary and by no means complete one could be a sense of "failure" due to being unable to *become* more themselves, both because of internal weakness and social impositions, the frailties of the self and the pathologies of society indifferent to their welfare. Each gospel writer understands the importance of Jesus' soteriological mission even if the metaphors are numerous and different. As Matthew writes, "the son of man is come to save (*sosai*) that which was lost" (Matt 18:11). The soteriology here is one of retrieving, of bringing back, of showing a path (a life) that seemingly was no longer possible. His *revelations* allow others to *see themselves*, for the first time, as human beings who have long endured impositions from within and without that have effectively made them resigned to the limits of their everyday life. For Luke, the healing involves a certain kind of knowledge, a "knowledge of salvation (*soterias*)" that leads him to define Jesus as a "*Soter*" (Luke 2:11).[1] "I came not to judge the world, but to save (*soso*) the world," (John 12:47) Jesus says, emphasizing his role not as someone who passes judgment on the vulnerable, but rather who provides

---

1. In *The History of the Synoptic Tradition*, Rudolf Bultmann's comments on Luke 2:11 specifically separate the idea of *soteria* between its Hellenistic and Palestinian meanings.

them with solace; he comes to their aid regardless of their moral or physical condition.

"The Son of man came ... to minister (*diakonesai*), and to give (*dounai*) his life (*psuchen*)," (Mark 10:45) Jesus proclaims and when he adds that he will dedicate his *psyche* (heart and mind and soul) to others, he does so as a "ransom," the *lutron* repeated at Matthew 20:28, and one intended to be for the release, for the freedom, of others. C. F. D. Moule believes that this is one of Jesus' most significant "sacrificial sayings,"[2] but another interpretation should at least be mentioned. Although this all-important declaration has been interpreted from the standpoint of his sacrificial death, *didomi* has the multifaceted sense of "to give, present, or devote oneself to." When *psyche* is translated as *life* (and therefore tending toward a sacrificial understanding of Mark's words), Jesus here seems to give himself up, in death, rather than give his life as someone capable of transforming the minds and lives of others in his everyday teaching.

Jesus served above all by giving himself to others. Filled with empathy and compassion, he above all expressed *feelings* during an age when people had been forced to become hardened, denying their emotions so as to protect themselves from the everyday experience of pain and deprivation. They had no choice but to endure. Jesus gave everyone his psyche as someone who could speak in a remarkable way, in substance and tone both, and by doing so bringing support and consolation to the most afflicted. Among them were (and to examine only a few) the psychologically troubled and the anguished, those "possessed" by "unclean spirits," and, most important in the context of his immediate society and its traditions, those suffering from illnesses that made them especially vulnerable because of their appearance, their skin ailments, or their "issue of blood." These stigmatized individuals were defined according to ancient Levitical laws that made them "unclean" and therefore shunned from family and community.[3] Jesus should be regarded as someone who directly challenged the most commonly held assumptions about the meaning of people's *religious* illnesses which resulted in them being shunned from their immediate families and communities. "Let not your heart be troubled," (John 14:1) Jesus tells all those who would listen to him, acting always in his capacity as someone who healed by consoling, by being a "Comforter" (John 14:16), the *parakletos* as someone with an extraordinary capacity to understand the specific suffering of others and bring them relief. The language of *paraklesis* that was so important

---

2. Moule, *Sacrifice of Christ*, 11.

3. In *Leviticus*, Knight argues that one of Jesus' "Satan temptations" was "to turn his back on the book of Leviticus," 94.

in John, though it first originated in Timothy's ministry to the church in Thessalonika,[4] involves a specific kind of speaking that brings consolation and reassurance most especially in the context of a life as a Christian among hostile and suspicious communities. "Learn of me," Jesus says to people, and "ye shall find rest (*anapausin*) unto your souls" (Matt 11:29), a tranquility and peace of mind they have not experienced for a long time. But it was above all in the way he spoke that he was able to heal people, as when he said, "these things I say, that ye might be saved (*sothete*)" (John 5:34). The vocabulary is constant and stresses relief, support, and consolation. The soteriology essential to his ministry—on his own, without acknowledgment from the religious authorities or following the prescribed rituals—was daily emphasized by Jesus. By doing so independently and with a singular ability, he made his service to others *unconditional*. Unlike the rituals of the temple leadership, those based on an exchange between human beings and Yahweh, with the *qorban olah* or "ascent offering" of sacrifice required, Jesus did not ask them for *things*, and certainly not dead animals; rather, he continually appealed to their inner spirit, and by reanimating it, giving it the life of the spirit, Jesus hoped they would become transformed human beings now capable of contributing to a slowly changing world for all.

In the four gospels, there are innumerable examples of Jesus' dedication to others and of his ability to heal many different kinds of ailments. At the time, the vast majority of the population had no access to medical care (physical or psychological) and there was also the suffering of those individuals unfortunate enough to have physical symptoms considered impure. These were especially grievous since they had to suffer from the condition itself and also feel a moral culpability, as if an outward mark on the body of their illness confirmed an inner imperfection, a flaw now exposed for everyone to see. However, despite the innumerable descriptions of his "miracles" (though the Greek *semeia*, or "sign," for example, has no such distinctive connotations and does not, as a consequence, imply any transcendence of natural law or metaphysical accomplishment), the only concern here will be to demonstrate how his relationship to others—first and foremost *how* he spoke (for example, with the "gracious words" of Luke 4:22), *what he said* to them, and the effect it had on their overall health—showed capacity for empathy and compassion as necessary in his capacity as a healer.[5] "Out of

---

4. *Paraklesis* appears first in 1 Thessalonians 2:3, and is essential in Timothy's visit to them.

5. In *Jesus of Nazareth*, Gerhard Lohfink writes that Jesus "healed sick people, not through mere words" (121), thereby minimizing his particular kind of speaking, one that again should be stressed. Others have drawn an unnecessary division between his speaking and his healing. In *The Aims of Jesus*, Ben Meyer concludes: "Jesus epitomized

the abundance of the heart the mouth speaketh," (Matt 12:34) Jesus says, emphasizing how a good man is one who can speak well, from the heart, with love, and is certainly not evaluated according to rhetorical standards of eloquence and persuasion even though his listeners could not always understand the demanding meanings, and intentions, of his words. "A good man out of the good treasure of his heart bringeth forth that which is good" (Luke 6:45). The reason Jesus couples goodness with the heart (with the importance of human emotions) is the recognition that, during this time of hardship, all kinds of people had stopped feeling, had turned themselves hard as a reaction to life's conditions. Many had been dehumanized by others, by the suffering that had become insupportable and endured only by turning away from one's *feelings*. Jesus restored them, bringing individuals back to themselves, their essential humanity, and allowed rejected individuals, the mad and the unclean, lepers and those with blood ailments, back into their families and communities. The ostracized and stigmatized were restored, saved from being outcasts and brought back into their essential and until now degraded (by the judgment of others) humanity. And so *soteria* was simultaneously a salvation from a previous condition as well as a healing, a renewed life in health and freedom. He lived up to the highest standards of the prophets not by observing rituals or merely adhering to the exacting details of the law without an accompanying disposition, as did some (though, of course, not all) of the priests of the temple,[6] but by his ability to "execute true judgment, and shew mercy and compassion every man to his brother: and oppress not the widow, nor the fatherless, the stranger, nor the poor" (Zech 6:9–10).

There will be only one overall emphasis in interpreting Jesus' many examples of teaching and healing. Each of the gospel writers represents Jesus as a specific kind of teacher and healer, one who does so only from the standpoint of what he says to people and how he speaks, and with less

---

his public career not as words but as exorcisms and cures," 154. To minimize Jesus' words is to emphasize a healing ability transferrable, somehow, through his body and miraculously rather than through the therapeutic, soteriological words he speaks to others, as individuals and in groups. To emphasize his acts over his words runs the danger of ignoring how the words of his teaching were a substitution of ritual. Those first listening to him, of course, had only a number of ways to understand and interpret him; the oral tradition, in part, has perpetuated Jesus as a magician and exorcist because that was their only point of reference.

6. It is important to note, as Rowley does in *From Moses to Qumran*, that "to think of prophets only in terms of the best and priests only terms of the worst is unwise," 137. As John himself emphasizes, the Jewish temple leadership was itself "divided" about Jesus (John 10:19), some of them because they understood how clearly he saw *through them*. He exposed them. Of course, there were others who also believed him (John 12:42).

emphasis on his preaching to many people at once than on his conversation with stricken *individuals*, at times privately, in extended conversation, which the gospel writers unfortunately do not preserve in part due to the necessity for them of presenting Jesus' acts as instantaneous. Their accounts of incidents is so often hurried, as if the time involved mattered much less than the result. Unfortunately, the need to stress the instantaneous moment of a so-called miracle rather than a substantive conversation fails to fully represent the teaching and healing of Jesus. As N. T. Wright notes in his discussion of the time involved in miraculous events, "most of them would have been over in about one minute."[7] The gospel writers are much more concerned with demonstrating Jesus' healing ability (as if his body emanated with a God-given power) than with his words, those revealed in lengthy conversations with those most needing to hear him acknowledge their humanity, their fundamental worth and dignity. Without hearing Jesus' words to the ill, we continue today to merely perceive him as a divine figure; doing so runs the danger of forgetting his teaching and how it has to be passed on, continued, his ministry accepted as an obligation for anyone who would like to serve others.

All references to Jesus' acts with the appearance of the miraculous will avoid any connection to the metaphysical (divine), much less magic[8] or exorcisms.[9] Thomas Martin describes him as, "Christ the healer (understood as comprehensively as possible: physician, surgeon, therapist, pharmacologist, specialist)."[10] There are (as one can imagine) countless descriptions of Jesus. He has been defined as a "magician covered social revolutionary."[11] Jesus is portrayed as a village psychiatrist.[12] Geza Vermes calls him a "Galilean Hasid."[13] The often-described miracles performed with his hands will also be interpreted less as a sign of his extraordinary abilities than how he

---

7. Wright, *Who was Jesus?*, 97.

8. Horsley, *Jesus and Magic*. "Application of the modern concept of miracle to the healing stories of Jesus in fact distorts them, makes them into something they are not in themselves. There appears to be no basis in the healing and exorcism stories themselves for categorizing them as miracles stories or for referring to the healings and exorcism of Jesus as miracles," 28.

9. Twelftree, *Jesus the Exorcist*.

10. Martin, *Our Restless Heart*, 31.

11. Frend, *Martyrdom and Persecution*, 497.

12. Capps, *Jesus, the Village Psychiatrist*. One of the many virtues of this particular study has been to reassess descriptions of certain illnesses in the gospels with a modern understanding of psychological illness. That Capps cites more than a dozen references to the work of Sigmund Freud's psychoanalytic theory allows for a thoroughly rational account of ancient psychological illness.

13. Vermes, *Jesus and the World*, 11.

conveys, with a gesture, a touch, a caress, his profound emotions for people, feelings which they, in turn, feel and are consoled by. A distinction will be made between the dynamic and therapeutic aspect of his speech and the healing power of his hands, or, for that matter, the unusual occurrences of healing with spittle. "Jesus went forth, and saw a great multitude, and was moved with compassion toward them, and he healed (*etherapeusen*) their sick," (Matt 14:14) the *therapeia* once again, as in Socrates, being the dedication of a *servant*. Rather than portraying the miracles, magic, and exorcisms attributed to him (an attempt, from antiquity, to give him exceptional authority by virtue of his association with the divine), he becomes all the more impressive if one only hears him *speak* to the ill. He conveys a particular message to them, about their humanity and how the world they live in has, wrongly, denied them a fundamental commonality.[14]

"If a man love me, he will keep my words" (John 14:24).[15] One must keep, preserve, and safeguard his words and also act on them; his listeners are also encouraged to memorize his sayings (as the followers of Epicurus were) so his teaching could be recalled and always present, repeated from one person to another, individually and in groups. "Whoever cometh to me, and heareth my sayings, and doeth them, I will shew you to whom he is like" (Luke 6:47). Moreover, what is striking about some of the individuals Jesus meets (especially those defined as "possessed with devils," that is, suffering from severe psychological disturbance) is their isolation from their families and communities, sometimes being bound and chained, living in tombs and in caves, and thereby reduced to being less than human, their condition exacerbated by a profound loneliness and loss of all dignity. They are, indeed,

14. In "The Quest for the Historical Jesus," Werner Kelber draws attention to Jesus as a speaker and someone "intent on retrieving Jesus' message has to come face to face with the intractably difficult issue of speech." He comes to the conclusion that "the words voiced by the historical Jesus are not available to us for purposes of classification or quantification," 107–8. The point, however, is not to capture some original saying but rather make the attempt to understand how he spoke, with what tone and emotion. Jesus' words can be understood when one presupposes his spoken words in context; surely we can recognize the tone he uses when accusing a Pharisee of being a hypocrite as opposed to when he is talking to someone about their illness. The gospels portray his character—his anger at injustice, his love for the vulnerable.

15. A remarkable saying indeed: Jesus tells his listeners that one of the ways to love him (and certainly among the most important) is to "keep"—that is, preserve, memorize, and also *guard*—his sayings so they will not be misinterpreted and corrupted. He was always aware that he would be slandered and his message, if at all possible, turned against him. According to Lamar Williamson, Jr. in *Preaching the Gospel of John*, "there is no significant distinction in meaning" (190) between words and commandments (of John 14:21). My emphasis calls attention to Jesus' awareness that his message will not be univocal; and so he tells his listeners to hear him, memorize him, so there will later be consensus and no doubt about what he said and how he said it.

demonized by the people who shun and ostracize them, by families who have disowned them, and communities that have banished them, in effect punishing them for afflictions they can in no way be responsible for and are simply unfortunate to suffer from. When Jesus then "cast out the spirits with his word (*logo*), and healed (*etherapeusen*) all that were sick," (Matt 8:16) it is his *therapeutic speech* that relieves them of their pain and suffering, healing them by welcoming them back into humanity once again, for the first time letting them hear that they are not culpable for their illnesses and that they have been wrongly, cruelly treated by those most responsible for their well-being: their families, friends, and fellow villagers. He heals by approaching individuals, such as the Gadarene, who are ostracized from families and communities and reintroduces them back to their own.

There are events (and certain acts reputed to have been done by Jesus) that seem to have the characteristics of ritualistic gestures. For example, in the case of a deaf person who had a speech impediment, Jesus "put his fingers into his ears, and he spit, and touched his tongue," (Mark 7:33) followed by the Aramaic *ephphatha*, "be opened," as if the words are commands to the organ that will suddenly be transformed by his words, in this case sounding like an Aramaic incantation. Mark prefaced the gesture with an important point: "And he took him aside from the multitude" (7:33). Jesus takes the man away so as to be alone—that is, unseen and unheard by others and in a deliberately private conversation. The acts were not *seen* by anyone; their conversation, and the event as a whole, must be reconstructed from the imagination of the reader. Mark has a similar incident with a blind person. "And he took the blind man by the hand, and led him out of the town; and when he had spit upon his eyes, and put his hands upon him, he asked him if he saw ought" (Mark 8:23). In this case, Jesus seems to spit directly into the man's eyes, in his face, a gesture of extreme insult and disrespect in their society, one he completely ignores and, in fact, understands in a unique way. Once again, Jesus and the man are alone; no one sees them, and therefore the incident has been recounted by the blind man or, more likely, by someone who had to account for the fact of healing. The events are not witnessed, and yet they are part of an important and enduring testimony.

Finally, in the third account (this time, with his disciples as witnesses) Jesus is once again reputed to restore the sight of the blind: "He spat on the ground, and made clay of the spittle, and he anointed the eyes of the blind man with the clay" (John 9:6). However, if the entire incident is followed from beginning to end, another meaning becomes evident. It begins, first of all, when his disciples ask Jesus, "Who did sin, this man, or his parents, that he was born blind" (John 9:2)? Following a common assumption at the time, it was believed that anyone born with a severe ailment such as blindness had

Jesus' *Soteria* 179

been punished due to some past sin, either individual or inherited, as if a physical malady was in fact a divine punishment. Jesus does nothing less than repudiate such a belief (that God punishes the living or the dead) when he tells them that "neither hath this man sinned, nor his parents" (John 9:3). The gospel writer, who shows himself to be familiar with rhetoric, provides descriptions of the scene with two readers in mind: one requiring eccentric gestures and a "miracle," the other being someone who can recognize the meaning of the scene beyond any appeal to the miraculous and instead juxtapose a condition of blindness (not reducible to the physical) to Jesus telling his disciples "I am the light of the world" (John 9:5). John's account therefore takes different readers into consideration: those who rely on the miraculous to intervene in the world and others who, more rationally disposed, can nevertheless understand the act of healing as restorative, a remedy that may involve a change in the blind man's self-conception.

In all three cases, the presence of spit has a meaning not entirely clear unless one recognizes what it means for Jesus to spit in someone's face in contrast to at least two members of the Jewish leadership who, after Jesus' apprehension, "then did they spit in his face," (Matt 26:67) and the Romans who will mock and scourge "and shall spit upon him" (Mark 10:34) in order to further degrade him. The spit he uses to heal is intended to challenge the traditional perception of the act as one of insult. Instead of understanding his gesture as somehow an instance of his miraculous healing powers, Jesus can be understood as someone who lives, by example, to directly challenge all the assumptions, beliefs, and prejudices taken for granted in his immediate society. Christians would later be defined as "these that have turned the world upside down," (Acts 17:6) directly overturning all the views of an age in order to inaugurate nothing less than a new history, one made possible by the teaching and specific *soteriology* of Jesus. His teaching is salvific in the sense of *rescuing* individuals from the limits of their own society and by denying the legitimacy of the categories (especially, as we shall see, the religious ones) accepted as a matter of fact and to separate the clean from the unclean, the pure from the impure. Jesus may often be portrayed as being a healer, but such repeated experiences of healing occur in a context of him being a teacher, someone capable of altering the idea of an individual, most especially in a self-conception imposed due to widespread religious beliefs. His soteriology was individual and conveyed by the power of his speech and the strength of his empathy. He had an extraordinary presence not by simply drawing attention to himself—and, of course, not to be in any way deified or worshipped—but by allowing people to once again recognize their own frail humanity, perhaps ill, stricken with disease, though never lessened despite the traditional beliefs long held and now more and more open to being rethought. Jesus' teaching and healing began with individuals and soon was felt in society. Those most threatened by his uncompromising life would soon plan to attempt to stop them. Anticipating their plan, Jesus had to fulfill the intentions of his ministry before the appointed time. Before entering the temple on Passover, he had to devote himself to others and therefore give everyone a sense that a new piety, a new testament, was now being proclaimed.

2. A Teacher

What, precisely, is the role of someone described, in Greek, as a *didaskale*?[16] He was certainly a teacher, as his followers were students or disciples, but with several crucial differences: Jesus was no traditional teacher, much less someone depending on a curriculum, though of course he often recalled Scripture (at least according to the gospel writers who always associate him with a scriptural precedent) and represented himself as someone related to the teachings of the prophets insofar as they held the priestly class accountable to their responsibilities. His speech, at least when treating the ill and not arguing with individuals from the temple leadership, had none of the rhetoric or sophistry associated with some philosophical teachers who, of course (and unlike Jesus) were paid for their services. Despite claims of a shared perspective between Jesus and the Cynics, as some have argued,[17] the connection is tenuous at best. Wisdom is attributed to him from the time he was a child (Luke 2:52), and *sophia* could obviously not be unfamiliar to him, whether the wisdom literature of the Jewish tradition or its importance in Hellenism. His use of a *general* philosophical vocabulary is not incidental; there are numerous and interrelated examples, though this crucial problem cannot be treated within the scope of the discussion to follow. Bruce Chilton believes that "as Christianity took on an increasingly Hellenistic character, its portraits of Jesus became more cerebral, almost philosophical," making a distinction between a tactile Mark who heals with his hands and the later

---

16. Jesus is most often labeled a *didaskale*, a teacher, though there are two others that are prominent. Understandably, given his immediate society and how others put him in a context they could understand, he is often called a rabbi. Finally, he is also called an *epistata*. For example, when he first meets his future disciple, Simon (Luke 5:5), the fisherman (obviously recognizing his intelligence in the way he speaks) calls him an *epistata* even before knowing anything about him. In other words, if an *epistata* is someone who is educated, who knows, Simon clearly recognized Jesus' intelligence.

17. See, for example, F. Gerald Downing's *Christ and the Cynics: Jesus and Other Radical Preachers in First-Century Tradition*.

gospels he describes as "logocentric."[18] The tactile/logocentric distinction is motivated less by the necessary attention to Jesus' language, words, and teaching (when neglected, his teaching can no longer be accurately or completely represented) than a desire to elevate Jesus' body and hands to a mediation between health and illness, and of course to the often-portrayed miraculous touch of the hands. A theological divine body of grace may be appealing; it displaces, however, the extraordinary and still enigmatic language of Jesus—and worse, consigns it to secondary importance.

In the Gospel of John, *didaskale* and *rabbi* are both mentioned so as to affirm a double source of Jesus' teaching and without emphasizing one over the other. Each example must be analyzed, both to recognize the context of each title and to notice specific individuals who call him. Calling him may determine their relationship to him, but like other, even more significant titles (i.e. Lord, King, Son of God), they do not, cannot, define his self-conception. He has many names,[19] yet noticeably, no one in any of the four gospels ever calls him by his birth names(s)—the ones given to him by angels, preferring "Master" (*didaskale, rabbi, epistates*) and many others, all of them with complicated significance. Without here developing the meaning of Jesus' only and many-times-repeated self-designation ("the son of man"), no single or several titles could hope to define him. These may be heuristic, but they cannot be definitive.

There are six different examples (to mention only the Gospel of John) of being called one of the three, though in the last one, at 20:16, an emphasis does seem to occur, perhaps giving it a more definitive sense. In any case, the speakers less than Jesus should be mentioned; they are not irrelevant for understanding the use of specific titles, of reverence and respect, each individual revealing more about themselves than Jesus. In the first incident, the scribes and Pharisees bring a woman charged with adultery and ask him to deliberate on her situation as it reflects the law of Moses: those who appeal to him for a judicial decision call him "Master," *didaskale* (John 8:4), a teacher, and by no means, in their eyes, a rabbi. In the next example, previously discussed in relation to the blind man, his disciples call him "Master," *rabbi* (John 9:2), thereby acknowledging his relationship to Judaism and his role as a specifically Jewish teacher versed in the Hebrew Bible and the law. In the incident leading to the tomb of Lazarus, again his disciples call him "Master," *rabbi* (John 11:8). When Jesus speaks with Martha, Lazarus's

---

18. Chilton, *Rabbi Jesus*, 131. The difficulty with the before and after argument is this: it presupposes an original, somehow uncontaminated message and one that, after being exposed to Hellenistic thought, becomes somehow corrupt.

19. See, for example, Sabourin's *Names and Titles of Jesus* and Taylor's *Names of Jesus*.

sister, she then tells her sister Mary that "the Master (*didaskalos*) is come" (John 11:28), using the Greek instead of the Hebrew so as to differentiate him (positively, it seems) from the temple leadership. Thus far, he has been defined according to two different terms by the scribes and Pharisees, his disciples, and Martha. During the last supper, however, Jesus talks to his disciples and reminds them that "ye call me Master (*didaskalos*) and Lord: and ye say well; for so I am. If I then, your Lord and Master (*didaskalos*), have washed your feet; ye also ought to wash one another's feet" (John 13:13–14). In this unique incident in John, Jesus appears to change one of the titles they have previously given him, *rabbi*, and instead affirms the Greek instead, and precisely in the context of a complete social reversal—the "master" washing the feet of his followers. Finally, in the last reference in the gospel of John, we have one last juxtaposition in the very same incident when Mary Magdalene, at Jesus' sepulchre, sees his apparition and after calling her she "saith unto him, Rabboni (*rabbouni*); which is to say, Master (*didaskale*)" (John 20:16). Although John intervenes to *translate* "rabbi" to "teacher," the titles are nevertheless related and, even if the gospel writer should prefer one over the other, there are simply no indications throughout making one of the other preferable, or, more difficult still, more accurate. Only one conclusion can be made: Jesus acts, in different contexts and in relation to different individuals, as a teacher understood as both Greek and Hebrew and who will represent simultaneous traditions as he heals—including, finally, often being called an *epistates* (Luke 5:5)[20], someone who is given a position of leadership due to his education and knowledge: his *episteme*. All the titles related to his leadership, however, may ultimately be insufficient to understand him as an unprecedented human being, certainly, and in the expression of a language that remains elusive, which is perhaps the single greatest challenge readers of the gospels face as they narrow the gap between Jesus and our present. All the titles given to him are no more than approximations reflecting the language and history of the first century AD. Jesus, however, cannot be limited by the language (or the consciousness) of his times.

Before providing, first, examples of his language and, second, particular events of healing (especially those afflicted with illnesses that made

---

20. In this case, Simon calls him an *epistata* the first time they meet and cannot possibly know anything about him—except, of course, one thing: the way he speaks which, in his society (as ours), was one indication of someone's intelligence. Noticeably, another disciple (Peter) calls him *epistata* (Luke 9:33) immediately following the experience of the transfiguration. It seems, to say the least, noticeable that Peter calls him with a title referring to education and knowledge immediately after witnessing the "transfiguration." The title appears to be at odds with the experience. Finally, John calls him *epistata* (Luke 9:49) during a moment when Jesus is attempting to teach them a lesson they seem unable to understand.

them stigmatized according to Levitical law) it is first necessary to at least partly trace the nature of his language and, in particular, the many references to *words*. "He preached (*lalei*) the word (*logon*) unto them," (Mark 2:2) *speaking* and teaching people ideas they have never heard before, and often doing so with parables, sayings which require the listener to interpret their meaning. "The sower soweth the word," (Mark 4:14) Jesus says, using one of his many agricultural metaphors and surely realizing his hearers may not understand, and certainly cannot begin to think of him as a "last Adam" as Paul did insofar as he understands how the imperative of "tilling the ground" was both an agricultural and an intellectual/spiritual imperative. For human beings are not similar to nature, plants, vegetables, and trees that can grow according to an internal development that has a definitive *telos*. The words he plants are, in principle, infinite and therefore cannot be determined to have a *telos*. When at the beginning of the Gospel of Luke he tells his first reader, Theophilus, that he writes to him "that thou might know the certainty of those things (*katechethes logon*)," (Luke 1:4) the sense of teaching by word of mouth can now be transferred to the written word. Luke, the writer of the gospel and of Acts, realizes the unique moments of Jesus' life and sayings can now be infinitely repeated, interpreted, and understood. "And they were astonished at his doctrine (*didache*): for his word (*logos*) was with power (*exousia*)" (Luke 4:32). *Exousia* does have the sense of power as well as authority. Another sense of *exousia*, however, more completely reveals how Jesus' words as powerful contain within them an unexpected sense such that they force the listener to hear meanings that compel one to rethink common beliefs and assumptions. The *exousia* is also an unparalleled *resource*, from out of Jesus himself, self-generated ideas without antecedents or parallels. They demand the listener to extend beyond the limits of their everyday comprehension. His sayings are often enigmatic because they are not easily traceable to a common idea, a prior source, scriptural or not, that would be well-known to his listeners and recognizable as part of traditional teaching. An unprecedented message does not easily reveal itself in intent or meaning. His authority does not come from a source that is easily, obviously traceable to past history. It comes from a sense of himself as being foundational, without a prior influence that could determine him. He does not, like the leaders in the temple, obtain his authority from a position within a hierarchy supported by tradition, much less one handed down to him by a father. His authority is not *conferred*; it does not originate in anyone but himself and the sense of his life and teaching.

Although John makes Jesus supremely conscious of his relationship to the past of the world, Hebrew and Greek both, there is also an unwavering sense of his uniqueness, as if he was an unprecedented human being, one, moreover, related to nothing less than the *logos* prior to creation itself. Surely no metaphysicians, even the officers commanded by the chief priests and Pharisees to apprehend Jesus, can report to them that "never man spake like this man" (John 7:46), emphasizing nothing more, though nothing less, than his ability to speak as no one had before him. Unfortunately, his manner of speaking (not only his words and message) is difficult to perceive. He impresses to such an extent that people can say of him that "it was never so seen in Israel" (Matt 9:33). Those who are considering whether to arrest him or not must nevertheless recognize that his words are unique and, despite being given orders, they seem to hesitate, questioning themselves when confronted with Jesus, provoked to reconsider beliefs of long-standing; and that was consistent with his own self-conception as someone capable of thinking—and articulating, even if his words were not always understood—meanings never before revealed. "I will open my mouth in parables; I will utter things which have been kept secret from the foundation of the world," (Matt 13:35) Jesus is reported to have said, confirming his belief that the world, as it now stands, will be transformed from its present condition. For many who had such hopes for the liberation of their people from occupation, he was easily understood to be eschatological even if he had no such intentions. The gospel writers were under tremendous pressure to make Jesus legitimate by giving him scriptural authority and defining him according to preexisting conceptions. In the gospels there is "the obvious desire of their writers to make Jesus behave in such a way as to fulfill the Messianic expectations."[21] But Jesus, in self-conception, does not consider himself a Messiah. He believes himself to be capable of recovering what until now has never has been possible, or perhaps bringing back into the world a relinquished possibility, again assuming the responsibility of someone who calls people back to their future, one that was closed off due to the seemingly irrevocable limits imposed upon the present. No one could have anticipated him and the future he envisions.

When John opens his gospel with "in the beginning was the Word," (John 1:1) he has simultaneously returned the reader to Genesis 1:3 (when God speaks in order for light to be—with language initiating the world of being) and to the teaching of Jesus that has always stressed how he speaks in order to create a new human being and a new world, that is, history. And if through his speaking he preached and taught, the most fundamental and important consequence of such a language is his healing, a care of others so crucial it could ignore all other laws, observances, and rituals in the temple. For John, the presence of Jesus in the world is intended to be nothing less

21. Wells, *Jesus of the Early Christians*, 183.

than a new beginning, and such a beginning can only become a possibility by the meaning of his words. They healed, but such a soteriology was only a preparation for a much more enduring form of being well, improving the health of others in order to prepare for the creation of another world, another history that could not be anticipated by any past conceptions. His language, later obscured by the fantastic events of miracles that the gospel writers hoped would confirm his divinity (and the insistence on his messianic purpose to give him legitimacy), has no need for any appeal to the metaphysical precisely because, if interpreted from the standpoint of his speech, it is itself a revelation intended to be seen by the understanding. As John leads his readers to the most decisive event of his ministry (Jesus in the temple, as we will see, and at the beginning of his gospel unlike the Synoptics) he has one concern above all: to place the entrance into Jerusalem as the primary meaning of his ministry so as to then return to the whole of his life since being baptized by John and thereby demonstrate the relation between his therapeutic healing and the end of the sacrifice of animals. John uniquely places the cleansing of the temple at the beginning of his ministry in order to abolish the sacrifices at the temple and replace them with a fundamentally new form of piety: the healing and soteriology of others. The events in the temple in Jerusalem are decisive for the life of Jesus of Nazareth because they are a culmination of his belief in teaching—beginning with a reconceptualization of religious practice, the abandonment of a tradition now no longer adequate for the worship of God since one commandment above all remains in effect. In order to concentrate exclusively on Jesus' ability as a speaker—and, specifically, as simultaneously a thinker who challenges the customs and traditions of his age and a therapeutic healer concerned above all with the suffering of others—many acts attributed to him by the gospel writers will have to be necessarily ignored, including those acts deemed "miracles," or the even more outlandish descriptions of him as a magician or exorcist. As Emerson tells us, "You can forget the miracles, but you can't forget the message."[22]

In often-repeated instances, Jesus shows himself to be concerned with being properly heard, first of all, and understood, knowing full well how human beings can so often misunderstand themselves, others, and the world due to preconceptions they cannot recognize, much less overcome. Finally, if his theology is to be part of the discussion here, it will have to be undertaken in the same way as with Socrates and Epicurus, a theology that does not so much define any attribute of the divine and our relationship, but rather our conceptions and how they determine *human life*. So when John tells us

---

22. Emerson Jr., *Jesus Story*, 66.

that Jesus gave people his "fullness," (John 1:16) such a *pleroma* has to be understood in the context of his belief that human beings suffer because they are torn, divided, not whole, which are his consistent descriptions of human maladies and the consequences of *hamartia*; human beings receive his *pleroma* in order to be healed, filled up (fulfilled), and made whole from a condition of suffering and destitution. His consistent understanding of human affliction and *hamartia* as a state of being, divided and incomplete (not whole, not wholly human), leads him to adopt his speech to particular individuals such that their transformation would spread; they in turn would speak, become witnesses, and teach. His idea of *pleroma*, then, needs to be contrasted with the idea of disease as *astheneia*, fullness instead of feebleness, a weakness and fragility as the deprivation of human emotions. Jesus allows us to witness the emotional destitution of the people during a time of extreme suffering. He provides a diagnosis of his times and holds those entrusted with taking care of the afflictions of people accountable. No doubt expressing a prevailing sentiment of the time and noticing an increasing dissatisfaction with the order of society, in and out of Jerusalem, Jesus was determined to both heal the various maladies of the body and of his social world, and thereby increase people's awareness of their freedom and ability to determine a different future for themselves. The long tradition of Judaism had reached one more critical moment, as it had done so often in the past.

3. *Afflictions of the Self, Afflictions of Society*

The attention to the maladies of individuals and their healing has given us one indication of Jesus' abilities; far less obvious, perhaps, has been the consciousness he had of the malaise affecting his immediate society and, much more, the condition of being during his life as it burdened virtually everyone. He has rightly been acknowledged as a healer; but before he could provide consolation, well-being, and soteriology, Jesus *felt* (in more than thought, viscerally) a particular symptom. As a unique physician, he consciously recognized a condition he diagnosed and that no one seemed to notice, because they were enveloped too tightly in its numbing consequences. People had been separated from their human emotions. They no longer had the necessary feelings—for themselves, or for others.

A particular description of the "diseased" (*asthenounton*) in John 6:2 further adds to Jesus' diagnostic and healing abilities, while also clarifying the specific meaning of a certain illness, one physicians could certainly not perceive. Doctors and physicians were at a loss, their learning and treatments ineffectual. By diagnosing many people suffering from a condition of *astheneia*, such an affliction cannot be simply interpreted as a physical malady, though to be sure, symptoms of the body cannot easily be excluded either. There were of course many psychosomatic ailments, physical symptoms arising from psychological pain and suffering. One important aspect of being *anaesthetic* is to be without feelings, that is, living in a state of general numbness, making it impossible to either sense anything in oneself or to feel for anyone else. People had become estranged from their human emotions, turning (more through weakness than malice) callous and insensitive. They had no choice but to defend themselves against an increasingly cruel world that was indifferent to the plight of their everyday lives. Jesus thereby makes it a condition of a healthy life to be emotionally related to oneself and others; and he also makes it imperative to *feel* for others, hence the importance of showing mercy, refraining from judging, and the all-important teaching of loving one's neighbor. Jesus does not concern himself primarily with the development of human rationality; he is above all intent on restoring the full capacity of human emotions, those most essential to individuals, in themselves, and their relationships with others. Jesus again provides a scathing critique of how his society has developed under the double yoke of the temple state and the Roman authorities, psychologically forcing common everyday people to numb themselves as a protective reaction to their present conditions, estranged as they are from themselves and others and suffering a perpetual trauma that has been accepted because it has been forcefully imposed—brutally by the Romans, and compulsively by the Jewish leadership. Jesus also defines more universally the vulnerabilities of human beings who at times can become indifferent to themselves (one wonders, for example, of the suicide rate at the time) due to the demands of their lives. So often Jesus refers to people being hard-hearted; they have turned themselves away, protectively, defensively, against feeling at all—as a way to cope with pain and suffering and learning to endure the only way they were capable of, without recourse to an alternative.

If the previous *astheneia* is now related to Jesus' teaching of perception and consciousness and *feelings*, it can now be understood in what way he sometimes heals in the Gospel of John. If not for the first time, Jesus has been a healer of people's emotional state, or more precisely, curing their lack of feelings for others, their hard-heartedness. The Gospel of John exemplifies Jesus' healing insofar as he revitalizes the emotions of others and allows them to understand how the single most important human characteristic is the empathy for others—ultimately *agape*, the love he calls a "new commandment." "A new commandment I give unto you, that ye love one another; as I have loved you, that ye also love one another" (John 13:34). His feelings, of course, can also be expressed with anger, with a reaction that everyone has no choice but to take into consideration and to reflect on; his demonstrations of rage, finally unequaled in the temple of Jerusalem, are always intended to rouse the emotions in any onlookers. Mark 3:5—"And when he had looked round about on them with anger, being grieved for the hardness of their hearts"—is a passage that shows him experiencing conflicting emotions, both anger and grief, due to people being unable or unwilling to become different than themselves—with a concept, *metanoia*, always decisive in the possible transformation of human beings and related, from the beginning of his ministry in baptism, to the all-important *regeneration*. Jesus can be indignant, an anger that cannot be disassociated from his considerable pain; he literally suffers when he sees a cold-hearted world, a diminished humanity. Such a hardness of heart makes it impossible to be attuned to his teaching, to perceive and to understand what he attempts to change, what he attempts to accomplish—revitalizing the human spirit and giving everyone the possibility of a new life, of being new creatures. When he asks "perceive (*noeite*) ye not yet, neither understand (*suniete*)? Have ye your heart yet hardened?" (Mark 8:17), Jesus asks these questions so as to force his listeners to think about the level of their noetic ability, doing nothing less than stressing how his teaching can enhance human consciousness and that understanding involves much more than a cognitive ability. It can overcome doubt, uncertainty, despair, and therefore reconcile human beings to themselves, to their own internal self-divisions, and to others who previously were a source of conflict and animosity. His soteriology is necessarily both individual and social. Jesus imagines humanity to be capable of much more than what it can presently see in itself; he urges self-awareness and the in-born ability to examine oneself, developing both human perception and consciousness. He can even be disappointed in his own disciples, the very people who have been with him and witnessed his teaching and, despite their life with him, can in effect deny their previous experience so as to return to the limits of their former selves. "Their heart was hardened," (Mark 6:52) and because of it, they are unable to fully see, fully believe, fully have the faith (the confidence) in the reality, the changed reality, unfolding before them. Jesus knows above all that unless people change their perceptions and consciousness, they will not be able to *convert*, to change their *minds*:

> For this people's heart is waxed gross, and their ears are dull of hearing, and their eyes they have closed; lest at any time they should see with their eyes, and hear with their ears, and should understand with their heart, and should be converted (*epistrepsosin*) and I should heal (*iasomai*) them. (Matt 13:15)

John's description of Jesus speaking with spirit—that animates and revitalizes and makes human beings, once more, conscious of themselves as living souls—now has to be related to the incident in Matthew when the Pharisees confront Jesus. Prior to the Pharisees accusing Jesus of being "the prince of devils," Matthew quotes from Isaiah and the prophet receiving the "spirit" (*ruach*) of Yahweh (Isa 42:1). "I will put my spirit (*pneuma*) upon him," (Matt 12:18) and when the Pharisees make their accusations, Jesus' extended, and extremely angry, response turns to the very opposite of the spirited word, what he calls *blasphemy*, the spoken word that does not revitalize but instead slanders. *Blasphemia* is profane speech since it slanders not so much the man as the spirit. "All manner of sin and blasphemy shall be forgiven unto men," Jesus says, "but the blasphemy against the Holy Ghost (*pneumatos*) shall not be forgiven unto men (*anthropois*)" (Matt 12:31). In this case, blasphemy is unforgiveable precisely because the *pneuma* has been in the world, both Hebrew and Greek, to sustain humanity and to make it conscious of itself as being more than all the limits it has imposed on itself. The spirit raises humanity from their relation to the world, of matter, and to realize it cannot be contained. "And whosoever speaketh a word against the Son of Man, it shall be forgiven him: but whosoever speaketh against the Holy Ghost, it shall not be forgiven him" (Matt 12:32) So serious is blasphemy against the spirit that it cannot even fulfill the precept in the one and most significant of Jesus' prayers—that is, to forgive the trespasses of others. Jesus opposed blasphemy since, in the social world, it attempted to reduce human beings to their physical conditions. The *pneuma* represented an idea of a humanity not simply limited to their physical conditions; they necessarily have an inner principle capable of rousing them from a debilitating condition of being in the world (to be more than their daily existence) and be enhanced by the spirit. The maladies of the body and the spirit of individuals had now become such a widespread contagion that it was no longer even recognized. Jesus tended to the difficult conditions of being; but he also opposed the *definitions* of certain illnesses that he vowed to change and also abolish from a dominant vocabulary. Jesus turned to Levitical illnesses in order to remedy conceptions more than actually cure signs on the body indicative of the unclean, the impure, the polluted. Jesus' healing cannot be disassociated from his particular relationship to Judaism and his commentary on its history, to say nothing of his anticipation of its future; and if he has been portrayed as in dialogues with learned Jews, his many examples of healing cannot be separated from the maladies specifically mentioned in Leviticus.

Thus far there has been a consistent emphasis on his ability to speak as a teacher who can explain his ideas and expound on their meanings, and as a healer who understands the nature of ailments and how to best cure them. His preaching remains central to the gospels. One element of his speaking, however, is underemphasized, and that is his *conversations* with the ill. He is shown, in many cases, to be "moved with compassion," expressing his deep feelings for others, and because of it, "he began to teach them many things" (Mark 6:34). He preaches and teaches to the crowds (numbered to be as many as five thousand) but he also has significant encounters with individuals. In many of these unique instances concerning those in pain, those who suffer, there are a few who are enduring their condition in two ways: the malady itself, and perhaps even more distressing to them, the way their community *judges* them. They are, first of all, stigmatized, ostracized, in many cases (such as the woman suffering from an issue of blood, "unclean spirits," lepers, and the mad) shunned from their communities and living isolated lives. Unless Jesus is recognized as a teacher who attempts to repudiate some aspects of Leviticus, then his ministry will remain incomplete; Jesus' healing cannot be separated from his care for those individuals suffering from illnesses especially defined as "unclean" due to their Levitical interpretation. Ethelbert Stauffer is extreme: "*Jesus broke officially with the Torah.*"[23] If overstated, unquestionable was Jesus' refusal to uphold the beliefs and practices related to Levitical law. His opposition to Jewish tradition would be one more act of defiance bringing him closer to an anticipated end.

4. Levitical Illness

Jesus' ministry of teaching and healing has been more precisely defined in terms of his soteriological words, a particular speech capable of alleviating may different kinds of illnesses, such as paralysis endured from birth. Jesus aspires to treat others, first and foremost, by words alone, with conversations that are intended to remake the consciousness of his listener. While refraining from making a judgment about the instantaneous descriptions of his healing, with the sudden touch of his hands, and with the consensus in the gospel of its sign as a miracle, the extraordinary dedication of the human Jesus to others was effective in restoring a lost humanity to the individual most in need of support. The designation "teacher," however understood as a *didaskale* or "rabbi," was acceptable to those around him who could not conceive of him beyond all the categories of their time and place; but he could not be reduced to a designation with a well-known linguistic or ethnic origin. The gospels may need to define Jesus to readers, possible

---

23. Stauffer, *Jesus and His Story*, 66.

converts, or during liturgy, but in his human essence and in self-conception, the reader today must extend beyond first-century history and attempt to reflect on his uniqueness, on his ability to recognize the afflictions of individuals no less than the malaise obvious in society as a whole and (from out of himself alone) to alter the world by teaching, preaching, and "curing (*therapeuon*) every disease and every sickness among the people" (Matt 4:23). As soon as Jesus began to heal and his reputation quickly spread over a wide geographical area beyond Galilee and to Jerusalem, he came to the attention of the religious establishment and the class of priests who had long enjoyed the privilege and status of being intermediaries between the people and God, healing not as doctors or physicians, but as groups associated with the temple and all of them endowed with divine purpose. Their social importance had no parallels. Any affliction had a possible aetiology and a cure as long as one followed protocol and consulted the proper authorities, followed all the time-tested procedures that alone guaranteed a favorable outcome. Once Jesus began to act alone, and with the authority everyone witnessed if not always acknowledged (doing so would reduce the reputation of scribes and priests) he was intruding upon an intensely preserved monopoly. And while the priestly class in charge of illness and the sacrifices offered for a cure or another beneficial intervention had previously been uniquely capable and qualified to offer a cure, Jesus had neither the formal training nor the religious legitimacy of someone in charge. His authority was self-conferred, and his healing, more importantly, neither demanded nor expected recompense—either for himself or for an offering to the temple. Despite the scholarly attention to his opposition to the temple leadership (with no consensus viable or perhaps possible even with the omnipresent Pharisees) Jesus' ministry has not been sufficiently recognized for its independence from all prior traditions, and certainly from the society of priests who were, it seems, assured of their positions as mediators. Some of the religious leaders accustomed to being obeyed and respected in all aspects of the law had to react with disbelief and resentment; they were outraged by his pretensions. That an individual—from Galilee of all places, a backward region of troublemakers and discontents—could act on his own accord to provide both teaching and healing had to seem preposterous to them, not yet as socially disruptive as a political radical, but immediately of concern. No wonder the first accusations against him, during his life and long after his death, maligned him by making him out to be a deceiver, a sorcerer, or most superstitious of all, someone supported by demonic powers.[24]

---

24. In Stanton's *Jesus and Gospel*, see especially 127–47, "Jesus of Nazareth: A Magician and a False Prophet Who Deceived God's People?"

There was, however, an even more critical problem. More daring still was his complete disregard for some of the most time-honored beliefs (indeed, inviolable laws) of Judaism. Ignoring precepts of the law was one more indication of this rabble-rouser's complete lack of respect for tradition; he did not wash his hands before eating, sat at the table with all kinds of unsavory characters, and acted on the Sabbath with complete disregard for its sanctity. His final and willfully intentional acts had reached a point where tolerance could no longer be extended to him. His healing turned to a class of people who had been deemed polluted and unclean; lepers, the mad, the unclean, even women suffering from the defiling issues of blood, were treated by him with care and without the severe prejudice common for the times. For some, Jesus' many acts of healing illnesses were inseparable from a commentary on Levitical law, with all their attendant prescriptions and their origins in the *wayyikra* or "call" of God (audibly) to Moses. Jesus' unprecedented care for the individuals of their society most shunned and stigmatized—to the point of being exiled from a town and chained in empty tombs—surely left an impression; onlookers had to be stunned by his courage and audacity in defying the very distinctions that were essential to the proper order of society. Though the subject of the Jerusalem leadership's relation to Jesus will culminate with his actions in Jerusalem, one development must be now mentioned. For pious men, deeply committed to Scripture, and absolutely devoted to the service of God, Jesus' unselfish care for the most vulnerable of their society left them with an abiding respect, even when it conflicted with other responsibilities and the rancor of others within their immediate groups. Although this important topic cannot be undertaken here, there were significant individuals in the temple leadership of Jerusalem who were drawn, if slowly, reluctantly, and with hesitation, to him as a teacher and healer and as someone who could not be doubted in terms of his genuine devotion to *all* human beings.

When Jesus many times repeated how his message would create dissension in families, dividing them, making enemies within a household and in communities, no one has considered how many Jews in positions of power began to think about him with far less hostility than has been previously assumed. The gospel writers are, so it seems, unequivocal about the many groups of Jerusalem and their constant harassment and intimidation of Jesus; the scribes and priests and most especially the Pharisees are singled out for their initial suspicion, hatred, and ultimately murderous intent. Such an absolute consensus cannot reflect the much more complicated situation at the time, one in which the Jerusalem leadership—long before Jesus' appearance—were far less in absolute agreement than in a state of almost perpetual negotiation and the need, as it were, to stay one step ahead of the authority of the Romans that could be unleashed with the most innocuous provocation if the situation served their ends. The military and bureaucratic organization of the Romans had little hesitation to be brutal and murderous if the occasion called for it. The ones most devoted to the service of God must have been in a constant state of awareness and anxiety since the temple could be threatened at any time. One of the most recent provocations by an emperor (Caligula, demanding a statue of himself to be erected on the temple grounds) threatened any momentary stability. The division among the leaders of Jerusalem became even more vulnerable if not fractured once they had to deliberate on the Galilean healer who dared to even heal lepers, the mad, and the unclean. Jesus provoked a wider crisis, and this time the Romans could not be looked upon as the cause. This was an intranational problem. Now that Jesus was engaged with a rethinking of some of the fundamental laws of Judaism, all the learned among them (those who dared to admit it) had to consider how Jesus represented the very language of the prophets of old—most especially those who had repeatedly called for the abrogation of sacrifice in the temple for a more authentic expression of piety. Levitical law was now a central issue; Jesus' teaching had made this unequivocal.

By specifically following Jesus' healing of Levitical illnesses, we repeatedly witness much more than the cure of individuals in and through the extensive conversations the gospel writers do not adequately describe or report. Jesus develops the meaning of his ministry as it leads inexorably to the city of Jerusalem during Passover. In the meantime, as the planning becomes more firm and exact, with two or more disciples no doubt sent to give him a more precise sense of the temple layout, he continues with fulfilling the greatest commandment of all, the one in Leviticus on the love of neighbor and the responsibility to do more than feel, but to act and to do everything possible to alleviate the suffering of others. Jesus will not be forgiven for his love. Four examples are necessary so as to follow Jesus' dedication to a class of people whose illness made them so repulsive that, in many cases, they were shunned by their families, expelled from their villages, social outcasts who had no place. Once Jesus begins attending to the people suffering specifically from Levitical illnesses, he has now forced the Jerusalem leadership to confront an unprecedented teaching and healing. No one but the most loving and devoted individuals had ever given those suffering from these maladies any attention. They were so defined by their immediate society and the Scriptures ensuring their identity and continuity that any seeming reappraisal of such laws would be regarded with outrage and disbelief. One unmistakably glimpses Jesus as a teacher (who above all speaks to the ill, relieving them of their judged condition) and a healer when he turns to the most loathed of all. By coming close to them, establishing once more a severed human bond, Jesus brought them back into the family of human beings who, through no fault of their own, and who certainly did not become ill due to some perceived moral fallibility, had succumbed to a physical malady and an even worse social stigmatism. His therapeutic healing could not be more in evidence than when he repeatedly turned to those suffering from issues of blood, those deemed unclean, the possessed and mad, or the lepers whose various marks on their physical bodies made them so repulsive they were the objects of aversion and stone-throwing from children and adults, keeping them outside the boundaries of all settlements. In his healing, however, Jesus was not ultimately concerned with their "reintegration."[25] His teaching was much more comprehensive; the very definition of a polluted and unclean human being had to be abolished, and it began, first of all, with his acceptance of their plight and, more importantly, their frail humanity.

One woman in particular suffers from what in the Synoptic Gospels is described as "diseased with an issue of blood twelve years" (Matt 9:20; Mark 5:25; Luke 8:43), a degrading condition of the worst kind. The incident of healing is important for two reasons: 1) suffering from such an illness, more than likely a menstrual condition, would have made her especially stigmatized in her Jewish community and shunned as ritually unclean, and 2) she was obviously unmarried, therefore childless, and considered to be suffering from a double curse. That she was considered to be one who contaminated *objects* degraded her to being a person with less value than a thing. Her anguish was beyond estimation. The gospel writers, however, fail to mention how she would have *first* gone to the religious authorities for help. No doubt she was initially given instructions by the priests for someone suffering from such an ailment, a particularly abhorrent one that was cause for revulsion:

> And if a woman have an issue, and her issue in her flesh be blood, she shall be put apart seven days: and whosoever toucheth her shall be unclean until the even. And every thing that she lieth upon in her separation shall be unclean: every thing also that she sitteth upon shall be unclean. And whosoever touched her bed shall wash his clothes, and bathe himself in water, and be unclean until the even. And whosoever toucheth any thing that she sat upon shall wash his clothes, and bathe himself in water, and be unclean until the even (Lev 15:19–22).

Her temple offerings, sacrificial or not, did nothing to alleviate her pain. After twelve years, the good news of the gospels must have seemed a

---

25. Pilch, *Visions and Healings*.

blessing to her. Desperation could not make her sceptical; magical thinking at least gave her consolation, some hope.

The manner in which the unnamed woman will be healed (such is her belief, from rumors she may have heard) involves nothing more than touching the hem of Jesus' garment. His reputation has traveled far and wide; apparently touching any part of him is enough to be healed. She believes some power actually emanates from his *body* and can be transferred out of him unto his clothes. "For she said within herself, If I may touch his garment, I shall be whole (*sothesomai*)" (Matt 9:21). In Matthew, she does not in fact touch Jesus' clothes; all he does is turn around and, as if he has read her mind, tell her that she is healed; more specifically, "thy faith (*pistis*) hath made thee made whole" (Matt 9:22). The healing, as well, appears to be instantaneous. The woman believed that she would be "saved" (*sozo* has the sense of being *rescued*—from the judgment of others). For some reason, the account in Matthew omits significant details of the incident. In Mark, we are told that she has consulted many physicians and spent all the money she had. None of them have been able to cure her; on the contrary, "she grew worse" (Mark 5:26). Obviously turning to any possibility of hope, and no doubt discouraged by any and all traditional methods, she has heard of Jesus by reputation and therefore believes that he will be able to heal her.

The woman actually touches Jesus' garment, without his knowledge, "and straightaway the fountain of her blood was dried up; and she felt in her body that was healed of that plague (*mastigos*)" (Mark 5:29). Again, the healing appears instantaneous and, in this case, not directly attributed to any intention on Jesus' part. He does, however, have a unique experience. After the woman touched his garment, Jesus knew "in himself that virtue (*dunamin*) had gone out of him" (Mark 5:30). He can sense that a dynamic ability has been transferred from out of himself. He therefore asks who touched his clothes. The woman, understandably, is terrified, so apprehensive is she that she may be in a permanent traumatic state. A woman in her condition is perceived to be polluted and, in fact, capable of transferring her "plague" to others. She had to be extremely careful, constantly on guard; the slightest touch could lead to someone being unintentionally harmed. An everyday man would have been horrified by the *reputation* of such a woman; any physical contact with her would be regarded almost as an act of violence and the worst kind of defilement.

The entire incident with Jesus, then, is intended as a *reversal*. Instead of the woman being contagious and infecting others (with a real plague or by herself being polluted) the dynamism of Jesus' own body and clothes can, by themselves and without his will, cure; such is the meaning of the reversal and one that necessarily would have included a conversation, as he does

196 SOTERIOLOGY AND THE END OF ANIMAL SACRIFICE

with others, that would have informed her of Jesus' ideas concerning the irrelevancy now of the meaning of her illness or, to be more precise, the difference between illness and disease, "illness as a social construct as distinct from a disease as a biological condition."[26] When Jesus finally tells her to "go in peace (*eirenen*), and be whole (*hugies*) of thy plague (*mastigos*)" (Mark 5:34), only Mark uses the word for being healed rather than the previous saved and preserved. Moreover, when Jesus tells her to go in peace (also in Luke 8:48) he makes a comment about her psychological disposition; previously, she was devastated by being considered polluted and impure by her community. Jesus has healed her, as he will many others, by telling her that a physical condition (and through no fault of her own) will no longer be considered as before, will no longer be the reason for treating others differently, as lesser or worse than others. The scourge or plague, then, does not refer to her physical ailment; the scourge is a *belief* that people suffering from various forms of physical ailments can be considered polluted according to Levitical law. The scene reported to be another example of a miracle, therefore, should be understood in its social context and reflect the new humanity of Jesus. He heals by talking to people and giving them an argument for abandoning certain beliefs that are detrimental to the well-being of a community and to its afflicted individuals. According to Annette Weissenrieder, "*Jesus calls into question and overrides the Israelite law of purity.*"[27] Of the many sicknesses in the gospels, the majority (if not all) would have been looked upon with disapproval and aversion, and not only those suffering from ailments inimical to Levitical law, but also the lame and the blind, individuals who were regarded to be inferior because of the widespread belief that they—or their progenitors, near or distant—were guilty of an offence so grievous God had punished them with physical sickness. Despite so often reporting what Jesus says, at length, in the form of preaching, as, for example, the extended Sermon on the Mount, the gospel writers fail to report the conversations he would have had with such individuals. By showing the woman with an issue of blood that her touch does nothing to him, does not harm him in any way, she recognizes how her ailment cannot be transferred to others. By reversing the transference from Jesus to the woman—which Jesus would have explained, with specific references to a prevalent social belief—he brings peace to her, relieves her of the overwhelming conflict she has suffered from during the twelve years of her illness. The dynamism of Jesus is not in his garment, in his body, or in the use of his hands to heal; he has the unique ability to share a different worldview with others,

26. Freyne, *Jesus Movement and its Expansion*, 153.
27. Weissenrieder, "Plague of Uncleanness?," 208.

which is in fact a repudiation of those beliefs (based on "law") that are so firmly entrenched in their society and that defines individual character according to outward manifestation. Admittedly speculative, but also highly probable given Jesus' compassion, he may have also *embraced* the woman, an act unthinkable and unheard of in his time and place. The touch, with the whole of his arms, is a gesture of absolute acceptance. He is, in Marcus Borg's definition, a "religious revolutionary"[28] because of his opposition to convention. He does not merely oppose the Jewish leadership in Jerusalem or the temple sacrificial system he soon physically confronts, he must also be seen as someone who returned to Scripture and challenged the beliefs and practices of his fellow Jews. There are simply too many cases in the gospels when Jesus heals individuals who are suffering from maladies directly related to Leviticus, including individual considered especially revolting, anyone suffering from a skin disease generally, though inaccurately, defined as "leprosy."

When the leper (*lepros*) pleads with Jesus—so desperate does he seem that he is "beseeching him, and kneeling down to him"—he specifically asks him to "make me clean (*katharisai*)," (Mark 1:40) to be relieved, freed, of his condition, one that cannot be reduced to his physical symptoms and the pain associated with them. First of all, the description of his ailment should not be narrowly understood as leprosy, that is, Hansen's disease and caused by the *Mycobacterium leprae* microorganism.[29] A prime misunderstanding of Jesus' therapeutic healing occurs here. It is revealing how Jesus' actions are first described: "And Jesus, moved with compassion, put forth his hand, and touched him" (Mark 1:41). Are we to understand, in this and other instances, that Jesus' touch itself is the source of his *healing ability*, as if he had particular powers transferrable to others from his body? Or is there a more plausible explanation, one ignoring the miraculous power of his touch? In this case, Jesus does indeed use his hands, perhaps his arms too, and touches him, but Jesus uses his body to be close to him, in the contact so dreaded by others, to let the man know that Jesus will not be influenced by any Levitical law that judges someone suffering from a skin ailment to be unclean, a pariah due only to his outer self. Socially reviled and outcasts, lepers had to wear raggedy clothes, cover their faces, and were required to wear bells so as to warn anyone when they were approaching.[30] By his touch (by his physical presence) Jesus places himself between the leper and the law and denies the intermediary role of the priest:

28. Borg, *Jesus: The Life, Teachings, and Relevance of a Religious Revolutionary*.
29. Ferngren, *Medicine and Health Care*.
30. Lavin, *People Who Met Jesus*.

> When a man shall have in the skin of his flesh a rising, a scab, or bright spot, and it be in the skin of his flesh like the plague of leprosy, then he shall be brought unto Aaron the priest, or unto one of his sons the priests. And the priest shall look on the plague in the skin of the flesh: and when the hair in the plague is turned white, and the plague in sight be deeper than the skin of his flesh, it is a plague of leprosy: and the priest shall look on him, and pronounce him unclean (Lev 13:2–3).

In Jesus' society, priests are given the authority of a physician making a diagnosis with theological implications, as if illness (in this case, a skin ailment) was a moral condition, the flesh itself being indicative of a moral failure. What needs to be explained in such scenes of Jesus' touch is his intentions as a healer, a healing taking place not through some miraculous or magical ability but through his exemplary behavior in relation to others. Jesus touches lepers to show that he absolutely ignores those social beliefs based on law and intends to repudiate the customs and traditions whose consequences are injurious to human beings who, through no fault of their own (and certainly not through any transgression or sin), have been stricken with skin diseases, whether such an ailment is in fact leprosy, or, more generally, lesions caused by all kinds of factors such as allergies, psoriasis, eczema, cysts, boils, etc. Equally important, and again consistent with his identification with Jewish prophets, Jesus questions the authority of the priests who, by virtue of their social standing in the community, can define someone as unclean. By relating himself to so-called lepers, Jesus both puts into doubt the legitimacy of priests and their authority to judge others according to Levitical law. Jesus separates the moral from the medical. Illness is not a form of punishment; and that is the reason he tells the man he has healed to go show himself to the priest so as to reveal to him his new *self-understanding*. The encounter between Jesus and the leper also clarifies one of the purposes of his ministry: Jesus does not simply begin to confront the long-held views of the Jerusalem religious authorities, he directly challenges their appointed vocations. Interpretations have tended to ignore the consequences of the act of healing and the instructions given to the man after he had been made clean.

We must now examine a neglected idea; far from the traditional miracle, Jesus' touch and the conversation that ensues is nowhere reported though it involves nothing less than a complete repudiation of the stigma imposed on the unfortunate individuals afflicted with Levitical illness. Their conversation, and so many others, had to focus on the social belief—inviolable and traceable to the most authoritative individual possible, Moses himself—of the illnesses most injurious to the community. Jesus is not a prophet. He is a historian. Jesus realizes that the ordinances necessary to safeguard the health of the community are now no longer applicable or relevant. Jesus' instructions to the leper are revealing. First, he tells him "say nothing to anyone" (Mark 1:44). Nothing is to be communicated to anyone—with one exception: "But go, show yourself to the priest, and offer for your cleansing what Moses commanded, as a testimony to them" (Mark 1:44). Here, at the beginning of Mark's Gospel, we have nothing less than one of the primary motivations of Jesus' entire ministry; such a beginning will reverberate throughout Mark's Gospel and beyond, creating a long-lasting impression culmination in Jerusalem during Passover. Jesus' instructions should not be misunderstood, as they have been repeatedly. Far from supporting the offering to the priest—the giving of a sacrificial animal to be slaughtered as an offering of thanks—Jesus in fact prompts the healed man to show himself as cleansed without the need of a priest or a sacrifice. The revolutionary act has not been perceived much less affirmed. Commentators guided by their unfailing dedication to Scripture have not heard Jesus' unprecedented acts and words as an affirmation of his own ability outside all boundaries and proper jurisdiction of Judaism. Equally important, with a highly provocative and daring intention, he has sent the individual to the priest. The final intention is exemplary: the individual has not, in fact, been healed at all. Jesus did not heal him of his condition—whatever specific one he suffered from. No, what Jesus accomplished with his conversation (and with a touch that may have been an embrace) was the complete and absolute acceptance of the man as no longer stigmatized by a Levitical definition imposed on him by his society. Jesus abolishes Levitical definitions of uncleanness and restores the man's humanity back to him. When the priest then faces the man and hears of his experience, the reactions are swift and will only become more dangerous in time. The man then begins to "spread the word," (Mark 1:45) not as a testimony of his healing as is so often assumed, but the words spoken to him by Jesus on restoring his humanity and abolishing his Levitical stigma. No wonder that "Jesus could no longer go into town openly," (Mark 1:45) for the radical nature of his teaching, incomprehensible to the authorities, would soon be met with opposition and acrimony. Mark's Gospel therefore opens with a decisive set of doctrines as taught by Jesus, none more resented than the affirmation of the presence of his speech against the writings handed down by tradition.

A continuing problem in the understanding and interpretation of Jesus' public activity occurs due to the translation of the word catharsis—such as the "unclean spirit" (*akarthato*) in the synagogue of Mark 1:23. By using the language of clean and unclean, the specific events are always understood through the perspective of the Judaic law concerning purity. But Jesus has no interest at all in the handed-down idea of purity. On the contrary, denouncing someone of being unclean runs counter to the very ideals of his teaching, one clearly separating the body from the spirit and its analogue in the law/grace distinction first made by Paul and repeated in John 1:17. Returning to the case of the leper, his healing does not occur with a touch of Jesus' hand: "And as soon as he had spoken, immediately the leprosy was departed from him, and he was clean" (Mark 1:42). Once again, as previously with the woman suffering from an "issue of blood," Mark presents the event of healing as instantaneous; it happened immediately. The leprosy, in this case, is not healed by his touch, but rather by a speech that conveys an important message. Leprosy is a disease of the body, with natural causes; it has no relation at all to a condition of the spirit.

The inherited tradition of his healing—whether from Q or another supplemental oral source—portrays Jesus as a miraculous healer. But if his touch is separated from his words (that, in principle, could involve a *conversation* directly challenging the precepts of Levitical law) then these reports of miraculous healing are better understood as a consequence of his radical beliefs and his teachings; they are unique, to be sure, but certainly comprehensible and welcomed as an alternative to tradition and commonly-held beliefs. His healing occurs as a consequence of what he says to people, in what he tells them; he does indeed expose them to the good news because all the people previously ostracized (so much so that lepers were barred from Jerusalem and all walled towns[31]) are welcomed back into the human family, back into their communities and their homes. "And he straitly charged him, and forthwith sent him away" (Mark 1:43). Not only does he share his assessment of Levitical law, Jesus speaks with emotion, even anger as he attempts to persuade and convince the man to stop believing in the worthiness of the law and, consequently, seeing himself as somehow culpable. He can now change his *self-conception* previously imposed on him by priests and by members of his society, his immediate family, first, and his community. Jesus heals by allowing his individuals to see themselves, for the first time, as free from the social imposition placed upon them. He restores them to themselves, relieving them of experiences as terrifying as episodes of psychological imbalance interpreted by the superstitious as a form of possession.

In the events surrounding the man from the "country of the Gadarenes," he "had devils (*daimonia*) for a long time" and, noticeably, did not wear any clothes and also did not live in a human community, "neither abode in any house, but in tombs" (Luke 8:27). In what would have been understood

---

31. Barclay, *Gospel of Matthew*.

at the time as a form of possession, rather than a serious psychological illness—a form of psychosis, perhaps, with terrifying hallucinations—what needs to be emphasized is his isolation. Without human contact, the spoken word by others, he continued to experience projections without being able to reflect on their origin or meaning. He has also been crying, an indication of anguished weeping, showing the desperation of someone overcome with grief and bereft of any support or help. He has been shunned by family, friends, and community, a predicament Jesus understands and identifies with, for he knows, and several times repeats, "no prophet is acceptable in his own country" (Luke 4:24). Indeed, his message is so resisted, and so contemptible to some, that he runs the danger of being killed. In one instance, the people "rose up, and thrust him out of the city" (Luke 4:29). In this case defined as both an unclean spirit and possessed by a devil, Jesus significantly asks him his name. The situation is unique. Whatever his source of suffering, he has a name, has been given a name by his mother and father. When the man answers, "Legion,"[32] in effect naming himself as an indication of his illness—being plural, more than himself, unable to be an individual—Jesus understands his predicament; and without, here, discussing the peculiar episode and the transfer of his demons to a herd of swine, there are two consequences of being healed. When people learn about what has happened, they "came to Jesus, and found the man (*anthropon*), out of whom the devils were departed, sitting at the feet of Jesus, clothed, and in his right mind (*sophronounta*)" (Luke 8:35). He has become a human being again—wearing clothes—and he is in his right mind, capable once more of using his *phronesis*, his rational intelligence. As a physician himself, Luke's use of *phronesis* shows him to be aware of the man's ailment not in relation to any demons, but as in fact a psychological illness he has rightly diagnosed. Luke's use of *phronesis* relies on Greek philosophical lexicon so as to oppose the irrationality of superstition.

"He preached (*elalei*) the word (*logon*) unto them," (Mark 2:2) and if this kind of speaking, and the logos, needs to be more precisely defined, it can only be done in the context of innumerable examples. When his healing is defined as emanating from some power—as in Mark 3:15, "to have power (*exousian*) to heal sicknesses (*therapeuein*)"—such an authority comes from both his considerable reputation, which had become extensive and

---

32. Here and so often elsewhere, John Dominic Crossan in *The Historical Jesus* has brought a considerably expanded understanding of Jesus' healing ministry and its relationship to the social/political times and, in particular, the consequences of the Roman occupation on the psychological health of the population. In this case, specifically drawing attention to "Legion," the name points directly to "Roman power," its abuses during their occupation, and the adverse effects it would have had on the population.

geographically wide-ranging, and from the obvious trust he inspires in others. Furthermore, he also achieves authority due to the fact that the doctrine he talks about has a salvific effect on people—at least those who are capable of it, hence the repetition and insistence by Jesus on people's ability (and, more importantly, willingness) to listen and be prepared to relinquish ideas most held in common. No wonder he often repeats the phrase "he that hath ears, let him hear" (Mark 4:9). Jesus knows, above all, how people who are accustomed to their beliefs and will under no circumstance evaluate much less change them, find it difficult and threatening to expose themselves to a thorough evaluation of what they have accepted as true their entire lives. Jesus expects everyone who has grown up in a particular time and place and one with a significant and binding tradition to be able to reflect on its overall meaning in the here and now, comparing it to the past and thereby make it possible to rethink the nature of the present. Jesus accomplishes many different kinds of healing; and one of the most significant ones occurs in the context of his immediate society and how certain maladies and conditions (lepers, unclean spirits, the possessed) were considered impure and unclean and therefore were branded as stigmatized individuals. Those who believe that he in no way defied Judaism have neglected to consider how many of his examples of healing could not be separated from his challenge to tradition and Jewish law. Jesus initiates a new religion by emphasizing a bifurcation in Judaism, one to be abandoned, the other inherited and developed, thereby reflecting the announcements of the prophets. He does not repudiate Judaism as a whole; he does, however, abandon ideas no longer necessary to maintain the health and cohesion of the community so important in the past, as in Sinai, when the survival of the community was all-important. Since the Jewish people are now dispersed, they no longer need to defend themselves against a contagion that could, in principle, kill everyone and destroy the community. Old laws no longer serve the present; on the contrary, their continuity has made a different future both inconceivable and impossible.

In the incident described by both Mark and Luke, Jesus comes into the synagogue in Capernaum and begins to teach. At one point, a man with an "unclean spirit" (*pneumati akatharto*) (Mark 1:23)—in Luke 4:33 he is described as "a spirit of an unclean devil (*pneuma diamoniou akathartou*)"—tells Jesus "let us alone" (Mark 1:23, Luke 4:34). If one reflects on being *akathartos*, he has, in himself, something he cannot get rid of, again a plurality, the inability to achieve any constancy owing to the many-sided influences and conflicts bearing upon him. Ignoring the idea of spirit (and, of course, any relation to a *daimon*), he can best be understood as someone who is psychologically troubled, unable to be himself. He does not have a constancy of character; he may be suffering from compulsions and obsessions, with perhaps physical manifestations as well—tics or seizures, spasms or convulsions. For some reason related to Jesus' teachings in the synagogue—and we do not know at all what the teachings are about—the man seems to resent him and believes that Jesus has come to "destroy" the people in the synagogue. When Jesus then says "hold thy peace, and come out of him," (Mark 1:25, Luke 4:35) it seems as if he is talking directly to the spirit in him—who has *possessed* the man—and forces him to come out. If, however, all metaphysical language is avoided so what is expeled is not some entity, what Jesus has accomplished with *his words* is to heal the man of some kind of psychological disturbance. Those who saw the incident then ask a pointed question: "What new doctrine (*kaine didache*) is this" (Mark 1:27)? In Luke there is a statement rather than a question: "What a word (*logos*) is this" (Luke 4:36). Here we encounter one of the fundamental problems of the gospels: in the transition between the first experience of the event, its oral transmission, and its writing, specifics have been omitted, keeping only what the writer believes to be most essential—in both cases, here, dealing with doctrine and the word. In both cases, the apparent exorcism is accomplished with words alone and, to stress again, a conversation that may have well lasted for some time, a period impossible to define but certainly longer than any rapid moment of healing. Although some individuals are consistently described as being witness to the man being liberated from an unclean spirit, in both accounts there is an equal emphasis on both his teaching and the words he speaks. Likewise, when people who are brought to Jesus that were possessed with devils, he does not perform any kind of action (as he does, for example, with spitting); "he cast out the spirits with his word (*logo*), and healed (*etherapeusen*) all that were sick (*kakos*)" (Matt 8:16). The language of exorcism is appropriate only when the casting out is understood to be a release—not from a possession, but from a difficult condition. One can define his new doctrine and teaching as soteriology, healing by talking to those suffering from various psychological disorders and making them feel better by his ability to change them. "Now ye are clean through the word which I have spoken unto you" (John 15:3). John recognizes how Jesus does not *make* anyone clean; he simply tells them that the social definition of uncleanness is no longer relevant because in fact it harms the very community such a category was intended to protect. His words defy the archaic definitions of the unclean, the mad, the possessed.

Whatever may be the origin of the four gospels (Q, and other oral traditions according to consensus) there are many instances of the same event being important enough to be recalled; however, as in Luke, there are often descriptions which are noticeable by their uniqueness. For example, there are countless episodes of Jesus and his particular kind of speaking—and yet, each gospel writer seems to find a unique expression and vocabulary, as if supplementing the oral tradition with an individual language so as to capture, in detail, the range of Jesus' acts and the specific words used to describe them. The extensive range of his vocabulary, as portrayed by the gospel writers, shows Jesus to be dynamically related to the languages of his times (i.e. Aramaic, Hebrew, and Greek) while at the same time developing their meanings specifically to be relevant to the present. The uniqueness of *his* language continues to elude us.

In a remarkable passage reminiscent of (but also distinct from) Isaiah 61:1, Luke provides one more unique description of Jesus and his particular kind of healing of injuries not usually associated with illness as such. Jesus tells those in the synagogue that he has been appointed

> to preach the gospel to the poor; he hath sent me to heal the brokenhearted, to preach deliverance (*aphesin*) to the captives, and recovering sight to the blind, to set at liberty (*aphesei*) then that are bruised. (Luke 4:18)

In each case (the poor, broken-hearted, captives, blind, bruised), the affliction can be interpreted from the standpoint of a psychological rather than a physical condition; they suffer, but it is due to their particular situation, as a prisoner that now will be set free. More importantly, in two instances Jesus uses the word *aphesis*—with the strong sense of a "remission" (as in Matt 26:28), of first of all the elimination of a previous condition of illness, and at the same time being "forgiven." However, contrary to traditional interpretations of this *forgiveness*, it is not Jesus who places himself in the position of someone who can judge (to pronounce one guilty and therefore, in principle, pardonable), but rather speaks to people so that they can fundamentally *forgive themselves* by, in part, also forgetting burdens recalled from the past. He allows them to become free from the constant memory of a past experience that has left them traumatized and perpetually tied to the consequences of an original harm, stating, "I came not to judge the world, but to save the world" (John 12:47). Jesus teaches others how to forgive themselves for some past event (inflicted by or on an individual), such that the forgiveness can be accomplished only when there is also sufficient forgetting, that is, the ability to be released from the constant thought and memory. Jesus releases people from their traumas, from the painful experiences that for some have had lifelong consequences. This is what is meant by his speech when it is described in terms of "gracious words (*logois tes charitos*)" (Luke 4:22), words perceived to be generous and well-received, this *charis* previously understood as divine favor has now been accomplished by someone, a man, who simply cares above all for the well-being of others. The grace does not have a divine source; nor is it obtainable through either sacrifice or prayer. Jesus gives his grace freely to others for their benefit and health. The grace previously received in an exchange initiated with a human offering a sacrificial animal at a temple has now begun to be contravened. Jesus will give others grace through his presence. Luke presents Jesus as someone who speaks with grace, a sense of being disposed to others in love and kindness and goodwill. In one of the most poignant examples of Jesus and his relationship to others insofar as he reveals his *charis* occurs when, in the house of a Pharisee during dinner, a woman described as someone suffering from *hamartia* shows, above all, her emotions:

> and stood at his feet behind him weeping, and began to wash his feet with tears, and did wipe them with the hairs of her head, and kissed his feet, and anointed them with the ointment. (Luke 7:38)

In a remarkable scene of pathos, Luke presents the woman as suffering unbearable anguish, such that her actions—weeping and washing Jesus' feet with tears, drying them with her hair, kissing his feet—show her unbearable desperation. We know nothing about the woman, no reason for being considered a sinner, no reason for her emotions except that they are intense and undeniable. She is one of the despised.[33] The emotions of others as portrayed in the gospels have not always been emphasized, though Jesus is extremely conscious of their range in others, whether they have become numb (in part to protect themselves, making themselves hard) or have endured such pain and suffering that resistance is no longer possible. Jesus' feelings are too often taken for granted; he has an unparalleled capacity for directly experiencing the anguish of others, and by himself feeling their pain, he is compelled to bring them solace. To love others as oneself becomes an act of absolute identification; he feels for them and, in a real way, achieves complete empathy *with* them, *as* them. Jesus understands how feelings can be transferred, from one person to another—him taking on their pain, them receiving his *paraklesis* such that he already is a comforter.

Despite the objections of the Pharisee, Jesus tells him that "her sins, which are many, are forgiven (*apheontai*)" (Luke 7:47), and they are forgiven because "she loved much," as if Jesus is not only showing empathy to her emotional state, but also reciprocates her feeling, in herself, for Jesus. He then demonstrates his own particular *charis* by speaking to the woman and telling her "thy sins are forgiven" (7:48). How is the forgiveness of sins

---

33. Baggett, *Seeing through the Eyes of Jesus*.

to be explained psychotherapeutically? In terms of the distressed woman who begins to cry in front of Jesus, washing his feet with her tears, holding and kissing his feet, and anointing him, she is suffering from an act she may have committed (or perhaps endured) and her contrition or anguish is overwhelming. She cannot forgive herself because she cannot forget. Psychologically in anguish due to the past, Jesus realizes the nature of her grief. When he says, then, "thy sins are forgiven (*apheontai*)" (Luke 7:48), the forgiveness requires interpretation. Jesus helps her *to be released* from the haunting, relentless memory that has made her unable to live in the present; Jesus' insight here sees how the woman has lost herself due an incident in the past. Jesus literally brings her back into the present, releasing her from her bind to a past long distant but urgent in its effects. His therapy, in this case, is nothing less than healing her of an idea that has confined her to a binding experience in the past and made any future all but impossible. "Thy faith has saved thee (*pistis sou sesoken*); go in peace (*eirenen*)" (Luke 7:50), Jesus tells her. Peace is now possible since she is no longer in conflict. If we understand Jesus' role as a therapeutic healer of people's psychological afflictions, we can then put into context how his teaching was first announced by John the Baptist and his role as one who would "give knowledge of salvation (*soterias*) unto his people by the remission of their sins (*aphesei hamartion*)" (Luke 1:77), and repeated at 3:3 with one crucial addition: "and he came into all the country about Jordan, preaching the baptism of repentance (*baptisma metanoia*) for the remission of sins (*aphesin hamartion*)." The idea of the forgiveness of sins should not then be interpreted from the standpoint of Jesus as a judge who can morally exculpate someone from their wrongdoing. Rather, and if we relate the forgiveness of sins to *soteria*, what Jesus accomplishes is not so much a moral action of forgiveness, but in his relationship with the woman (explicitly demonstrating his actions to be in opposition to the conventional morality of the Pharisees), providing her with a different evaluation of her past; he allows her to relate to herself differently than before in a moment in time. Clearly, the woman experiences visceral emotional pain. What Jesus does, first of all, is allow her to release herself from the thoughts, memories, and emotions stemming from a recollection that has made her life unbearable.

One aspect of Jesus' speaking and healing cannot be overlooked, and must be reemphasized: in Luke and with the other gospel writers, it seems as if his healing occurs almost instantaneously, either with a simple *declaration* or with the touch of his hand. However, the way Jesus is represented cannot take into consideration the length of time for his healing to take place. In other words, rather than witness Jesus' words and act leading to immediate results, it is necessary to take into account the passage of time and, in particular with the distraught woman, how a possible conversation takes place between them. If Jesus is to be regarded as a psychotherapeutic healer rather than a miracle-worker, magician, or exorcist, the accounts provided by the gospel writers are necessarily brief to the point of being almost instantaneous. Just as his words and healing are not immediate, so too are Jesus' expectations of others as they listen to him. He knows all too well how his words are radical and, in many ways, unprecedented. Therefore, he prepares his listeners, gives them time to listen to his message, interpret his meaning, and understand its significance for their changed lives.

One incident in particular can be a preliminary summary of Jesus' ministry as teaching and preaching and soteriology, one that heals by exposing the ideals of a society now no longer tenable. When the Pharisees approach Jesus and attempt to lead him to a self-betrayal, to "catch him in his words" (Mark 12:14) and therefore denounce him with the Herodians present, they begin with the language of flattery, something Jesus would have immediately noticed. "We know that thou art true (*alethes*)," they begin, not realizing, as he does, what it means to be the embodiment of *aletheia*, the truth. By then adding how Jesus "carest for no man: for thou regardest not the person of men" (Mark 12:14), their particular rhetoric involves disregarding, literally, the faces of human beings, all outward appearance. Jesus can in no way be delimited by the values of a world he has vowed to change; and the Pharisees themselves, despite attempting to entrap him into making a seditious comment, completely fail to understand him at all when they present him with the challenge of whether or not it is *lawful* to pay Caesar's tax. The Pharisees, so accustomed to believing unfailingly in their own declared truth, cannot possibly understand Jesus when he asks them for a coin with the image (the face) of Caesar on it, and then tells them, absolutely, that there can be no reconciliation between Caesar and God, each of them separated by an absolute divide. "A good man out of the good treasure of his heart bringeth forth that which is good" (Luke 6:45). He concludes his speech by defining himself as a teacher and asking everyone who is listening to heed his sayings and act on them—that is, change themselves so that one fulfills his precepts and principles. The abundant heart is shown above all by his speech, "for of the abundance of the heart his mouth speaketh" (Luke 6:45). Jesus has had twelve disciples—his main students—but with a speech such as this one, he has also made it the responsibility of every listener that they too must change their heart such that it will be reflected in their actions and in their own speech. Jesus therefore turns to the single most important commandment, already announced in Leviticus 19:18 ("Thou shalt love thy neighbor as thyself"), as a foundation of his teaching. Although John writes that Jesus is giving everyone "a new commandment" (John 13:34), there is nothing new in this directive, only a reemphasis on the need to love, in empathy and compassion, and therefore overcome the social conditions that have led to such widespread destitution. Only when people once again devote themselves to each other as the first requirement of a flourishing humanity will health and peace be restored. "This is my commandment. That you love (*agapate*) one another as I have loved you" (John 15:12). Jesus now makes perhaps the single most important statement of his ministry, one related to his opposition to the temple sacrifices and to the imminent transformation of religious life. For now love has a formidable imperative, and an urgent necessity that can always be fulfilled: "Greater love (*agapen*) hath no man than this, that a man lay down his life (*psychen*) for his friends (*philon*)" (John 15:13). From such a statement, traditionally understood as the announcement of his sacrificial death, it is now time to turn to the last days of Jesus' life, not so much to determine how he understood his imminent death (predictable given the plan he has prepared), but to witness his acts in the temple and to interpret them as anticipated in the Synoptic Gospels and in John. The entire period of his ministry, whatever its length, was sustained for a definite period so his teaching and healing would be recognized not as simply an individual accomplishment, but as an essential part of a comprehensive view he would soon complete in Jerusalem. The acts in the temple during Passover would be a long-prepared culmination of his entire life.

CHAPTER 6

Jesus' Anti-sacrificial Acts in the Temple of Jerusalem

1. *The Essenes of Qumran*

ALL FOUR ACCOUNTS IN the gospels of Jesus' acts in the temple of Jerusalem during Passover are decisive in revealing an unmistakeable intention on his part, one where his enraged attack on the merchants of sacrificial animals carries out a well-thought-out plan both in terms of its meaning, and leading, he well knows, to the arrest and execution he has prepared himself for during the entire period of his ministry. Jesus' acts in the temple are one culminating statement on his part as to his teaching and its relationship to the traditions of the past, the ones he had repeatedly called into question and, as pertains to the law, ignored and willfully contested as now being irrelevant. Certain rituals and the spirit have been absolutely separated; one law above all has now been established. During the period of his teaching and healing, Jesus had repeatedly defied some of the universal precepts of Judaism; his indifference to everyday observances—for example, washing one's hands before eating, the strict regulation of the Sabbath, socializing with pariahs—would now *culminate* with an unthinkable display in the temple. It was inconceivable for a human being to physically intervene and attempt to end animal sacrifice with one act of defiance. No one would dare because the thought itself would be considered outrageous. Jesus surely knew his act (and its meaning, which the four gospel writers anticipate and actually explain) would be regarded as scandalous and understood by most in the Jerusalem leadership as nothing less than an assault on the temple and on its most important ritual; an assault, furthermore, possibly construed as anti-imperial and therefore brought to the attention of the Roman authorities who, as occupiers, were always concerned with periodic outbreaks of rebellion and the threat to the always precarious social stability of the region. Jesus may have anticipated and expected to be apprehended, brought before the Jewish authorities and denounced as someone who had dared to directly criticize the observances at the temple and its normal, everyday processes. Jesus would be denounced as a threat to the stability the Romans and the Sanhedrin had established as part of their necessary, if much resented, collaboration. His anti-sacrificial acts were not simply impious; they were seditious and could be interpreted as a challenge to a politicoreligious institution ultimately in the service of the Roman state and the *divine* emperor. The Sanhedrin led by Caiaphas easily persuaded the Roman authorities that Jesus' acts in the temple were criminal because they were anti-sacrificial, and therefore a direct challenge not only to Judaism, but also to the politicoreligious apparatus of the Roman state and to its most important representative: the emperor. If they could inculpate him further with a statement of sedition, his arrest would be simply a matter of time.

Far from reflecting the limits of his immediate world, Jesus first of all conceived of himself as someone in opposition to the values of the times—the Romans[1] without question, but also almost the whole of the Jewish leadership and (more importantly) the religious rituals and observances of the temple that a particular class organized, controled, and carried out. Following, in part, the tradition of Jewish prophets from Isaiah to Micah, animal sacrifice was by no means a religious ritual without conflict and ambiguity, uncertainty and opposition. It had long come under the scrutiny and forceful criticism of the prophets who recognized the temptation of substituting an ancient ritual for an authentic piety. Human weakness could choose and rely on the expediency of ritual rather than the more difficult demands of ethical self-examination and on serving others, most especially those most in need. "To what purpose is the multitude of your sacrifices to me? saith the Lord: I am full of the burnt offerings of rams, and the fat of fed beasts; and I delight not in the blood of the bullocks, or of lambs, or of he goats," Isaiah writes at 1:11, in effect allowing his readers to hear the words of Yahweh directly. For the first time (though related to a long history of criticism of animal sacrifice, in the Jewish prophets as well a the Greek

---

1. The literature on Jesus and the social and political implications of his life and teaching is extensive. See in particular Horsley's *Jesus and the Politics of Roman Palestine*. Titles are themselves indicative of Jesus' political motivations. Among them, Storkey's *Jesus and Politics*, and Hendridk's *The Politics of Jesus*.

philosophers) Jesus will place himself in the position of being the *singular individual* who will demonstrate, with physical force and emotional outrage, his opposition to animal sacrifice as the central observance in the temple of Jerusalem, thereby returning himself during Passover to the events leading to the Israelites led by Moses and leaving Egypt and thereby reinstituting the practice of animal sacrifice. If the so-called "cleansing of the temple"—a term itself in need of reconsideration and a new interpretation—remains the *unique* act of Jesus' life and teaching and the one that led inevitably to his death, it becomes all the more necessary to again read all four accounts in the gospels and understand the specific meanings of its language and the motivations that led Jesus to commit an act he knew would be regarded as both impious and criminal.

Many commentators insist again and again that Jesus should not be understood as in any way defying Judaism, or for that matter as influenced by thoughts other than that which was culturally and intellectually determined by Judaism. But such an argument fails to consider that the tradition of the Judaic prophets necessarily includes bitter, relentless invectives against their own people due to their inability to live up to its highest standards of conduct and belief. Jonathan Klawans may critique the language of "supersession," and in the case of Jesus and his confrontation with the temple write that "the record is less clear,"[2] but at this juncture, as it pertains to Jesus as a critic of Judaism, we must now introduce a possibility thus far neglected. Jesus cannot be simply understood as a critic of the Jerusalem temple and its sacrificial rituals without understanding his intentions as much wider in scope and intention. At the appropriate time, then, Jesus will be presented as a more radical thinker than previously conceived: his acts in the temple around the festival of Passover, when Jerusalem was filled with as many as two million visitors (Jews, of course, but also many gentiles from all over the Mediterranean world and beyond), was a display intended for *everyone* to see. Jesus' acts in the temple were meant to abolish *all* animal sacrifice as a religious institution.

Before turning to the most decisive event in the life of Jesus of Nazareth—his entrance into the city of Jerusalem for the one and sole purpose of overturning the entire edifice of the sacrificial temple, and its cleansing is only one aspect of his actions there, and one that certainly requires some deliberation and an honest appraisal of its meaning—it is first necessary to briefly mention not so much other interrelated influences on his thought and teaching but rather current ideas which were prevalent at the time. Among the most relevant may be how Jesus was related in any way,

---

2. Klawans, *Purity, Sacrifice, and the Temple*, 145.

in thought if not association, to the group of people who abandoned the city of Jerusalem and established a separate and independent community in Qumran, in part due to their opposition to the Jewish leadership and, more significantly, their rejection of the long-standing practice of animal sacrifice, and therefore envisioned themselves as an independent if not a new form of Judaism. The Roman occupation only made them more determined to pursue their own vision of Judaism—most especially when they realized how their most important ritual at the temple of Jerusalem, animal sacrifice, was also observed and considered all-important by the Romans. Sacrifices offered for the emperor were unacceptable and offensive; such a compromise was a betrayal of their most deeply held beliefs.

The manuscripts discovered in the caves around Qumran represent an invaluable source for understanding both the members of the community of the Essenes (their social organization, beliefs, and practices) and their relationship to the religious authorities in Jerusalem. In the often extremely critical language evident in the Dead Sea Scrolls, the community of the Essenes had separated themselves from the Jerusalem leadership due to what in their eyes were serious faults that made it impossible to maintain a relationship with their leaders, most especially to someone referred to, enigmatically, as "the Wicked Priest" and to be distinguished from their own "Teacher of Righteousness."[3] Their rhetoric is as uncompromising as it is precise. Some aspects of their criticism are general; others are more specific. If Josephus and Philo are consulted, it becomes possible to form a clearer idea of what the Essenes considered most objectionable about the Jerusalem leadership and their practices at the temple.

Recalling the Jewish prophets who repeatedly and insistently denounced the practice of animal sacrifice, instead hoping for a renewed dedication to others less fortunate, to the reaffirmation of everyone's individual responsibility to those most vulnerable and suffering, the reasons that the Essenes left the city of Jerusalem and established an independent community in Qumran was their disapproval of the religious authorities and how they conducted temple rituals, though returning to the wilderness could also be interpreted as a reversal, first by relating themselves back to a sacred *topos* of the desert, to return to their origins, and to symbolically renew themselves and their relationship to Yahweh. The Essenes established their community in a remote desert location so as bring themselves back to a historically traceable origin and, overlooking the Dead Sea, redefine what Robert Sack calls a "view of the self" such that an "ontological issue"[4]

---

3. As cited in Stone, *Jewish Writings of the Second Temple Period*, 510.
4. Sack, *Homo Geographicus*, 127.

once again becomes essential. They were intent on recreating themselves by adhering to principles they believed had been corrupted and estranged from the original intentions of Judaism. They returned to nothing less than an inception; by recollecting the origins of their past in Scripture, they could attempt to emulate an original relationship to God. As Robert Cohn writes, "The student of religions must take account of geographic factors in its effort to understand the dynamics of the biblical imagination."[5] A return to the desert (the wilderness of the gospels) was a separation from the city of Jerusalem and a return to Jewish origins so as to separate themselves from the times; only by a physical distance from the city of Jerusalem and a return to the desert as a sacred place of foundations could the Essenes renew themselves and dedicate themselves to a religious practice devoted to what they believed to be all-important—purity.

Early Christians made urban centers[6] essential in the development of their faith, most especially in the foundation of churches, but pious Jews at the time of Jesus were, more often than not—and evident, first, with John the Baptist—living in the wilderness, though itinerant preachers and the Essenes related to their geographical lives completely differently, the first as wanderers, the second in a specific place and within a precisely prescribed community of followers. Preaching in the cities was dangerous; the authorities were omnipresent, though concealed by a well-organized intelligence network. Infiltrators and spies were common. Any indication of subversion could lead to arrest and, as in the case of John the Baptist, death. With the number of Romans and Herodians, collaborators and provocateurs, and spies in the imperial and Sanhedrin service, any deviation from the expected norm could lead to severe consequences. Laws were absolute and enforced with cruelty and impunity by the Romans. There are numerous indications, beginning with "Jesus could no more openly enter into the city, but was without in desert places" (Mark 1:45), that attest to his movement from place to place and the avoidance of large cities as necessary for his and his disciples's safety. There are also significant instances of Jesus being tracked down and followed by the authorities; he was becoming well known to them and, due to his reputation and growing following (that he preached to an audience of five thousand may be hyperbole but does tell us his followers were numerous, his gatherings conspicuous) posed a threat to

---

5. Cohn, *Shape of Sacred Space*, 25.

6. This is the well-known thesis by Wayne Meeks. See *The First Urban Christians*. Though the first Christians may have been urban, there would eventually be a return to an isolated existence in the desert with the foundation of monasteries, as with Anthony in Egypt. Meeks's position has been recently reappraised by Robinson's *Who Were the First Christians?*

their authority; a radical teaching could certainly undermine the monopoly of proper religious ideas as perpetuated by the law. The Essenes, as far as we know and in part due to their isolation, seemed not to have been of any concern to the temple leadership in Jerusalem, or to the Romans until the Jewish War when members of the community were tortured and killed; but those events were still in the future even if revolutionary sentiments were common. The Romans were despised except by those who had profited from their collaboration and by Hellenistic Jews who had, if not renounced ancestral ways, also adopted a culture of leisure and entertainment consistent with baths and the gymnasiums, theatres and athletic competitions. The austerity of Jewish virtues was offset by the much more comprehensive ideas of Greek *arete,* or excellence.

If the accounts provided by Josephus and Philo are consulted, it seems there was *one* reason above all that compelled the Essenes to refrain from contact with the temple in Jerusalem. Granted, the Essenes were anti-urban in their sentiments—again attesting to the fact that both philosophical schools (like the Pythagoreans and Epicureans) were estranged from city life and therefore found an alternative in what the gospels call the wilderness, a place of profound significance for Judaism. One should mention, first of all, Pliny's description of the Essenes as "remarkable beyond all other tribes in the whole world."[7] It is noticeable for a Roman to make such a statement for reasons related to their dedication to a certain life of purity and austerity and, perhaps, to their scriptorium as a place that revered the written word and its central place in study and education.[8]

In *Every Good Man is Free*, Philo begins identifying the Essenes, a name related to holiness—Greek, *hosiotes,* Hebrew *Hasidim*—and then specifically contrasts the idea of holiness with animal sacrifice: "Indeed, they are men utterly dedicated to the service of God (*therapeutai theou*); they do not offer animal (*zoa*) sacrifice, judging it more fitting to render their minds truly holy."[9] He singles them out for their "exceeding holiness."[10] Further-

---

7. Pliny, *Nat. His.,* 5.15.

8. In *The Scriptural Universe of Ancient Christianity*, Guy Stroumsa argues that the religious book (and its development from the scroll to the codex) replaced animal sacrifice.

9. Philo, *Prob.,* 75–76. This is the decisive passage for those who believe the Essenes did not sacrifice. Among them are Geza Vermes in *The Dead Sea Scrolls in English,* and Lena Cansdale's *Qumran and the Essenes.* There are dissenting voices. Among the most recent, see Joan Taylor's *The Essenes, the Scrolls, and the Dead Sea.* It is important to emphasize, once again, the commonality of language and the consistent idea of *therapeia* being a *new* service to God. They served God with their lives, not through a scapegoat substitute.

10. Philo, *Hy.,* 11.1. He further comments on their "love of gentleness and humanity,"

more, in Philo's *On the Contemplative Life* and his description of the Jewish sect called the Therapeutae living outside the city of Alexandria in Egypt, he says, "The table is free from animal food, which would pollute it."[11] Their vegetarianism is unquestioned. While inconclusive, it is possible the Essenes were also vegetarians and of course would have separated themselves from temple sacrifices in part due to their objection of animal slaughter and consumption, most especially in the context of a religious observance. The resolve to make their minds holy (as a substitute for the ritual of piety *in the temple*) differentiates them from Judaism in so far as it founded itself, at least partly, on observances related to material matters—i.e. cooking containers and utensils—a fact specifically ignored by Jesus when in the company of fellow Jews, to demonstrate his own rethinking of the history of Judaism. Philo represents our single most important and reliable source insofar as he himself visited Judea between the 30s and early 40s. His writings on the Essenes could therefore be evaluated for its accuracy by the many Jews from Alexandria who visited the region.[12]

In Josephus's *Jewish War* and his account of the Essenes being tortured by Romans, he specifically writes that they endured extreme physical suffering rather than blaspheme their God "or to eat forbidden (*nomotheten*) food."[13] Unlawful food, not in keeping with their *nomos*, could refer to pork and other animals excluded from consumption. Or it may include meat eaten after being sacrificed. Submission to sacrificial slaughter in honor of the emperor would long continue to be the Romans' preferred method of forcing believers to apostasy. Being forced to eat sacrificial meat and thereby show subservience to Roman law and the emperor would have been abhorrent to the Essenes. Furthermore, adding one more intriguing comment, in Josephus's *Antiquities* he writes that the Essenes were "a group which employs the same daily regime as was revealed to the Greeks by Pythagoras."[14]

11.2.

11. Philo, *Vit. Cont.*, 1.73. The question of vegetarianism could here be considered ancillary, though it certainly was not for the early Greeks discussed in the Introduction.

12. Nesbit, *Christ, Christians and Christianity*. Identifying Jesus as an Essene is now much more in doubt.

13. Josephus, *War.*, 2.152.

14. Josephus, *Ant.*, 15.371. Given Josephus's provocative statement that the Essene community was influenced by Pyathagorean life and thought, several publications have pursued the connection. Among them are Justin Taylor's *Pythagoreans and Essenes* and John Collins's *Beyond the Qumran Community*. Josephus is important here insofar as a possible influence on the Essene community may have come from Pythagoreans. However, it is unnecessary (and, perhaps, even undesirable) to trace a direct influence since the Essenes, as pious Jews, are unlikely to have adopted a Greek idea. What remains beyond doubt is the existence of individual philosophers and their communities as

The Pythagoreans were vegetarians; of course, there was much more to their daily regime than their diet though not eating meat singled them out as a group indifferent to temple observances. In another section of the *Antiquities*, Josephus writes:

> They send offerings to the Temple, but perform their sacrifices using different customary purifications. For this reason, they are barred from entering into the common enclosure, but offer sacrifice among themselves (*thusias epitelousin*). (18.19)

If, then, Josephus (now living in Rome) wrote for an audience mostly made up of polytheists, he may have wanted to minimize the difference between them and the Essenes's rejection of animal sacrifice. Philodemus of Gadara, as we noticed previously in his relationship to Rome, adopted a similar attitude to the people he felt indebted to and relied upon for support.

In the collection of his essays on the Essenes of Qumran, Geza Vermes writes that "owing to quarrels among the ranks of the priesthood, our community turned its back on the Temple and settled in the wilderness."[15] Unfortunately, at least here, he does not specify the nature of the quarrels despite providing a date on the origin of the community around the middle of the first century BCE. If the disagreements between the priests are not discussed, even conjecturally, one point cannot be disputed: the Essenes decided to abandon the city of Jerusalem and, with it, all the observances associated with the temple—the principal one, of course, related to the sacrifice of animals, including all the transactions related to the ancient practice. To return to the wilderness was, for the Essenes (and for John the Baptist and Jesus), the responsibility of reclaiming a calling that they interpreted as somehow forsaken. Hence, also, their turn toward the copying, preservation, and interpretation of the writings from the Hebrew Bible that, comprehensively, were to be called The Dead Sea Scrolls when discovered in the caves around Qumran in 1947 and later excavations. In his overview of the history of Encratism, Gilles Quispel argues that the Essenes formed "as a reaction against the priesthood of the Temple, which invested the enormous capital obtained from the Temple tax and had monopolized the trade in

---

examples of being independent from the status quo. The commonality of both Jewish and Greek sources—and, of course, Roman ones such as Lucretius—makes it evident that opposition to animal sacrifice in the ancient world was much more common than previously considered. The point here is not to trace any direct influence, however interesting it may be. The argument is this: two traditions of thought upheld similar ideas, and to deny that Jesus was familiar with them is simply to see him as an insular preacher rather than someone acutely aware of his age.

15. Vermes, *Scrolls*, 39.

sacrificial animals."[16] In *The Dead Sea Scrolls*, Timothy Lim adds that the Essenes "refused to participate in the Temple Service, objecting to the sacrifice of animals."[17] Hartmut Stegemann argues, however, that the Essenes' rejection of sacrifice was due to the adoption of a calendar that effectively compromised the correct days of festivals and the Sabbath.[18] Perhaps. There has been no consensus on the Essenes and their views on sacrifice or, for that matter, their relationship to the temple in Jerusalem and the religious authorities. One point, however, cannot be argued—and it will ultimately lead us to a reconsideration of the meaning of the temple cleansing, one that involves not simply the rejection of temple economics, the buying and selling of animals, but the much more serious aspect of the temple and its sacrifices—that is, the temple as a *slaughterhouse*. Commentators repeatedly defend the slaughter of animals in the temple as essential to Judaic piety as if it was simply accepted and unquestioned by everyone, but this is precisely the point now to be raised as it relates to Jesus' acts.

Although Jesus as represented in the gospels has significant similarities with the Essenes, it is neither necessary to establish a direct relationship with them (that is, any real contact, in Qumran or elsewhere) or to somehow have been influenced, in part, by their beliefs. It is important to point out, however, that for some the relationship seems likely.[19] Yizhar Hirschfeld goes as far as writing that both John the Baptist and Jesus visited the Essene community and adds that "the Essenes' way of life was certainly a source of inspiration for the earliest followers of Jesus."[20] It is virtually impossible that Jesus, as a preacher and as someone who traveled extensively in southern Galilee and its environs, did not have any knowledge of the Essenes or, for that matter, other itinerant preachers, whose number was significant. Although Jesus' acts in the temple were radical and unprecedented, the philosophy that motivated him was by no means unique either in the Greek-speaking world of Socrates, the Hellenism of Epicurus, the culture that spread into Judaea after the death of Alexander the Great, or in Rome and its numerous colonies. There were many reasons for a noticeable resentment (if not direct opposition, difficult in any case) to the Jerusalem leadership and its necessary, if coercive and imposed, relationship to Rome, and if it was exacerbated by the Sanhedrin's necessary relationship to the

16. Quispel, "Study of Encratism," 76.
17. Lim, *Dead Sea Scrolls*, 60.
18. Stegemann, *Library of Qumran*.
19. On the numerous and fundamental ways in which Jesus and the Essenes were similar, see Charlesworth's "The Dead Sea Scrolls and the Historical Jesus."
20. Hirschfeld, *Qumran in Context*, 230.

Romans, its origin was nevertheless long standing. The aristocratic priestly class could not have had universal approval; the many benefits they enjoyed, economic and otherwise, naturally made them vulnerable to criticism, and worse. The general population, under considerable pressure (from over-taxation, for one) could not easily accept how the leaders of the temple had lost none of their wealth despite the Roman occupation. As aristocratic landowners, with farms capable of rearing significant amount of animals (some of them to be sold for sacrifice) the priestly Jerusalem class, especially the aristocratic Sadducees, would have enjoyed economic benefits that were related to religion. A peasant class working daily in the fields could not be faulted for being cynical and for resenting a priestly class who enjoyed social and economic privileges.

2. *Opposition to the Temple Leadership*

Prior to his entrance into Jerusalem, Jesus is portrayed in the gospels as consistently and, at times, with language of extreme aggression and insult, opposed to the Jerusalem leadership as a whole, whether it is the priests, scribes, Pharisees, or Sadducees. They confront him and demand to know his intentions and purpose. It is simply impossible to view Jesus as in any way sympathetic to the Jerusalem leadership and, in fact, he can often be seen as one of their strongest critics and opponents precisely because he challenges the custom and tradition of Judaism in neglecting to observe the Sabbath, for example, and in repeatedly opposing some aspects of Levitical law. The examples of his criticism, though in many cases in the context of an ongoing dialogue and during the sharing of a meal, are numerous and relentless. He can provoke and insult, criticize and offend, and with a directness that ignores self-restraint and diplomacy. Jesus is compelled, his teaching urgent, and always with the need to be vigilant about persecution and (being aware of the death of John the Baptist) possible arrest and worse. Jesus anticipated such a possibility—it was, perhaps, inevitable—but it had to occur according to his overall plan and at the most appropriate time. No doubt already anticipating his entrance into Jerusalem for Passover, Jesus continues with his relentless dialogue—at times, in the manner of that "bold speaking" reflective of *parresia* (John 7:26)—with various individuals of the temple leadership, some of them, it must be stressed, who are by no means ill-disposed to him as a man and a teacher and are, in fact, sympathetic to some of his ideas.

In one noticeable incident however, and by no means unique and affirmed by all the gospel writers, the scribes and the Pharisees indirectly criticize Jesus as a teacher by asking him a question related to respecting and upholding tradition: "Why do thy disciples transgress the tradition (*paradosin*) of the elders (*presbuteron*)" (Matt 15:2)? The question is also repeated in Mark 7:5: "Why walk thy disciples according to the tradition of the elders?" they ask, holding him responsible (as their teacher) for the beliefs and actions of his students. As with Socrates, the authorities recognize the influence of a teacher on his students/disciples and how they in turn can continue to spread the message and increase its followers and, consequently, its social influence. Groups defined and motivated by ideas are potentially dangerous; they can disrupt the balance now maintained so precariously within a society pressured by different and competing interests. They represented a seemingly growing alternative to the authority so guarded by the temple leadership. Jesus' followers obviously had a reputation; and they were often sent out alone by Jesus, teaching independently in pairs—"And he called unto him the twelve, and began to send them forth two by two" (Mark 6:7)—now instructing them to spread Jesus' ideas: what he stood *for* and *against*. He often begins one of his speeches (that are also arguments) with the phrase: "You have heard that it was said by them of old times (Matt 5:21) . . . "but I say unto you," (Matt 5:22) explicitly contrasting his teaching with tradition, the present and all prior history. Jesus understands himself, his teaching, his purpose, as motivated by the urgent call to announce what he will soon call a new testament and represented, ultimately, by one profound symbolic substitution: the Eucharist for animal sacrifice, his body and blood instead of the body and blood of a sacrificed animal. The revolution he has envisioned in religious worship will soon be demonstrated; for the time being, his teaching (his service, his *therapeia* and healing) is a wholehearted dedication to others, a new piety that will represent an alternative to what has been perpetually guaranteed by a sacred history.

For those who argue that Jesus in no way challenges the precepts of Judaism, they must necessarily ignore both his numerous transgressions of everyday observances and his conversations with many individuals from the Jewish leadership, including every single group,[21] in which he made statements like "To eat with unwashen hands defileth not man" (Matt 15:20). Jesus often answers the questions of his interlocutors by telling them that they are hypocrites, literally actors who merely represent themselves publicly by observing the laws when in fact (in their heart) they are themselves impi-

---

21. For an overview of the difference in groups, see Stemberger, *Jewish Contemporaries of Jesus* and John Bowkder's *Jesus and the Pharisees*. He provides references that include post-AD 70 writings such as the Mishnah, Tosefta, and the Talmuds. An especially informative work is Anthony Saldarini's *Pharisees, Scribes, and Sadducees in Palestinian Society*.

ous. By exposing the mere "doctrines" and "commandments of men," (Mark 7:7) Jesus exposes the everyday practice of, for example, the washing of pots and cups as indicative of a religious faith more concerned with cleanliness, externals, than with authentic belief oriented to the internal self. Again, Jesus differentiates himself from other human beings (especially those with social and religious authority), first of all to undermine both their beliefs and practices and, ultimately, to present himself as an example, the first, of a new humanity coming into being, one capable of radically transforming individuals and the world with a unique wisdom and a "new doctrine" (Mark 1:27). Paul, himself a Pharisee prior to his conversion, defined himself as someone who in the past was "exceedingly zealous of the tradition of my fathers" (Gal 1:14). It was therefore important for the writers of early Christianity to present themselves, as followers of the teachings of Jesus, as a group that in part defined itself by being distinct from tradition; they could acknowledge the heritage of their past, and their relationship to it, while insisting on the newness of their message and, equally important, the world being inaugurated as they spoke. Such a belief was central to Jesus' teaching since he wanted to be foundational and bring a change into the world. Jesus opposes tradition insofar as he announces the possibility of a different history to come, a new age, and a renewed humanity.

Those who have learned from him are now behaving in defiance of tradition, of the handed-down beliefs that fundamentally organize human social life in the region and perpetuate the *status quo* as a whole. Prior to the one and definitive act in the temple, then, Jesus was widely considered to be "impious"—a word, *asebeia*, and description oddly (and noticeably) missing from the gospels. From the beginning, that is, when he came to the attention of the Jewish authorities (he was by all accounts unknown to the Roman leadership or military until he was denounced), Jesus was widely considered to be a teacher whose beliefs were in marked opposition to the prevalent teachings of Judaism. There were many reasons for Jesus opposing the tradition of the Pharisees. For one, as a priestly organization, it was entirely based on inheritance, the office passing from the father to the son. Therefore, Jesus opposes a social institution founded upon nothing more than a biological or familial relationship, ensuring that succession remains determined by family and therefore makes it impossible for someone other than a son to become a member of the Jerusalem priestly class. Such an act has the consequence of announcing the ability of a human freedom to become something other than his past, in other words, inaugurating another history, what will be called rebirth and regeneration. A. I. Baumgarten[22]

---

22. Baumgarten, "Pharisaic Paradosis."

makes the argument that Jesus' opposition to the Pharisaic tradition was not unique but was prevalent among other Jewish religious groups, among them the Essenes. Jesus, then, was only one individual opposing the Pharisees and their traditions; he was reflecting a common, unquestioned view and one shared by many, most especially those most exploited and marginalized.

Sufficient historical context to the ideas of Jesus and some of his precursors have been mentioned; now we can turn to the description of the particular incident at the temple and, equally important, the philosophical opposition to the practice of animal sacrifice (along with its ancillary needs, i.e., the sale of animals) in the gospels as they lead up to the cleansing of the temple (in Matthew, Mark, and Luke) and its more deliberate presentation by John. If, as Baumgarten argues, Jesus was by no means unique and was only one of several individuals and groups who opposed the status quo (certainly true of the Essenes) his actions in the temple, however, do make him unprecedented and—as far as we know—the only individual to *actively* and directly intervene in the temple itself. Ben Meyer describes the cleansing of the temple as "an event without known parallel in the tense history of Palestinian Judaism under the Romans."[23] The event is indeed without parallel—in history period. Jesus' acts in the temple are to be regarded as the decisive and culminating act of his ministry of teaching and healing, at once a rejection of animal sacrifice as the central ritual in religious worship of *all cultures* and its permanent substitution by soteriology as the care for and healing of others.

3. Jesus' Rejection of Animal Sacrifice

Jesus' acts in the temple of Jerusalem before Passover remain a source of continuing and unresolved interpretations. Their range is noticeable for being extreme and one can certainly understand the reluctance, even apprehension, in attempting to once again turn to the four gospel accounts and reconsider the meaning of what has often been described, not without disagreement, as the temple *cleansing*. Many other definitions have been proposed, though none of them have been willing to consider a possibility thus far ignored. Despite putting forward his own argument, P. M. Casey seems to resign himself when he writes that it is "difficult to see a way forward for scholarship dealing with this sort of topic, because the cultural constraints affecting the investigators are so strong."[24] There may very well be cultural constraints making an investigation of the account

23. Meyer, *Aims of Jesus*, 238.
24. Casey, "Culture and Historicity," 327.

difficult. History and hermeneutics are, however, all (everything) we have and everything we need to assume the responsibility of interpreting what took place at the temple in Jerusalem before Passover and understanding Jesus' singular motivations, both his acts as presented by the gospel writers and the words attributed to him before and after the fact. Victor Eppstein judicially believes that "the student may reflect meaningfully upon what may have actually occurred and why."[25] In all four of the gospels, Jesus' entrance to the city of Jerusalem, the meaning of the incident at the temple, and his subsequent arrest and crucifixion are described; however, each of the writers has a particular relationship to Jesus' acts, anticipating them and also giving us individually specific words that together provide a consistent reason for disrupting the day-to-day normalcy of the rituals at the temple. In all four accounts, Jesus acts with a characteristic rarely witnessed during his ministry: extreme anger, physically expressed by overturning tables and man-handling the money changers and, in the case of John's account, whipping them with a knotted rope as well as scattering (that is, freeing) the animals intended for sacrificial slaughter. The scene is one of physical force and rage and indignation. The reason for Jesus' emotions (and they are perhaps the most intense in any one description of him) have been given in part, but a further account is both possible and necessary. And this we will do at the conclusion.

Leaving aside the obviously nonstoic reaction once he sees how the temple has been used, Jesus directly attacks a long-established tradition, and consequently his actions would have been regarded as both extremely *impious* and subversive, both directed at religious and political sensibilities. The variously described temple functionaries (Pharisees, chief priest, and scribes) are continuously confronting Jesus during his ministry, a conflict between the radical teacher and the individuals whose social status gave them legitimacy, influence, and a certain amount of power, even if in the context of submitting to Roman rule. Jesus' act in the temple had to be understood as brazen and provocative. For some, it would have been unimaginable that a sacred sanctuary could be so disrupted, its most important ritual challenged and repudiated. Any *gentile* witnessing such an event would be immediately struck by its singularity of purpose and intent. Many knew precisely what Jesus was doing. The gentile reaction has been overlooked, a serious omission since observers were unlikely to interpret his acts as simply in relation to Judaism. Jesus acted against a ritual observed by *everyone*.

---

25. Eppstein, "Historicity of the Gospel Account," 58.

Jesus knew, without a doubt, that his acts were revolutionary and the consequences, certainly the judicial ones, could be severe. E. P. Sanders argues that "the notion that the temple should serve some function other than sacrifice would seem to be extremely remote from the thinking of a first-century Jew."[26] Geza Vermes likewise insists of defining Jesus as a "first-century AD Galilean Jew, a man firmly situated in time and space."[27]

We are not discussing, *pace* Sanders, *any* "first-century Jew," but the man who would engender a radical and, what is more, a world-altering movement whose effects would ultimately bring to an end the very empire responsible for his execution. To simply ignore the possibility that Jesus (precisely because of his uniqueness) acted against the sacrifice of animals as a religious ritual is to deny what may have been one of his culminating motivations. When the descriptions are then related to the anticipation of his entrance into Jerusalem and, in particular, when his acts in the temple in all four gospels are examined, some conclusions are difficult to avoid. Each of the gospels give us the details of certain *preliminary* facts that together provide a comprehensive meaning to Jesus' actions. He has been preparing for such an act from the beginning of his ministry. It would be final and decisive. A noticeable statement has also been made by the many members of the Jesus Seminar. "While the Fellows argued that Jesus did speak some word against the temple or *temple practices*, they were skeptical that the evangelists preserved his words."[28] Although his remembered words are extremely few, when related to his acts they become much more clear and meaningful. Denials, however, seem common.

Jesus, like the Essenes, as well as other philosophical groups influenced by the history of Greek philosophy, rejected animal sacrifice as a religious ritual, and in so doing also, necessarily, questioned the legitimacy of the

---

26. Sanders, *Jesus and Judaism*, 64. Sanders further argues that "there is no indication that Jesus' action was directed only against some particular practice," 69.

27. Vermes, *Jesus the Jew*, 16. The problem with such insistence is the accompanying assumption that Jesus could only understand himself within the immediate context of his society. If simply determined by his time and place, Jesus makes no sense whatsoever.

28. Funk, *Five Gospels*, 98. So, by consensus apparently, the very pithy words ascribed to Jesus during the incident at the temple are very much in doubt. What is clear is that, so unlike many other instances of Jesus speaking, at the temple he says very little—this despite teaching a doctrine that his hearers found extraordinary. What was he teaching at the temple in relation to his acts? My conclusion is not sceptical; on the contrary, his words had to somehow be related to (and be an explanation of) his acts. So, their conclusion is correct: the evangelist did not preserve his words. There was no need to: everyone knew them.

priests who were in charge of killing the animals in its specifically religious context. Bruce Chilton argues that

> if we wish to speak of Jesus in historical terms, he must be located in the space of Judaism. Any language that alleges Jesus' rejection or transcendence of Judaism is to be dismissed from the outset as an instance of apologetic.[29]

At the very least, however, the actions in the temple are certainly an expression of Jesus' outrage at the one central and now no longer relevant expression of piety. To be unequivocal, Jesus' actions at the temple are a rejection of animal sacrifice, a belief he holds not simply in relation to Judaism but to *all* sacrificial cultures. All four gospels are a testimony of that belief. Each of them will be interpreted in turn. To begin with, and to respond to Chilton (and many others), we have completely diminished Jesus as a religious revolutionary when we continue to insist on his narrow concern with the practices of Judaism and not consider how he was attempting to transform the very idea of religious piety, worship, and service in *all cultures* of the ancient world.

One view, expressed by Daniel Ullucci, argues that "nowhere in the New Testament is the historical Jesus portrayed as explicitly rejecting sacrifice."[30] A reinterpretation of the gospels and, in particular, Jesus' actions at the temple prior to his arrest, will attempt to present Jesus as a critic of animal sacrifice and, with it, also a critic of the priestly society that controlled the most important aspect of ritual observances in Judaism. Craig Evans writes that "Jesus' protest apparently was directed not against sacrifices but against the trafficking of sacrificial animals."[31] The economic critique is much too narrow as a concern. Jesus had a much more comprehensive idea. The commercialism at the temple was, perhaps, an ancillary reason; it was not the sole (and certainly not the most pressing) of Jesus' motivations.

---

29. Chilton, *Temple of Jesus*, 120

30. Ullucci, "Sacrifice in the Ancient Mediterranean," 421. A preliminary argument, and one to frame the four readings of the gospels: Jesus' acts in the temple were a culmination of a ministry that consistently, repeatedly, called into question the role of the various factions of the temple leadership. Jesus knew, well in advance (and obviously through no prophetic expectation but from an awareness of the religio-political consequences of his acts) that what he was about to do in the temple—and, it should be emphasized, through the very festival day commemorating Passover and, therefore, the sacrificial death of an animal for each household so as to free the Jewish people from Egypt—would lead to severe consequences. The Jewish temple leadership could tolerate his teachings as long as he roamed the Galilean countryside. Once he dared enter Jerusalem and with an act of unprecedented defiance, the consequences could be predicted.

31. Evans, "Opposition to the Temple," 246.

Jesus' Anti-sacrificial Acts in the Temple of Jerusalem   225

His repudiation of the sacrificial system is not merely economic. Not only does Jesus explicitly reject animal sacrifice, in each of the narratives of Jesus' acts in the temple there are clear anticipations, indeed preparations (with the exception of John, who places the temple incident early), that provide specific commentary on Jesus' motivations with singular examples. In every case, the acts at the temple are both anticipated and related to prior events that serve as explanations for his purpose and intent. The gospel writers have never been more unified than in this one presentation of Jesus. His entrance in the temple, and the meaning of his acts, are prepared by the Synoptic writers with prior examples of his teaching and speaking, both directly and in parables, with Jesus' words explicit. Can anyone honestly misinterpret his argument for showing mercy instead of carrying out a sacrifice? To repeat: an almost unanimous majority simply accepts the ritual of animal slaughter in the Jerusalem temple as normal, straightforward, and traditional. Its supposed normality—so readily accepted—conceals what should be most objectionable about such a practice. The vast majority of scholars have established an apologetic (to use Chilton's word) that can no longer be sustained. Others, in part recognizing Jesus' intent, can write that "Jesus symbolically destroys the temple by attacking its fiscal, sacrificial, and cultic necessities."[32] There are a few who have, if only partly and without extending their argument to the conclusion it deserves, at least mentioned Jesus as a critic of animal sacrifice, and with the description of cleansing we must soon not only acknowledge but also investigate a meaning everyone has avoided—and with an understandable reason. "In its historic immediacy the cleansing aimed at putting an end not only prepassover money changing in the court of the gentiles and to secular traffic using the court as a short-cut, but perhaps to the cult itself."[33] The careful "perhaps" shows the extent of the hesitation. Without being more specific and detailed, Martin Hengel writes that Jesus "was shaking both the foundations of Jewish community life and the order of temple worship."[34] There are also a very few who reflect on the temple in a particular way, writing that "the temple resembled a butcher shop" more than "a place of worship."[35] On the other hand, we

---

32. Crossan, *Who Killed Jesus?*, 63.

33. Meyer, *Early Christians*, 59.

34. Hengel, *Charismatic Leader and His Followers*, 40.

35. Akers, *Lost Religion of Jesus*, 103. Though "butcher shop" begins to more properly define one aspect of the temple, *slaughterhouse* is much nearer to emphasizing the scale of the butchery involved. And then one should add: a certain class of priests were, in fact, butchers, just as a related class were responsible for what had to be a far from agreeable duty, that is, the *real cleansing*. We will see the reason why the term "temple cleansing" has been so often rejected as of late; the denial seems like the avoidance of a

have the peculiar statement (so often repeated, both for the prescriptions in Leviticus and for the Jerusalem temple) that "the blood and fat of animals was especially dear to God."[36] Such an assumption could be sustained by priests and pious readers; it can be defended by the theologically conservative who read the writings of Scripture as originating in Yahweh and not within the limits of a historical imagination Jesus had repeatedly defied. But in each of the gospels (interpreted, in order), and with subtle language and equally subtle arguments, such a belief in the relationship of animal sacrifice to *the desire* of God (or the polytheistic gods in the case of non-Jews) will no longer be defensible. Jesus does nothing less than categorically suspend the religious imagination of antiquity and inaugurate a new conception of the spirit in its service to God. In the city of Jerusalem, Jesus simultaneously confronted Judaism and all the sacrificial cultures now unified by the Roman empire and exposed how the Latin *sacer facere* (the supposed "making sacred" by sacrifice) was no longer tenable. The belief that the sacrificial slaughter of animals, their death, "points to humanity's desire for renewal: to 'make sacred' and participate in the source of life,"[37] had become inimical to the life of the spirit and the consciousness of a religious piety dedicated to others as the expression of the love of God. Each of the examples from the gospel writers are now to be examined, beginning with Jesus' very first entrance into the temple of Jerusalem.

Early in his gospel, Luke prefaces Jesus' acts in the temple of Jerusalem by returning to his birth and the requirements imposed on his parents to fulfill the law and therefore take their new-born infant to the temple of Jerusalem and "offer a sacrifice according to that which is said in the law of the Lord, a pair of turtledoves, or two young pigeons" (Luke 2:24). As they prepare to make a sacrifice in accordance with the law, they meet Simeon, a man defined as just and devout and somehow associated with the temple. Although not described specifically as a priest, a functionary with specific responsibilities, he is clearly in charge of the sacrifices performed after the birth of a child. However, when Jesus is presented to him, there is no indication of an animal sacrifice being performed; the typical and expected rites are neither mentioned nor at all involved. Instead, and with Simeon somehow recognizing the importance of the child's future, he says: "Lord, now lettest thou thy servant depart in peace" (Luke 2:29). Simeon makes the announcement, directly to Jesus, that he has seen "thy salvation," the

---

most unpleasant but unavoidable fact of ancient Mediterranean religion.

36. Neville, *Symbols of Jesus*, 64. That such a statement can be made with no self-consciousness whatsoever is, in part, what has allowed scholarship (the majority of theologians and historians of religion) to simply avoid a fuller inquiry.

37 Sedley, "Sacrifice, Transcendence, and 'Making Sacred'," 268.

soteria or healing that he will bring to the gentiles as well as to the people of Israel. The connection (or rather, the distinction between animal sacrifice and human healing) is further strengthened when Anna, a prophetess, is described as someone who "departed not from the temple" and who "served (*latreuousa*) God with fasting and prayers" (Luke 2:37), *latreia* the repeated word used by Socrates during his trial when he defined himself as a servant of God. In other words, although Anna did not withdraw from the temple (as John the Baptist did to become a preacher in the wilderness) she does not serve God except through fasting and prayer, thereby offering herself as a sacrifice rather than the body of an animal, a reevaluation of faith ultimately recognized by Paul when he writes: "Present your bodies a living sacrifice (*thusian*), holy, acceptable unto God, which is your reasonable service (*latreian*)" (Rom. 12:1). To understand the renewed meaning of *latreia* as service means that one no longer needs to perform the ritual of animal sacrifice but instead offers oneself (and, as Jesus will soon make clear) and one's *soteria* and *therapeia* to others.

In the Gospel of Matthew, there are two repeated passages that not only are important in themselves, they are also unique; no other Synoptic writer mentions them. They are especially relevant since the idea of human healing and sacrifice (at the temple), are specifically related and contrasted; more than that, Jesus replaces sacrifice with healing. In one of the events when Jesus is sharing a meal with someone that the Pharisees consider inappropriate, they ask his disciples why Jesus would eat with "publicans and sinners" (Matt 9:10). Those that are sinners, or suffering from *hamartia*, are too general to define precisely; however, the publicans or tax-collectors would be bureaucrats in the service of the Roman state and individuals who would have been looked upon with particular contempt. They were perceived to be extortionists, inflicting hardships on those already burdened by their marginal social status, the reason he tells the tax collectors to "exact no more than that which is appointed you" (Luke 3:13). He does not simply judge; Jesus encourages and exhorts, prompting others (because of the temptation to exploit their social position) not to take advantage of those who cannot demand to be treated justly. Jesus responds to the disapproval of the Pharisees by telling them that "they that be whole (*ischuontes*) need not a physician (*iatrou*), but they that are sick (*kakos*)" (Matt 9:12), a first statement later to include the significant (and many times repeated) insult of being hypocrites, for they too collected money, if for the continued function of the temple, a necessity they of course thought to be perfectly legitimate and necessary in the day-to-day organization of the temple. The relationship of the tax collectors and a meal is, for Jesus, a reflection of the Pharisees who, in and through their duties at the temple, would have also managed the collection of taxes while also enjoying the benefits of eating the sacrificial animals, in fact being fed by what was symbolically offered to God. By defining those who suffer as, in part, weak, Jesus recognizes the particular frailty of human beings and how, in weakness, they may lead a life that compromises their character; self-deception and rationalization are easily maintained when the immediacy of personal pain allows you to neglect others. His next words are both clear in terms of the prior message and how he needs to be interpreted. "But go ye and learn what *that* meaneth," (Matt 9:13a) he tells the Pharisees, first of all saying that they have not understood either his actions or his words. Jesus is both exposing their ignorance and telling them to reflect on the meanings he has now revealed for the first time. That Jesus is so often misunderstood, and not only by those who despise him and consider him a threat to be eliminated, but also by the very disciples he is attempting to teach, reveals the extent of his message as unprecedented and almost impossible to fully understand; his ideas are simply inconceivable to the Jerusalem leadership. His next declarations may even be more enigmatic than the first: "I will have mercy, and not sacrifice (*thusia*)" (Matt 9:13). The relationship between Jesus' mercy (and understanding) and sacrifice seems to indicate that the sinners will not be conveniently exploited precisely by those who need to see themselves as holy, as comparisons. Jesus juxtaposes mercy and sacrifice, echoing Hosea 6:6, but he does not, during this particular conversation, make the all-important addition. He saves it for another moment. For the time being, he wants the Pharisees to reflect on his difficult saying, hopefully understanding his meaning, that is, substituting sacrifice with healing others and then adding, with mercy being shown to the animals slaughtered as well as the compassion shown to those most in need of support: "For I am not come to call the righteous, but sinners (*hamartolous*) to repentance (*metanoian*)" (Matt 9:13). Sacrifice and healing are opposed, set against each other; the opposition is also a substitute.

Jesus responds to the accusations by the Pharisees by, first of all, telling them that they too "profane the Sabbath," and particularly in the temple; he does not specify, precisely, what leads to their profane acts, but he does make the assertion (provocative for the Pharisees) that the field of corn is greater than the temple. "But I say unto you, that in this place is one greater than the temple" (Matt 12:6). To call the sanctuary of the temple less than a field of corn would have been incomprehensible to the Pharisees, and again Jesus has to tell them that they will misunderstand the meaning of his words: "but if ye had known what this meaneth, I will have mercy, and not sacrifice (*thusian*)" (Matt 12:7), repeating an earlier declaration and saying it twice for emphasis. In this case, however, he also makes a significant addition. Not only will he not sacrifice due to his mercy (and this can only be the mercy shown to the animal as a *victim*), he makes this explicit when he continues: "ye would not have condemned (*katadikasate*) the guiltless (*anaitious*)" (Matt 12:7). The judicial language could not be clearer: Jesus does nothing less than declare that a sentence of death has been passed on an animal without fault, a statement he understands but, for those listening to him, is all but incomprehensible; their consciousness is unprepared for such a realization. No one but Jesus can possibly conceive that the sacrificial system depends on imposing a death sentence on an animal so as to (somehow, and with divine approval) relieve human beings of *their* faults. Jesus has exposed the sacrificial machinations once and for all even if it will take the first generation of Christians to understand the implication of his teaching and finally repudiate sacrificial ritual as a religious observance.

For the second time, he tells the Pharisees that they have to understand his meaning and contrasts mercy with sacrifice while at the same time making the statement (again, incomprehensible to his listeners) that the sacrificial system depends on slaughtering an animal he pronounces innocent, that is, innocent despite its subjection by theological law as that which suffers for the faults of human beings. Animals are innocent victims of the sacrificial system. Or, to use René Girard's language, scapegoats, surrogate victims. Jesus places himself between the human actors of a failed religious system and the animal to be sacrificially slaughtered, now fully representing Yahweh "who encompasses all divinity and does not depend at all on what happens among humankind. This is the God who reproaches human for their violence and has compassion on their victims."[38] Is Jesus telling the Pharisees that his mercy is directed at the slaughtered animals? Is this the reason he will not sacrifice, introducing an idea that, already known to the Essenes and, perhaps, other pious Jews, may have questioned the practice? Jesus' language of mercy, innocence, and the compassion for a victim—implies that the sacrificial system appears as a form of what Girard has called nothing less than a "crime."[39]

Does the reference to mercy and *thusia* anticipate his entrance into Jerusalem? In his first act once he enters the city, Jesus fulfills what he had promised the Pharisees. "And Jesus went into the temple of God, and cast out all them that sold and bought in the temple, and overthrew (*katestrepse*) the tables of the moneychangers, and the seats of them that sold doves" (Matt 21:12). The first recorded action related to Jesus' entrance into the city of Jerusalem involves him expelling (by force) those who frequented the temple for the purpose of selling animals for sacrificial slaughter. He is

38. Girard, *I See Satan Fall like Lightning*, 119.
39. Girard, *Violence and the Sacred*, 197.

sufficiently motivated (and physically strong) to grab the merchants, shoving and pushing them, even forcing some to the ground and, perhaps, injuring them. When Jesus overturns the tables of the moneychangers, the meaning of "overthrow" implies that such an act is also intended to bring their practice *to an end*. His single act is intended to be absolute. After throwing out some people from the temple, overturning tables and chairs with a violence perhaps never witnessed before, he says "My house shall be called the house of prayer; but ye have made it a den (*spelaion*) of thieves (*leston*)" (Matt 21:13), he tells everyone, in part recalling Isaiah 56:7 and Jeremiah 7:11, uttering words echoing prophetic statements, ones intended as disapproval and castigation. Instead of being an *oikos* of prayer, the temple has become a cave filled with robbers—a robbery he defines more clearly when he equates the sacrificial system with a form of violence that takes the lives of innocent animals. The robbery is first and foremost the taking of an animal's life—"theft" is, therefore, a circumlocution—and the economic commercialism is only a consequence of a more serious practice. Once in the temple, and immediately after violently disrupting the normal, everyday practice of the commerce of animals (including those that are the less costly, the doves, and therefore made available to the poor) he turns to the people who have come to see him and heals them. "And the blind and the lame came to him in the temple; and he healed them" (Matt 21:14). *Healing follows the rejection of animal sacrifice.* Jesus does so precisely so that human healing (taking care of others as an ethical responsibility) replaces the mere ritual of animal slaughter in the context of a religious tradition he now rejects and requires everyone to abandon. The announcement of the temple being destroyed is fundamentally related to a religious practice he no longer considers to be an adequate expression of piety. Jesus' temple acts are not accidentally related; they constitute the essence of his entire ministry: to end the religious observance of animal sacrifice and initiate a new form of piety and service, dedicating one's life to the healing and well-being of others. Many have grappled with the meaning of Jesus' acts (while also refraining from seeing him as rejecting sacrifice at the temple), though the consequences are difficult to deny. In tracing the events at the temple to a source prior to the evangelists—that they all inherited, with obvious approval—Wilfred Knox points out that the remembrance of (at least some, though not many) of his words was essential in the oral tradition preceding the writing of the gospels. "The cleansing of the temple came from a source which rightly or wrongly regarded that action as the turning point which led the authorities to decide to get rid of Jesus."[40] Jesus' death has often been hoped-for, an-

---

40. Knox, *Sources of the Synoptic Gospels*, 81. It is also highly unlikely it came from

ticipated, and planned. His acts in the temple have now given the religious authorities all the judicial evidence they will ever need to denounce him to the Romans as both a political rebel and religious agitator who conspired to disrupt animal sacrifice, and therefore the very observance of religious cultures, and,more importantly for the Romans, as a necessary submission to the symbol of Caesar.

After the actions taken in the temple, the Pharisees meet and "took counsel how they might entangle him in his talk" (Matt 22:15), apparently trying to get Jesus to inculpate himself, though strangely he has obviously been guilty (in their eyes) of both an impious and illegal act according to Jewish and Roman law. However, in order for Jesus to be arrested and tried by the Romans, he must be heard to utter something that could be interpreted as seditious and a political threat to the Roman state. The act itself could be interpreted as no more than a petty squabble between merchants and a disaffected buyer. An excuse could certainly be provided. For him to be denounced to the Romans, arrested, and tried (and executed), he must be shown to be a threat to Roman rule and law. His disruptive acts would not in themselves be punishable by the Romans since they might consider his show of anger as a petty squabble and therefore nothing more than an internal matter to be decided by the Jewish leadership, unless of course certain high-ranking individuals could persuade the Romans—and Pontius Pilate in particular—that Jesus' anti-sacrificial acts were attacks on the emperor and on Rome. The questions they ask him, therefore, are directly related to the animal sacrifice in the temple as, in part, a tribute to Caesar. "Is it lawful to give tribute unto Caesar, or not?" (Matt 22:17) they ask Jesus, in part justifying their acceptance of Roman law as it pertains to their worship in the temple, for the Jewish leadership in the temple and the Romans had one thing in common: they both charged a tax. The sacrifice in the temple served in part as a tribute to Caesar. Recognizing that they are attempting to make his own speech treasonous, Jesus accuses them again of being hypocrites, the most often-repeated word for them. When he asks them to show him a coin (that would have had both the image of the emperor as well as an inscription), he then tells them to "render therefore unto Caesar the things which are Caesar's, and unto God the things that are God's" (Matt 22:21). What does he mean? Jesus shows himself to be in opposition to the relationship between religion and the economy, in both cases—in the temple and in talking to the Pharisees—explicitly denouncing the use of money. More than that, when he then turns to the people to preach, he begins an extended

---

one source. Jesus' acts in the temple soon became universally known. His notoriety, especially among non-Jews, may well have this one event as the cause.

criticism of the scribes and the Pharisees, several times calling them hypocrites, denouncing the rituals in the temple, the economic burden suffered by the people, and the privileges enjoyed by the Pharisees who are overly concerned with appearances and, in particular, enjoying their social status. The intense denunciation of the Pharisees begins, first of all, with telling people that their religious leaders "bind heavy burdens and grievous to be borne, and lay them on men's shoulders" (Matt 23:4). All they care about is their social status and receiving privileges and material wealth. His list is extensive. Jesus does not accept the difficult positon of the Pharisees, the necessary cooperation with the Romans for the sake of the continued existence and function of the temple. He refuses to rationalize a necessary collaboration, as would the Zealots, sicarii, and the other revolutionaries soon to initiate an all-out war against the Romans and, if victorious, no doubt anticipating the appointment of a new temple leadership. More seriously, Jesus mentions for the first time the fact of Jewish proselytizing and, in the context of converting others to Judaism, making these converts "more the child of hell (*Gehenna*) than yourselves" (Matt 23:15). By making new converts children of Gehenna (otherwise known as the valley of Hinnom), Jesus accuses the Pharisees of turning converts into people who pray to gods who demand child sacrifice. The reference to Gehenna turns back, historically, to the prophets and the condemnation of child sacrifice. He connects the present to the past and, by doing so, hopes to bring animal sacrifice to an end just as child sacrifice, called an "abomination" by Jeremiah, was abolished:

> They have set their abominations in the house which is called by my name, to pollute it. And they have built the high places of Tophet, which is in the valley of the son of Hinnom, to burn their sons and their daughters in the fire; which I commanded them not, neither came it into my heart. Therefore, behold the days come, saith the Lord, that it shall no more be called Tophet, nor the valley of the son of Hinnom, but the valley of slaughter: for they shall bury in Tophet, till there be no place. (Jer. 7:30–32)

Jesus' reference to Gehenna is also a testament of himself as the individual, like Jeremiah, who assumes the responsibility of bringing a historical period *to an end*. The substitution of animal sacrifice for child sacrifice is now abolished. Jesus makes the attempt to make them aware of a historical fact and its consequences for the present; for if the sacrifice of children (historically practiced in the past as an act of the most demanding religious devotion) could be abolished, so could animal sacrifice now also be replaced. Jesus' actions are not simply some rejection of the commercialism involved in the temple; the specific economic transaction, the buying and selling of animals for sacrifice, is only the context of the much more serious challenge to the ritual as such that Jesus now replaces with teaching and healing.

Although the twice-repeated statement on mercy and sacrifice in Matthew is not mentioned in the gospel of Mark, the incident at the temple is nevertheless anticipated, again with a *culminating* metaphor related to food and, in particular, the seasoning of salt. Prior to the end at 9:50, however, there are a series of enigmatic, difficult sayings attributed to Jesus that deal with fire, "hell," and worms. "And if thy hand offend thee, cut it off: it is better for thee to enter into life maimed, than having two hands to go into hell, into the fire that shall never be quenched" (Mark 9:43). The significant juxtaposition involves the preference for an incomplete life—one hand instead of two—rather than being in the *fire of Gehenna*, the fire where children were previously sacrificed and now is the site of a garbage dump south of Jerusalem, a sizeable mound that also contains the carcasses of animals as well as executed criminals.[41] The fire that is never quenched is Jesus' allusion to the perpetual sacrifices at the temple. Jesus continues with a word (the sternest of warnings) he will repeat three times when referring to Gehenna and its predominant feature: "Where their worm (*skolex*) dieth not, and the fire is not quenched" (Mark 9:48). He has never been more emphatic. The worm here can be more clearly defined as a "maggot," and its presence would be noticeable in such a place as Gehenna; maggots would multiply and never die, that is, they would be continually present in and around the garbage, especially as they fed on the remnants of dead animals and other organic matter. If, in this speech, Jesus anticipates the culmination of his message in verses 49–50, then he has prepared the end of the statement with a prelude, one related to the Jewish past and to the present sacrificial system.

"For every one shall be salted with fire, and every sacrifice (*thusia*) shall be salted with salt," (Mark 9:49) making a distinction between how human beings will be salted, changed with the fire of the spirit while animal sacrifices will continue to be salted merely with something to give meat its flavor, a mere act prior to eating. That salt mediates the relationship between the dead body of an animal and the living spirit of a human beings begins Jesus' reflections in Mark on the sacrificial system. Soteriology replaces sacrifice; the salt of *soteria* replaces the salt used in the *thusia*. In this one speech, containing elements of the Sermon on the Mount, and remembering how he has anticipated his confrontation with the Jerusalem authorities

---

41. See Berlin and Grossman, *Oxford Dictionary of the Jewish Religion* and Livingstone, *Concise Oxford Dictionary*.

("The Son of Man is delivered into the hands of men," [Mark 9:31]), Jesus begins a series of interrelated statements culminating with 9:50.

Jesus draws his first conclusion: "Salt is good: but if the salt have lost his saltness, wherewith will ye season it? Have salt in yourselves, and have peace with one another" (Mark 9:50). The salt previously used to salt the body of the sacrificed animal prior to eating it has been now transformed into the salt "in yourselves," no longer a thing, specks of mineral, but rather an inner transformation of the psyche, the metamorphosis previously discussed during his time on a mountain with his disciples. His comments on the difference between salting a sacrificed animal and being, oneself, the salt that changes, anticipates Jesus' arrival in Jerusalem and his entrance into the temple. And the peace has two simultaneous meanings, one individual (individual being reconciled, finally, and their self-division healed), the other social (the peace that now reconciles people and their differences—their socially imposed differences—from each other). The peace attainable by a sacrificial act no longer has any pertinence; peace can only be experienced by first returning to oneself and then establishing a relationship. The previous reciprocity, between human beings and God, has now been replaced by Jesus with the human-to-human relationship, each sharing in the peace now evident as a dedication to others and the world. It seems probable that his disciples, as so often before, did not understand Jesus' pronouncements and the role of salt, how symbolic was its discussion, divided between soteriology and sacrifice. They have been unclear. Jesus, however, realized how significant the comparison was between the salt used to add flavor to sacrificed animals and the salt (also, of course, used to preserve, to keep, to maintain) as it pertained to human beings who are perpetually vulnerable to *spoiling*, being rotten. Salt has been removed from the external body of a dead animal before being consumed (as a mere superficial additive) into the internality of a human being who will be seasoned, that is, saved, changed, and preserved. Human beings will now be kept, each responsible for the other—indeed, a brother's keeper and the reemphasized commitment to the love of the neighbor.

Unlike Matthew, who portrays Jesus immediately confronting the merchants who buy and sell sacrificial animals as he enters Jerusalem, Mark has him first arriving at Bethphage and Bethany, at the mount of Olives, then going to Jerusalem, but only as a reconnaissance. He appears methodical, so as to plan his assault and, trying to avoid the temple guards, act quickly and decisively so as to elude those who could apprehend him on the spot. "And when he had looked upon all things," (Mark 11:11) as if he first inspects the place so as to decide on the best way to act at a later time, he went back to Bethany in the evening. Jesus does not act in haste; he has been carefully,

Jesus' Anti-sacrificial Acts in the Temple of Jerusalem 235

methodically anticipating and planning his act based on his evaluation of the lay-out of the temple, possibly also on the movement of the temple constabulary and their periodic movements and shifts. No doubt there was a changing of the guard at a prescribed time, one that could be anticipated and serve as an appropriate moment to act. He will not, as it later seems, act simply out of spontaneous anger. He fully knows his disruption at the temple must have the desired results; Jesus must come to the attention of the authorities and, by doing so, now confront the people who have been his detractors from the beginning and also to be seen by the people in his role as a teacher and a healer in contradistinction to the temple priests. His acts must come to the attention of the religious authorities as well as *all the people* attending the festival of Passover, Jews and all other *ethne*. Needless to say, his plan is unprecedented, bold, and extremely dangerous, most especially considering the number of guards present and the fact that the walls were manned day and night.[42]

The next day, "Jesus went into the temple, and began to cast them that sold and bought in the temple, and overthrew (*katestrepsen*) the tables of the moneychangers, and the seats of them that sold doves" (Mark 11:15). The actions of Jesus at the temple have been the subject of many interpretations. They are as divergent as they are extensive. Many will be recalled at the appropriate time and in relation to the description known as "the temple cleansing." For the time being, one decision seems the most perplexing—and completely unacceptable:

> The possibility will be entertained that the act is simply a literary creation by Mark. This possibility will, in the end, be preferred as manifesting the fewest difficulties of interpretation.[43]

Fortunately, not everyone avoids difficult interpretations. Not only does Jesus overturn the tables of the money changers, the "overthrow" (as in Matthew—perhaps, then, originating in Q) has the sense of bringing them to an end, that is, the tables no longer having a function. "And he would not suffer that any man should carry any vessel (*skeuos*) through the temple" (Mark 11:16). What is the meaning, here, of *any* vessel? It can be a thing, equipment, or an implement of sorts—such as a sacrificial knife,

---

42. On the security operations of the temple, see Goldhill, *Temple of Jerusalem*.

43. Seeley, "Jesus' Temple Act," 1. The suggestion that the entire incident is nothing but literary fiction by Mark (and repeated by the other three gospel writers) does not ask *why* it has been included. What motivation would Mark have for making up such a story? Equally important, the other gospel writers (if using Mark) had to have their own reasons for including it. Seeley's decision to see the incident as "fiction" (because it poses interpretive difficulties) should be dismissed.

or a platter for carrying parts of an animal. Whatever the various possible meanings, and it is significant that Jesus does not permit *any* vessel to be carried, he concludes his act with a teaching, repeating Matthew's reference to a den of thieves. "Is it not written, My house shall be called of all nations (*ethnesin*) the house of prayer? But ye have made it a den of thieves" (Mark 11:17). Noticeably, as we shall see, John does not refer to the den of thieves (which clearly has biblical precedent) but an altogether different term—one remarkably used by Socrates in the *Euthyphro*. Notice, too, how the people respond not only to his actions, but equally if not more importantly to what has been defined as his "doctrine (*didache*)" (Mark 11:18), how it astonishes them for being so unexpected, surprising, and new—for everyone, that is, for everyone from all nations. Jesus is much more absolutely radical than previously conceived. His words are spoken to everyone present. *All the temples of the world* are dens of thieves. As Jesus physically overturns the tables of the moneychangers and the sellers of animals, he is also speaking to the whole crowd who, at this point, understand him to be making statements much more comprehensive than to the Jews.

Jesus has not planned his actions as some arbitrary expression of anger; it has been essential to his new and unprecedented *teaching* and on nothing less than a reevaluation of the practice of animal sacrifice in the temple of Jerusalem and in all other temples of the world who continue to maintain one ritual as the highest expression of religious piety. The scribes and chief priests of the temple actually hear, for the first time, the extent of his message. They are both incredulous and outraged. The leaders of the Jerusalem temple suddenly realize how Jesus has not merely addressed his fellow Jews and attacked only the Jewish temple; he has called into question all religions as they presently observe their most important ritual in the service of their God. The chief priests and scribes can in no way tolerate Jesus' acts and declarations. They therefore "sought how they might destroy (*apolesosin*) him: for they feared him, because all the people was astonished at his doctrine (*didache*)" (Mark 11:18). The sense of "destroy" is, more precisely, to kill. The priests want to kill Jesus on the spot but, of course, cannot because of all the people present. A man killed by the religious authorities would have been scandalous to Jews and non-Jews alike. Only one teaching could have roused the temple leadership to kill him. His teaching is a call for the abolition of animal sacrifice in the temple and its replacement by *soteria*, healing instead of death. People were obviously astonished with a doctrine that for many would have been unthinkable and, in fact, completely out of the realm of the possible—except, of course, to people from other cultures (at the very least, both Greek speakers and Romans) who were more than aware of precedents in their respective cultures, from both philosophers and poets. But Jesus' words must have been effective precisely when he began to question the motives of those in the temple leadership for the continuity of the practice. He exposes the priestly class to the very people who had no choice but to follow and obey the politicoreligious doctrines of their respective culture. That the tradition has not preserved more words of this doctrine raises serious questions. Are the gospel writers unable or unwilling to report what Jesus said? Has the memory been preserved and not recounted? Or is it much more likely that the teaching is so well known among Christians—and, by the time of the first gospel of Mark, animal sacrifice no longer practiced and certainly not a part of any liturgy—that it did not have to be written, in part due to their now precarious position of being nonsacrificers within the limits of the Roman empire?

Jesus tells his disciples that, now that animal sacrifices have been repudiated, what is essential is their prayer, most especially concerning "what things soever ye desire, when ye pray, believe (*pisteuete*) that ye receive them" (Mark 11:24). In the past, in the relationship of gift-giving, one gave to God in the temple in order to receive—atonement, for example—but now Jesus makes human beings free from the relationship of gift-giving and instead makes everyone dependent on prayer and *pistis*, that is, belief, trust, and faith. The desire, previously in the nature of a request to God, now becomes a self-demand—a prayer to ask of oneself that which seems difficult, like forgiveness. The prayer is no longer a request; it has become a self-demand, an ongoing responsibility to *be* a certain person. Noticeably, the previous atonement, made possible by God after receiving the sacrificial offering, has been replaced by a human act, by an overcoming of oneself and a previous conviction held and rationalized: "And when ye stand praying, forgive, if ye have ought against any" (Mark 11:26). The house of prayer for all *ethne* now also has an appeal to universality, overcoming distinction based on any and all differences—what Paul will initially express in his "neither/nor" formulation. Inherent in the gospel is much more than the fragile sense of Roman cosmopolitanism, with all the privileges given to a citizen; it demands nothing less than an absolute universality along with the all-embracing ethics first articulated (and understood to be distinction from animal sacrifice) in Leviticus 19:18 with the commandment, "Thou shalt love your neighbor as yourself."

Another day when Jesus enters the city of Jerusalem (he does not pass the night there) he is again confronted by the chief priests, scribes, and elders (Mark 11:27). They demand to know by what authority he acted (and spoke) in such a way in the temple precinct. He does not answer directly, instead asking them a question (related to the ministry of John the Baptist) on his authority. After speaking to them in parables—in a parable that criticizes the temple priests—they went away and urged the Pharisees, this time accompanied by Herodians, Jewish soldiers, to confront him. As in Matthew (and as will be repeated in Luke), Jesus is asked if it is lawful to give a tribute to Caesar, at which time Jesus mentions the image, *eikon*, and inscription, *epigraphe*, on the coin. One final incident is crucial for two interrelated reasons: it follows his critique of animal sacrifice and its *substitution*.

Overhearing a conversation between Jesus and a Sadducee, a scribe—portrayed as sympathetic, admiring his answers—asks him his own question: "Which is the first commandment of all?" (Mark 12:28) Not only does he tell him the first commandment (that one acknowledge the one and only God and love him with all one's heart, soul, and mind) but he also tells him the importance of the second commandment: "Thou shall love (*agapeseis*) thy neighbor as thyself" (Mark 12:31). The declaration becomes the single most important indication of a *reemphasized* piety: the substitution of prayer and love of neighbor instead of the sacrificial slaughter of animals, in effect recalling an initial distinction when the Jewish people were establishing themselves after their release from Egypt. This one individual scribe, unnamed, then makes a statement that shows him to have understood Jesus' actions in the temple, understood and confirmed his teaching as not simply in opposition to the practice of animal sacrifice, but as a call for its abolition and its replacement. For the first time, someone else, a scribe from the temple and one whose responsibility includes interpreting the meaning of the law, is shown to have understood Jesus' teaching. He says to Jesus: "And to love him with all the heart, and with all the understanding, and with all the soul, and with all the strength, and to love his neighbor as himself, is more than all whole burnt offerings (*holokautomaton*) and sacrifices (*thusion*)" (Mark 12:33). This one unnamed scribe, so different from the lawyer in Matthew 22:35, who asks him the same question but never reaches the same conclusion, shows him not only to have understood Jesus and confirmed his teaching[44]; more importantly, and surprisingly given his knowledge of his tradition and his responsibility as a religious leader, he has acknowledged

---

44. The extraordinary quality of their conversation (uniquely in Mark) should raise questions about the particular meaning of the incident and the reason(s) why the later accounts omit it. If, as is the overriding consensus, the Gospel of Mark is the first one written, one must wonder why it was later omitted. The incident in Mark must certainly stand as one of the single most important testimonies about individuals in the Jewish leadership who exemplified the highest standard of conduct and belief. The overwhelming evidence of Jesus' critique (that is, the number of incidents portrayed that are critical) should now be much more balanced and lead the reader of the gospels as a whole to consider whether the accounts are heavyhanded and polemical. Such a reappraisal should also consider the not-to-be-neglected Gospel of John and his own recognition that it is only *some* members of the temple leadership who are acting inappropriately.

how Jesus' new precepts—different, in principle, from commandments as impositions—have replaced the sacrificial system with one overreaching idea, *agape*. As we will see, this one comprehensive idea (of *agape and* its relation to *soteria* and *therapeia*) will replace the sacrificial system and lead ultimately to its transformation. Mark's Gospel culminates with one unmistakable substitution: love instead of animal sacrifice—indeed, the *agape* so profound it can lead to one's own sacrifice for a friend—as Epicurus first understood. Jesus' giving of himself, however, does not necessarily have to be interpreted from the standpoint of a theology of sacrifice related to his crucifixion and death. His sacrifice was exemplified by his acts in the temple and his willingness, for the sake of others (for the sake of those who were compelled to sacrifice animals), to risk his life to present a teaching he knew would be welcomed by many who heard him, but also extremely resented by most of the individuals in the temple leadership. The scribe in this case is portrayed favorably, for as someone knowledgeable about the textual tradition of his people, he knows that Jesus' teaching reflects the distinctions made in the Torah between a "nation of priests" and the all-encompassing commandment to be holy.

Jesus not only brings sacrifices to an end; he affirms the most important law of all. The love of one's neighbor replaces the sacrificial system, in effect transforming the traditional understanding of piety and worship. If, previously, sacrifices were intended to help one draw near God, Jesus now makes a radical change in the very nature of piety and worship. One will now "draw near" to others in love and service.

While the Synoptic Gospels present the incident at the temple well into their narrative on the life and death of Jesus, and prepare it with significant episodes that place the series of events within a context of opposition to the Jerusalem leadership and their control of the temple, its importance, and its ritual in the Gospel of John, the acts are presented early, completely ignoring any sense of chronology and, even more significantly, with unique, unprecedented language when compared to Matthew, Mark, and Luke. The early descriptions, provided by John the Baptist as his witness as the one who gives a testimony of him to others such as the priests and Levites and Pharisees, define him unmistakably and in anticipation of the events to unfold on the day of his entrance into Jerusalem, his acts at the temple and their *judicial consequences* that were definitely known to him, expected, and yet his defiance was more compelling than any apprehension about his life. He had prepared for this one decisive event in his life immediately after being baptized and when, in the desert, alone and confronting the all-too-human fear of being imprisoned, tortured and killed, he had anticipated the events about to unfold. His forty-day sojourn in the desert had led him directly to the anguished night in the garden of Gethsemane and the following horrendous day at the hands of the Romans.

On two occasions when first describing Jesus as he approached him, John uses animal metaphors, first by calling him "the Lamb of God," (1:29 and 1:36) and then "a dove," (1:33) animals that are to be juxtaposed with his conception of the spirit and the holy ghost. The two animals—each of them replaced with the spirit (*pneuma*) and the holy ghost (*pneumati hagio*)—were routinely slaughtered at the temple and served a ritual that will soon come to an end. The *bodies* of sacrificial animals are now transformed into radically new ideas expressing a human possibility previously neglected, if not completely unrecognized. The transformation of physical animals is, moreover, echoed in the testimony of John the Baptist (as he speaks to the Jerusalem leadership) when he tells them "for the law (*nomos*) was given by Moses, but grace (*charis*) and truth (*aletheia*) came by Jesus Christ" (John 1:17). However, the gospel writer understands the statement to be much more comprehensive than merely revealing the juxtaposition between the law (the Judaic law) and grace. By calling upon *charis* as an aspect of divine favor usually associated with the human/divine reciprocity involved in animal sacrifice, John writes essentially to a Hellenistic audience, and then by adding *aletheia* and the language of philosophical truth he has simultaneously related Jesus back to a prophetic and philosophical tradition—individual, a minority, and unheeded—that has consistently attempted to change the very ideas and practices of piety and worship. John presents Jesus as inheriting two countercultural traditions of thought—Judaic and Hellenistic, prophetic and philosophical.

During the incident at the temple, the reference to the dove will be exemplary. Especially important was the dove given that it was the most affordable animal to be bought for sacrifices along with pigeons and, as we learned in Luke, the dove was also offered after the birth of a child (Luke 2:24). The relationship of John's animal metaphors can be related to Luke insofar as Jesus will replace the slaughtered lamb and dove and attend not to the birth of a single child, but to the entire regeneration of everyone. Previously, one lamb was slaughtered for one child; in the future to come, no lamb will be slaughtered for anyone, sacrifice replaced with a symbolic internalization as exemplified with the Eucharist. John's Gospel therefore emphasizes from the beginning how Jesus' symbolic body and blood will first nullify the ritual of animal sacrifice at the Jerusalem temple and prepare for a transformation of belief—about God (what has previously been assumed about God's demands) and what is expected from one whose faith is exemplary. Unlike the other gospels that culminate in the language of Jesus himself as sacrifice, in John he begins with the unmistakable association.

For John, the significance of Jesus, above all, is his impending sacrifice as a substitution (that is, a *once and final replacement*) of the sacrificial system as perpetuated in the temple of Jerusalem.

"And the Jews' Passover was at hand, and Jesus went up to Jerusalem" (2:13). Jesus chose his time well for many reasons. First, there was its association with the foundation of one of the three festivals celebrated yearly, Passover, and the death of animals whose death and blood ensured Jewish families would be spared the imminent death of first-born children; and second, guaranteeing his acts, committed during the festival with, arguably, the most people attending from the whole of the region (to say nothing of the diaspora), would quickly become well known and later attested. "And found in the temple those that sold oxen and sheep and doves, and the changers of money sitting" (2:14). The animals are named, in order, in terms of their value. The dove, the most affordable animal, has earlier (1:32) been used as an analogy for the *pneuma*, thereby putting first what has been considered last; he completely overturns previous values, economic and otherwise, and by doing so also repudiates the idea of economic value being in any way significant for the demonstration of piety. John then adds a detail and an accompanying action and emotion that were nowhere present in the other three accounts. Jesus does not act in haste. He first of all "made a scourge of small cords" (2:15) and then uses it to chase both the merchants and the animals out of the temple. His actions are demonstrative, unrestrained; he whips people so forcefully, in anger, in outrage, that they are forced to flee. "He drove them all out of the temple, and the sheep, and the oxen" (2:15). The detail cannot be overlooked. Both human beings and animals are driven from the temple; Jesus' relationship to the sacrificial animals has not been sufficiently considered, in part because (if Matthew 12:7 is ignored) commentators do not consider his actions as directly related to *saving* animals that are "guiltless." "And poured out the changers' money, and overthrew the tables" (2:15). He scatters money on the floor as a protest of the economy of exchange for the purchase of sacrificial animals. The overthrowing of the tables, however, is not simply a physical act; it has the sense (as in Mark and Matthew) of making the buying and selling of animals for sacrificial slaughter at the temple *null and void*. Here John makes the same announcement as in the Synoptics; the descriptions have been interrelated and sustained.

Finally, specifically addressing those that *sold doves*, now a metaphor of the spirit, he tells them to "take these things hence; make not my Father's house an house of merchandise (*emporiou*)" (2:16). Unlike the other three descriptions and the quote attributed to him concerning the "den of thieves," echoing Isaiah and Jeremiah, here John provides a unique saying. The "house of merchandise" or emporium is the exact word used by

Socrates in the *Euthyphro* when considering the purpose of sacrificing animals as a form of exchange between humans and the divine. When Jesus is asked by bystanders to explain his actions, he tells them that he will "destroy the temple" and he will then build it again ("raise it up") in three days, a reference that John translates. "But he spake of the temple of his body," (2:21) John interjects, thereby offering what he believes to be the proper interpretation of Jesus' saying. Not only does he prophetically announce his resurrection, meaning that physical death cannot prevent the continuity of his meaning, he simultaneously informs those listening that the temple, as it now stands, will be destroyed; but with its physical destruction (that is, the destruction of the physical place central to Judaism that, at the time of writing, would already have been fact) there will also be a comparable resurrection—its rabbinic transformation, a return to the reading of Scripture, and embodying its teachings rather than relying on a cultic act. Therefore, John's Gospel presents Jesus' action at the temple as the beginning of another kind of ministry—which he then narrates from chapters 3 to 21. Since the arrival in Jerusalem, his actions at the temple as the episode that leads to his arrest and crucifixion, John now presents Jesus' ministry as one dedicated to the care of others, beginning first with his concern for the bride and groom and the wedding guests who need wine to celebrate, an opening parable of serving others as individuals and in their relationship of love. In John's Gospel, as in the others, Jesus is presented as someone who performs miracles but who does so as a consequence of his desire to serve others while also urging people to "love one another," (John 13:34) the very love that has inspired his ministry from the beginning and turned his love into a soteriology. John narrates the events at the temple early in his gospel so as to accomplish two goals: one, to emphasize that Jesus' acts were the culmination of his teachings as it related to sacrifice, and two, to then turn to the whole of his ministry so as to show how Jesus was fundamentally motivated to be a healer, someone who (whatever the characteristics of individuals) loved and took care of others with no regard to their status either within Judaism or society as such. We may end, and provide a transition to Jesus' creation of the Eucharist, with two points. Referring once again to E. P. Sanders, he believes that Jesus' acts in the temple were not directed at some specific practice; but he cannot bring himself, it seems, to the conclusion he both draws and ignores. He adds, "He made a symbolic gesture by overturning tables in the temple area. This is *the crucial act which led to his execution*."[45] But could the act, admittedly controversial, of simply overturning tables—which, by the way, an angry merchant or disaffected client might have easily done—lead

---

45. Sanders, *Jesus and Judaism*, 334.

to his execution, as Sanders believes? Was there not an additional reason for Jesus being apprehended by the Jewish authorities and then handed over, with some perfectly legitimate reason in the eyes of the Romans, for trial and execution? The answer must lie in what Jesus *taught* immediately after his temple act, one the gospel writers do not need to include in their accounts precisely because it would have been known by *everyone*; and it is nothing less than the reason for overturning the tables of the money-changers as the denunciation of the ritual of sacrifice, one that can now be related to what has been described as the *cleansing of the temple*. Now that each of the gospel writers has provided us with suggestive indications on the interpretation of Jesus' temple acts, it is necessary to turn, first of all, to the creation of the Eucharist as the single most important substitution of animal sacrifice as a ritual—indeed, as the repudiation of all death in religious worship; for in the events of the Last Supper and the creation of the Eucharist, Jesus annuls the *therapeia* previously inherent in animal sacrifice and substitutes the ritual with a new testament founded on the care of others—what John defines as love.

4. *The Eucharist*

Several experiences of the Last Supper as reported by the gospel writers indicate how Jesus (acting and speaking in relation to the tradition of Passover) begins to reveal unprecedented and, for at least some of his disciples, inconceivable ideas and practices; they have been precisely conceived and well thought out in terms of putting them into practice at the appropriate time. Those preparing to share a meal with him would have been bewildered by his acts, first and foremost, as John tells us, by ending the supper "before the feast of the Passover" (John 13:1). In other words, the supper was not a commemoration of Passover; their meal, in fact, was eaten on a Wednesday evening—a day before Thursday, the 14th day (Nisan) in the Hebrew month. Their last supper together, then, cannot be equated with Passover at all. Jesus has planned his last supper so that he will *not eat* the Passover meal.

Again in an act that the disciples could not all understand, and that Peter in particular resists as unthinkable, Jesus "began to wash the disciples' feet," (John 13:5) in effect replacing the customary law of washing his hands prior to eating with the washing the feet of others. The observance of a law has been effectively replaced by not so much an act of profound humility as the demonstration of one's selfless dedication to others; all concerns with ritual cleanliness have become irrelevant. In John, there is no mention of the

Eucharist, no explicit announcement of the flesh and blood, bread and wine, involved in the meal. There is, however, a direct consequence of the meaning of the Eucharist, that is, Jesus' announcement of a "new commandment," the commandment "that ye love one another; as I have loved you, that ye also love one to another," (John 13:34) with the significant addition that their love will become public, a way of life. "By this shall all men know that ye are my disciples, if ye have love one to another," (John 13:35) Jesus adds, indicating their love will be an *emulation* of Jesus. "As I have loved you" now becomes the responsibility of those listening to his words and a principle not simply to be taught, but to be shown.

The love they will show each other and to others, however, cannot be the same as the love Jesus himself displays; its purpose and end are different. Although it may seem as if Jesus is doing nothing less than equating the greatest love with his *sacrifice* (that is, his death, theologically, is being interpreted as sacrificial), the precise use of *psyche* in one memorable declaration may give us pause for a reconsideration of the message that the greatest love is the giving of one's mind and heart and soul to those now considered brothers and sisters, the *adelphoi* soon to congregate after his death to form a new community and inaugurate the idea of a new history. When Jesus calls himself the son of humanity and defines his ministry, his service to others, "to give his life (*dounai ten psuchen*) a ransom (*lutron*) for many," (Mark 10:45, Matt 20:28) one can at this point raise doubts about a sacrificial interpretation of such an announcement. For in giving himself—more precisely, giving his psyche as a gift—he intends it to be a kind of exchange. If the ransom is given, Jesus expects there will be a *return*; one, however, that replaces the sacrificial system of the dead animal offering with the benevolent gift from God. By giving himself as a ransom, Jesus has dedicated himself to people's freedom from the bondage of a prior and now no longer sustainable belief, from their prior *conviction*. The return, however, cannot be a simple restitution, a return to a previous state of affairs; it must involve reclaiming a previously forsaken possibility, something *missed*, something missing, the meaning latent in *hamartia*.

While the history of theology, at least since the letter to the Hebrews, has reaffirmed the death of Jesus as sacrificial, René Girard's compelling argument can now be given due consideration: "It is important to insist that Christ's death was not a sacrificial one. . . Jesus dies, not as a sacrifice. . . but in order that there may be no more sacrifices."[46] While Girard separates the

---

46. The extended argument may be found in René Girard's *Things Hidden Since the Foundation of the World*. See especially the entirety of Book II, the Judaeo-Christian Scriptures and, more particularly, chapter 2, "A Non-Sacrificial Reading of the Gospel Text," 181–223. Girard is quite right to point out that the theological tradition on the

death of Jesus from being a sacrifice—in effect, denying the crucifixion as sacrificial—one additional and final argument must be made. Not only does Jesus repudiate and nullify the sacrificial system, he does so, precisely, in the context of a last supper eaten prior to (and as a substitute for) the Passover meal. There have been many decisive moments during his life and ministry. The Last Supper, which has no indication whatsoever of meat being eaten (there has been, of course, no symbolic slaughter of a sheep to commemorate the event of the Jewish people leaving Egypt), is now radically transformed by Jesus since he invents a substitution—one, furthermore, which is unthinkable in the context of Judaism.

When Jesus takes a loaf of bread, breaks off pieces, and gives one each to his disciples, he tells them "Take, eat; this is my body" (Matt 26:26, Mark 14:22). By doing so, he has now (and forever) replaced the slaughtered body of a sacrificed animal with the body his disciples, and everyone after them, will *internalize* so as to make the attempt, in principle always renewed as a commitment, to emulate him. Jesus does not consider the Eucharist a meal; rather, eating bread and drinking wine become the internalization of his essence so that it transforms those who receive it and become, with the unparalleled effort involved, like him. Everyone sharing in the Eucharist is given a part of him, perpetually, so as to allow them—with sufficient purpose—to become more than themselves. And when he took the cup of wine and told his disciples "drink ye all of it," (Matt 26:27) he is about to introduce nothing less than a shocking idea into religious worship, and one all his disciples would have found without precedent and, at first, difficult to understand. For when he says "this is my blood of the new testament," (Matt 26:28, Mark 14:24) he has now turned a previous prohibition—under no condition should one drink the blood of a sacrificed animal, as stated in Leviticus 17—into a necessary act and one representing one of the two new symbols of his new testament: his body and his blood. The Eucharist becomes the supreme *ontological* sacrament. Matthew preserves the additional statement that the blood to be drunk is done so "for the remission of sins (*aphesin hamartion*)," (Matt 26:28) that is, not so much the forgiveness of that which has been missed, but rather a release, becoming free, now again given the possibility to fulfill one's dynamic ability as a human being that, until now, has been relinquished.

Finally, in the Gospel of Luke and to complement John, we have Jesus making the announcement that "With desire I have desired to eat this

---

question of Jesus' sacrifice has been so formidable that to think counter to it is by no means easy. In the short discussion to follow, the Eucharist (rather than his sacrificial death) will be emphasized along with the substitution of the slaughter of an animal and its consumption as a commemorative event.

passover with you," (Luke 22:15) followed immediately by, "For I say unto you, I will not any more eat thereof" (Luke 22:16). Jesus does not in fact eat the paschal meal or drink the wine accompanying it. He replaces himself as the meal to be eaten and the wine to be drunk. The events of the last supper do nothing less than bring all sacrifices to an end; and it is Luke who alone reveals two additional meanings of the Eucharist and makes them explicit. The Eucharist will be a memorial. "This is my body which is given (*didomenon*) for you: do this in remembrance (*anamnesin*) of me" (Luke 22:19). Among the four gospel writers, Luke is unique in also recounting the event and Jesus' words. Jesus' death may have become recognized as sacrificial, but in this one moment, he gives himself as a "gift" (a *didomi*) so as to replace the animal as a sacrificial offering, and he will do so in ritual to be infinitely repeated so as to remember, recollect, and "bring back" (into the present, always) the meaning of his life. By becoming a gift and an offering, he has replaced the tradition of a slaughtered animal given to God; he has himself become the infinite gift to be repeatedly and always given, but not as a sacrifice (not in death) but in the giving of his *psyche*. By recalling Jesus in memory, however, he has at the same time substituted himself for the remembrance of the freedom from Egypt. By doing so, Jesus introduces a caesura into history, a before and after indicated by the Eucharist and the inauguration now of a new human being and a new creation. With the creation of the Eucharist and its repetition to be observed forever, Jesus knows he will, in fact, die but nevertheless remain an absolute presence (a *parousia*) in the world. Although the night of the creation of the Eucharist requires him to undergo the experience of another day in the world prior to his death, his acts in the temple and his astonishing doctrine heard by everyone will now be recalled. His disciples at the Last Supper will soon have sufficient time to reflect, precisely, on the substance of his teaching and on the abolition of animal sacrifice for a new kind of piety, the soteriology dedicated to the well-being of others as expressed in love and healing.

Postscript: A Dialogue with Paula Fredriksen on the Cleansing of the Temple

A previous argument, with particular examples—the nonsacrificial service in the temple in Luke, on the guiltless animals in Matthew and the requirement of mercy, the salt used to savor the sacrificial meat in Mark, and the expression of love in John—has presented Jesus' acts in the temple of Jerusalem as the repudiation of animal sacrifice and as a call for its abolition, in effect demanding the closure (the "destruction") of the temple and its operations. Overthrowing the tables of the moneychangers, physically ejecting the merchants, and forcing the animals to flee (releasing them), were all intended to be a part of a well-thought-out plan that was much more comprehensive than merely an economic critique, as if Jesus simply objected to the buying and selling of animals. The fundamental problem is not the temple (a term used by both Socrates and John) as an *emporium*. Nor was it a confrontation with "*ceux qui pratiquaient le culte sacrificial sans reel sincerité.*"[47] Irving Zeitlin's argument is also too narrowly focused on the political consequences of his acts when he writes, "Jesus shared the outrage of the Zealots toward the sacrifices offered daily for the well-being of the emperor."[48] Jesus objects to the temple—a supposed place of worship, with acts intended for God—as an immense *slaughterhouse*, a place of perpetual ritual killing, with the consequences of such a place no one, it seems, has been willing to consider; understandably, the one truth of the temple has been too overwhelming to consider, the precise details ignored.

Very few have interpreted Jesus' acts in the temple as anti-sacrificial. His intentions have been mentioned here and there with passing allusions, hesitation, and restraint, but no one has presented the explicit analysis it demands. But Jesus' perception of the holy site, and the meaning of his acts, can no longer be doubted and must now be put forward for consideration. Denial can no longer be accepted, rationalizations less so. Jesus' acts were intended to separate the temple as a house of prayer from its function as a slaughterhouse, what the three Synoptics report as being a "den of thieves," a *theft* that is neither ambiguous nor unclear. Thieves cannot give the gifts they have stolen. One cannot, in fact or in spirit, *own* an animal. The transfer or possession of the animal to its sacrificial death can only be accomplished by the perpetrator with an elaborate set of ideas inherited from the past and used as both justification and exculpation. Girard is unequivocal. The idea of a surrogate victim "provides the only feasible explanation of how a sacrificial murder . . . can literally be transformed into an act of piety."[49] Finally, the temple *cleansing*—a term some deem inappropriate and which has resulted in innumerable challenges as to its definition—could not, in fact, be more revealing; it has been obvious and, because of it, completely unnoticed. The cleansing of the temple has seemingly remained outside our imaginative consciousness and experience. John Crossan writes that the temple cleansing is "an unfortunate term for what was actually a symbolic

---

47. Boyer, *Jésus contre le temple?*, 106.
48. Zeitlin, *Jesus and the Judaism*, 136.
49. Girard, *Violence and the Sacred*, 197.

destruction of the temple."[50] Kenneth Matthews, using the same language, writes that it is "unfortunate since it suggests actual purification rites."[51] Alfred Edersheim refers to the act as a "purgation of the temple."[52] It has variously been called an intervention,[53] as well as a cursing.[54] The definitions are as numerous as the explanations. Hans-Dieter Betz writes that "the modern title 'The Cleansing of the Temple' is ambiguous."[55] No ambiguity exists at all; on the contrary, cleaning the temple could not be more exact. Despite J. D. G. Dunn's claim that "some sort of 'purifying' (cleansing!) was bound to be at least part of Jesus' motivation,"[56] the equation of purifying with cleansing cannot be made; they are completely different from each other. Jesus has no interest in purifying the temple. His *cleansing* should be much more exact than previously considered. It is not "misnamed."[57] Indeed, what should be equated (absolutely related) is the meaning of the cleansing of the temple and its related destruction.

Rather than call upon a number of scholars on the issue of the temple cleansing—and the commentaries are innumerable, much debated, and with no consensus since they range from a complete denial of its historicity to it being "an unexpected, even implausible incident"[58]—a dialogue will be initiated with Paula Fredriksen due, in part, to several unavoidable passages in *Jesus of Nazareth, King of the Jews* where she more than adequately defines the meaning of the temple cleansing without, however, acknowledging or pursuing the implications of her own conclusions. In the sections called "The Cleansing of the Temple" to "The Temple, Again"[59] she begins her extended argument with a recapitulation of the scene in the gospels of Mark and John, and then, as is customary, puts the "Cleansing of the Temple" in quotations marks and attributes the scene to church tradition. The incident then has been invented by the church. The blame here is much too convenient. Her first and most exemplary question, intended rhetorically here but, stunningly, *answered later*, is simply: "Cleansed of what (207)"?

---

50. Crossan, *Jesus*, 147.
51. Matthews, "John, Jesus and the Essenes," 1.
52. Edersheim, *Life and Times of Jesus*, 557.
53. Domeris, "The 'Enigma' of Jesus' Temple Intervention."
54. Watty, "Jesus and the Temple."
55. Betz, "Jesus and the Purity," 459.
56. Dunn, "Jesus and Purity," 466.
57. Freyne, *Jesus and the Gospels*, 225.
58. Clarke, *Gospel of Matthew*, 176.
59. These sections are found in 207–34 of Fredriksen, *Jesus of Nazareth*. All further references to this will be given in page numbers in the text.

Jesus' Anti-sacrificial Acts in the Temple of Jerusalem 249

Others have followed with questions like, "But from what must it then be cleansed?"[60] The answer, forthcoming, fully reveals what Jesus thought most objectionable about the temple and its sacrifices of animals. The temple must be imagined (viscerally, with all our senses) so as to fully grasp its day-to-day reality and one to the extreme during a time such as Passover when an estimated number of visitors to Jerusalem approached as many as two million people, which means, to provide a conservative number, the slaughter of a half million sheep as well as other, less costly animals for those unable to afford the recommended Passover sheep per family.

The first interpretation of the cleansing can now be analyzed. Jesus' primary objection to temple sacrifices is not, simply, reductively, the references to the temple as a place of commerce, of buying and selling of animals—though, certainly, members of the temple leadership were also landowners and therefore produced the very animals that would be sold and butchered at the temple. The privileges of the priestly aristocracy can here be set aside. Two points require emphasis: one, the aspect of theft, and two, the meaning of an *emporium* that, if simply understood as a marketplace and reduced to an economics *between people*, fails to recognize Jesus' much more radical message. John's account, let us remember, should not be separated from the other Synoptics and the significant, if subtle, perhaps under-perceived references—for example, to the guiltless animals in Matthew. The theft involves a *crime*; and worse, a *profit* from the crime. The crime involves killing, the profit is its supposed compensation. The sacrificial system is a criminal enterprise. Equally important, Robert Eisler's translation of "den of robbers" from Isaiah 56:7 into the Aramaic (*me' ārath pārīsīm*) should be rendered "den of slaughterers" and suggests that "*pārīsīm* could be used for butcher's work."[61] Even if John was unaware of any traditions related to Mark, Matthew, or Luke (or Q, or for that matter, anyone else) his account and the one uniquely calling the temple a "house of merchandise" (John 2:16) cannot be separated in meaning from the other gospels; for in relating the theft to a crime, and more precisely to a killing, we are now in a position to understand the entire relation of the sacrificial system: human beings kill as an offering to God and so as to receive some necessary compensation—peace, for example. The emporium does not refer simply to the buying and selling of animals. There is an additional and more important point: the emporium has been established so that *livestock* are investments, dead animals offered for a return. Religious worship and piety in Judaism and *everywhere else*, in all other sacrificial cultures (rationalized to be a gift or

---

60. Wedderburn, "Jesus' Actions in the Temple," 1.
61. As discussed in Burkitt's "Cleansing of the Temple," 387.

an offering, giving to God so God can provide some return), has turned into an economic theology, human beings effectively buying peace, forgiveness, or atonement through the slaughter of an animal. Jesus has no intention to restore some ancient purity to Judaism since, as Fredriksen points out, such purity has never existed; the temple has always been a place of sacrifice. "If by this gesture he [Jesus] were repudiating the sacrifices themselves, he would be utterly unique among both Jews and Gentiles of his own period" (209). But of course he is utterly unique. He was an *unprecedented* human being who can in no way be compared to any of his contemporaries, either within Judaism or in any other sacrificial society. That Fredriksen mentions both Jews and Gentiles is, despite her claims, precisely *how* he is unique. Jesus is not repudiating animal sacrifice as a merely Jewish observance; his intentions have been much more absolute. Unless we are willing to consider Jesus as unique (can this be in doubt historically or theologically?) and as an individual who was most certainly not like anyone else, that he was not simply a reflection of his time and place but was unprecedented, then the Jesus present to the writer here simply has no relevance at all. And when Fredriksen then comes to the conclusion that Jesus' acts were intended to be eschatological, we have passed (seemingly without noticing) from a historical inquiry to a metaphysical conclusion of world-altering proportions. The alternative is certainly telling: Fredriksen and many others to prefer Jesus as an eschatological prophet who arrives in the world to announce an imminent end of days, with outrageous fantasies of cataclysms for the natural world and in the lives of human beings, instead of Jesus the religious visionary who absolutely repudiated the historically most common form of religious worship. The people of Jerusalem enduring Roman occupation—and perhaps even some of Jesus' own disciples—may have desired a metaphysical event that could change the world of their time. Jesus had no such plans or ambitions.

Two more crucial comments will be made now to lead to lead us to a conclusion concerning Jesus' acts in the temple and the meaning of the cleansing. Once again, allow me to quote Fredriksen and her very noticeable question, "Cleansed of what?," first raised at the very beginning of the section called "The Cleansing of the Temple." Here is the answer she gives without, it seems, being aware of it:

> The Thursday day of Jesus' arrest, 14 Nisan, they [the temple priests] would have overseen the slaughter of *tens of thousands* of lambs and goats in a few hours before sunset, the beginning of the night of the meal. They then would have ensured that the Temple—all courts which had been used as a theater for

sacrifice—*had been washed down and cleaned* for the next day's worship. (223, my italics)

The number of animals killed was almost unimaginable; and the testimonies of the temple as a slaughterhouse are numerous and consistent. 1 Kings 8:5 tells us that they were sacrificing "sheep and oxen, that cannot be told nor numbered for the multitude." Josephus writes that "the number of their (sacrifices) it would be impossible to give, for it would exceed our power to give a true estimate."[62]

To draw to a conclusion that is now more than evident in Fredriksen, the temple cleansing has moved from its assumed symbolism to an unavoidable reality. That the temple was a slaughterhouse and some segment of the priestly class were both butchers and cooks cannot be disputed. These are historical facts. One must also consider the high number of *janitors* that would have been necessary. Indeed, one noteworthy case points out that the Levite priests literally "occupied themselves with the cleansing of the Temple,"[63] even if John Kilgallen cannot quite bring himself to define, precisely, what he means by the cleansing. The reality has never been in doubt. But what has been avoided until now (ignored and disavowed because it is, frankly, too disturbing for virtually everyone who has commented on the event) is the state of the temple throughout the day and the conditions that needed constant attention from a segment of priests (young, in training, specially designated) whose sole job must have been to continuously clean up the unbelievable amount of discharge, of all kinds, from the animals. One description in the temple is provided by a letter written in the second century BCE. "The number of ministers in attendance is more than seven hundred, in addition to a large number of assistants bringing forward animals for sacrifice."[64] The assistants who were taking the animals to be killed were also janitors and cleaners. Fredriksen recognizes the problem and believes a solution is possible; the temple was also organized, spatially, for such an occurrence:

> No large sacrificial animals like sheep and oxen would have been kept within the courtyard itself. *They would have fouled the precincts.* Rather, they would have been sold in the market area below the Temple. (232, my italics)

---

62. Josephus, *Ant.*, 15.422.
63. Kilgallen, *Guida alla Terra Santa Seguendo*, 176.
64. Letter to Aristeas, as quoted in Hanson and Oakman, *Palestine in the Time of Jesus*, 143.

And this is now the concluding point. Even conceding that the animals to be slaughtered were sold in one specific area separated from any holy site, once they were led from the market inside the temple precincts to the place of slaughter there would have been unavoidable consequences.

At the risk of being indelicate (but this is known to people who have animals living in their house—especially if the animals are ill, or very old and in need of constant care, and is known surely to people living on farms with animals) when we talk about "fouling," Fredriksen's word, such a description cannot be limited to feces and urine but must also include other natural processes—most especially as a consequence of the animals' understandable apprehension and fear, in part due to the smell of blood, smoke, sizzling meat, the considerable noise of the bellowing of other animals, the clattering as they were led to slaughter, as well as the cacophony of music and singing. Not only was there a sizable amount of feces and urine to be cleaned up continuously from the temple floor as can be expected, there would be other animal discharges such as occasional vomit, bile, saliva, not to mention the continuous flow of blood cleaned by priests and directed toward the sewers on the temple floor. The acrid stench may have been partly covered up by the burning of incense; but the temple floor would have been filled with all manner of animal discharge and continuously cleaned up by priests and forced into sewers that led the waste outside the temple precinct. Despite the Talmudic claim, in Pirkei Avot 5, that there was no smell in the temple at all (due to a perpetual miracle) the stench would have been almost overwhelming.[65] The claim is expanded:

> The temple was, among other things, a giant slaughterhouse in which livestock were butchered by the thousands every day. Yet the odour of the meant never caused a woman to miscarry. That meat was never putrid. No fly was ever seen in the slaughterhouse.[66]

When we take into consideration the massive scale of the slaughter on a festival such as Passover, it is almost incomprehensible to the modern imagination to realize how visceral the scene must have been. Archaeological evidence has revealed an extensive sewer system, with sizable conduits, that would have been necessary to collect as much as a million liters of blood alone, without taking into consideration the amount of water, readily available, needed to wash the stones of the temple floor.[67] As Dan Bahat notes, "A

---

65. Sichel, "Air Pollution."
66. Kirsch, *People and the Books*.
67. Bahat, *Carta's Historical Atlas of Jerusalem*.

Jesus' Anti-sacrificial Acts in the Temple of Jerusalem 253

sewer at the south-west corner of the altar carried the blood and the rinsing water to the Kidron valley. Other installations around the altar and the ramp were meant to dampen the refuse from the sacrifices."[68] "Refuse" is, of course, a euphemism. The temple as a slaughterhouse, in evidence in Ezekiel 40:39–43, is specifically mentioned in terms of the tables where the animals were slaughtered, the instruments used, and the hooks to hang the animals before being skinned, disemboweled, and butchered prior to being roasted. In the Jerusalem Scroll from Qumran, there is a detailed description of the temple as a slaughterhouse; goats and rams were tethered to columns before being killed.[69] In the tractate *Middot*, the places where the animals were killed, flayed, and hung are also mentioned.[70]

It can no longer be avoided that Jesus' temple cleansing was a repudiation of the sacrificial system, and soon to be its abolition in Christianity, because the holiest places in religious worship (the temple in Jerusalem, but also temples used in the polytheistic worship in Rome, Greece, and elsewhere) had become—indeed, had always been—places of violence and death. Animals, alive or dead, simply had no place in any temple. A place intended to be sacred and holy had become filthy. Jesus is an unprecedented individual because, despite the centuries-old tradition extending to the Jewish prophets and the Greek philosophers, he did not simply oppose animal sacrifice as a form of religious worship, he created another form of piety as an alternative. He decided to physically intervene and, for the first time in history (as far as we know—and there are no accounts anywhere remotely like him) make both the act and the teaching preliminary to the end of sacrifice. This is the reason he was apprehended by the Jewish leadership and crucified by the Romans. He was not executed for claiming to be the king of the Jews—which, in any case, he never claimed to be and attempted numerous times to tell his disciples he should not be associated with any such title—but by acting against the sacrificial system as such, he was charged with directly intervening and disrupting its day-to-day observances and, with it, the entire politicoreligious edifice of both Judaism and Rome. Jesus defined the traditions of the past and the central place of the temple both in Judaism and in the observances dedicated in part to Caesar.

Jesus' acts in the temple of Jerusalem (planned well in advance to coincide with Passover—that is, the festival commemorating the reinstitution of animal sacrifice after the Israelites' release from Egypt) are unique in world history since he is not only an individual who repudiates animal sacrifice

---

68. Bahat, "Herodian Temple," 55.
69. Lundquist, *Temple of Jerusalem*.
70. Chyutin, *New Jerusalem Scroll from Qumran*.

as a form of religious worship as was common with Jewish prophets, Greek philosophers, and Roman poets, but he *acted* physically against the temple so as to destroy it as a place that equated animal slaughter with divine worship. By doing so, he is the first individual whose teaching and exemplary acts led some of his followers (the Christians independent from the Jerusalem church led by James, his brother) to repudiate animal sacrifice as a religious ritual and to replace it with the new commandment he announced during the Last Supper and the creation of the Eucharist—to internalize and emulate him and doing so as the highest expression of faith, loving and taking care of others so as to be responsible to their life and well-being.

Conclusion
Christians, Jews, Polytheists, and the End of Animal Sacrifice

THREE DECISIVE EVENTS ARE crucial in tracing the long, drawn-out history of the end of animal sacrifice and, more generally, what has been defined by some as the end of "paganism:" the credo of early Christianity as determined by Paul's gospel in the late 40s AD and its consideration of the ritual slaughter of an animal as an "abhorrent rite"[1], the destruction of the temple in Jerusalem by the Romans at the end of the Jewish War in AD 70; and Constantine's conversion in AD 312 and subsequent edicts by emperors outlawing polytheistic practices and closing down shrines and temples (though as historians realize, laws imposed on the population by authorities were not always effective, a fact repeatedly shown by those early Christians who had to suffer persecution for their belief and endure the harrowing experiences of the martyrs in prisons and as spectacles in Roman amphitheatres). Alan Cameron concludes that the polytheistic aristocracy remained a "powerful force" well into the fifth century; beliefs, if associated with certain social privileges, were not easily relinquished,[2] as were practices that provided common people with understandable consolation such as the drinking at the graves of ancestors that Augustine observed as the bishop of Hippo.

Prior to his death in Rome, Paul's remarkable individuality and insistence on his gospel being revealed to him rather than merely adopted from a human tradition in history, becomes evident first in Acts in several pronouncements in his letters (none, perhaps, more meaningful than a noteworthy passage in Romans) and finally in the letter to the Hebrews, an all-important document of Pauline Christianity insofar as it announces the

1. Brown, *Authority and the Sacred*, 21.
2. Cameron, *Last Pagans of Rome*.

end of sacrifice and its substitution by Jesus who has now been proclaimed a high priest and who represents the end of sacrifice through the symbol of the Eucharist. The letter also seems to indicate knowledge of the impending Jewish rebellion against the Roman occupation and advises the recipients, with some trepidation, against a military confrontation the writer(s) of the letter expect to end in catastrophic failure. The powers of the world will continue to be perpetuated and to flourish precisely through confrontation and violence. The apprehension proved to be right. After a four-year struggle, the Roman forces overwhelmed the city of Jerusalem and by the early 70s AD, the city lay in ruins, the population killed or enslaved, and the temple completely destroyed. The hilltop fortress of Masada, the last bastion of resistance, would soon also fall, the people choosing collective suicide of defiance rather than capitulation in any form to the Romans who, with their knowledge of engineering, made their advance on the lofty citadel and the breach of its fortifications inevitable.

In the less than two decades following the death of Jesus and the emergence of the first Christian churches other than the one in Jerusalem and, most especially, the effect on numerous cities throughout the Mediterranean by the teaching of Paul and his co-workers, the religious tradition and officially sanctioned practice of animal sacrifice was decisively repudiated and abolished—even if, for converts from polytheism, the new credo and its practices took time for readjustment. After all, the celebrations of periodic festivals alleviated the often harsh difficulties of daily life, the reason some polytheistic practices such as the commemorative banqueting at burials was adopted by Christianity.[3] Paul's mission to the *ethne*, independent from the church in Jerusalem led by James, the brother of Jesus, no longer observed the ritual of animal sacrifice and therefore (from its beginnings) distinguished itself from what can be called Jerusalem Christianity and its continuing affiliation to the temple and to other observances consistent with Judaic law. Paul's early Christianity understood itself as a singular gospel, different from the practices of Judaism and polytheism (which had animal sacrifice in common) and one initiating a new religious sensibility.

For Paul, the gospel was nothing if not a new testament, as Jesus had proclaimed during the last supper and with the meaning of the Eucharist; the symbolic internalization of the body and blood of Jesus (unthinkable for a pious Jew respecting the precept of Leviticus 17) had definitively replaced the ritual slaughter of animal sacrifice. Insisting on his independence from the Jerusalem church and developing the radical innovation of his teaching as it related to his unique understanding of the message of Jesus, Paul

3. Leone, *End of the Pagan City*.

determined animal sacrifice to be irrelevant as a religious ritual—a belief that made him and the early Christian churches controversial and separated them from the rest of their society, both Jewish and all other *ethne*. Such a unique teaching was not easily ignored; traditionalists and conservatives regarded it with a mixture of incredulity and animosity, though a few in a cultural minority were reminded of various sects in the Greek-speaking world with a history extending over five centuries and, more recently, Roman poets whose pastoralism turned to a less bloody past for animals, for human beings. In the book of Acts, we have an all-important episode that not only makes Paul's rejection of animal sacrifice unequivocal, the event that precedes it foregrounds its substitution and replacement, a ministry to others (a taking care of others) in terms of their health and healing. As a former Pharisee, Paul had intimate knowledge of the prophetic substitution of sacrifice with the language of love, one of course with judicial consequences and the executions of prophets such as Isaiah. He too would suffer and be executed for the message he proclaimed.

In one episode in Lystra, Timothy's hometown, Paul encounters a man who had been unable to walk since birth, a condition perhaps more socially than physically distressing. Someone considered a cripple had a marginal place in his society; at best he could expect pity, at worst, contempt:

> The same heard Paul speak: who steadfastly beholding and perceiving that he had faith to be healed, Said with a loud voice, Stand upright on thy feet. And he leaped and walked. (Acts 14:9–10)

The act of healing itself is not as significant as the events about to unfold, and certainly does not emphasize any miraculous capacity on the part of Paul except for his emphasis on the words he speaks and the recognition of the man's belief that he could be healed. The people of the region, Lycaonia, are obviously impressed by Paul's ability to heal, doing it by a simple declaration as reported in Acts that, no different than in Jesus' ministry, does not account for the extent of the conversation and his ability to alter his listener's perception of himself and his immediate society. They believe Paul (and Barnabas, who has accompanied him on his missionary journey) to be gods and "are come down to us in the likeness of men," (Acts 14:11) actually calling them Jupiter and Mercury, Paul being called Mercury because "he was the chief speaker" (Acts 14:12). Like the Roman god Mercury, who was known for being eloquent among other attributes, Paul is recognized for his ability to speak. As was so often the case in the ministry of Jesus, and what has not often been emphasized, Paul too is recognized by the people— Greek-speakers—that his voice and words carried meanings with them that were in some way unusual; in the context of his healing, the instantaneous event must be filled in by a much longer conversation that would have involved Paul's words to the paralytic as to his social condition, and not only his physical infirmity. The *pistis* cannot be reduced to a religious faith; it involves a belief and conviction and assurance in the meaning of his life overall despite his physical condition. A paralytic was worthy of consideration and respect, was a human being despite a world reducing itself and others to appearances and merely physical capacities. The physical body, especially when compromised, could no longer contain the meaning of the spirit. The gospel made one more than a physical presence.

The people of the town are so impressed with Paul that they want to thank him, to reciprocate, in the only way they know how: they want to offer the "gods" a sacrifice so as to thank them, no doubt a customary gesture. "Then the priest of Jupiter, which was before their city, brought oxen and garlands unto the gates, and would have done sacrifice with the people" (Acts 14:13). The understandable reaction of these devout polytheists, and of their priest, is to prepare oxen (the most expensive of sacrificial animals) to be slaughtered in their honor. Paul and Barnabas, however, turn to the people and tell them, first of all, that they are not gods at all and that they are "men of passions with you (*homoiopatheis*)," (Acts 14:15) have the same feelings and emotions. And yet, despite their similarity, they also distinguish themselves from these people and their traditions by asking them to "turn from these vanities unto the living God," (Acts 14:15) a significant juxtaposition insofar as it differentiates the *death* of a sacrificial animal as an act of piety from the "living" God—one, moreover, who cannot be "worshipped (*therapeuetai*) with men's hands, as though he needed any thing," (Acts 17:25) a declaration Paul soon makes, of all places, in Athens to the philosophers. The observation first made by Socrates in his conversation with his friend Euthyphro before his trial on the charge of impiety is now reaffirmed by Paul to the very people who would have immediately understood his argument. A central tenet of Epicureanism was the indifference of the gods to the human world and their independence from lack, want, need; the gods could not be served or complemented in any way by a human act. Paul's declaration has the consequences of rejecting what the purpose of sacrifice had always been, one of *charis* and reciprocity, the offering of a dead animal for some compensatory return. Paul's God does not need a thing, an object; the worship it demands can only be fulfilled by turning to others and attending to *their* needs.

The piety they now teach introduces a new conception of the divine and, therefore, makes unnecessary the most important ritual of their devotion and worship. The turning away from the one fundamental ritual of serving the divine inaugurates nothing less than another history—even though its complete cessation would take a considerable period of time and not be without postponement and resistance by those most tied to tradition. "And with these sayings scarce restrained they the people, that they had not done sacrifice unto them" (Acts 14:18). They are not simply restrained; they are stopped from performing a sacrifice in this one particular instance and from then on. There are still many people who are suspicious of the new teaching, both Jews and Gentiles. Paul and Barnabas, however, are not simply introducing a new teaching. Ideas on their own are insufficient in part because both Jews and polytheists are *organized*, are led by institutions such as the temple leadership, and sustained by custom. Therefore, Paul and Barnabas "ordained them elders in every church," (Acts 14:23) that is, elected leaders who become responsible for a consistent teaching, one in no way related to the tradition of ancient *practices*. Christianity and polytheism were not involved in competing *discourses*, as if their respective views were reduced to the level or rhetoric or argument, as George Heyman[4] believes. Maria-Zoe Petropoulou's extensive study "is offered to prove that second-century evidence for Christian attitudes to animal sacrifice is not only confined to rhetoric, but also contains implications relating to concrete situations."[5] All-important were religious observances and the relation between an act and a certain way of being, as evidenced by John Scheid's study on the sacrificial acts of the Romans.[6] Nor were they merely involved in what Daniel Ullucci calls "on-going debates" between "cultural producers" about the meaning of animal sacrifice.[7] The *critique* of animal sacrifice was an attempt to bring an end to a ritual that equated divine worship with the slaughter of animals. The refusal to sacrifice was a testimony of a new belief,

---

4. Heyman, *Power of Sacrifice*. He concedes when he writes that "*religio* was the proper behavior that characterized the life of the Roman citizen. Roman religion was not concerned with distinguishing *true* from *false* beliefs," 12. Indeed, it had no concern at all with faith, but only in observing what was ordained by law. Religion had to be obeyed since it was political.

5. Petropoulou, *Animal Sacrifice in Ancient Greek*, 251.

6. Scheid, *Quand faire, c'est croire*.

7. Ullucci, *Christian Rejection of Animal Sacrifice*. Given my earlier debate (in the Introduction on the very first page of this study) let me finally add one more disagreement. Ullucci believes that the critique of animal sacrifice "serves only to reinscribe a modern (largely Christian) narrative upon the history of animal sacrifice," 5. My argument overall has attempted to show that the critique of animal sacrifice was consistent and longstanding in two different traditions long before Christianity. The critique of animal sacrifice is not a narrative, and if Ullucci insists that the critique is largely Christian, so be it. The end of animal sacrifice is, indeed, a great Christian revolution in the history of religion.

a new social identity, and a new way of life. A future history inaugurated in the present could no longer inherit an exhausted past.

Due to their unwillingness to sacrifice, and increasingly to avoid the society of polytheists during their festivals and processions, Christians will eventually come to the attention of the imperial authorities. By making it imperative that they "abstain from meats offered to idols," (Acts 15:29)—in effect now avoiding meat-eating if the animal had been ritualistically slaughtered—they were creating a fundamentally radical doctrine that would be regarded as both religiously impious and, for Romans, *anti-imperial*. At the very least, as Pliny writes in a letter to the emperor Trajan, the Christian doctrine of refusing to eat sacrificial meat[8] had several consequences. According to Pliny, with the imperial authorities forcing Christians to renounce their belief—and doing so by being compelled to offer sacrifices to the emperor, that is, someone considered quasi-divine,

> the temples, at least, which were once almost deserted, begin now to be frequented; and the sacred rites, after a long intermission, are again revived; while there is a general demand for the victims, which till lately found very few purchasers.[9]

The Roman authorities understood how the refusal to participate in a sacrificial cult and avoid eating meat slaughtered at a temple had political consequences, as it had at the time of the Orphics and Pythagoreans. Christian independence would have to be thwarted, their freedom (of worship) eliminated as anti-social, most especially because their God was a man who had been crucified for his seditious act against temple sacrifice and, therefore, against the ritual that bound together the gods, the state, and Caesar.

The incident in Acts, as a historical event showing how Paul's Christianity would abandon animal sacrifice, is developed into a well-defined doctrine by simultaneously using the language of the ritual and transforming it into a disposition—one reflecting Paul's distinction between the body and the spirit. "I beseech you therefore, brethren (*adelphoi*), by the mercies of God, that ye present your bodies a living sacrifice (*thusian zosan*), holy, acceptable unto God, which is your reasonable service (*logiken latreian*)" (Rom 12:1). Paul's remarkable request has several consequences, all of them indicative of an innovative thinking consistent with the teaching of Jesus. First of all, those reading the letter or listening to it being read understand

---

8. There were, at the same time, Christians who were wondering if all meat consumption should be stopped and if vegetarianism should be adopted as a Christian ideal, as is evident in the correspondence between Paul and Timothy. See my "The Christology of Shame and the Reevaluation of Hellenic Ideas in 1 and 2 Timothy."

9. Pliny, *Ep.*, 10.96.

themselves as bonded by new social relations, being brothers and sisters beyond all ties to a biological family, much less the groups so indicative of Roman classes and hierarchies. Second, the idea of *thusia* has been transformed from the death of an animal to a "living sacrifice," a perpetual one that is characterized by reason and intellect and logic (by a "logical service" and therefore not irrational) and, finally, again invokes the idea of a service—reminiscent of Socrates during his trial and his *latreia*—as a now-humble relationship to the divine in terms of oneself, not simply a ritualistic act. One does not serve up a sacrificed animal; one becomes a servant. The Christian self cannot be substituted. Paul continues:

> And be not conformed to this world (*aioni*): but be ye transformed (*metamorphousthe*) by the renewing of your mind, that you may prove what is good, and acceptable, and perfect, will of God. (Rom 12:2)

Abandoning animal sacrifice has further consequences. Paul urges everyone to be nonconformists, to reject the ideas of the times, thereby teaching that their developing doctrines can no longer reflect the state of the world. By doing so, they will begin to change, achieving a metamorphosis; their minds will be renewed. Paul rightly understood that a metamorphosis had to simultaneously involve a change of heart along with different *acts*; one had to be different, inside and out, and no mere observance could accomplish such a transformation.

Finally, with one more reference that could be extended in the cowritten letter to the Philippians, Paul and Timothy thank the church for gifts they have sent them. In describing the gift, they now appropriate traditional language of sacrifice from the Hebrew Bible and transform it to their own ends and purpose, connecting to an archaic past so as to establish a separation. The offering they have received is "an odour of a sweet smell, a sacrifice acceptable, wellpleasing to God" (Phil 4:18). The sacrifice is no longer a slaughtered animal and the fragrance, or taste, or its meat; it is an offering made to others, for their benefit and welfare. Paul's ministry to all *ethne*, as always essential to Jesus' message, radically disassociates the emergence of Christianity from the violence and killing inherent in both Judaic and polytheistic worship and instead affirms the most important commandment made by Jesus insofar as he inherits the love of one's neighbor as oneself from Leviticus in contradistinction to sacrifice. By the end of Paul's life and his execution in Rome, estimated to be circa 64 CE, two interrelated events will soon bring animal sacrifice in Judaism to an end.

The letter to the Hebrews may be rightly seen as a culmination of Christian teaching as it relates to the words of the prophets (recalling them so as to define the uniqueness of the present), especially as it pertains to the healing words of Jesus. Once again, as if recalling Isaiah, the letter to the Hebrews juxtaposes sacrifice with healing—replaces the ritual of animal sacrifice with the healing words of Jesus who now has also become a priest, and one, moreover, who has announced a new testament. The letter begins with God "who at sundry times and in divers manners spake in time past unto the fathers by the prophets," (Heb 1:1) and then, more recently, "spoken unto us by his Son." (1:2) The letter also makes the most direct statements on the irrelevance of animal sacrifice as a ritual; it has been definitively replaced. In the letter there is both continuity with the prophets as well as an unprecedented proclamation. Before turning repeatedly and incessantly to the abolition of animal sacrifice, the author of the letter, whoever he may be, presents a fundamental teaching of the gospel: *soteria*. Regarding himself as one of the "ministering spirits," the author knows that he has been "sent forth to minister for them who shall be heirs of salvation (*soterian*)" (1:14). Without necessarily relying on the sacrificial language adopted and then transferred to Jesus, recalling the tradition of the prophets and Jesus' recollection of their words, of their teachings as emanating from the words of God, the letter now makes it explicit that to be a minister involves one comprehensive responsibility: to bring *soteria* to others. Soteriology has replaced animal sacrifice as an expression of piety and service to God; and Jesus has himself become a priest so as to replace the priests of the temple—an institution now about to be physically destroyed in the aftermath of the Jewish war against the Romans.

Once again, the *soteria* so central to the development of Jesus' teaching is intimately related to none other than his speech. "How shall we escape, if we neglect so great a salvation (*soterias*); which at first began to be spoken (*laleisthai*) by the Lord, and was confirmed unto us by them that heard him" (2:3). Those who heard and listened to him were seized above all by Jesus' words; they understood themselves, others, and the world as never before. The letter also makes an important proclamation—or rather, an additional one after the previous separation between Jesus and the prophets—those individuals naturally assumed to be related to him since, for many, he fulfilled their prophecy. The letter, however, far from simply equating Jesus with the tradition of the prophets, announces that he has been acknowledged as a "high priest," (4:14) a clear allusion to the temple leadership in Jerusalem that he now replaces. The provocative letter makes a series of declarations on the meaning of Jesus—beginning with the interrelated aspect of his healing speech (even though some are "dull of hearing," [5:11]), his identity now as a high priest, and the obligation he now assumes to simultaneously abolish animal sacrifice in the temple for the reason that he has announced another kind of offering altogether, one intended as a replacement. However, as Girard has argued, Jesus' death should not be understood as a sacrificial one since the abolition of the ritual of sacrifice (for example, the death of the lamb during Passover) has now been substituted and definitively replaced by the body and blood of Jesus as represented, symbolically, by the Eucharist. One could certainly rely on a theology of sacrifice, traditionally understood, to interpret the following passage and concerning Jesus as a high priest "who needeth not daily, as those high priests, to offer up sacrifice" (7:27). Jesus does not have to offer up any temple sacrifices since "he did once, when he offered up himself," (7:27) a statement related to the Passover meal rather than his sacrificial death. Rather than the traditional offerings made by priests on the altar of the temple, Jesus as a high priest presiding over a new disposition "hath obtained a more excellent ministry, by how much also he is the mediator of a better covenant, which was established upon better promises," (8:6) and by doing so has done nothing less, as the letter also reaffirms, than to separate itself from the history of the Exodus and of the leadership of Moses—no doubt provocative and unthinkable for any pious man or woman still adhering to the Torah and who are now listening to the letter being read. Without here presenting further claims made by the letter to the Hebrews, a summary can be presented in terms of its emphasis on Jesus' rejection of animal sacrifice, its substitution in and through the Eucharist, and the role of the high priest who, from the beginning, emphasized a *soteria* conveyed through his words alone.

One final note is, however, necessary, most especially considering the historical events about to unfold in Palestine and the consequences for Judaism. Though the letter sets out to differentiate an *ethne* Christianity from the Jerusalem church, it also is more than aware of imminent plans (including Zealots who may have entered the church so as to influence its political decisions) for the Jewish revolt against the Romans and therefore attempts to dissuade those involved from confronting Rome by military means.

If the letter to the Hebrews is written shortly before Paul's execution in Rome, it also marks a transition to two historical events that will determine the future of both Judaism and Christianity: the first persecution of Christians in Rome during the reign of Nero in AD 64 and, only a few years later, the defeat of the Jews by the Romans in the early 70s and the destruction of the temple in Jerusalem. Both events will be paramount: for the Christians it will initiate an extended period of animosity and conflict (and even more pronounced episodes of intense persecutions and martyrdoms under various emperors), and for the Jews, it will mark the end of animal sacrifice in the temple and the beginning of rabbinical Judaism. In both cases, early Christianity ended animal sacrifice as a matter of credo, the Jews from an imposed necessity. In Book 5 of *The Histories*, the Roman historian Tacitus tells us of "the death-agony"[10] of a famous city as it is besieged by the legions under the leadership of Titus. Josephus concludes *The Wars of the Jews* with

> As soon as the army had no more people to slay or to plunder, because there remained none to be the objects of their fury, (for they would not have spared any, had there remained any other work to be done,) Caesar gave orders that they should now demolish the entire city and temple.[11]

And so, with the defeat of the city of Jerusalem and the destruction of its temple, the central ritual of Judaism effectively ended and led to its rabbinical development; even if private sacrifices continued to be carried out for a period of time, the centrality of the temple had been lost forever despite, by some, the hope for its future restoration.

In a period of only a few years, Pauline Christianity and Judaism had altogether stopped the religious ritual of animal sacrifice, though of course for different and unrelated reasons. The apparent announcement by Jesus that the temple would be destroyed was not prophetically interpreted, though to be sure by the time of Mark's Gospel (the first written) the event had already taken place. History had made prophecy possible. Despite these two events, polytheists continued their traditional practices as they had from a beginning now long-forgotten and perhaps no longer relevant to the present. In any case, not until Constantine's conversion to Christianity in AD 312 did polytheism begin to be reconsidered and, eventually, made illegal. The momentous event of Constantine's conversion led, slowly and inevitably, to the gradual closing of temples and the passing of edicts making sacrifice illegal. Many followed the one issued by Theodosius in AD 390. Traditions were not, however, easily abandoned. Although the ritual may have been officially prohibited, it was not absolutely discontinued. Animal sacrifice may have been done in secret; but it had not been definitively abandoned. Indeed, it continued to be observed, even if now the emphasis was less on the religious ritual, per se, as on its relation to commensality. Two closely related events can bring our study to a close. When the emperor Theodosius wrote a letter on April 9, 423 to a prefect asserting that pagans were now non-existent, he was reflecting a social reality that had been definitively altered. Fergus Millar tells us that while some sacrifices, perhaps in private and certainly unrelated to a city's official observances, may have continued, "in general the enormous change in communal life

---

10. Tacitus, *Hist.*, 5.2.
11. Josephus, *War.*, 7.1.1.

represented by the cessation of public sacrifice had already taken place."[12] The longstanding festivals and the public sacrifices that accompanied their celebrations had come to an end. That they required repeated edicts demonstrated their persistence.

From the singular voices of the Jewish prophets to the teachings of Greek philosophers, from the poets of the Augustan era to the earliest Christians, there had been a persistent and often repeated call to abolish animal sacrifice and to replace the idea of piety and worship with a new service, one that would culminate, finally, with the end of the civic ritual slaughter of animals and the adoption of a comprehensive therapeutic care dedicated to the psychological well-being of others. That most difficult of imperatives, to love one's neighbor as oneself, required even more dedication when love had not only to be felt as an authentic disposition, but shown in one's dedication to others, in taking care of those most distressed and afflicted. In the end, soteriology as healing first emerged when the ritual of animal sacrifice became of doubtful merit in serving the divine, indeed completely antithetical to a new conception of the divine and what is most reflective of piety. And when Socrates as represented in Plato's dialogues emerged as a philosopher and defined himself as such in his confrontation with the sacrificial polis religion of Athens, he both inherited the visions of a few philosophically motivated individuals and prepared what would eventually become the Hellenistic thought of Epicurus and culminate—after Lucretius's great Epicurean poem as well as the works of the Augustan poets—in the life and teaching of Jesus of Nazareth and the persistent idea to be transformed into a new testament for the world. Animal sacrifice did ultimately come to an end; the imperative of love continues as a fundamental obligation in the ongoing and infinite history of humanity proceeding toward its *telos*—not so much its end but its ultimate purpose.

Toronto
March 30, 2018
Good Friday

---

12. Millar, *Greek Roman Empire*, 116.

Bibliography

Adamson, Peter. *Philosophy in the Hellenistic and Roman Worlds: A History of Philosophy Without Any Gaps, Vol. 2.* Oxford: Oxford University Press, 2015.
Akers, Keith. *The Lost Religion of Jesus: Simple Living and Nonviolence in Early Christianity.* New York: Lantern, 2000.
Allen, R. E. *Plato's Euthyphro and the Earlier Theory of Forms.* London: Routledge & Kegan Paul, 1970.
Allen, R. E., trans. "Comment." *Euthyphro.* New Haven: Yale University Press, 1984.
———. "Comment." *Symposium.* New Haven: Yale University Press, 1991.
Annas, Julia. *The Morality of Happiness.* Oxford: Oxford University Press, 1993.
Armstrong, David. "Introduction." In *Vergil, Philodemus, and the Augustans*, edited by David Armstrong et al., 1–24. Austin: University of Texas Press, 2004.
Arrighetti, Graziano, ed. *Epicuro: Opere.* Torino: Einaudi, 1973.
Aslan, Reza. *Zealot: The Life and Times of Jesus of Nazareth.* New York: Random House, 2013.
Baggett, John. *Seeing through the Eyes of Jesus: His Revolutionary View of Reality and His Transcendent Significance for Faith.* Grand Rapids: Eerdmans, 2008.
Bahat, Dan. *Carta's Historical Atlas of Jerusalem.* Jerusalem: Carta, 1986.
———. "The Herodian Temple." In *The Cambridge History of Judaism. Vol. 3. The Early Roman Period*, edited by William Horbury et al., 38–58. Cambridge: Cambridge University Press, 1999.
Balentine, Samuel E. *Leviticus.* Louisville: John Knox, 2002.
Baltzly, Dirk, and Nick Eliopoulos. "The Classical Ideals of Friendship." In *Friendship: A History*, edited by Barbara Caine, 1–64. London: Routledge, 2009.
Barclay, William. *The Gospel of Matthew, Vol. 2.* Louisville: Westminster John Knox, 1975.
Baumgarten, A. I. "The Pharisaic Paradosis." *HTR* 80.1 (1987) 63–77.
Beckman, James. *The Religious Dimension of Socrates' Thought.* Waterloo, ON: Wilfred Laurier University Press, 1979.
Benardete, Seth. *Plato's Symposium.* München: Carl Friedrich von Siemens Stiftung, 1994.
Berlin, Adele, and Maxine Grossman, eds. *The Oxford Dictionary of the Jewish Religion, Second Edition.* Oxford: Oxford University Press, 2011.
Betz, Hans-Dieter. "Jesus and the Purity of the Temple (Mark 11:15–18): A Comparative Religion Approach." In *JBL* 116.3 (1997) 455–72.

Bloch, Ernst. *Natural Law and Human Dignity*. Translated by Denis J. Schmidt. Cambridge, MA: The MIT Press, 1986.

Bluck, R. S. "The Origin of the Greater Alcibiades." *CQ* Vol. 3, Nos. 1/2 (Jan-Apr., 1953) 46–52.

Bollack, Jean. *La pensée du plaisir: texts moraux, commentaires*. Paris: Les éditions minuit, 1975.

Bonnechere, Pierre. "Divination." In *Greek Religion*, edited by Daniel Ogden, 145–60. Chichester, UK: Wiley-Blackwell, 2010.

Borg, Marcus J. *Jesus: The Life, Teachings, and Relevance of a Religious Revolutionary*. New York: HarperCollins, 1989.

———. *Jesus: Uncovering the Life, Teachings, and Relevance of a Religious Revolutionary*. New York: HarperOne, 2006.

Bowkder, John. *Jesus and the Pharisees*. Cambridge: Cambridge University Press, 1973.

Boyancé, Pierre. *Lucrèce et l'épicurisme*. Paris: Presses Universitaires de France, 1963.

Boyer, Chrystian. *Jésus contre le temple? Analyse historico-critique des textes*. Montreal: Editions Fides, 2005.

Bracht Branham, Robert. *Unruly Eloquence: Lucian and the Comedy of Traditions*. Harvard: Harvard University Press, 1989.

Bremmer, Jan N. *Greek Religion*. Oxford: Oxford University Press, 1994.

Brown, Eric. "Politics and Society." In *The Cambridge Companion to Epicureanism*, edited by James Warren, 179–96. Cambridge: Cambridge University Press, 2009.

Brown, Peter. *Authority and the Sacred: Aspects of the Christianisation of the Roman World*. Cambridge: Cambridge University Press, 1995.

Bryant, Joseph M. *Moral Codes and Social Structures in Ancient Greece: A Sociology of Greek Ethics from Homer to the Epicureans and Stoics*. Albany, NY: State University of New York Press, 1996.

Bultmann, Rudolf. *The History of the Synoptic Tradition*. Translated by John Marsh. Oxford: Basil Blackwell, 1963.

Burkert, Walter. *Greek Religion: Archaic and Classical*. Translated by John Raffan. Oxford: Basil Blackwell, 1985.

———. *Homo Necans: The Anthropology of Ancient Greek Ritual and Myth*. Translated by Peter Bing. Berkeley: University of California Press, 1983.

———. *Lore and Science in Ancient Pythagoreanism*. Translated by Edwin L. Minar Jr. Cambridge: Harvard University Press, 1972.

Burkitt, F. C. "The Cleansing of the Temple." *JTS* 25.100 (1924) 386–90.

Burnyeat, M. F. "The Impiety of Socrates." *AP* 7 (1997) 1–12.

Cameron, Alan. *The Last Pagans of Rome*. Oxford: Oxford University Press, 2011.

Cansdale, Lena. *Qumran and the Essenes: A Re-valuation of the Evidence*. Tübingen: J. C. B. Mohr/Paul Siebeck, 1997.

Capps, Donald. *Jesus, the Village Psychiatrist*. Louisville: Westminster John Knox, 2008.

Caratini, Roger. *Initiation à la philosophie*. Paris: Éditions Archipoche, 2012.

Casey, P. M. "Culture and Historicity: The Cleansing of the Temple." *CBQ* 59.2 (1997) 306–27.

Charlesworth, James H. "The Dead Sea Scrolls and the Historical Jesus." In *Jesus and the Dead Sea Scrolls*, edited by James H. Charlesworth, 1–74. New York: Doubleday, 1992.

Chilton, Bruce. *Rabbi Jesus: An Intimate Biography*. New York: Doubleday, 2000.

———. *The Temple of Jesus: His Sacrificial Program within a Cultural History of Sacrifice*. University Park, PA: The Pennsylvania State University Press, 1992.
Chyutin, Michael. *The New Jerusalem Scroll from Qumran: A Comprehensive Reconstruction*. Translated by Richard Fiantz. Sheffield, UK: Sheffield Academic, 1997.
Clark, Gillian. "Introduction." In *Porphyry: On Abstinence from Killing Animals*, translated by Gillian Clark, 1–28. London: Bloomsbury, 2000.
Clarke, Howard. *The Gospel of Matthew and its Readers: A Historical Introduction to the First Gospel*. Bloomington, IN: Indiana University Press, 2003.
Clay, Diskin. "The Athenian Garden." In *The Cambridge Companion to Epicureanism*, edited by James Warren, 1–28. Cambridge: Cambridge University Press, 2009.
———. "A Lost Epicurean Community." *GRBS* 30.2 (1989) 313–35.
Cohn, Robert L. *The Shape of Sacred Space*. Chico, CA: Scholars, 1981.
Collins, John C. *Beyond the Qumran Community: The Sectarian Movement of the Dead Sea Scrolls*. Grand Rapids: Eerdmans, 2004.
Connor, W. R. "The Other 399: Religion and the Trial of Socrates." In *Georgica: Greek Studies in Honour of George Cawkwell*, edited by Michael A. Flower and Mark Toher, 49–56. London: Institute of Classical Studies, 1991.
Copleston, Frederick Charles. *History of Philosophy: Vol. I: Greece and Rome: From the Pre-Socratics to Plotinus*. New York: Image, 1993.
Corrigan, Kevin, and Elena Glazov-Corrigan. *Plato's Dialectic at Play: Argument, Structure, and Myth in the Symposium*. University Park, PA: The Pennsylvania State University Press, 2004.
Crossan, John Dominic. *The Historical Jesus: The Life of a Mediterranean Jewish Peasant*. San Francisco: Harper, 1991.
———. *Jesus: A Revolutionary Biography*. San Francisco: Harper Collins, 1994.
———. *Who Killed Jesus? Exposing the Roots of Anti-Semitism in the Gospel Story of the Death of Jesus*. New York: HarperCollins, 1995.
De Lacy, P. H. "Lucretius and the History of Epicureanism" *TP* 79 (1948) 12–23.
DeMaris, Richard E. "Sacrifice, an Ancient Mediterranean Ritual." *BTB* 43.2 (2013) 60–73.
Detienne, Marcel. "Culinary Practices and the Spirit of Sacrifice." In *The Cuisine of Sacrifice among the Greeks*, translated by Paula Wissing, 1–20. Chicago: The University of Chicago Press, 1989.
———. *Dionysos Slain*. Translated by Mireille Muellner and Leonard Muellner. Baltimore: The Johns Hopkins University Press, 1979.
———. *The Gardens of Adonis: Spices in Greek Mythology*. Translated by Janet Lloyd. Princeton: Princeton University Press, 1994.
DeWitt, Norman W. "Epicurean Contubernium." *TPJA PA* 67 (1936) 55–63.
———. *Epicurus and His Philosophy*. Minneapolis: University of Minnesota Press, 1954.
Diamon, Eli. "Parallel Trials: The Dramatic Structure of Plato's *Euthyphro*." *CQ* 62.2 (2012) 523–531.
Diogenes of Oenoanda. *The Fragments*. Translated by C.W. Chilton. London: University of Hull Publications, 1971.
Dodds, E. R. *The Greeks and the Irrational*. Berkeley: University of California Press, 1959.

———. *Pagan and Christian in an Age of Anxiety: Some Aspects of Religious Experience from Marcus Aurelius to Constantine*. Cambridge: Cambridge University Press, 1965.

Dombrowski, Daniel A. "Philosophical Vegetarianism and Animal Entitlements." In *The Oxford Handbook of Animals in Classical Thought and Life*, edited by Gordon Lindsay Campbell, 535–55. Oxford: Oxford University Press, 2014.

Domeris, William. "The 'Enigma' of Jesus' Temple Intervention: Four Essential Keys," *HTS TS* 71.1 (2015) 1–8.

Dorandi, Tiziano. Edizione, Traduzione, e Commento. *Filodemo: Storia dei Filosofi, La Stoà da Zenone a Panezio (P. Herc. 1018)*. Leiden: Brill, 1994.

Douglas Minyard, John. *Lucretius and the Late Republic: An Essay in Roman Intellectual History*. Leiden: Brill, 1994.

Dover, K. J. "Aristophanes' Speech in Plato's Symposium." *JHS* 86 (1966) 41–50.

Downing, F. Gerald. *Christ and the Cynics: Jesus and Other Radical Preachers in First-Century Tradition*. London: Continuum, 1988.

Drummond, W., and R. Walpole. *Herculanensia; or Archaeological and Philological Dissertations, containing a Manuscript Found among the Ruins of Herculaneum*. London: Bulmer and Co. Cleveland-Row, 1810.

Dunn, J. D. G. "Jesus and Purity: An Ongoing Debate." *NTS* 48.4 (2002) 449–67.

Edersheim, Alfred. *The Life and Times of Jesus the Messiah*, Vol. 2. London: Longmans, Green, 1883.

Ellery Leonard, William, and Stanley Barney Smith, eds. *De Rerum Natura, Libri Sex*. Madison, WI: The University of Wisconsin Press, 1942.

Ellis, E. Earle. *The Gospel of Luke*. Grand Rapids: Eerdmans, 1966.

Emerson, William A., Jr. *The Jesus Story*. New York: Harper & Row, 1971.

Eppstein, Victor. "The Historicity of the Gospel Account of the Cleansing of the Temple." *ZNW* 55.1 (1964) 42–58.

Erler, Michael. "Epicurus as deus mortalis. Homoiosis theoi and Epicurean Self-cultivation." In *Traditions of Theology: Studies in Hellenistic Theology, its Background and Aftermath*, edited by Drothea Frede and André Laks, 159–82. Leiden: Brill, 2002.

Evans, Craig A. "Opposition to the Temple: Jesus and the Dead Sea Scrolls." In *Jesus and the Dead Sea Scrolls*, edited by James H. Charlesworth, 235–53. New York: Doubleday, 1992.

Faraone, Christopher A., and F. S. Naiden, eds. *Greek and Roman Animal Sacrifice: Ancient Victims, Modern Observers*. Cambridge: Cambridge University Press, 2012.

Farrington, Benjamin. *Head and Hand in Ancient Greece: Four Studies in the Social Relations of Thought*. London: Watts, 1976.

Ferngren, Gary B. *Medicine and Health Care in Early Christianity*. Baltimore: The Johns Hopkins University Press, 2009.

Festugière, A. J. *Epicurus and His Gods*. Translated by C. W. Chilton. Oxford: Basil Blackwell, 1955.

Fischel, Henry A. *Rabbinic Literature and Greco-Roman Philosophy: A Study of Epicurea and Rhetorica in Early Midrashic Writings*. Leiden: E. J. Brill, 1973.

Foucault, Michel. *The History of Sexuality, Vol. 2: The Use of Pleasure*. Translated by Robert Hurley. New York: Vintage, 1986.

———. *The History of Sexuality, Vol. 3: The Care of the Self.* Translated by Robert Hurley. New York: Vintage, 1986.

Fratantuono, Lee. *A Reading of Lucretius' De Rerum Natura.* Lanham, MD: Lexington, 2015.

Frend, W. H. C. *Martyrdom and Persecution in the Early Church: A Study of a Conflict from the Maccabees to Donatus.* Oxford: Basil Blackwell, 1965.

Freyne, Seán. *Galilee, Jesus and the Gospels: Literary Approaches and Historical Investigations.* Dublin: Gill and MacMillan, 1988.

———. *The Jesus Movement and its Expansion: Meaning and Mission.* Grand Rapids: Eerdmans, 2014.

Friedländer, Paul. *Plato, Vol. 1.* Translated by Hans Meyerhoff. New York: Pantheon, 1958.

Frischer, Bernard. *The Sculpted Word: Epicureanism and Philosophical Recruitment in Ancient Greece.* Berkeley: University of California Press, 1982.

Fuhrmann, Manfred. *Cicero and the Roman Republic.* Translated by W. E. Yuill. Oxford: Basil Blackwell, 1992.

Funk, Robert W. *The Five Gospels: The Search for the Authentic Words of Jesus.* New York: HarperCollins, 1997.

Furley, David J. "Lucretius the Epicurean: On the History of Man." In *Lucretius*, edited by Monica R. Gale, 158–81. Oxford: Oxford University Press, 2007.

Fusaro, Diego. *La farmacia di Epicuro: La filosofia come terapia dell'anima.* Padova, Italy: Il Prato, 2006.

Gale, Monica R. *Myth and Poetry in Lucretius.* Cambridge: Cambridge University Press, 1994.

Ghisalberti, Giosuè. *Augustine's Passions: His Transformation from a Roman Citizen to a Catholic Bishop.* Milwaukee: Marquette University Press, 2016.

———. "The Christology of Shame and the Re-evaluation of Hellenic Ideas in 1 and 2 Timothy." *HJ* 54.5 (2012) 625–37.

Gigante, Marcello. *Philodemus in Italy: The Books from Herculaneum.* Translated by Dirk Obbink. Ann Arbor, MI: The University of Michigan Press, 1995.

Girard, René. *I See Satan Fall like Lightning.* Translated by James G. Williams. Maryknoll, NY: Orbis, 2001.

———. *Things Hidden Since the Foundation of the World.* Translated by Stephen Bann and Michael Metteer. London: The Athlone, 1987.

———. *Violence and the Sacred.* Translated by Patrick Gregory. Baltimore: The Johns Hopkins University Press, 1977.

Giussani, Carlo. *Studi Lucreziani.* Torino: Ermanno Loescher, 1896.

Glad, Clarence E. *Paul and Philodemus: Adaptability in Epicurean and Early Christian Psychagogy.* Leiden: E. J. Brill, 1995.

Glidden, David K. "Epicurus on Self-Perception." *APQ* V16.4 (1979) 297–306.

Goldhill, Simon. *The Temple of Jerusalem.* Cambridge: Harvard University Press, 2005.

Goldman, Harvey S. "Re-examining the 'Examined Life' in Plato's Apology of Socrates." *PF* 35.1 (2004) 1–33.

Gordon, Pamela. *The Invention and Gendering of Epicurus.* Ann Arbor, MI: The University of Michigan Press, 2012.

Green, Steven J. "Save Our Cows? Augustan Discourse and Animal Sacrifice in Ovid's Fasti." *GR* 55.1 (2008) 39–54.

Gunkel, Hermann. "Prophet as Writers and Poets." In *Prophecy in Israel: Search for identity*, edited by D. L. Peterson, translated by J. L. Schaaf. 22–73. Philadelphia: Fortress, 1987.

Guthrie. W. K. C. *The Greeks and their Gods*. London: Methuen, 1950.

———. *A History of Greek Philosophy, Vol. 1: The Early Presocratics and the Pythagoreans*. Cambridge: Cambridge University Press, 1962.

Hadot, Pierre. *Philosophy as a Way of Life: Spiritual Exercises from Socrates to Foucault*. Translated by Arnold I. Davidson. Oxford: Blackwell, 1995.

Hamerton-Kelly, Robert G., ed. *Violent Origins: Walter Burkert, René Girard, and Jonathan Z. Smith on Ritual Killing and Cultural Formation*. Stanford: Stanford University Press, 1987.

Hanson, K.C., and Douglas E. Oakman. *Palestine in the Time of Jesus: Social Structures and Conflicts*. Minneapolis: Fortress, 1998.

Harrington, Daniel J. *The Gospel of Matthew*. Collegeville, MN: Liturgical, 1991.

———. *Wisdom Texts from Qumran*. London: Routledge, 1996.

Haussleiter, Johanees. *Der Vegetarismus in der Antike*. Berlin: Verlag von Alfred Töpelmann, 1935.

Hecht, Jamey. *Plato's Symposium: Eros and the Human Predicament*. New York: Twayne, 1999.

Hendridk, Obery M. *The Politics of Jesus: Rediscovering the True Revolutionary Nature of Jesus' Teachings and How They have been Corrupted*. New York: Doubleday, 2006.

Hengel, Martin. *The Charismatic Leader and His Followers*. Translated by James Greig. New York: Crossroad, 1981.

———. *Jews and Hellenism: Studies in their Encounter in Palestine during the Early Hellenistic Period*. Translated by John Bowden. Minneapolis: Fortress, 1974.

Heyman, George. *The Power of Sacrifice: Roman and Christian Discourses in Conflict*. Washington D. C.: The Catholic University of America Press, 2007.

Hibler, Richard W. *Happiness through Tranquillity: The School of Epicurus*. New York: University Press of America, 1984.

Hirschfeld, Yizhar. *Qumran in Context*. Peabody, MA: Hendrickson, 2004.

Hopper, Anthony. "The Greatest Hope of All: Aristophanes on Human Nature in Plato's Symposium." *CQ* 63.2 (2013) 567–79.

Horsley, Richard A. *Jesus and Magic: Freeing the Gospel Stories from Modern Misconceptions*. Eugene, OR: Cascade, 2014.

———. *Jesus and the Politics of Roman Palestine*. Columbia, SC: The University of South Carolina Press, 2014.

———. "Popular Messianic Movements around the Time of Jesus." *CBQ* 46 (1984) 409–32.

Iles Johnston, Sarah. *Ancient Greek Divination*: Chichester, UK: Wiley, 2008.

Inwood, Brad. *The Poem of Empedocles: A Text and Translation with an Introduction*. Revised Edition. Toronto: University of Toronto Press, 2001

Jaeger, Werner. *The Theology of the Early Greek Philosophers*. Oxford: The Clarendon, 1947.

Janko, Richard. "Reconstructing (Again) the Opening of the Derveni Papyrus." *ZPE* 166 (2008) 37–51.

———. Review of *The Derveni Papyrus: Cosmology, Theology and Interpretation*, by Gator Betegh. *BMCR* 200.01.27 (2005) no pages given.

Jay, Nancy. *Throughout Your Generations Forever: Sacrifice, Religion, and Paternity*. Chicago: The University of Chicago Press, 1992.

Jeremias, Joachim. *Jerusalem in the Time of Jesus: An Investigation into Economic and Social Conditions during the New Testament Period*. Translated by F. H. Cave and C. H. Cave. London: SCM, 1969.

Johnson, Luke Timothy. *Among the Gentiles: Greco-Roman Religion and Christianity*. New Haven: Yale University Press, 2009.

———. "The New Testament's Anti-Jewish Slander and the Conventions of Ancient Polemic." *JBL* 108.3 (1989) 419–41.

———. *The Real Jesus: The Misguided Quest for the Historical Jesus and the Truth of the Traditional Gospels*. New York: Harper Collins, 1997.

Johnston, Sarah Iles. *Ancient Greek Divination*. Oxford: Blackwell, 2008.

Kahn, Charles H. *Plato and the Socratic Dialogue*. Cambridge: Cambridge University Press, 1996.

Keener, Craig S. *A Commentary on the Gospel of Matthew*. Grand Rapids: Eerdmans, 1999.

Kelber, Werner H. "The Quest for the Historical Jesus: From the Perspectives of Medieval, Modern, and Post-Enlightenment Readings, and in View of Ancient, Oral Aesthetics." In *The Jesus Controversy: Perspectives in Conflict*, edited by John Dominic Crossan et al, 75–115. Harrisburg, PA: Trinity, 1999.

Kilgallen, John J., S.J. *Guida alla Terra Santa Seguendo il Nuovo Testamento*. Roma: Editrice Pontificio Istituto Biblico, 2000.

Kirsch, Adam. *The People and the Books: 18 Classics of Jewish Literature*. New York: W. W. Norton, 2016.

Klawans, Jonathan. *Purity, Sacrifice, and the Temple: Symbolism and Supercessionism in the Study of Ancient Judaism*. Oxford: Oxford University Press, 2006.

Knight, G. A. F. *Leviticus*. Philadelphia: Westminster, 1981.

Knox, Wilfred Lawrence. *The Sources of the Synoptic Gospels*. Edited by H. Chadwick. Cambridge: Cambridge University Press, 1953.

Konstan, David. *Some Aspects of Epicurean Psychology*. Leiden: E. J. Brill, 1973.

Lain-Entralgo, Pedro. *The Therapy of the Word in Classical Antiquity*. Edited and translated by L. J. Rather, and John M. Sharp. New Haven: Yale University Press, 1970.

Lännström, Anne. "A Religious Revolution? How Socrates' Theology Undermined the Practice of Sacrifice." *AP* 31 (2011) 261–73.

Lavin, Ron. *People Who Met Jesus: Another Look at the Suffering, Death, and Resurrection of the Lord*. Lima, Ohio: CSS, 2006.

Leone, Anna. *The End of the Pagan City: Religion, Economy, and Urbanism in Late Antique North Africa*. Oxford: Oxford University Press, 2013.

Levenson, Jon D. *The Hebrew Bible, the Old Testament, and Historical Criticism: Jews and Christians in Biblical Studies*. Louisville: Westminster/John Knox Press, 1993.

Lieu, Judith. *Neither Jew nor Greek? Constructing Early Christianity*. London: T & T Clark, 2002.

Lim, Timothy H. *The Dead Sea Scrolls: A Very Short Introduction*. Oxford: Oxford University Press, 2005.

Livingstone, E. A., ed. *The Concise Oxford Dictionary of the Christian Church*. Oxford: Oxford University Press, 2013

Lohfink, Gerhard. *Jesus of Nazareth, What He Wanted, Who He Was.* Translated by Linda M. Maloney. Collegeville, MN: Liturgical, 2012.

Long, A. A. *Hellenistic Philosophy: Stoics, Epicureans, Sceptics.* Berkeley: University of California Press, 1986.

Lucas, Ernest C. "Sacrifice in the Prophets." In *Sacrifice in the Bible*, edited by Roger T. Beckwith, and Martin J. Selman, 59–74. Eugene, OR: Wipf & Stock, 1995.

Lundquist, John M. *The Temple of Jerusalem: Past, Present, and Future.* Westport, CT: Praeger, 2008.

Mack, Burton L. *A Myth of Innocence: Mark and Christian Origins.* Philadelphia: Fortress, 1988.

Manning, Aubrey, and James Serpell, eds. *Animals and Human Society: Changing Perspectives.* London: Routledge, 1994.

Mansfeld, Japp. "Aspects of Epicurean Theology." *M* 46.2 (1993) 32–57.

Marion, Jean-Luc. *God without Being.* Translated by Thomas A. Carlson. Chicago: The University of Chicago Press, 1991.

Martin, Thomas F. *Our Restless Heart: The Augustinian Tradition.* London: Darton, Longman and Todd, 2003.

Masson, John. "M. Guyau and the Epicurean Doctrine of Free-Will and Atomic Declination." *JP* 11 (1882) 34–55.

———. "The Religion of Lucretius." *CR* 37.7–8 (1923) 149–52.

Matthews, Kenneth A. "John, Jesus and the Essenes: Trouble at the Temple." *CTR* 3.1 (1988) 101–26.

McPherran, Mark L. *The Religion of Socrates.* University Park, PA: The Pennsylvania State University Press, 1996.

Meeks, Wayne. *The First Urban Christians: The Social World of the Apostle Paul.* New Haven: Yale University Press, 1983

Meier, John P. *A Marginal Jew: Mentor, Message, and Miracles.* New York: Doubleday, 1994.

Mendels, Doron. "Hellenistic Utopia and the Essenes." *HTR* 72.3–4 (1979) 207–22.

Meyer, Ben F. *The Aims of Jesus.* London: SCM, 1979.

———. *The Early Christians: Their World Mission and Self-Discovery.* Wilmington, DE: Michael Glazier, 1986.

Meyer, Matthew. "Peisestairos of Aristophanes' Birds and the Erotic Tyrant of Republic IX." In *The Political Theory of Aristophanes: Explorations in Poetic Wisdom*, edited by Jeremy M. Mhire and Bryan-Paul Frost, 275–302. Albany, NY: State University of New York Press, 2014.

Mikalson, Jon D. *Greek Popular Religion in Greek Philosophy.* Oxford: Oxford University Press, 2010.

Milgrom, Jacob. *Leviticus: A Book of Ritual and Ethics.* Minneapolis: Fortress, 2004.

Millar, Fergus. *A Greek Roman Empire: Power and Belief Under Theodosius II (408–450).* Berkeley: University of California Press, 2006.

Minyard, J. D. *Lucretius and the Late Republic: An Essay in Roman Intellectual History.* Leiden: Brill, 1985.

Mitsis, Phillip. *Epicurus' Ethical Theory: The Pleasures of Invulnerability.* Ithaca, NY: Cornell University Press, 1988.

Montarese, Francesco. *Lucretius and His Sources: A Study of Lucretius, De rerum natura I 635–920.* Boston: De Gruyter, 2012.

Morris, Leon. *The Gospel According to John.* Grand Rapids: Eerdmans, 1995.

Moule, C. F. D. *The Sacrifice of Christ*. Philadelphia: Fortress, 1956.
Nesbit, Edward Planta. *Christ, Christians and Christianity: Jesus the Essene*. London: Simpkin, Marshall, Hamilton and Kent, 1895.
Neutel, Karin B. *A Cosmopolitan Ideal: Paul's Declaration "Neither Jew nor Greek, Neither Slave nor Free, Neither Male or Female" in the Context of First-Century Thought*. London: Bloomsbury, 2015.
Neville, Robert Cummings. *Symbols of Jesus: A Christology of Symbolic Engagement*. Cambridge: Cambridge University Press, 2001.
Nilsson, Martin Persson. *Greek Piety*. Translated by Herbert Jennings Rose. Oxford: Clarendon, 1948.
———. *A History of Greek Religion*. Translated by F. J. Fielden, Oxford: Clarendon, 1949.
Nock, Arthur Darby. *Essays on Religion and the Ancient World*. Edited by Zeph Stewart. Oxford: Clarendon, 1972.
———. "Religious Attitudes of the Ancient Greeks." *PAPS* 85.5 (1942) 472–82.
Nussbaum, Martha C. *The Fragility of Goodness: Luck and Ethics in Greek Tragedy and Philosophy*. Cambridge: Cambridge University Press, 1986.
———. *The Therapy of Desire: Theory and Practice in Hellenistic Ethics*. Princeton, NJ: Princeton University Press, 1994.
Obbink, Dirk. "The Atheism of Epicurus." *RBS* 30.2 (1989) 187–223.
———. "Commentary" to Philodemus's On Piety. Oxford: Oxford University Press, 1994.
———. "Hermarchus, against Empedocles." *CQ* 38.2 (1988) 428–35.
———. "How to Read Poetry about Gods." In *Philodemus and Poetry: Poetic Thinking and Practice in Lucretius, Philodemus, and Horace*, edited by Dirk Obbink, 189–209. Oxford: Oxford University Press, 1995.
———. "The Origin of Greek Sacrifice: Theophrastus on Religion and Cultural History." In *Theophrastean Studies: On Natural Science, Physics and Metaphysics, Ethics, Religion, and Rhetoric*, edited by William W. Fortenbaugh and Sobert W. Sharples, 272–95. New Brunswick, NJ: Transaction, 1988.
———. *Philodemus On Piety, Part 1*. Oxford: Clarendon, 1996.
O'Keefe, Tim. *Epicurus on Freedom*. Cambridge: Cambridge University Press, 2005.
Onfray, Michel. *Les sagesses antique: contre histoire de la philosophie 1*. Paris: Bernard Grasset, 2006.
O'Sullivan, L. L. "Athenian Impiety Trials in the Late Fourth Century B.C." *CQ* 47.1 (1997) 136–52.
Owens, J. Edward. *Leviticus*. Collegeville, MN: Liturgical, 2010.
Panagiotou, Spiro. "Plato's Euthyphro and the Attic Code on Homicide." *H* 102.3 (1974) 419–37.
Pancera, Carlo. *La formazione dell'uomo in Socrate*. Bologna: Clueb, 2003.
Paratore, Ettore. *Epicureanism and its Diffusion in the Latin World*. Roma: Edizioni dell'Ateneo, 1960.
Parker, Robert. "The Trial of Socrates: And a Religious Crisis?" In *The Trial and Execution of Socrates: Sources and Controversies*, edited by Thomas C. Brickhouse and Nicholas D. Smith, 145–61. Oxford: Oxford University Press, 2002.
Pascual, José. "Epicuro y Atenas: La creación de una communidad identitaria distinta de la Pólis." *SH* 29 (2011) 39–63.
Peirce, Sarah. "Death, Revelry, and Thysia." *CA* 12.2 (1993), 219–66.

Penella, Robert J. *Man and World: The Orations of Himerius.* Berkeley: University of California Press, 2007.

Petropoulou, Maria-Zoe. *Animal Sacrifice in Ancient Greek Religion, Judaism, and Christianity, 100 BC–AD 200.* Oxford: Oxford University Press, 2008.

Pieper, Josef. *For the Love of Wisdom: Essays on the Nature of Philosophy.* Edited by Berthold Wald and translated by Roger Wasserman. San Francisco: Ignatius, 2006.

Pilch, John J. *Visions and Healings in the Acts of the Apostles: How the Early Believers Experienced God.* Collegeville, MN: Liturgical, 2004.

Price, Simon. *Religions of the Ancient Greeks.* Cambridge: Cambridge University Press, 1999.

Quasten, Johannes. *Music and Worship in Pagan and Christian Antiquity.* Translated by Boniface Ramsey. Washington, D. C.: National Association of Pastoral Musicians, 1983.

Quispel, Gilles. "The Study of Encratism: A Historical Survey." In *La Tradizione dell'enkrateia: Motivazione ontologiche e protologiche*, edited by Ugo Bianchi, 35–82. Roma: Edizioni dell'ateneo, 1985.

Radner, Ephraim. *Leviticus.* Grand Rapids: Brazos, 2008.

Reale, Giovanni. *Il pensiero antico.* Milano: Vita e Pensiero, 2001.

———. *Storia della filosofia antica, Vol. IV: Le scuole dell'età imperiale.* Milano: Vita e Pensiero, 1989.

Reeve, C. D. C. "Introduction." In *Plato on Love*, edited by C. D. C. Reeve, xi–xviii. Indianapolis: Hackett, 2006.

———. *Socrates in the Apology: An Essay on Plato's Apology of Socrates.* Indianapolis: Hackett, 1989.

Renaud, François, and Harold Tarrant. *The Platonic Alcibiades I: The Dialogue and its Ancient Reception.* Cambridge: Cambridge University Press, 2015.

Rinella, Michael A. *Pharmakon: Plato, Drug Culture, and Identity in Ancient Athens.* Lanham, MD: Lexington, 2010.

Robinson, Thomas A. *Who Were the First Christians?: Dismantling the Urban Thesis.* Oxford: Oxford University Press, 2016.

Rooker, Mark F. *Leviticus.* Nashville: B&H, 2000.

Rosen, Stanley. *Plato's Symposium.* New Haven: Yale University Press, 1968.

Rosivach, Vincent J. *The System of Public Sacrifice in Fourth-Century Athens.* Atlanta: Scholars, 1994.

Rowley. H. H. *From Moses to Qumran.* New York: Association, 1963.

Rüpke, Jörg. *Religion of the Romans.* Translated and Edited by Richard Gordon. Cambridge, UK: Polity, 2007.

Sabourin, Leopold. *The Names and Titles of Jesus.* Translated by Maurice Carroll. New York: Macmillan, 1967.

Sack, Robert David. *Homo Geographicus.* Baltimore: The Johns Hopkins Press, 1997.

Saldarini, Anthony J. *Pharisees, Scribes, and Saducees in Palestinian Society: A Sociological Approach.* Grand Rapids: Eerdmans, 2001.

Sanders, E. P. *Jesus and Judaism.* London: SCM, 1985.

Saxonhouse, Arlene. "The Net of Hephaestus: Aristophanes' speech in Plato's Symposium." *I* 13.1 (1984) 15–32.

Saylor, Charles F. "Man, Animal, and the Bestial in Lucretius." *CJ* 67.4 (1972) 306–16.

Scheid, John. *Quand faire, c'est croire: Les rites sacrificiels des Romains.* Paris: Aubier, 2005.

Schnackenburg, Rudolf. *The Gospel of Mattew*. Translated by Robert R. Barr. Grand Rapids: Eerdmans, 2002.

Scott, Gary Allan, and William A. Welton. *Erotic Wisdom: Philosophy and Intermediacy in Plato's Symposium*. Albany, NY: State University of New York Press, 2008.

Sedgwick, Henry Dwight. *The Art of Happiness, or the Teachings of Epicurus*. Freeport, NY: Books for Libraries, 1933.

Sedley, David N. *Lucretius and the Transformation of Greek Wisdom*. Cambridge: Cambridge University Press, 1998.

Sedley, Douglas. "Sacrifice, Transcendence, and 'Making Sacred.'" *RIPS* 68 (2011) 257–67.

Seeley, David. "Jesus' Temple Act." *CBQ* 55.2 (1993) 263–83.

Sichel, Meier. "Air Pollution—Smoke and Odor Damage." In *The Jewish Law Annual, Vol. 5*, edited by Bernard Jackson, 25–43. Leiden: Brill, 1985.

Smith, Jonathan Z. *Drudgery Divine: On Comparisons of Early Christianities and the Religions of Late Antiquity*. Chicago: The University of Chicago Press, 1990.

Smith, Nicholas D. "Did Plato Write Alcibiades I?" *A* 37.2 (2004) 93–108.

Stanton, Graham N. *Jesus and Gospel*. Cambridge: Cambridge University Press, 2004.

Stauffer, Ethelbert. *Jesus and His Story*. London: SCM Press, 1960.

Stegemann, Hartmut. *The Library of Qumran: On the Essenes, Qumran, John the Baptist, and Jesus*. Grand Rapids: Eerdmans, 1998.

Stemberger, Günter. *Jewish Contemporaries of Jesus: Pharisees, Sadducees, Essenes*. Translated by Allan W. Mahnke. Minneapolis: Fortress, 1995.

Stone, Michael E., ed. *Jewish Writings of the Second Temple Period: Apocrypha, Pseudepigrapha, Qumran Sectarian Wrings, Philo, Josephus*. Philadelphia: Fortress, 1984.

Storkey, Alan. *Jesus and Politics: Confronting the Powers*. Grand Rapids: Baker, 2005.

Stowers, Stanley K. "Does Pauline Christianity Resemble a Hellenistic Philosophy?" In *Paul Beyond the Judaism/Hellenism Divide*, edited by Troels Engberg-Pedersen, 81–102. Louisville: Westminster, 2001.

———. "Greeks Who Sacrificed and Those Who Do Not: Towards an Anthropology of Greek Religion." In *The Social World of the First Christians: Essays in Honour of Wayne A. Meeks*, edited by L. Michael White and O. Larry Yarbrugh, 293–333. Minneapolis: Fortress, 1995.

———. "The Religion of Plant and Animal Offerings Versus the Religion of Meanings, Essences, and Textual Mysteries." In *Ancient Mediterranean Sacrifice*, edited by JenniferWright Knust and Zsuzsanna Várhelyi, 35–56. Oxford: Oxford University Press, 2011.

Strauss, Leo. *On Plato's Symposium*. Edited by Seth Bernadete. Chicago: The University of Chicago Press, 2001.

———. *Spinoza's Critique of Religion*. Translated by E. M. Sinclair. Chicago: The University of Chicago Press, 1965.

Strenski, Ivan. *Theology and the First Theory of Sacrifice*. Leiden: Brill, 2003.

Stroumsa, Guy G. *The End of Sacrifice: Religious Transformations in Late Antiquity*. Translated by Susan Emanuel. Chicago: The University of Chicago Press, 2009.

———. *The Scriptural Universe of Ancient Christianity*. Cambridge, MA: Harvard University Press, 2016.

Strozier, Robert M. *Epicurus and Hellenistic Philosophy*. Lanham, MD: University Press of America, 1985.

Summers, Kirk. "Lucretius and the Epicurean Tradition of Piety." *CP* 90.1 (1995), 32–57.
Tarrant, Harold. "Elenchos and Exetasis: Capturing the Purpose of Socratic Interrogation." In *Does Socrates Have a Method? Re-Thinking the Elenchus in Plato's Dialogues and Beyond*, edited by Gary Allen Scott, 61–77. University Park, PA: The Pennsylvania State University Press, 2002.
Tatti-Gartziou, Ariadni. "Blindness as Punishment." In *Light and Darkness in Ancient Greek Myth and Religion*, edited by Menelaos Chrstopoulos et al., 181–90. Lanham, MD: Rowman & Little Field, 2010.
Taylor, A. E. *Epicurus*. New York: Dodge, 1910.
Taylor, Alfred Edward. *Varia Socratica*. Oxford: James Parker & Co., 1911.
Taylor, Joan E. *The Essenes, the Scrolls, and the Dead Sea*. Oxford: Oxford University Press, 2012.
Taylor, Justin. *Pythagoreans and Essenes: Structural Parallels*. Leuven: Peeters, 2004.
Taylor, Margaret. "Progress and Primitivism." *AJP* 68.2 (1947) 180–94.
Taylor, Vincent. *The Names of Jesus*. London: Macmillan, 1954.
Travis, Roger. *Allegory and the Tragic Chorus in Sophocles' Oedipus at Colonus*. Lanham, MD: Rowman & Littlefield, 1999.
Twelftree, Graham H. *Jesus the Exorcist: A Contribution to the Study of the Historical Jesus*. Peabody, MA: Hendrickson, 1993.
Ullucci, Daniel. *The Christian Rejection of Animal Sacrifice*. Oxford: Oxford University Press, 2012.
———. "Contesting the Meaning of Animal Sacrifice." In *Ancient Mediterranean Sacrifice*, edited by Jennifer Wright Knust and Zsuzanna Várhelyi, 57–74. Oxford: Oxford University Press, 2011.
———. "Sacrifice in the Ancient Mediterranean: Recent and Current Research." *CBR* 13.3 (2015) 388–439.
Vamvacas, Constantine J. *The Founders of Western Thought—The Presocratics: A Diachronic Parallelism between Presocratic Thought and Philosophy and the Natural Sciences*. Translated by Robert Crist. New York: Springer, 2009.
van Straten, F. T. *Hierà Kalá: Images of Animal Sacrifice in Archaic and Classical Greece*. Leiden: E. J. Brill, 1995.
Vermes, Geza. *The Dead Sea Scrolls in English*. Harmondsworth, UK: Penguin, 1968.
———. *Jesus and the World of Judaism*. London: SCM, 1983.
———. *Jesus in His Jewish Context*. Minneapolis: Fortress, 2003
———. *Jesus the Jew: A Historian's Reading of the Gospels*. New York: Macmillan, 1973.
———. *Scrolls: Scriptures and Early Christianity*. London: T&T International, 2005.
Vermes, Geza, and Martin D. Goodman, eds. *The Essenes According to the Classical Sources*. Sheffield, UK: SJOT, 1989.
Vernant, Jean-Pierre. *Mortals and Immortals: Collected Essays*. Edited by Froma I. Zeitlin. Princeton, NJ: Princeton University Press, 1991.
———. "Théorie générale du sacrifice et mise a mort dans la ΘΥΣΙΑ grecque." In *Le sacrifice dans l'antiquité*, edited by Jean-Pierre Vernant et al., 2–21. Genève: Vandoeuvres, 1980.
Versényi, Laszlo. *Holiness and Justice: An Interpretation of Plato's Euthyphro*. Washington, D. C.: University Press of America, 1982.
Vlastos, Gregory. *Platonic Studies*. Princeton, NJ: Princeton University Press, 1973.

Voelke, André-Jean. *La philosophie comme thérapie de l'âme: études de philosophie hellénistique*. 2nd edition. Fribourg, Switzerland: Fribourg Academic, 1993.
Von Staden, Heinrich. "Body, Soul, and Nerves: Epicurus, Herophilus, Erasistratus, the Stoics, and Galen." In *Psyche and Soma: Physicians and Metaphysicians on the Mind-Body Problem from Antiquity to Enlightenment*, edited by John P. Wright and Paul Potter, 79–116. Oxford: Clarendon, 2000.
Warren, James. "Diogenes Epikouros: Keep Taking the Tablets." *JHS* 120 (2000) 144–48.
Watts, Edward J. *City and School in Late Antique Athens and Alexandria*. Berkeley: University of California Press, 2006.
Watty, William. "Jesus and the Temple—Cleansing or Cursing?" *ET* 93.8 (1982) 235–38.
Wedderburn, Alexander J. M. "Jesus' Actions in the Temple, A Key or Puzzle?" *ZNW* 97.1–2 (2006) 1–22.
Weiss, Roslyn. "Euthyphro's Failure." *JHP* 24.4 (1986) 437–52.
Weissenrieder, Annette. "The Plague of Uncleanness? The Ancient Illness Construct Issue of Blood in Luke 8:43–48." In *The Social Setting of Jesus and the Gospels*, edited by Wolfgang Stegemann et al., 207–22. Minneapolis: Fortress, 2002.
Wells, G. A. *The Jesus of the Early Christians*. London: Pemberton, 1971.
Williamson, Lamar, Jr. *Preaching the Gospel of John: Proclaiming the Living Word*: Louisville: Westminster John Knox, 2004.
Wilson, Stephen G. *Related Stangers: Jews and Christians, 70–170 C.E.* Minneapolis: Fortress, 2005.
Wollheim, Richard. *The Sheep and the Ceremony*. Cambridge: Cambridge University Press, 1979.
Wright, N. T. *Who was Jesus?* Grand Rapids: Eerdmans, 2014.
Young, Richard Alan. *Is God a Vegetarian? Christianity, Vegetarianism, and Animal Rights*. Peru, IL: Carus, 1999.
Zeitlin, Irving M. *Jesus and the Judaism of his Time*. Cambridge: Polity, 1988.

www.ingramcontent.com/pod-product-compliance
Lightning Source LLC
Chambersburg PA
CBHW070237230426
43664CB00014B/2332